Get the eBook FREE!

(PDF, ePub, Kindle, and liveBook all included)

We believe that once you buy a book from us, you should be able to read it in any format we have available. To get electronic versions of this book at no additional cost to you, purchase and then register this book at the Manning website.

Go to https://www.manning.com/freebook and follow the instructions to complete your pBook registration.

That's it!
Thanks from Manning!

100 Java Mistakes
and How to Avoid Them

100 Java Mistakes
and How to Avoid Them

TAGIR VALEEV

FOREWORD BY CAY HORSTMANN

MANNING
SHELTER ISLAND

For online information and ordering of this and other Manning books, please visit www.manning.com. The publisher offers discounts on this book when ordered in quantity. For more information, please contact

Special Sales Department
Manning Publications Co.
20 Baldwin Road
PO Box 761
Shelter Island, NY 11964
Email: orders@manning.com

 Manning Publications Co.
20 Baldwin Road
PO Box 761
Shelter Island, NY 11964

Development editor:	Connor O'Brien
Technical editor:	Jean-François Morin
Review editor:	Radmila Ercegovac
Production editor:	Kathy Rossland
Copy editor:	Christian Berk
Proofreader:	Mike Beady
Technical proofreader:	Cosimo Damiano Prete
Typesetter and cover designer:	Marija Tudor

ISBN 9781633437968
Printed in the United States of America

To my mother, Nadya

brief contents

contents

7 Comparing objects   177

foreword

In August 2023, I got this in my inbox: "Hello, Cay! I'm Tagir Valeev. You may remember me from some discussions in mailing lists. Also, we met in person during a conference...."

I thought that was odd. *Of course* I knew Tagir—and not just from those mailing list discussions. I am the author of the classic *Core Java* book that, since Java 1.0, aims to explain modern Java to professional programmers. As I update the book (for its 13th edition), I need to poke around many obscure and tricky aspects of the Java language and library. Every so often, I am thoroughly stumped about some subtle point, fire up my favorite search engine, and find a thoughtful discussion by none other than Tagir. This man really knows his way around Java. He ought to write a book....

That's what his email was about. "I'm writing my very first book," he wrote and asked me to write a foreword. He pitched his book as follows: "In the book, I concentrate on common and recurring mistakes that developers make in Java programs and try to advise on how to avoid them."

This is not a new idea. Many years ago, I had to learn to program in C. I was horrified that anyone would use such an obviously dangerous language, but what choice did I have? It was the only language with bindings to the libraries I needed to use. I made all the usual mistakes, and only afterward, found Andrew Koenig's delightful *C Traps and Pitfalls*. My life would have been so much more tranquil had I been able to learn from that book instead of the school of hard knocks.

Of course, Java is not C. It is a very thoughtfully designed language, and so is its standard library. Nevertheless, while Java 1.0 was simple, the current version of Java layers on over a quarter century of added complexity. And we have learned a few things, too, during that period. Not everything that seemed a good idea 25 years ago has withstood the test of time.

Therefore, there is ample opportunity to present a hundred pitfalls in the Java language and API, which Tagir has set out to do in this book. Each item is motivated by actual code Tagir has seen in the wild. And he has seen a lot of code, thanks to his position at JetBrains, the makers of IntelliJ IDEA, which is by far the most popular Java IDE.

I assure you that you will learn a lot by reading through those pitfalls, understanding why they are dangerous, and learning how to avoid them. Having programmed in Java since version 1.0, I found myself nodding in agreement many times. At other times I said, "Whoa, I've used Java since version 1.0, and I never knew this!" The problematic items Tagir selected are important. They occur in real code, and Java programmers need to be aware of these issues and how to address them.

There is no better path to success than to learn from failure and no cheaper way than to learn from the failure of others. Follow Tagir's path through those mistakes, and profit from the lessons learned so that you become a better and more confident Java programmer! You could not hope for a more competent guide.

—CAY HORSTMANN
PROFESSOR EMERITUS, SAN JOSÉ STATE UNIVERSITY

preface

I've been developing commercial software for about 20 years, mostly in Java, though I have experience with other languages as well. I have written hundreds of thousands of lines of code, and I've read even more code written by other programmers. If I've discovered one truism in my career, it is that humans are not perfect. Every programmer makes mistakes. Even the smartest software developers can introduce seemingly obvious bugs.

Mistakes always cause struggles. The program does not behave as expected; it fails with exceptions; users complain; and you spend hours reproducing, analyzing, and fixing the problem. Even a very small mistake, like a typo, may require a lot of effort to find.

Around 10 years ago, I discovered a Java static analyzer called FindBugs. It was a revelation to me. We had never used such a tool in our company before, and in a matter of a few minutes, it found dozens of real mistakes in the project I was working on at the time. It pointed exactly to the incorrect piece of code; I didn't need to wait until the mistake actually affected users, and I didn't need to investigate the problem. I could just fix it.

I became a big fan of static analysis. However, I soon discovered that FindBugs has its limitations. It often reports false positives and problems that are not really important, but it takes time to get through them in the report. On the other hand, it doesn't relay many actual bugs that could be reported. For a while, I started to contribute to FindBugs, trying to improve it. A few years later, I joined the incredible team at IntelliJ IDEA, which has its own great static analyzer inside. Since then, helping developers reduce the number of bugs they make became my primary job.

Around that time, I changed my attitude toward the mistakes I was fixing. I was no longer just fixing them—I was always asking myself questions: Why did this happen?

Was it possible to avoid this mistake in the first place? Can a similar problem occur in the future? What can my team do to prevent us from running into this again?

I've found there's no panacea against mistakes. Sometimes, static analysis can help you; sometimes it's better to rely on testing or assertions; sometimes, you should improve your code style, generate code automatically, or use library methods instead of coding something manually. Still, many mistakes have a repetitive nature; they can be categorized, and there are common approaches to avoid them. If you know about possible pitfalls in advance, you'll be prepared to avoid them. So I decided to write a book to summarize my experience and list the most common mistakes that can appear in Java programs, in the hopes that, after reading it, other developers will be prepared without needing to encounter these problems themselves.

acknowledgments

This is my first book. I was really surprised by how many people are involved in the creation of a single book and how all of them are working hard toward making the book better. It's really a huge amount of work.

First of all, I'd like to thank Daniel Zingaro, the first person in Manning who read my book proposal and believed it had potential, despite being submitted by a first-time author. Thanks to him, the proposal went through the initial review, and I signed the contract with Manning. Also, it was Daniel who suggested the title of the book.

The person who helped me the most was my development editor, Connor O'Brien. Before this book, I had experience in writing blog posts and preparing conference talks, so I was pretty self-confident, thinking that I knew how to deliver my thoughts to the reader. But a whole book is a completely different experience! You really need a professional, like Connor, who will guide you toward making the book well structured and understandable (but not boring!) for readers with different background knowledge. He was always convincing me to add more diagrams and tables to make the content easier to comprehend and sharing his ideas on what to draw there. If you like the figures in this book, you should thank Connor as well. Finally, he was very tolerant of the thousands of grammar mistakes, fixing the most blatant of them patiently to avoid scaring off the reviewers.

I was very lucky to have such a great technical editor, Jean-François Morin. Jean-François Morin is a senior Java developer and architect at Laval University in Quebec City, Canada. He holds a BSc in mathematics, an MSc in computer science, and six Sun/Oracle Java certifications. He is also an experienced Java teacher and a regular Manning collaborator. I arrogantly thought my text was technically perfect because I had reread it many times, and, after all, I know the topic pretty well. It turned out I was wrong, and a second pair of eyes from an expert was really useful. Jean-François found a handful of actual mistakes in code snippets, diagrams, and explanations. He also provided very useful suggestions to expand the text and explain things I took for granted.

To make the book even better, several external review rounds were performed. Radmila Ercegovac did the hard work of finding the reviewers and convincing them to spend their time on reviewing my book. It was quite scary to read the reviews, but to my relief, most of them were positive, and even the negative ones contained useful points that helped improve the book. My appreciation to all the reviewers: Akin Kaldiroglu, Amit Basnak, Andrea Silva, Andres Sacco, Arijit Dasgupta, Ashaar Riaz, Bob Shock, Bonnie Malec, Brent Honadel, Carl Hope, Chikkanayakanhalli Krishnegowda Purushotham, Cicero Zandona, Clifford Thurber, Cosimo Damiano Prete, Daut Morina, Deshuang Tang, Gandhi Rajan, Giampiero Granatella, Gianluigi De Marco, Greg Gendron, Gregorio Piccoli, Harsh Gupta, Jakub Jabłoński, Javid Asgarov, Jean-François Morin, Jerome Baton, John Zoetebier, Julia Varigina, Ken W. Alger, Krzysztof Kamyczek, Lakshmi Narayanan, Maksym Prokhorenko, Marcus Geselle, Matthew Greene, Matthew M. Nelson, Matt Welke, Michael Wall, Mikael Byström, Mikhail Malev, Oliver Korten, Oscar Gil, Rahul Kushwaha, Rajeshkumar Muthaiah, Raushan Jha, Ruben Gonzalez-Rubio, Simeon Leyzerzon, Steve Prior, Suhasa R. Krishnayya, Victor M. Perez, and Walter Alexander Mata López.

Before the final publication, the book was released in MEAP, the Manning Early Access Program. Readers could buy the book in advance and read the parts of the book which were available so far. This would not be possible without the work of the MEAP team, including coordinator Matko Hrvatin as well as Dragana Butigan-Berberovic and Ivan Martinović, who prepared nine preliminary versions of the book. Sometimes, they had to do the same work twice, as I applied my edits to the draft concurrently, screwing up the formatting they did. I'm sorry for this! Version control while you're writing a book is a complex thing.

The book was bought more than 500 times in MEAP. Thanks to all of you. I could monitor the sales in real time, and every new sale motivated me to continue working on the book. Some early readers went further and sent me feedback. I'd like to especially thank Piotr Żygieło, who reported the detailed errata.

I'm very grateful to Cay Horstmann, who not only agreed to write a foreword for my book but provided his own review comments. Having input from such a prominent author made me really happy. I am also grateful for the review of a partial draft and the useful feedback provided by the excellent software developer Brian Goetz.

Closer to publication, the book was checked by technical proofreader Cosimo Damiano Prete, who took every single code snippet from the book and checked whether they made sense, whether they worked as described, and whether static analysis tools actually produced the warnings I was speaking about. It was hard to find more mistakes after the technical editor, external reviewers, and MEAP readers, but Cosimo discovered a few very embarrassing issues. I'm very glad you won't see them.

After the draft is complete, the book goes to production, which is done by a separate team of professionals. Christian Berk was my copy editor. He fixed a lot of remaining grammar mistakes and rephrased many sentences to make them sound better. Marija Tudor did the meticulous job typesetting and laying out the book. Mike Beady did the final proofreading. You may think that at this stage there's not many things to fix, but during proofreading we had more than 1,000 individual edits! And I'd also like to thank Kathy Rossland, who coordinated the whole production process.

Writing a book is only a half of the process. The other half is to reach the readers and tell them about the book, which is also the hard work performed by the incredible marketing department of Manning. We are only at the beginning of this journey, but so far, many people have already participated in promoting the book in various ways. I'd like to mention Aira Dučić, Ana Romac, Radmila Ercegovac, Stjepan Jureković, Nikola Dimitrijevic, Christopher Kaufmann, Erik Pillar, Charlotte Harborne, and Paul Spratley.

Additionally, I appreciate the work of Manning management, including Rebecca Rinehart and Melissa Ice, who provided very detailed and comprehensive information about the publication process. I'm pretty sure many more people have worked on my book, whom I don't even know. Thank you to the whole Manning team.

This book would never have been written if I had not worked for JetBrains, the company that creates unique tools for programmers, including IntelliJ IDEA, which really helps programmers avoid many mistakes. Most of the book content was inspired by my everyday work. Also, some of my colleagues, including Trisha Gee, Dmitry Jemerov, Mala Gupta, and Andrey Akinshin, who are book authors already, shared their experience on how to write, how to approach the publisher, and so on. Thanks to them, this was not so scary for me.

Finally, I'd like to thank my wife, Ekaterina, and my sons, Artem and Maksim. They were very patient and supportive when I spent my free time writing the book—well, not every time. Right now, as I'm writing this, Maksim is trying to sit on my neck and tell me something right into my ear. But this is OK.

about this book

100 Java Mistakes and How to Avoid Them is a catalogue of mistakes that may occur in Java programs. Each mistake typically contains a code sample, a description of the mistake, its possible consequences, and the ways to avoid it. Many mistakes are accompanied by sidebars, in which I mention static analysis tools that can detect such a mistake. The appendixes describe ways to enhance existing static analysis tools to detect mistakes specific to your project.

Who should read this book

I believe this book is most useful for middle-level software developers who already know the Java language but may not have enough practical programming experience. Some bug patterns described in the book may be unfamiliar to senior software developers as well. Less-experienced developers or even advanced students might also find this book interesting.

How this book is organized: A road map

The book is organized into 10 chapters and 2 appendices. Chapter 1 explains common approaches used in software engineering to manage code quality and avoid bugs. The subsequent chapters cover various individual mistakes, grouped by category. The mistake sections are mostly independent of each other, so feel free to skip something if you already know the given pattern or feel it's not applicable to your daily work.

- Chapter 2 discusses mistakes inside individual expressions, such as problems with precedence, mixing one operator with another, or pitfalls with variable arity method calls.
- Chapter 3 concentrates on mistakes related to the structural elements of a Java program. This includes problems with statements like `for` loops as well as

higher-level structural issues, like circular initialization of superclasses and sub-classes.

- Chapter 4 covers problems working with numbers in Java, including the infamous problem with numeric overflow.
- Chapter 5 concentrates on several of the most common exceptions in Java, like `NullPointerException` and `ClassCastException`.
- Chapter 6 focuses on what can go wrong with string processing.
- Chapter 7 is devoted to comparing objects and is mostly concerned with using and implementing methods like `equals()`, `hashCode()`, and `compareTo()`.
- Chapter 8 concentrates on mistakes that come about when you use collections and maps.
- Chapter 9 covers some easy-to-misuse library methods not covered in previous chapters.
- Finally, chapter 10 describes mistakes that may happen when writing unit tests.

The appendixes briefly describe how to enhance some static analysis tools to catch problems specific to your project. These are optional to read, but if you are ready to introduce custom static analysis rules to your project, they can serve as a starter guide.

About the code

As the book is devoted to mistakes, aside from appendix B, it does not contain the complete programs intended to be compiled and executed. Instead, it contains short snippets of Java code that demonstrate the mistakes being discussed. The source code is formatted in a `fixed-width font`, `like this`, to separate it from ordinary text. I try to keep code samples as short as possible. In most cases, I omit the class declaration or even the method declaration, leaving only the method body. I also tend to use more compact code formatting than is usually seen in real-world Java programming. For example, I may omit the `@Override` annotation on the overriding method, despite the fact that it's recommended.

Appendix B describes sample plugins for static analysis tools, which are complete projects. The source code of these plugins can be found on GitHub at https://github.com/amaembo/100_java_mistakes_appendix. Alternatively, you can download the complete code for the examples in the book from the Manning website at https://www.manning.com/books/100-java-mistakes-and-how-to-avoid-them.

liveBook discussion forum

Purchase of *100 Java Mistakes and How to Avoid Them* includes free access to liveBook, Manning's online reading platform. Using liveBook's exclusive discussion features, you can attach comments to the book globally or to specific sections or paragraphs. It's a snap to make notes for yourself, ask and answer technical questions, and receive help from the author and other users. To access the forum, go to https://livebook .manning.com/book/100-java-mistakes-and-how-to-avoid-them/discussion. You can also learn more about Manning's forums and the rules of conduct at https://livebook .manning.com/discussion.

Manning's commitment to our readers is to provide a venue where a meaningful dialogue between individual readers and between readers and the author can take place. It is not a commitment to any specific amount of participation on the part of the author, whose contribution to the forum remains voluntary (and unpaid). We suggest you try asking the author some challenging questions lest his interest stray! The forum and the archives of previous discussions will be accessible from the publisher's website as long as the book is in print.

about the author

 **TAGIR VALEEV** is a technical lead at JetBrains GmbH. He belongs to the Java team, which is responsible for Java language support in IntelliJ IDEA. His primary interest is static analysis and code refactoring. Tagir designed and developed many code inspections for IntelliJ IDEA's built-in static analyzer. Previously, Tagir contributed to FindBugs, which is a Java bytecode static analysis tool. Tagir has 15 years of experience writing commercial software in Java and 10 years of experience in the field of static analysis. He holds a PhD in computer science (2006) and the title Java Champion (2020).

about the cover illustration

The figure on the cover of *100 Java Mistakes and How to Avoid Them* is *Habitant des Isles Philipines*, or *Inhabitant of the Philippine Islands*, taken from a collection by Jacques Grasset de Saint-Sauveur, published in 1788. Each illustration is finely drawn and colored by hand.

In those days, it was easy to identify where people lived and what their trade or station in life was just by their dress. Manning celebrates the inventiveness and initiative of the computer business with book covers based on the rich diversity of regional culture centuries ago, brought back to life by pictures from collections such as this one.

Managing code quality

This chapter covers

- Various techniques to improve the quality of your code
- Advantages and disadvantages of static analysis
- Approaches to make static analysis more useful
- Testing and assertions

Every software developer introduces bugs to the code—there's no way to avoid them completely. Some bugs cause very subtle changes to a program's behavior no user would reasonably care about. However, other bugs are much more severe and, depending on the project, could lead to millions of dollars in loss, a destroyed spacecraft, or even the loss of human lives. Most bugs fall somewhere in the middle: they don't have disastrous effects, but they annoy users and require hours of debugging and fixing.

Some bugs are caused by a misunderstanding of the specification requirements, a miscommunication between the software development team and the customer, or a similar human error. Other bugs are created by a miscommunication between the developer and the machine. That is, the developer correctly understands the problem but writes the wrong code, so the machine solves the problem incorrectly. This book is devoted to this second category.

Some bugs are complex and unique. For example, one module may fail to handle a rare corner case, and another may rely on that corner case—and everything might have been fine until these modules started talking to each other. In rare cases, three or more independent components are involved, and the problem appears only when all of them are connected to each other. Investigation of such problems can be as exciting as a good detective story.

However, programmers also produce repetitive bugs in many different programs. Experienced developers have seen many such bugs in their practice, so they know in advance what kind of code is dangerous and requires special care. They can spot these erroneous code patterns, simply because they've seen a similar type of bug in the past. Less-experienced developers overlook repetitive bugs more often, so the bug has a greater chance of slipping into production and causing serious consequences.

The purpose of this book is to summarize this experience. I list the common mistakes that appear in Java programs. For every mistake discussed in the book, I show a code example, explain why this problem usually happens, and advise on how to avoid the problem. I have seen most of the mistakes listed in this book in real production code bases. More often, though, I provide synthetic code samples based on real code, as this allows us to concentrate on each bug without going deep into the details of a particular project.

Each type of mistake discussed in the book is accompanied by a Ways to Avoid This Mistake section, which summarizes useful ideas to help you avoid this problem in your code. Just before this section, you will find a Static Analysis sidebar for each mistake known to be reported by static analysis tools. If you feel you already know about a particular mistake, feel free to fast-forward beyond the detailed description, straight to the Ways to Avoid This Mistake section. Most of the mistake descriptions are independent, so you can skip those that don't seem relevant to you now. For example, if you don't often work with numbers or bitwise arithmetic, you may want to postpone reading the corresponding sections until you actually need to maintain such code.

This book doesn't cover mistakes that cause a compilation error. Such mistakes also often occur, of course, but there's not much to say about them other than to read the Java compiler output and correct them. Luckily, the Java compiler is quite strict, and many things that are acceptable in other programming languages cause compilation errors in Java. This includes many instances of unreachable code, use of an uninitialized local variable, impossible type casts, and so on. Thanks to the compiler, I can omit these cases from the book and concentrate on the problems that will survive compilation and can slip into your production code.

The Java programming language is constantly evolving, and new versions may offer language constructs and library methods that help you avoid particular bugs. Unfortunately, they will not help if you don't know about them, so if you migrate to the new version of Java, take the time to learn about new capabilities. Throughout the book, I mention new features of Java (up to JDK 21) relevant to the discussed mistakes.

Over its decades-long history, several approaches to managing code quality have emerged in the software development industry. These approaches include code review; pair programming; static analysis; and various kinds of testing, including unit testing, property testing, integration testing, smoke testing, and several others. In this chapter, I provide an overview of some of the most notable of these approaches before we start discussing individual bugs later in the book.

1.1   Code review and pair programming

The *code review* technique involves an organized peer review of the changes committed by developers. Quite frequently, a second look at the code by someone with different experience and a unique background can be the difference between a bug being overlooked by the author and being caught before release. Code reviews are useful for more than simply catching bugs. They can also help improve the code architecture, readability, performance, and so on. Additionally, code review improves knowledge sharing and mentoring inside the organization. There are several notable books, conference talks, and blog posts on how to make code reviews efficient. For example, I recommend reading *What to Look for in a Code Review* by Trisha Gee (Leanpub, 2016).

Pair programming is a technique that emerged from the extreme programming methodology. It's an extreme version of code review, in which two programmers work together, either at one workstation or using a real-time collaborative code editing tool (aka remote pair programming). In this case, the code is reviewed while it's being written. Compared to code review, pair programming is more efficient, but it requires more discipline. Again, there are many excellent resources on how to use pair programming practically—for example, I recommend *Practical Remote Pair Programming: Best Practices, Tips, and Techniques for Collaborating Productively with Distributed Development Teams* by Adrian Bolboacă (Packt Publishing, 2021). *Extreme Programming Explained* by Kent Beck (Addison-Wesley, 2000), a classic programming text, also promotes the idea of pair programming.

1.2   Code style

In Java, a program can be written in many different ways and still achieve the same end goal. You can use conditional expressions instead of `if` statements, replace `while` loops with `for` loops, wrap statement bodies into braces or omit them, consistently mark local variables as `final` or avoid using this modifier, use different indentation styles, and so on. While many such decisions are a matter of taste, some invariably reduce the number of bugs in your code.

For example, to specify that a number has the `long` type, it's possible to use either a lowercase `l` or uppercase `L` suffix, as in `10l` or `10L`. However, it's generally agreed that uppercase `L` is better because it's possible to accidentally mix up a lowercase `l` with the digit `1`.

Another example is using braces around an `if` statement body that contains only one statement. The Java language allows you to omit them:

```
if (a < b)
  System.out.println("a is smaller!");
```
No braces—correct but error prone

However, this may cause an unpleasant mistake when a developer wants to add another line of code under the condition:

```
if (a < b)
  System.out.println("a is smaller!");
  System.out.println("and b is bigger");
```
Incorrect—this line is always executed.

In this case, the last line will be erroneously executed unconditionally. To avoid such a problem, many projects and development teams require programmers to wrap the `if` body in braces:

```
if (a < b) {
  System.out.println("a is smaller!");
}
```
Good—braces make the code more robust.

In your projects, you can create your own code style or follow an existing one. I recommend reading through the *Google Java Style Guide* (https://google.github.io/styleguide/javaguide.html). It does not cover every aspect of Java programming and usually lags in describing new features, but it's a good start for deriving your own style. You may also find *Code Conventions for the Java Programming Language* on Oracle's website, but unfortunately, it's not actively maintained and applies to a very old Java version. Many code style aspects can be configured in an integrated development environment (IDE) so that it will format code automatically for you. For example, in Eclipse IDE, you can find code style settings in the Preferences window, under Java > Code Style. You will find most of the interesting options under Clean Up. Press the Edit button, which displays the detailed configuration window (figure 1.1). There, you will find options for both of the previously listed examples (Use Uppercase for Long Literal Suffix as well as Use Blocks in `if`/`while`/`for`/`do` Statements) and many other interesting options. Now is a good time to experiment with the settings a bit. For example, try changing each option to see what changes in the Preview pane. Which settings do you think will help avoid bugs?

IntelliJ IDEA takes a somewhat different approach. Some aspects of the code style, such as spacing, line breaks, and braces, can be configured in Settings > Editor > Code Style > Java and stored in the project code style settings or EditorConfig files. However, many other options, such as long literal suffix, are configured as code inspections under Settings > Editor > Inspections and stored inside a separate file, called *inspection profile*. Consult the IDE documentation for instructions on sharing these settings within your team.

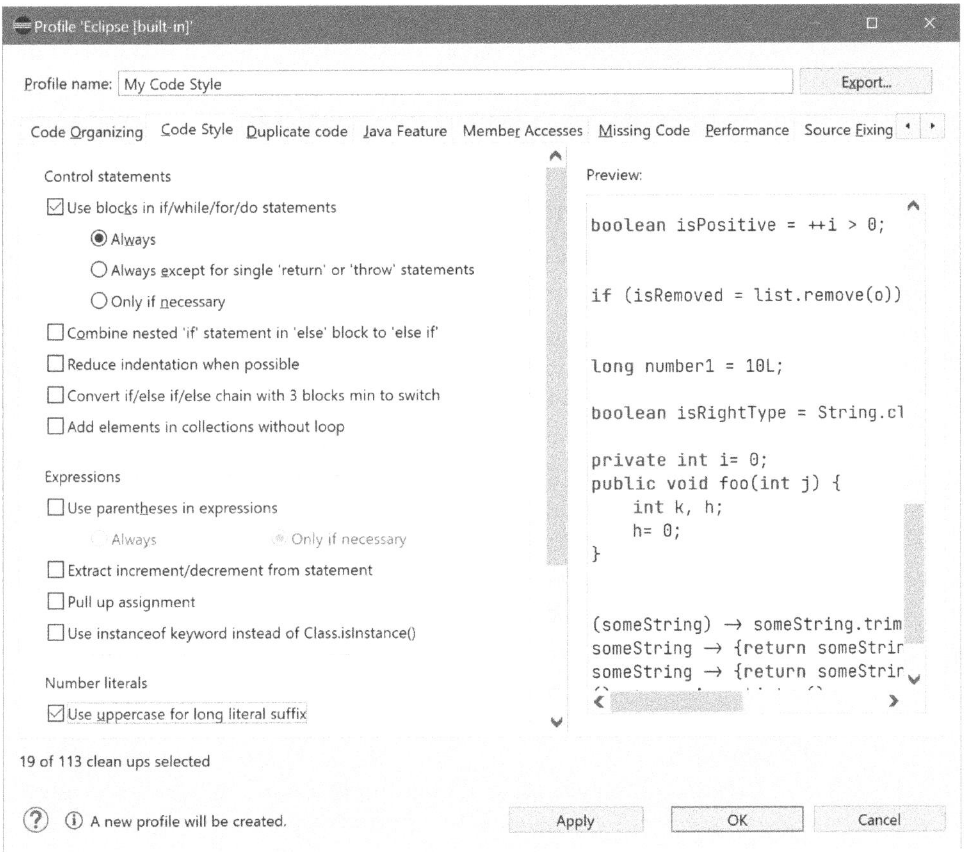

Figure 1.1   Eclipse Clean Up configuration window

While a consistent code style is helpful to make code more readable and less error prone, it protects you only against a small set of errors. Most of the mistakes covered in this book cannot be solved via code style alone, so you must use other approaches as well to make your code robust.

1.3 *Static analysis*

Static analysis is another very helpful technique that may help detect bugs. To some extent, it could be called an automated code review: it points to suspicious, confusing, or likely erroneous code, just like a human reviewer would. Still, it cannot replace code review. While static analysis is very good at detecting specific kinds of bugs, there are also many bugs that could be easily spotted by humans but will never be detected by a static analyzer. Often, static analyzers look at specific code patterns, and any deviation from these patterns may confuse the analyzer.

You may also encounter the terms *lint* or *linter* in programming-related articles or conference talks. Initially developed in 1978, Lint was the first well-known static analysis tool for the C language. Since then, the word lint has been commonly used to refer to static analyzers, with some even using lint in their name—notably, JSLint, which is a static analyzer for JavaScript.

1.3.1 Static analysis tools for Java

There are many static analyzers suitable for checking Java programs. Here's an incomplete list:

- *IntelliJ IDEA* (https://www.jetbrains.com/idea/)—A Java IDE with a powerful built-in static analyzer. It supports many languages, including Java. While it's a commercial IDE, a free and open source Community Edition is available, which includes most of the static analysis capabilities. In this book, we refer only to the functionality available in the free version of IntelliJ IDEA.
- *SonarLint* (https://www.sonarsource.com/products/sonarlint/)—A free static analyzer by Sonar, which is available as an IDE plugin. It supports many languages, including Java. This static analyzer is also integrated into the Sonar continuous code quality inspection platform, SonarQube.
- *Error Prone* (https://errorprone.info/)—An open source static analyzer developed by Google that works as a Java compiler plugin.
- *PVS-Studio* (https://pvs-studio.com/)—A proprietary static analyzer for C, C++, C#, and Java.
- *PMD* (https://pmd.github.io/)—An open source, rule-based, extensible, cross-language static code analyzer. In addition to Java, it detects problems in several other languages, including XML, JavaScript, Kotlin, and others.
- *SpotBugs* (https://spotbugs.github.io/)—A static analyzer that checks Java bytecode rather than source files.
- *Coverity* (https://mng.bz/0lol)—A proprietary static code analysis tool from Synopsys. It covers many languages and supports more than 200 frameworks for Java, JavaScript, C#, and more.
- *Klocwork* (https://www.perforce.com/products/klocwork)—A static code analysis tool owned by Perforce. It focuses on security and safety and covers a range of programming languages, including C, C++, C#, Java, JavaScript, and Python.
- *CodeQL* (https://codeql.github.com/)—A static analyzer integrated with GitHub. If your project is hosted on GitHub, you can set up a workflow to scan the project automatically. It supports many languages and is capable of providing deep, interprocedural analysis. It also includes a query language, which allows you to extend the analyzer.

There are many other analyzers in addition to those listed here, each with its own strengths and weaknesses. We won't compare them in this book—it's up to you to decide which to use. Just note that using any static analyzer is much better than using none. Some projects even use several analyzers at once to catch more bugs.

1.3.2   Using static analyzers

Some static analysis tools can be installed as IDE plugins or extensions. For example, you can easily install SonarLint as a plugin for popular Java IDEs. In the Eclipse IDE, open Help > Eclipse Marketplace, and then search for *SonarLint*. After installation, it will automatically report problems in the editor. For example, let's consider a simple mistake: shifting an `int` value by 32 bits. This operation has no effect in Java, and such code is likely a mistake, so it's reported by virtually any Java static analyzer. Figure 1.2 shows how this would look in the Eclipse IDE with the SonarLint plugin installed.

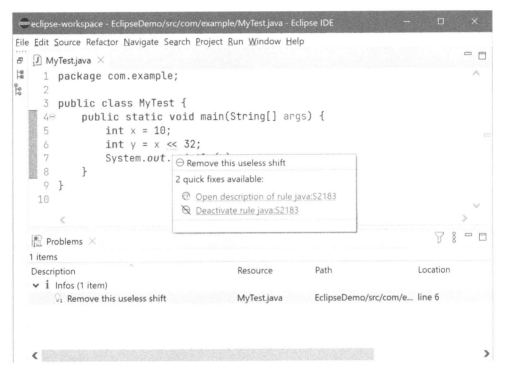

Figure 1.2   The Eclipse IDE with the SonarLint plugin installed shows a warning about an `int` value being shifted by 32 bits.

The mistake is underlined in the editor and listed in the Problems view. If you hover over the mistake, you have options to read the description or deactivate the rule. SonarLint also allows you to run the analysis on a whole project or some part of it (e.g., a particular package).

SonarLint is also available as an extension for Visual Studio Code. Select the Install Extensions action, and then search for and install *SonarLint*. It will immediately start analyzing your source code, and it looks very similar to Eclipse, as shown in figure 1.3.

Again, you have a problem listed in the Problems view and the ability to deactivate the rule or read its description.

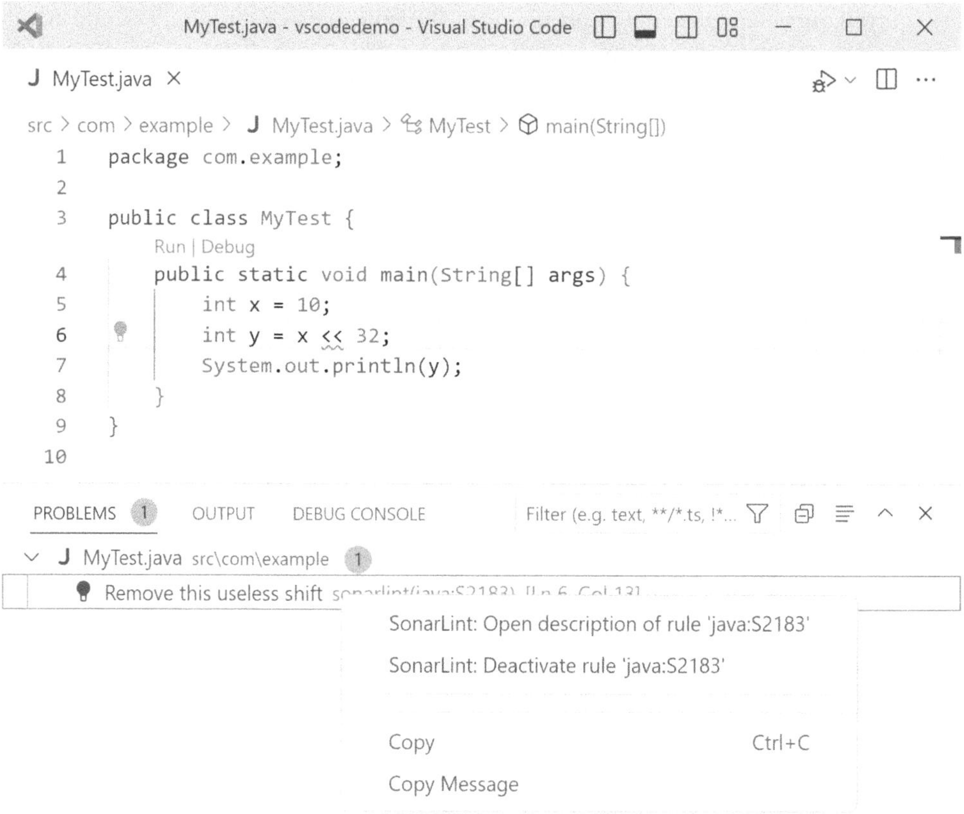

Figure 1.3   Visual Studio Code with the SonarLint plugin installed shows a warning about an `int` value being shifted by 32 bits.

Plugins and extensions for other static analysis tools, like SpotBugs or PVS-Studio, can be installed in a similar way. Note that PVS-Studio generally requires a paid license.

Static analyzers, like Error Prone, are better integrated into the build process. You can add the corresponding plugin to your Maven or Gradle build script, depending on the build system used. See the installation documentation (https://errorprone .info/docs/installation) for further information.

If you use an IDE, like IntelliJ IDEA, you get a powerful static analyzer automatically. Android Studio, an IDE from Google for Android developers, is based on IntelliJ IDEA and contains its static analyzer as well. In this case, you don't need to install or configure anything additional to start using static analysis. If you make a mistake, it will be automatically highlighted right in the editor as an inspection message, as shown in figure 1.4. Still, if you want to use SonarLint in IntelliJ IDEA, you can install it as a plugin from the plugin marketplace. You can also reuse the IntelliJ IDEA static analysis engine on a continuous integration server via JetBrains Qodana (https://www.jetbrains.com/qodana/).

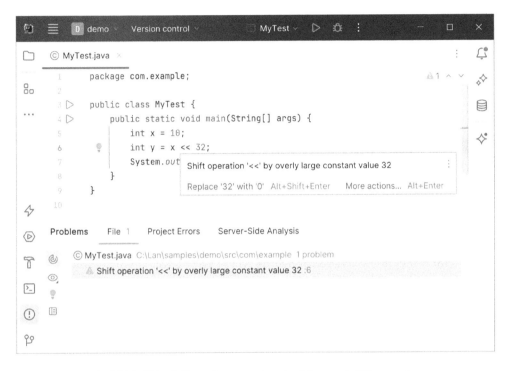

Figure 1.4   IntelliJ IDEA built-in static analyzer warning about incorrect shift amount

An inspection may suggest a quick-fix action to eliminate the mistake—don't be too eager to apply it though. Sometimes, quick-fix actions just simplify the code, preserving current semantics. But if it's really a bug, then the semantics should be changed. Here, for example, the quick fix is suggested to change the operation to x << 0. This preserves the code semantics, but it's unlikely to fix the problem. The author likely wanted to specify a different constant or use the long type instead of int, in which case shifting by 32 bits makes sense. We don't know for sure, but the suggested quick fix won't help us. Always investigate the root cause of the warning, instead of applying a quick fix blindly.

If you press Alt-Enter, you may see more fixes and context actions. Pressing the right arrow, you'll find options to edit the inspection settings, suppress the warning, or disable the inspection completely (figure 1.5).

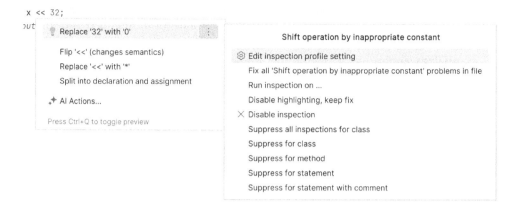

Figure 1.5   A static analysis additional warning menu that allows you to suppress the warning, edit inspection options, or disable the inspection

Static analyzers may know the behavior of standard library methods and warn if you use them incorrectly. However, they typically are not aware of the behavior of your own methods or methods used by third-party libraries. One way to teach static analyzers about the behavior of your own methods is using specific annotations analyzers recognize. I mention some of these annotations throughout the book, and they are covered in more detail in appendix A.

Many static analyzers are extensible. Usually, they provide a kind of plugin API that allows users to write a custom detector for new problems. Other analyzers offer a kind of flexible configuration or scripting, like the structural search and replace actions in IntelliJ IDEA. We discuss extending static analyzers in greater detail in appendix B.

> **Static analysis**
>
> Throughout the book, you'll see sidebars like this one, discussing the specifics of static analysis results for a given class of mistakes. In these sidebars, I mention the name of the corresponding inspection or rule in popular tools, like IntelliJ IDEA or SonarLint, and discuss the limitations of static analysis or additional configuration necessary to report a particular problem.

1.3.3   *Limitations of static analysis*

With Static Analysis sidebars included in most sections of this book, you might begin to wonder why you need to learn about a mistake if the analyzer will warn you anyway. While it may be tempting to overly rely on static analysis, unfortunately, it is not a silver bullet. Static analysis certainly helps prevent mistakes, but it has its limitations.

Static analysis tools can work either online or offline. Online, or in-editor, static analyzers are integrated with the code editor and update the result of analysis as soon as you type new code or save it to disk. Usually, an online static analysis tool only displays the bugs it has found in the currently opened editor. Offline analysis should be launched explicitly or performed on a continuous integration server and may take significantly more time to produce the report for the whole project. While online static analysis is convenient and powerful, it has limitations, due to its limited CPU resources and the necessity to process constantly changing code. Specifically, the online analyzer usually does very limited interprocedural analysis.

Another problem with online analysis is that changes in one class may introduce problems to a completely different class using the current one. In these cases, even if online analysis can detect the error, you may not notice it unless you explicitly check all the call sites of each of the methods you've changed. Offline analysis that checks the whole project would be more helpful in this scenario.

In modern IDEs, online code analysis does not require any configuration; however, sooner or later, you're likely to start finding it annoying. One reason is that, oftentimes, many of the problems the IDE reports are irrelevant to your project. For example, static analysis might suggest you avoid using `System.out.println()` and instead opt for logging frameworks. This is good advice for enterprise software, but if you have a small research project, it's probably OK to rely on simple console output rather than deal with logging configuration.

Other warnings may be technically correct but not a source of real problems in your project; in some cases, it would take too much effort to fix the warnings, resulting in less-readable code. For example, calculating average value as `(a + b) / 2` has an overflow risk if `a` and `b` are large enough (we discuss this in greater detail in mistake 27 in chapter 4). However, in your program, `a` and `b` may always be small enough that the problem never occurs, meaning dealing with this warning would be just a waste of time.

Static analyzers usually search for specific code patterns to report. So even if a static analyzer recognizes a particular kind of mistake, it may overlook it in your code if you use a different code shape. For example, most static analyzers check for odd and negative numbers (see mistake 30 in chapter 4) and will report an expression like `value % 2 == 1`, which doesn't work for negative values. However, if you decide to extract the `value % 2` part to a separate variable, some analyzers will not report it, even though it's technically the same code and mistake.

You may also notice that not every mistake is reported by every static analyzer. Even the best analyzers may not report mistakes known by their competitors. Some programmers use several analyzers at once, but this can be difficult, as you'll need to configure all of them and deal with many more false-positive and noise warnings.

Finally, sometimes, static analysis warnings are plain wrong, as even the most advanced static analyzer is not perfect and cannot analyze a program completely. Don't forget that static analyzers are programs as well, which means they also contain bugs. It's possible that the static analyzer authors never considered a code pattern used in your project and have mistakenly reported it as suspicious.

1.3.4 *Suppressing unwanted warnings*

When you start using a static analyzer, you might find yourself concerned about the large number of unwanted warnings it produces. Fortunately, analyzers provide several ways to remove them. Most static analyzers consist of individual tools called *diagnostics*, *rules*, *detectors*, or *inspections*. It's possible to turn them off selectively, either for the whole project or a specific part of it. Additionally, analyzers may provide configuration options for inspections. These options allow you to turn off the warning in specific situations or help the analyzer recognize your own classes, like custom logging frameworks.

Often, it's preferable to suppress a particular warning, rather than disable a whole inspection. Usually, this is done via code comments or annotations. IntelliJ IDEA supports both of these methods. Suppression comments start with the `noinspection` prefix. It's also a good idea to explain every suppression. For example, assume we create a local variable named `debugData`, whose type is `List`. We fill it but never read its content. IntelliJ IDEA does not like it and reports that the collection is written but never read. However, we are using it to be able to get useful information during debugging or memory dumps analysis when something goes wrong. We can suppress the warning like this:

```
//Collection is never read: intended (used for debug)
//noinspection MismatchedQueryAndUpdateOfCollection
List<String> debugData = new ArrayList<>();
```

Alternatively, it's possible to use an `@SuppressWarnings` annotation:

```
//Collection is never read: intended (used for debug)
@SuppressWarnings("MismatchedQueryAndUpdateOfCollection")
List<String> debugData = new ArrayList<>();
```

Annotations are less flexible, as they can only be applied to variable declarations, methods, or classes. If you put a suppression annotation on the method, no warning of a specified kind will be displayed inside that method. This would mean there's a risk that, later, another more useful warning of the same kind will appear in the same method, but it will be suppressed as well, causing you to miss it. I recommend applying suppressions to the narrowest scope possible.

Even if different analyzers report the same problem, the suppression ID and even the suppression annotation could be different. For example, table 1.1 shows how to suppress a warning on an `x << 32` expression in various analyzers.

Table 1.1 Suppression of bad shift amount in different static analyzers

Static analyzer	Suppression annotation
IntelliJ IDEA	`@SuppressWarnings("ShiftOutOfRange")`
Error Prone	`@SuppressWarnings("BadShiftAmount")`
SonarLint	`@SuppressWarnings("squid:S2183")`
SpotBugs	`@SuppressFBWarnings("ICAST_BAD_SHIFT_AMOUNT")`

This complicates things if you use several different static analysis tools (e.g., one tool in the IDE and another on the CI server). If your code triggers a warning by several tools, you will need to suppress it for each tool separately.

Sometimes, if you see an unwanted static analysis warning, it's better to modify the source code in a way that makes the analyzer happy, rather than add a suppression. One may argue we should aim to produce correct, performant, readable, and maintainable code, not code that pleases the analyzer; however, fixing the code for the analyzer often also makes it better for human readers. It's not always easy to understand how to avoid a warning, but there are some common techniques that might be helpful:

- If you are using an unusual code pattern in many parts of your program and your static analyzer does not like it, consider extracting the pattern to a utility method and calling that method everywhere instead. Now, you only need to suppress one warning inside that method. You can also write documentation for the method and explain the rationale behind the unusual code pattern. This might be helpful for future code readers as well.

- If you calculate the same nontrivial value twice, consider extracting it to a local variable. Aside from removing the duplication, this will inform the analyzer that recalculation yields the same value. Consider the following example:

```
@Nullable String calculateData(int value) {…}    ◁─┐  This method may return
                                                     │  null for some input values.
void printData() {
  if (calculateData(1000) != null) {
    System.out.println(calculateData(1000).trim());   ◁──────────────┐
  }                                                                   │
}                                         Warning: Method invocation  │
                                                  trim() may produce  │
                                              NullPointerException    │
```

Here, we are using the method `calculateData()` twice with the same parameter value. We assume the method result depends only on the input parameter and does not change between invocations. However, the static analyzer may not know this. As the method is annotated as `@Nullable` (we will cover this annotation in greater detail in mistake 41 in chapter 5), the analyzer assumes the resulting value should always be checked against `null`; hence, it produces an unwanted warning when `trim()` is called on the result of `calculateData()`. Instead of silencing the analyzer with a suppression, we can help it by extracting the repeating computation into a new local variable:

```
String data = calculateData(1000);
if (data != null) {                      │  No warning
  System.out.println(data.trim());   ◁──┘  anymore
}
```

Now, the analyzer knows that the value stored in the `data` variable was checked against `null`—thus, a warning is no longer issued.

1.4   *Automated testing*

Automated testing is another technique used to discover bugs. There are many kinds of automated tests, including unit testing, property-based testing, functional testing, integration testing, and several others. Some complete methodologies for testing even exist, like test-driven development (TDD), in which tests are written before the actual code. There are several excellent books on TDD if you'd like to learn more, including *Test Driven: Practical TDD and Acceptance TDD for Java Developers* by Lasse Koskela (Manning, 2007, https://www.manning.com/books/test-driven). To learn more about the JUnit testing framework, I recommend reading *JUnit in Action* by Cătălin Tudose (Manning, 2020, https://mng.bz/K9vZ).

I especially like the property-based testing approach, as it allows you to find bugs in new code without even writing any new unit tests. The idea is to perform random operations with your program and check that the program has some expected properties or its behavior is within the expected bounds. For example, you might check whether no unexpected exceptions happen, read-only operations don't actually modify anything, and so on. If the property you are checking is violated, the testing framework provides you with a way to replay the sequence of operations and reproduce the problem. It also tries to remove some operations from the replay sequence if the problem is still reproducible without them. If you want to create property tests for Java software, you can try the jqwik (https://jqwik.net/) framework.

Unfortunately, it's rarely possible to discover each and every bug with automated testing alone. Usually, the quality of tests is measured by a code coverage tool, like JaCoCo (https://www.jacoco.org/jacoco/). This tool instruments the Java bytecode and reports which fraction of the existing code is executed during automated tests. It can report covered percentage in terms of lines of code, bytecode instructions, or branches.

My experience has taught me that when coverage exceeds 80%, increasing it further requires much more effort, which continues to grow exponentially as coverage approaches 100%. So, if you set a very high bar for test coverage in your project, you may end up spending all your time writing tests instead of actual functionality. Some lines of code are simply impossible to cover. For example, assume you implement the `Cloneable` interface to be able to clone objects. As `Cloneable` is implemented, you don't want clients to deal with checked `CloneNotSupportedException`, as this would never happen, so you handle it by yourself:

```java
class MyObject implements Cloneable {
  public MyObject clone() {
    try {
      return (MyObject) super.clone();
    } catch (CloneNotSupportedException e) {
      // never happens as we implement Cloneable
      throw new AssertionError(e);
    }
  }
}
```

Java requires something to be inside the catch section, either a `return` or `throw` state-ment, even if it's never reachable. However, it's impossible to write a unit test that covers this statement, and it's likely that your code coverage tool will always report the corresponding line as not covered.

On the other hand, even 100% test coverage doesn't mean your code has no bugs. Consider a simple Java method that averages two `int` values:

```
static double average(int x, int y) {
  return (x + y) / 2;
}
```

Assume we call it once in unit tests with a single pair of values, like

```
assertEquals(5, average(0, 10));
```

This test passes, and the coverage tool will show 100% coverage. Does this mean the method is free of bugs? No. In fact, it contains two problems:

- It uses integer division in a floating-point context. As a result, `average(0, 1)` returns `0.0` instead of `0.5`.
- If an input number is too large, the result may overflow. For example, if you call `average(2000000000, 2000000000)` it will return `−1.47483648E8` instead of `2.0E9`.

It appears that both problems can be reported by static analysis tools. We discuss these in greater detail in chapter 4.

Another problem with coverage analysis is that it cannot check whether your tests actually assert the expected behavior. There are many ways to write a test incorrectly—so that it executes your code but doesn't test its correctness. The most trivial mistake is to forget the assertion call. If your test simply calls `average(0, 10)`, you'll still have the method covered, even if you don't check whether the result is correct.

Again, don't forget that tests are also code, so they may contain bugs that prevent them from functioning properly. For example, an incorrectly written test may not fail if the code being tested functions improperly. We discuss some bug patterns related to testing in chapter 10.

1.5 *Mutation coverage*

There's a better approach to evaluate the quality of automatic tests: *mutation coverage.* When the tests are launched with a mutation coverage engine, it instruments the code, adding trivial edits. For example, it may change a `>=` comparison to `>` or `<=`, replace a numeric variable x with `x + 1`, negate `boolean` variables, remove some calls, and so on. Then, for each edit (usually called *mutations*), it checks whether any of the tests now fail. If any do fail, the mutation is killed; if none fail, it survives. The final report contains the percentage of killed mutations, with higher numbers indicating better test suite quality. The report also contains detailed information about the mutations that survived, so you can quickly understand which code requires more tests. The most popular mutation testing system for Java is Pitest (https://pitest.org/).

Mutation coverage analysis helps to detect some problems not detected by normal coverage. For example, if you ignore the result of a method in an automated test, most mutations introduced in that method will survive (some of the mutations may lead to exceptions or infinite loops and, thus, may be killed even if the method result is ignored). However, there are also downsides of this approach. First, complete mutation analysis is many times slower than the run time of normal tests. Mutation coverage is acceptable if you have a small project, in which running all the tests normally takes just a few minutes. However, for bigger projects, it might be too slow. There are ways to perform mutation testing incrementally, but it complicates the continuous integration process.

Another problem is that some mutations cannot be killed at all. For example, consider the following method:

```
public static int length(int from, int to) {
  if (from > to) return 0;
  return to - from;
}
```

It returns the length of the interval, assuming the length is zero if `from` is greater than `to`. The method is very simple, and leaving these tests to cover it should be sufficient (let's ignore the possible overflow problem):

```
assertEquals(0, length(1, 1));
assertEquals(100, length(0, 100));
assertEquals(0, length(100, 0));
```

However, if we run Pitest 1.7.6 with default options for this code, it says that only 75% of mutations (3 of 4) are killed. That's because one of the mutations (created by the conditionals boundary mutator) replaces the 'from > to' condition with 'from >= to'. As you can see from the code, this change doesn't affect the method result for any input, so it cannot be caught by any test. While changing the comparison operator can break the code in some cases, whether to use the > or >= operator is a matter of preference here. Of course, Pitest cannot know whether a particular mutation actually changes the code behavior, so even if you write every possible test, you cannot kill all the mutations.

Finally, you should really check all the survived mutations to find possible omissions in your automated test suite. If your coverage is not close to 100%, too many mutations may have survived. Therefore, it's a good idea to increase line coverage to at least 90% before using mutation coverage.

1.6   *Dynamic analysis*

In addition to static analysis, there are also tools that perform *dynamic analysis* to find bugs when executing your code. These tools are tailored to detect very specific bugs, mostly related to concurrency. One example of such a tool is Java Pathfinder (https://github.com/javapathfinder), which can detect data races, unhandled exceptions, potentially failed assertions, and more. It requires quite a complex set up process and a lot of system resources to analyze even a small application.

Another tool worth mentioning is Dl-Check (https://github.com/devexperts/dlcheck) by Devexperts. It's a Java agent that aims to find potential deadlocks in multithreaded programs. Dl-Check is quite simple to run and very useful.

These tools don't replace static analysis but can augment it. Usually, dynamic analysis finds problems that are difficult to identify via static analysis, and vice versa. Static analysis tools usually detect many more bug patterns than dynamic analysis tools. Also, dynamic analysis only detects problems in executed code, so if you use dynamic analysis with a test suite, problems will only be found in code covered by tests. In contrast, static analysis can detect bugs in any part of the code, even if it's not covered by tests.

1.7 Code assertions

A technique similar to unit testing is adding *code assertions* directly into the production code. This way, you can assert the expected state of your program, and if it falls into an unexpected state, it will immediately fail. This doesn't prevent all bugs, but it helps you find them earlier and increases the chance bugs will be found during testing and before release. Also, if the code is well covered with assertions, the assertion failure happens close to the actual bug, so it becomes much easier to debug the problem. Without assertions, the system might remain, unnoticed, in the incorrect state for a much longer period of time.

Java provides a standard mechanism for assertions: the `assert` statement. It contains a `boolean` expression that must be true in a correctly written program and, optionally, an additional expression that may add some explanation or context when the assertion is violated:

```
assert condition;
assert condition : explanation;
```

When Java programs are executed, assertions can be enabled via the JVM command-line option `-ea` (enable assertions). They are disabled by default, and it's expected that they are disabled in production. If you use assertions, make sure they are enabled during testing. It's also possible to enable or disable assertions for particular classes or packages, using additional parameters for the `-ea` and `-da` (disable assertions) command-line options, though this functionality is rarely used.

Starting in chapter 2, I will describe individual bug patterns so that you can recognize them early and understand how to avoid them.

Summary

- There are several techniques to help you reduce the number of bugs in your code and find them more quickly, but there's no silver bullet.
- Different approaches are effective against different types of bugs, so it's reasonable to use several (e.g., static analysis, code reviews, and automated testing) to some extent instead of concentrating all your efforts on one approach.
- Static analysis may help you to avoid many common mistakes; however, it may create unwanted warnings. You can reduce the number of unwanted warnings

you receive by configuring the static analyzer, using suppression annotations, or rearranging your code to make it easier to understand for the analyzer.

- Dynamic analysis tools may discover specific problems, notably concurrency-related bugs. Such problems are unlikely to be detected by other tools.

- Unit tests are very important to use, as they allow you to ensure the code works as expected and get notified if there are regressions. Test coverage and mutation coverage metrics can be used to control how much of your code is actually covered; however, these metrics are not perfect. Full test coverage is usually impossible to achieve, and even if it is achieved, this isn't an indication the program is necessarily bug free.

Expressions

This chapter covers

- Precedence-related errors
- Common mistakes stemming from one operator being used instead of another
- Pitfalls when using a conditional expression
- Common problems when using method calls and method references

This chapter discusses common bugs localized inside the single Java expression, such as using an incorrect operator or assuming the wrong operator precedence. Such bugs may result in an unexpected value being produced by the expression. I will also briefly discuss the bugs caused by the expression value being calculated correctly but ignored.

This chapter does not cover bugs related to specific data types, like numbers, strings, or collections. These are covered in subsequent chapters.

2.1   Mistake 1: Incorrect assumptions about numeric operator precedence

Many programming languages, including Java, provide a number of operators with different priorities, each affecting the order of expression evaluation in different ways. The precedence can be changed using parentheses. Table 2.1 shows the operator precedence in Java.

Table 2.1   Operator precedence in Java

Precedence	Category	Operators
1	Postfix	`++, --`
2	Prefix	`++, --, +, -, ~, !`
3	Multiplicative	`*, /, %`
4	Additive	`+, -`
5	Shift	`<<, >>, >>>`
6	Relational	`<, >, <=, >=, instanceof`
7	Equality	`==, !=`
8	Bitwise and	`&`
9	Bitwise xor	`^`
10	Bitwise or	`|`
11	Logical and	`&&`
12	Logical or	`||`
13	Conditional	`?:`
14	Assignment	`=, +=, -=, *=, /=, %=, &=, ^=, |=, <<=, >>=, >>>=`

Some priorities are pretty natural and rarely cause mistakes. For example, we all know from school that the multiplication and division operations have higher precedence in terms of order of operations than addition and subtraction. Java follows the same convention, so no surprises there.

2.1.1   Binary shift

Problems start to appear if you use more exotic operators, such as *binary shift*. Binary shift is semantically similar to multiplication and division, so it's natural to expect that their precedence is higher than addition; however, this is not the case. Consider the following method:

```
int pack (short lo, short hi) {
  return lo << 16 + hi;
}
```

Here, the code author expected that the binary shift would be evaluated before the addition, like in `(lo << 16) + hi`. However, as addition's precedence is higher, this will be evaluated as `lo << (16 + hi)`, resulting in an incorrect value. This kind of mistake cannot be caught by the compiler because there's no type mismatch. Normally, this could be caught by unit tests, but sometimes, such bugs appear in production code. I have seen such mistakes in manual `hashCode()` method implementations:

```
public int hashCode() {
  return xmin + ymin << 8 + xmax << 16 + ymax << 24;
}
```

Here, shift operators are executed after summation, so the result will be completely unexpected (figure 2.1). While this doesn't result in a behavioral error, the hash code distribution becomes extremely poor. In particular, during the last step, the intermediate result is shifted left by 24 bits, nullifying the least significant 24 bits of the final hash code. This may produce unexpected performance problems if the object is used as a `HashMap` key.

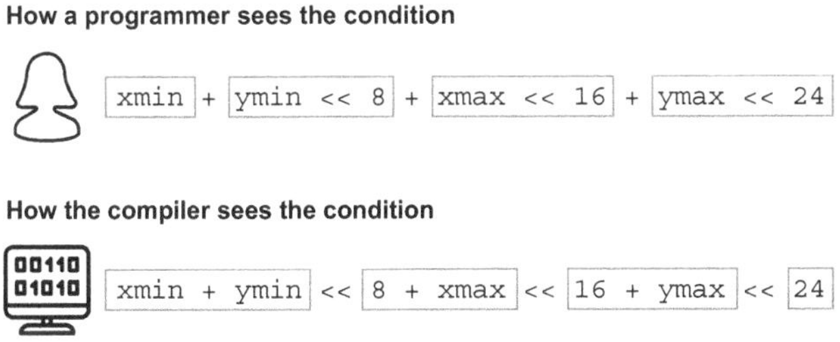

How a programmer sees the condition

`xmin` + `ymin << 8` + `xmax << 16` + `ymax << 24`

How the compiler sees the condition

`xmin + ymin` << `8 + xmax` << `16 + ymax` << `24`

Figure 2.1   Numeric addition has higher precedence than bitwise shift.

A similar problem may occur if you want to add 25% or 50% to some amount (usually, a size of some buffer). I saw the following code in the Apache Avro project:

```
class OutputBuffer extends ByteArrayOutputStream {
    static final int BLOCK_SIZE = 64 * 1024;
    ...
    public OutputBuffer() {
        super(BLOCK_SIZE + BLOCK_SIZE >> 2);
    }
}
```

Here, the author wanted to specify the initial capacity of `ByteArrayOutputStream` to be 25% larger than the `BLOCK_SIZE` constant. Unfortunately, it was overlooked that bitwise shift has a lower precedence than addition. As a result, the size is computed as `(BLOCK_SIZE + BLOCK_SIZE) >> 2`, which is equal to `BLOCK_SIZE / 2`.

Static analysis

It's interesting to note that the authors of the Apache Avro project actually used a static analyzer, and it reported this problem, saying that it's better to add parentheses to an expression that contains both addition and bitwise shift. The authors followed the recommendation blindly and added the parentheses to preserve the current semantics as part of their bigger cleanup. After that, the code looked like this:

```
public OutputBuffer() {
    super((BLOCK_SIZE + BLOCK_SIZE) >> 2);
}
```

The static analyzer was happy with this, and it didn't report anything else. It took several years before the code was revisited and finally fixed. This is quite a didactic case. If your static analyzer highlights suspicious code, don't blindly accept the suggested quick fixes. They may simply hide the problem instead of solving it.

WAYS TO AVOID THIS MISTAKE

- Remember that all bitwise shift operators have lower precedence than addition and subtraction. Always add explicit parentheses around them. For example, `(lo << 16) + hi` or `BLOCK_SIZE + (BLOCK_SIZE >> 2)`.
- Avoid using bitwise shift operators in favor of multiplication or division. For example, the expressions in the previous point could be rewritten as `lo * 0x10000 + hi` and `BLOCK_SIZE * 5 / 4` (or `BLOCK_SIZE + BLOCK_SIZE / 4`, if overflow is possible), respectively. Now, parentheses are unnecessary, and the code is probably even more readable. Please note that just-in-time (JIT) and ahead-of-time (AOT) compilers used in modern Java virtual machines (JVMs) are capable of rewriting multiplication and division with the shift operation when emitting the machine code, so the performance will be the same.
- Avoid writing `hashCode()` methods manually. Instead, rely on code generators, which are available in most Java IDEs. For example, in Eclipse, you can use the Source > Generate `hashCode()` and `equals()` menu actions. Alternatively, you may use the library method `Objects.hash()`.

2.1.2   *Bitwise operators*

Another group of operators whose precedence is often confusing is bit manipulation operators, like `&` (bitwise and) and `|` (bitwise or). Consider the following code sample:

```
int updateBits(int bits) {
  return bits & 0xFF00 + 1;
}
```

Try to guess how this expression is evaluated. Which comes first between `+` (addition) and `&` (bitwise and)?

Many developers associate addition and subtraction as low-priority operators. However, it appears that they have higher precedence than bitwise operators. So in this case, contrary to the author's intention, the expression is computed as `bits & 0xFF01`, and the least significant bit will be copied from `bits`, rather than set unconditionally.

The simplest advice for avoiding this kind of mistake is to stop mixing bitwise and arithmetic operators in a single expression, as this is rarely necessary and may only add confusion. In this sample, it's better to use the bitwise or operator:

```
return bits & 0xFF00 | 1;
```

Note that while the new code is correct, it may still be confusing to readers. Bitwise `&` has higher precedence than bitwise `|`, but not every developer remembers this. It would be clearer to add parentheses:

```
return (bits & 0xFF00) | 1;
```

> ### Static analysis
> Some static analyzers may report expressions where it's desired to use parentheses to explicitly specify the precedence. For example, SonarLint has rule S864: Limited Dependence Should Be Placed on Operator Precedence, and IntelliJ IDEA has the inspection Multiple Operators with Different Precedence. Both are turned off by default, as they may produce too many warnings, which some programmers may find annoying. However, if you consistently use this style from the very beginning of your project and fix warnings as they appear, you can avoid such unpleasant bugs.

WAYS TO AVOID THIS MISTAKE

- Avoid mixing bitwise and arithmetic operations within a single expression.
- Add parentheses when using uncommon operations. Even if you know Java operator precedence perfectly, another developer on your team may not and may interpret your code incorrectly.

2.2 *Mistake 2: Missing parentheses in conditions*

In Java, there's no implicit conversion between the Boolean type (either primitive `boolean` or boxed `Boolean`) and any other type. Thanks to this, it's quite rare for unexpected operator precedence in condition to cause an error that cannot be detected during the compilation. For example, a common mistake is not including parentheses around a negated `instanceof` operator; this will be immediately detected by the compiler:

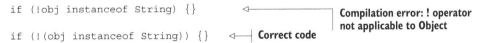

```
if (!obj instanceof String) {}          ◄─────────────┐  Compilation error: ! operator
                                                       │  not applicable to Object
if (!(obj instanceof String)) {}   ◄──┤ Correct code
```

Another common problem originates from & (bitwise and), | (bitwise or), and ^ (bitwise xor) operations. As we have previously seen, their precedence is lower than addition precedence. However, even more unexpected that it is lower than comparison precedence:

```
         if (flags == Flags.ACC_PUBLIC | Flags.ACC_FINAL) {}
Correct  └→
code     └→  if (flags == (Flags.ACC_PUBLIC | Flags.ACC_FINAL)) {}
```

Compilation error: |
operator cannot be applied
to boolean and int

Luckily, the compiler also helps us here.

2.2.1 *&& and || precedence*

Unfortunately, the compiler cannot report all the problems in conditions. One common source of confusion is the precedence of the && (and) and || (or) logical operators. Both operators work with `boolean` operands and produce a `boolean` result, so compiler type checking does not help us here.

Similar to bitwise & and |, logical && has a higher precedence than ||. This is because in math, logical and is commonly associated with multiplication, while logical or is associated with addition. This is more intuitive if you imagine `false` is replaced with 0 and `true` is replaced with 1 or any other positive number. After such a replacement, logical && will work exactly like regular multiplication, as shown in table 2.2.

Table 2.2 Comparison of logical && and multiplication

Logical &&	Multiplication
false && false == false	0 * 0 == 0
false && true == false	0 * 1 == 0
true && false == false	1 * 0 == 0
true && true == true	1 * 1 == 1

Similarly, logical || works like addition, as shown in table 2.3. Note that 1 + 1 = 2, which is still a positive number.

Table 2.3 Comparison of logical || and addition

Logical ||	Addition
false || false == false	0 + 0 == 0
false || true == true	0 + 1 == 1
true || false == true	1 + 0 == 1
true || true == true	1 + 1 == 2

Once you understand the similarity between logical and math operations, the precedence of && and || will no longer be a surprise. However, this is easy to forget, leading developers to write a condition like this:

```
if (index >= 0 && str.charAt(index) == ' ' ||
                 str.charAt(index) == '\t') { … }
```

This code was intended to protect against a negative index value before using the `charAt()` method. However, the `&&` operator has a higher precedence, so the last `charAt()` call is not protected by the `index >= 0` guard expression (figure 2.2). So if a negative index is possible at this point, an exception is inevitable. The correct code would be

```
if (index >= 0 && (str.charAt(index) == ' ' ||
                   str.charAt(index) == '\t')) { … }
```

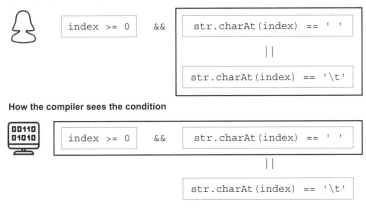

Figure 2.2 `&&` has higher priority than `||`.

Ways to avoid this mistake

- Take special care when the condition contains both the `&&` and `||` operators. Reread it, think about all the possible inputs, and make sure the output will be what you expect. Consult the Java operator precedence table if you have any doubts about precedence.
- Consider using parentheses every time the `&&` and `||` operators appear in a single expression.
- Split complex conditions into simpler ones in separate `if` statements. This not only helps to avoid mistakes but also makes the code more readable. The previous condition could be rewritten in the following way:

```
if (index >= 0) {
  if (str.charAt(index) == ' ' ||
      str.charAt(index) == '\t') { … }
}
```

Unfortunately, SonarLint doesn't like such nested `if` statements and reports the following problem: *Collapsible* `if` *statements should be merged*. In my opinion, this rule is not useful, and it's best to disable it.

- Consider extracting parts of complex conditions into separate methods. For example, you can extract the `isWhitespace()` method:

```
static boolean isWhitespace(char ch) {
  return ch == ' ' || ch == '\t';
}
```

Now, the condition can be rewritten as

```
if (index >= 0 && isWhitespace(str.charAt(index))) { … }
```

Again, the code became both more readable and less error prone, as precedence mistake is impossible now.

- When you have complex conditions, pay attention to the unit test coverage. Ensure that you have tests that execute every operand of the complex condition, both for a `true` and a `false` result.

2.2.2 *Conditional operator and addition*

The *conditional operator* (`?:`), also known as the *ternary operator*, has one of the lowest priorities, which can often be irritating. Luckily, most mistakes involving conditional operator precedence will be easily caught by the compiler:

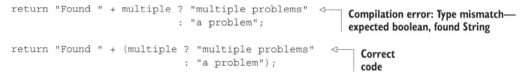

```
return "Found " + multiple ? "multiple problems"    ⟵  Compilation error: Type mismatch—
                          : "a problem";                 expected boolean, found String

return "Found " + (multiple ? "multiple problems"   ⟵  Correct
                          : "a problem");                code
```

However, the following is valid Java code, and the compiler is silent here:

```
static String indentString(String str, int indent) {
  int capacity = str.length() + indent < 0 ? 0 : indent;   ⟵  Incorrect precedence:
  StringBuilder sb = new StringBuilder(capacity);              plus is the part of
  for (int i = 0; i < indent; i++) {                           condition
    sb.append(' ');
  }
  sb.append(str);
  return sb.toString();
}
```

The idea is to add the requested amount of whitespace before the passed string, doing nothing if the negative amount is specified. For the sake of allocation optimization, the code author tried to precalculate the capacity of the `StringBuilder`. However, because parentheses are missing, the calculation is wrong (figure 2.3).

At first, `str.length() + indent` is calculated and compared to zero. Depending on the result of the comparison, the initial capacity is either set to `0` or `indent`. For positive indents and negative indents smaller than `-str.length()`, the method works correctly, even though the initial capacity is completely wrong. However, if the `indent` is between `-str.length()` and `-1` inclusive, the method fails with `NegativeArraySizeException`,

How a programmer sees the condition

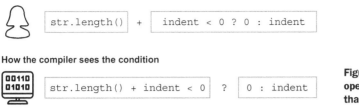

How the compiler sees the condition

Figure 2.3   The conditional operator has lower priority than addition.

as `StringBuilder` tries to allocate the array to have `indent` elements, which is a negative number.

> **WARNING** This problem can hardly be detected by a static analyzer, as there's nothing particularly suspicious in this calculation. In another context, it could be correct.

WAYS TO AVOID THIS MISTAKE

- Always include parentheses around a conditional expression when it's used as part of a more complex expression, as it likely has the lowest precedence.
- In this case, the problem could have been avoided by using the library method to calculate the max value:

```
int capacity = str.length() + Math.max(indent, 0);
```

In general, gravitate toward using standard library methods over manual computation, even if the computation looks very simple.

- If you need to create a string repeating the same character several times, don't do this manually. Since Java 11, a method called `repeat()`, in the `String` class, has been available, which can be used instead:

```
static String indentString(String str, int indent) {
  if (indent < 0) return str;
   return " ".repeat(indent) + str;
}
```

2.2.3   *The conditional operator and null check*

Another flavor of the same problem occurs when you compare a reference to `null` after a string concatenation and produce string values in conditional expression branches. For example, consider the following method:

```
String format(String value) {
  return "Value: " + value != null ? value : "(unknown)";
}
```

Here, the intent was to return `Value: (unknown)` if the value is `null` and concatenate with an actual value if it's non-null. However, the `return` expression is parsed as follows (figure 2.4):

```
(("Value: " + value) != null) ? value : "(unknown)";
```

As a result, the concatenation is executed first, and then the `null` check is performed, which is always successful, as concatenation can never produce `null`. So the method will always return `value` without a prefix, and `null` will be returned as is. This could go unnoticed during manual testing, as the tester might assume this behavior is intended. I discovered a bug like this in the procedure that generated some internal diagnostics information.

How a programmer sees the condition

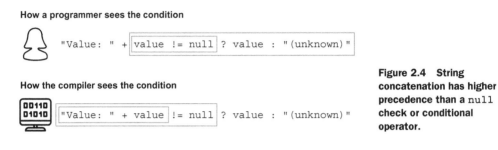

How the compiler sees the condition

Figure 2.4   **String concatenation has higher precedence than a `null` check or conditional operator.**

A similar problem was discovered in the Elasticsearch project, in code that initializes an `ArrayList` object with initial capacity. The original code is roughly equivalent to this method:

```
List<String> trimAndAdd(List<String> input, String newItem) {
  List<String> result = new ArrayList<>(
    input.size() + newItem == null ? 0 : 1);       Incorrect initial
  for (String s : input) {                          capacity calculation
    result.add(s.trim());
  }
  if (newItem != null) {
    result.add(newItem.trim());
  }
  return result;
}
```

Here, the number of elements in the resulting `List` is known in advance, and it looks like a good idea to pre-allocate it. However, due to the lack of parentheses, the plus operator is interpreted as string concatenation rather than numeric addition. Since the result of concatenation is never `null`, the `ArrayList` always has the initial capacity of one element now, which is likely worse than the default value (figure 2.5).

Static analysis

This scenario can be easily caught by static analyzers, as it's very suspicious to compare the result of concatenation to `null`. IntelliJ IDEA reports the Condition Is Always True warning here, and SonarLint reports S2583: Conditionally Executed Code Should Be Reachable.

How a programmer sees the expression

How the compiler sees the expression

The string concatenation
is never null.

**Figure 2.5
Addition is interpreted
as concatenation.**

WAYS TO AVOID THIS MISTAKE

- Split complex expressions involving different operators using intermediate variables:

```
String displayedValue = value != null ? value : "(unknown)";
return "Value: " + displayedValue;
```

Similarly, the `ArrayList` initialization in the `trimAndAdd()` sample could be rewritten as

```
int additionalElements = newItem == null ? 0 : 1;
List<String> result = new ArrayList<>(input.size() + additionalElements);
```

- Avoid string concatenation in favor of formatting calls:

```
return String.format("Value: %s",
                     value != null ? value : "(unknown)");
```

Or, since Java 15, you could write

```
return "Value: %s".formatted(value != null ? value : "(unknown)");
```

Unfortunately, in modern JVMs, formatting calls are significantly slower than string concatenation, so this might be undesirable on hot code paths. However, if the result of concatenation is about to be displayed in the UI, then UI rendering code performance will likely dominate the formatting performance.

- Since Java 9, the `Objects.requireNonNullElse()` API method has been able to replace such conditional expressions. It may look quite verbose, but sometimes, it adds clarity and solves the problem with operator precedence (use static import for this method):

```
return "Value: " + requireNonNullElse(value, "(unknown)");
```

I don't recommend always using it, but that's a matter of taste.

- In general, setting the initial capacity of `ArrayList` and `StringBuilder` is a fragile optimization. Even if you never forget the parentheses, changes in the subsequent logic (e.g., adding one more element to the list) may require changes in initial capacity as well, which is often forgotten, and it's unlikely that the mismatched capacity will be caught by any test.

2.3   Mistake 3: Accidental concatenation instead of addition

One of the problematic aspects of Java syntax is a *binary + operator*, which can be used both for string concatenation and numeric addition. Along with implicit conversion of numbers to strings inside the concatenations, this may cause unexpected bugs:

```
String entryName = "Entry#" + index + 1;
```

Here, the code author wanted to adjust the zero-based index, so for `index = 4`, for example, it was desired to produce the string `Entry#5`. However, Java executes the `+` operations left to right and interprets this line as a sequence of two string concatenations, resulting in the string `Entry#41`. Depending on the context, this may result in a runtime error, querying irrelevant data, or displaying an incorrect message in the UI.

WAYS TO AVOID THIS MISTAKE

- Always put arithmetic operations inside string concatenations in parentheses:

  ```
  String entryName = "Entry#" + (index + 1);
  ```

  Add them, even if parentheses are redundant, like here: `(price + tax) + "$"`. This will make the code more readable.

- Do not mix arithmetic operations and string concatenation in a single expression. Extract all the arithmetic operations to the intermediate variables:

  ```
  int adjustedIndex = index + 1;
  String entryName = "Entry#" + adjustedIndex;
  ```

- Again, using the formatting method will make the code more robust (at the cost of some performance degradation):

  ```
  String entryName = String.format("Entry#%d", index + 1);
  ```

  or

  ```
  String entryName = MessageFormat.format("Entry#{0}", index + 1);
  ```

2.4   Mistake 4: Multiline string literals

Before Java 15 introduced text blocks, it was common to represent long multiline string literals as a concatenation, like this:

```
String template =
  "<html>\n" +
  "  <head><title>Welcome</title></head>\n" +
  "  <body>\n" +
  "    <h1>Hello, $user$!</h1>\n" +
  "    <hr>\n" +
  "    <p>Welcome to our web-site</p>\n" +
```

```
"   </body>\n" +
"</html>\n";
```

There's nothing wrong with this approach if you cannot upgrade to Java 15 or newer. However, care should be taken if you need to process the whole concatenation somehow. For example, imagine you want to perform replacement of the `$user$` placeholder right here. It's quite easy to make the following mistake:

```
String greetingPage =
  "<html>\n" +
  "  <head><title>Welcome</title></head>\n" +
  "  <body>\n" +
  "    <h1>Hello, $user$!</h1>\n" +
  "    <hr>\n" +
  "    <p>Welcome to our web-site</p>\n" +
  "  </body>\n" +
  "</html>\n".replace("$user$", userName);
```

It might not be evident at first glance, but the replacement is applied to the last string segment `</html>\n` only. As a result, the `replace()` call does nothing, and the placeholder is not substituted. This will result in neither a compilation error nor a runtime exception, but users will see the `$user$` placeholder instead of the correct username.

Static analysis

Pay attention to static analysis warnings. IntelliJ IDEA features the Replacement Operation Has No Effect inspection, which can sometimes detect if the string replace operation does nothing. This can help to detect bugs like this.

WAYS TO AVOID THIS MISTAKE

- Don't forget that string concatenation has lower precedence than a method call. Always wrap a method call qualifier in parentheses, unless it's array element access, another method call, or a `new` expression.
- Avoid calls on complex qualifiers. Extract a complex qualifier to a separate variable whenever possible.
- Update to Java 15 or newer, and use text blocks instead of string concatenation when possible. In this case, such a mistake would not be possible:

  ```
  String greetingPage = """
          <html>
            <head><title>Welcome</title></head>
            <body>
              <h1>Hello, $user$!</h1>
              <hr>
              <p>Welcome to our web-site</p>
            </body>
          </html>
          """.replace("$user$", userName);
  ```

2.5   *Mistake 5: Unary plus*

Java features a *unary + operator*. In most cases, it's completely harmless and does nothing. Note, however, that it performs a widening conversion from the `byte`, `char`, and `short` types to the `int` type. This may cause an unpleasant bug when it's accidentally used inside a string concatenation before a character literal:

```
String error(String userName) {
  return "User not found: " +
        + '"' + userName + '"';
}
```

Can you spot the problem? Here, a duplicate `+` was accidentally written around the line break. In this case, the second plus is interpreted by the compiler as a unary `+` applied to the " character. This results in a widening conversion, changing the " character to its code (34). So the method will return `User not found: 34User"` instead of the expected `User not found: "User"`. Exact UI messages are not always covered by unit tests, especially if they are displayed in error-handling code. As a result, such mistakes may slip into production.

Another typo is possible due to the existence of unary plus:

```
x =+ y;         ⟵⎯   x += y was intended
```

Here, `=+` was mistakenly used for compound assignment instead of `+=`. This code successfully compiles and can be executed, but the result will be different, as the old variable value will be ignored.

> ### Static analysis
> Some static analyzers may recognize adjacent `=+` and issue a warning. SonarLint has a rule named S2757: "=+" Should Not Be Used Instead of "+=" to report this. Unfortunately, it's possible that automatic formatting will be applied to the code later, and the code will look like this:
>
> ```
> x = +y;
> ```
>
> Now, the static analyzer sees that there's a space between `=` and `+` and may assume unary plus was intended, so the warning is not issued anymore. I found a similar problem in an old codebase when I looked for all unary plus instances.

WAYS TO AVOID THIS MISTAKE

- Avoid using character literals in favor of string literals where possible. For example, in this case, it would be better to use a one-character string `"\""` instead of the character literal `'"'`. Any arithmetic operation, including unary plus applied to a string literal, will result in a compilation error. The performance penalty is marginal in most cases.
- Avoid string concatenation in favor of formatting calls like `String.format()`.

- Avoid blindly reformatting the code if it contains static analysis warnings. Fix the warnings first. It's quite possible that automatic reformatting will only hide the problem.
- Avoid unary + completely, and configure your static analyzer to report all instances of the unary + operator. In this case, automatic formatting will not suppress the static analysis warning.

Unfortunately, a similar problem may appear with *unary – operator* as well:

```
x =- y;   ◁———| x -= y was intended
```

It's not practical to ban unary - from the code base. Again, static analyzer may help you, unless automatic formatting is applied to the code. Still, you can rely on careful code review and unit tests. Luckily, compound subtraction is used much less frequently than compound addition. I checked a big project and found that += occurs seven times more frequently than -=.

2.6 *Mistake 6: Implicit type conversion in conditional expressions*

Conditional expressions, or *ternary expressions*, are quite similar to if statements. Many, developers assume that a conditional expression like this

```
return condition ? thenExpression : elseExpression;
```

is completely equivalent to the following if statement:

```
if (condition) {
  return thenExpression;
} else {
  return elseExpression;
}
```

Often, this is so, but when you deal with numbers, the semantics may be different.

2.6.1 *Boxed numbers in conditional expressions*

The problem is that conditional expressions perform nontrivial, and sometimes counterintuitive, type conversions on then expressions and else expressions. This is especially important when you have boxed numbers. For example, consider the following method:

```
Double valueOrZero(boolean condition, Double value) {
  return condition ? value : 0.0;
}
```

It looks like when the condition is true, we just return the argument unchanged. However, this is not what the *Java Language Specification* says (see JLS § 15.25, https://docs.oracle.com/javase/specs/jls/se21/html/jls-15.html#jls-15.25). The procedure to determine the final type of conditional expression is rather complex, and it's not practical to learn it by heart, but it's useful to remember a few things.

First, it's helpful to know that there are two types of expressions in Java, namely *standalone expressions* and *poly expressions*. The type of a standalone expression is defined by the expression itself, ignoring its surrounding context. For example, the expression a + b is a standalone expression. If you know the types of a and b, you can always determine what the type of the whole expression is. In contrast, `Collections` `.emptyList()` is a poly expression. Its type could be `List<Integer>`, `List<String>`, or any other `List`, depending on the surrounding context, like the type of variable to which we are assigning the result of this expression.

If you have a conditional expression that deals with primitive types or primitive wrappers, it will always be a standalone expression, so the surrounding context is not used to determine its type. In our example, the fact that the method return type is `Double` is completely ignored when determining the expression type. To determine the type, we only use the expression itself: `condition ? value : 0.0`.

Another thing to remember is that when a `then` expression has a boxed type, like `Integer` or `Double`, and an `else` expression has the corresponding primitive type, like `int` or `double` (or vice versa), the primitive type wins, so the result of the conditional expression here is the primitive `double`.

Only after the conditional expression is executed is its result boxed again, as the method return type is boxed `Double`. Java implicitly calls static methods like `valueOf()` for boxing conversion (to get a boxed type from the primitive one) and instance methods like `doubleValue()` for the opposite unboxing conversion. So if we make all the implicit operations explicit, this code will be equivalent to

```
Double valueOrZero(boolean condition, Double value) {
  return Double.valueOf(
        condition ? value.doubleValue() : 0.0);
}
```

Now, the problem is pretty clear. First, the `value` is always reboxed, so you may inadvertently waste more memory having two separate boxed values. Second, and more importantly, what will happen if you call `valueOrZero(true, null)`? Looking at the original code, one may expect that the `null` will be returned. However, as we have an implicit `value.doubleValue()` call, we will get `NullPointerException` instead, which is probably unexpected.

WAYS TO AVOID THIS MISTAKE

- Avoid using boxed primitives. Sometimes, they are necessary if you work with generic types. However, it's better to convert them to primitive values as early as possible. This will also show clearly that the variable cannot be `null`.
- If you still need a boxed primitive, try not to use it with a conditional expression. Instead, use an `if` statement. While it's more verbose, it will make the code much less confusing. Even if you totally understand all the subtleties of

the conditional expression, the code could be fragile, and a slight change in types may cause an unexpected behavior change.

- Remember that numeric conditional expressions are standalone expressions, which means the surrounding context does not affect its type.

2.6.2   Nested conditional expressions

Unexpected behavior may also be observed if you use nested conditional expressions with the boxed primitive type:

```
static Integer mapValue(int input) {
  return input > 20 ? 2 :
         input > 10 ? 1 :
         null;
}
```

This may look OK at first glance; we return a boxed `Integer` value, so 2, 1, or `null` look like valid return results. However, this method throws `NullPointerException` if the `input` happens to be 10 or less. Even more amusing is that if you change the order of conditions, it will work as expected:

```
static Integer mapValue(int input) {
  return input <= 10 ? null :
         input <= 20 ? 1 :
         2;
}
```

Here, the rules we saw previously are also helpful. But we need one more rule: when `null` meets primitive (like `int`), the resulting type is a boxed primitive (like `Integer`). So, in the first sample, the conditional expression type is determined according to the scheme shown in figure 2.6.

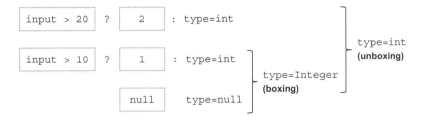

Figure 2.6   A type calculation resulting in an `int` type

On the other hand, the second method has a different pattern, and thus a different result type, as in figure 2.7.

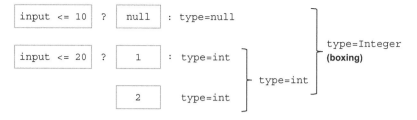

Figure 2.7   A type calculation resulting in an `Integer` type

As a result, the second code sample does not involve unboxing `null`; therefore, it's safe. It will likely be easier to understand if we make all the boxing conversions explicit. The first sample has two implicit auto-boxing conversions and one auto-unboxing conversion:

```
return Integer.valueOf(input > 20 ? 2 :
    (input > 10 ? Integer.valueOf(1) : null).intValue());
```

The second sample is simpler; it has only one implicit auto-boxing conversion:

```
return input <= 10 ? null :
        Integer.valueOf(input <= 20 ? 1 : 2);
```

It's OK if you don't fully understand all the type conversions here. What you should remember is that conditional expressions have nontrivial and counterintuitive rules when it comes to boxing.

Static analysis

IntelliJ IDEA reports that the `NullPointerException` is possible as a result of unboxing (inspection name: Nullability and Data Flow Problems). PVS-Studio also reports this problem with the V6093: Automatic Unboxing of a Variable May Cause `NullPointerException` warning. Unfortunately, SonarLint doesn't report a possible exception here. It complains, however, that the ternary operators should not be nested and suggests to extract the inner one into a separate variable. After doing this, it becomes happy and doesn't highlight this code anymore, though the problem is still there.

WAYS TO AVOID THIS MISTAKE

- Avoid nested conditional expressions. Use `if` statements instead.
- Avoid conditional expressions whose branches return different types. It's especially dangerous when at least one of the branches has a primitive type. The automatic type conversions are sometimes counterintuitive. It's much safer to use an `if` statement.

2.7 Mistake 7: Using non-short-circuit logic operators

Java provides two kinds of logical and and or operators. *Short-circuit operators* && and || do not evaluate the next operand if the resulting value does not depend on it. *Non-short-circuit operators* & and | evaluate all the operands, regardless of the intermediate result. It appears that, in most cases, short-circuiting logic is much more natural, so it's usually recommended to use them. However, accidental use of non-short-circuit operators is possible and will not be reported as a compilation error. Sometimes, such a typo is harmless (e.g., if the condition is like a == null & b == null). Occasionally, you may have unnecessary performance degradation, if the second condition takes a considerable amount of time to execute. However, unpleasant consequences, like runtime exceptions, may also happen. Take the following example:

```
boolean isPositive(int[] data, int index) {
  return index >= 0 && index < data.length & data[index] > 0;
}
```

Due to the typo, the second part of the bounds check doesn't work as expected. If the index exceeds the array length, the array will still be queried, resulting in Array-IndexOutOfBoundsException.

Note that compound assignment operators in Java never short-circuit. For example, sometimes, programmers write a series of checks in the following way:

```
boolean result = true;
result &= check1();
result &= check2();
result &= check3();
```

This may look pretty and uniform, but you should note that the methods check1(), check2(), and check3() will be always called, even if the result is already false. This does not always make your program incorrect, as the checks might be independent. However, this approach may require redundant computation. Unfortunately, there's no short-circuiting compound assignment operator in Java, like &&=, so to avoid unwanted computations, you need to write this in its full form:

```
boolean result = true;
result = result && check1();
result = result && check2();
result = result && check3();
```

Another possible problem with accidental use of non-short-circuit operators is different precedence. A bug can stem from a complex condition like this:

```
interface First {}
interface Second {}
interface Third {}
interface Exclude extends Second {}

boolean checkObject(Object obj) {
  return obj instanceof First && checkFirst((First)obj) |
```

```
        obj instanceof Second && !(obj instanceof Exclude) ||
        obj instanceof Third && checkThird((Third)obj);
}
```

Here, we have three acceptable interfaces, and we want to perform some additional checks for them. As we saw previously, logical or has lower precedence than logical and, so it looks safe to use a mix of && and || without additional parentheses. However, due to an accidental edit, the first || was replaced with | (according to the version control history; initially, the condition was correct). Non-short-circuiting logic operators have higher precedence than short-circuiting ones, so now the condition is evaluated like this (figure 2.8):

```
return (obj instanceof First &&
        (checkFirst((First) obj) | obj instanceof Second) &&
        !(obj instanceof Exclude))
        ||
        (obj instanceof Third && checkThird((Third) obj));
```

How a programmer sees the condition

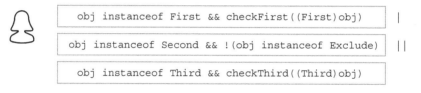

How the compiler sees the condition

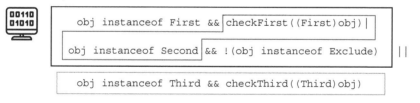

Figure 2.8 Non-short-circuiting logic operators have higher precedence.

In particular, if the obj happens to implement the Second interface, it cannot satisfy the condition unless it implements the First interface at the same time. This cannot be encoded in the Java type system, but according to the program logic, First, Second, and Third interfaces are mutually exclusive, so now, objects of type Second have stopped passing this condition.

Static analysis

Dataflow-based static analyzers can detect some dangerous uses of non-short-circuit logic. For example, a classic null check before dereference is reported in IntelliJ IDEA by the Nullability and Data Flow Problems inspection if & is used instead of &&:

```
if (str != null & str.isEmpty()) {}
```
◁─┐ **Warning: Method invocation isEmpty may produce NullPointerException.**

However, this inspection may not report more complex cases, like the one shown in figure 2.8. A simple solution would be to ban non-short-circuit logic operators in the project completely. SonarLint reports every use of & or | in conditions with the rule S2178: Short-Circuit Logic Should Be Used in Boolean Contexts. IntelliJ IDEA has a similar inspection called Non-Short-Circuit Boolean Expression, but you need to switch it on in the inspection profile, as it's turned off by default.

WAYS TO AVOID THIS MISTAKE

- Do not use non-short-circuiting logical operators, as they may lead to unwanted computations and even produce mistakes if the next condition depends on the previous one.
- Note that the compound assignment operators &= and |= are not short-circuiting.
- In a complex condition that involves a mix of && and || operators, use clarifying parentheses, even if you know the precedence of Java operators by heart. The accidental edit in the previous checkObject example would be harmless if the && expressions were initially parenthesized.
- Extract parts of complex conditions involving different operators. You can use intermediate variables, extract short methods, or split the condition into several statements. This way, the code will be more readable and less error prone. For example, you can extract instanceof checks to separate if statements:

```
if (obj instanceof First) {
  return checkFirst((First)obj);
}
if (obj instanceof Second) {
  return !(obj instanceof Exclude);
}
if (obj instanceof Third) {
  return checkThird((Third)obj);
}
return false;
```

Now, you don't need to use && and || operators at all. If you are using Java 16 or newer, you can use pattern matching in instanceof to eliminate cast expressions:

```
if (obj instanceof First first) {
  return checkFirst(first);
}
if (obj instanceof Second) {
  return !(obj instanceof Exclude);
}
```

```
if (obj instanceof Third third) {
  return checkThird(third);
}
return false;
```

Finally, starting with Java 21, it is possible to use pattern matching for `switch`, making code more uniform and readable:

```
return switch (obj) {
    case First first    -> checkFirst(first);
    case Second second -> !(second instanceof Exclude);
    case Third third    -> checkThird(third);
    case null, default -> false;
};
```

Evaluating both operands

Sometimes, it's still desired to have non-short-circuit logic, if both operands produce an intentional side effect. It may look like this:

```
if (updateA() & updateB()) {
  ...
}
```

Such code could be confusing to readers, as they might not be sure whether `&`, instead of `&&`, was intentional or a typo. If you configured your static analyzer to report all non-short-circuiting logic operators, an explicit suppression comment will be necessary here. While some developers don't like suppressions and prefer to disable static analysis checks altogether, in such a case, the comment may add clarity not only for the static analyzer but also for readers. For example, you can write a comment like this:

```
//Evaluating both operands is intended!
//noinspection NonShortCircuitBooleanExpression
if (updateA() & updateB()) {
  ...
}
```

A better alternative, though, is to refactor the code to avoid non-short-circuit logic completely:

```
boolean isAUpdated = updateA();
boolean isBUpdated = updateB();
if (isAUpdated && isBUpdated) {
  ...
}
```

This way, it's evident that evaluating both `updateA()` and `updateB()` is intended. In general, avoiding side effects in conditions leads to clearer and less error-prone code.

2.8 Mistake 8: Confusing && and ||

Human developers have trouble using logical `and` and logical `or` correctly. I have seen many bugs caused by one of them being used instead of another. One of the error patterns that frequently occurs looks like this:

```
void validate(int byteValue) {
  if (byteValue < 0 && byteValue > 255) {
    throw new IllegalArgumentException(
            "byteValue is out of range");
  }
}
```

Here, the author of the code wanted to reject parameter values outside of the range of 0 to 255. However, due to an unfortunate mistake, the `&&` operator was used instead of the `||` operator. As you can see, no value can be less than 0 and greater than 255 at the same time. As a result, this validation does nothing, and any `byteValue` is actually accepted.

I have found and fixed more than 10 bugs like this. Here's an example of such an erroneous method:

```
private static boolean isPrintableAsciiString(byte[] array) {
  for (byte b : array) {
    char c = (char) (b & 0xFF);
    if (c != '\t' && c != '\n' && c < 0x20 && c > 0x7E) {        ◁── Mistake: || should
      return false;                                                  be used instead of
    }                                                                 the last &&
  }
  return true;
}
```

The method should indicate whether a given byte array contains only printable symbols. However, due to the incorrect check, it always returns true, so the `byte[]` array was always displayed as a string. The correct condition would be

```
if (c != '\t' && c != '\n' && (c < 0x20 || c > 0x7E)) {
  return false;
}
```

When you are coding a condition that involves Boolean logic operators, it's essential to remember De Morgan's laws:

- `!(a || b)` is equivalent to `!a && !b`;
- `!(a && b)` is equivalent to `!a || !b`.

Some developers apply these laws in an incorrect manner when manually negating a condition. For example, assume that you are processing the text input and need to treat the lines starting with # or // as comments. You may use the following method:

```
void processLine(String line) {
  if (line.startsWith("#") || line.startsWith("//")) {
```

```
    processCommentLine(line);
  } else {
    processContentLine(line);
  }
}
```

Later, you decide no special processing of comment lines is necessary, and you just need to skip such lines, so you only need to keep the `else` branch:

```
void processLine(String line) {
  // Ignore comments
  if (!(line.startsWith("#") || line.startsWith("//"))) {
    processContentLine(line);
  }
}
```

Now, you may think that eliminating the parentheses would be a good idea. According to De Morgan's law, `!(a || b)` is equivalent to `!a && !b`, so if you eliminate the parentheses, you should also change `||` to `&&`. But it's quite possible to forget this and make a mistake instead:

```
void processLine(String line) {
  // Ignore comments
  if (!line.startsWith("#") || !line.startsWith("//")) {
    processContentLine(line);
  }
}
```

Such code is treacherous, as, even for a seasoned developer, it will take a while to understand that no comment lines will be ignored. If a line starts with # it cannot start with // at the same time, so all the lines will be passed to the `processContentLine()` method, and one can only guess what will happen next.

Static analysis

Some mistakes of this kind can be reported by static analyzers capable of performing range analysis of numeric values. For example, IntelliJ IDEA has a Constant Values inspection that will report a Condition Is Always False warning on the `validate()` sample at the beginning of this section. However, static analyzers may fail to detect the mistake if the code is more complicated:

```
void validate(int value) {
  if (Math.abs(value) < 10 && Math.abs(value) > 20) {
    throw new IllegalArgumentException();
  }
}
```

Not every static analyzer is aware that two calls of the `Math.abs()` method with the same argument will always yield the same value, so the problem is basically the same.

Static analyzers may not help when mutually exclusive conditions are more complex. For example, the `processLine()` sample shown previously is not reported by most static analyzers, despite the fact that the conditions `line.startsWith("#")` and `line.startsWith("//")` are mutually exclusive. That's because many static analyzers don't know the semantics of the `startsWith()` method and don't track the already filtered prefixes.

WAYS TO AVOID THIS MISTAKE

- Pay attention to static analyzer warnings. Use advanced static analyzers capable of tracking value ranges, and understand the semantics of various library methods. They may help you identify always-true and always-false conditions.

- Extract the repetitive parts of conditions to temporary variables. This may help static analyzers track the values. For example, IntelliJ IDEA doesn't warn you in the preceding `Math.abs()` sample; however, it will warn you if you extract the `Math.abs()` call to the intermediate variable:

```java
void validate(int value) {
    int abs = Math.abs(value);
    if (abs < 10 && abs > 20) {
        throw new IllegalArgumentException();
    }
}
```

This may also improve the performance and code readability.

- Pay attention to the conditional logic when writing the unit tests. Test uncommon code paths like validation logic. When testing a method returning `boolean` type, write at least one test for the case in which the method returns true and one for the case in which the method returns false. This way, you can easily detect if the method always accidentally returns the same value.

- To negate complex conditions, use IDE functions instead of doing it manually. If you want to keep only the `else` branch of an `if` statement, you can use the Invert `if` Condition action in IntelliJ IDEA or Eclipse to swap branches and then delete the `else` branch. If you already have a condition in the form of `!(a || b)`, there's a Replace `||` With `&&` in IntelliJ IDEA and an equivalent Push Negation Down action in Eclipse. These actions will correctly apply De Morgan's law to the condition, preserving the code semantics.

2.9   Mistake 9: Incorrectly using variable arity calls

Since Java 1.5, it's been possible to declare the last method parameter as a *variable arity* parameter. This allows passing an arbitrary number of arguments when calling this method. Upon the method call, all the passed arguments are automatically wrapped into an array. This is a convenient feature but also a source of specific mistakes.

2.9.1 *Ambiguous variable arity calls*

When variable arity calls were introduced, it was decided to also allow passing an array explicitly. For example, assume you have the following variable arity method:

```
static void printAll(Object... data) {
    for (Object d : data) {
        System.out.println(d);
    }
}
```

Now, these two calls have the same result:

```
printAll("Hello", "World");
printAll(new Object[]{"Hello", "World"});
```

The ability to pass either an explicit array or a flat list of arguments is useful for code evolution; you can upgrade the fixed arity method with an array parameter to a variable arity method, and this change will not break the existing call sites. However, this convenience comes at a cost. When you have exactly one argument passed, it's not immediately clear whether it will be wrapped to an array or not. For example, consider the following call:

```
printAll(obj);
```

Here, it's unclear whether `obj` will be wrapped into an array. It depends on its type: if it's a non-primitive array, it will not be wrapped. It's very important to understand that the decision is taken based on the declared type, not on the runtime type. Consider the following code:

```
Object obj = new Object[]{"Hello", "World"};
printAll(obj);
```

The variable `obj` contains an object array, so one may expect that no wrapping is necessary. However, the declared type of the variable is simply `Object`, not array. The decision on whether to wrap is performed during the compilation, and the compiler does not know the real type of the object stored inside `obj`. Therefore, it decides to wrap an array into another array. As a result, this code prints something like `[Ljava.lang .Object;@7106e68e`, a default string representation of an array.

The situation becomes more confusing if you pass `null` to a variable arity method:

```
printAll(null);
```

Some developers might expect that a single `null` will be wrapped to an array, and as a result, a `null` string will be printed. However, according to the *Java Language Specification* (see JLS § 15.12.4.2, https://docs.oracle.com/javase/specs/jls/se21/html/ jls-15.html#jls-15.12.4.2), the argument is not wrapped to an array if it can be assigned to a variable of the corresponding array type. As `null` can be assigned to any array variable, it's not wrapped into an array, so the data parameter becomes `null` inside the `printAll` method, and this call results in `NullPointerException`.

> ### Static analysis
>
> Static analyzers can warn you about ambiguous calls, as in this scenario. IntelliJ IDEA has the Confusing Argument to Varargs Method inspection for this purpose. Sonar-Lint reports this problem as S5669: Vararg Method Arguments Should Not Be Confusing.

WAYS TO AVOID THIS MISTAKE

- Be careful when passing only one argument as a variable arity parameter. When an ambiguity is possible, add an explicit type cast:

```
// I want an array containing null
printAll((Object)null);
// I want just null array reference
printAll((Object[])null);
```

- Avoid using nulls where possible, especially when you are dealing with arrays and variable arity methods.

2.9.2   Mixing array and collection

Another problem I've encountered with the variable arity method is using a collection instead of an array. For example, assume you have the following utility method to check whether an array contains a given element:

```
@SafeVarargs
static <T> boolean contains(T needle, T... haystack) {
    for (T t : haystack) {
        if (Objects.equals(t, needle)) {
            return true;
        }
    }
    return false;
}
```

For convenience, the method was declared as a variable arity method, so it could be used to compare a value against the set of predefined values:

```
boolean isDayOfWeek = contains(value,
    "SUN", "MON", "TUE", "WED", "THU", "FRI", "SAT");
```

Again, this convenience comes at a cost. Now, it's possible to call this method with a collection argument:

```
static final List<String> allLanguages =
    List.of("Java", "Groovy", "Scala", "Kotlin");

static boolean isLanguage(String language) {
    return contains(language, allLanguages);
}
```

As arrays and collections are semantically similar, a developer may forget that `allLanguages` is actually not an array. Another potential way for this mistake to happen is if `allLanguages` was previously an array, but the developer decided to change it to the `List` and fix all compilation errors after that. However, the `contains (language, allLanguages)` call can still be compiled without errors. Now, the compiler infers type parameter `T` as `Object` and wraps the collection into a single-element array. As a result, we have a `contains()` method call that compiles successfully but always returns `false`.

> **Static analysis**
>
> IntelliJ IDEA reports suspicious calls when a collection is passed as the generic variable arity parameter. The corresponding inspection name is Iterable Is Used as Vararg.

WAYS TO AVOID THIS MISTAKE

- Be careful when changing the variable type from an array to a collection. Check every occurrence of the variable, not only compilation errors, as it's possible that at some places, no compilation error will appear but the code semantics will change.
- When you call a method having `boolean` return type, write tests that cover both true and false results. This way, you will immediately notice if this call always returns the same value.

2.9.3   *Using primitive array in variable arity call*

A similar problem may occur with the `Arrays.asList()` method. This method is a handy bridge between arrays and collections. Some developers use it to wrap arrays to lists, as it provides useful methods like `contains()` and `indexOf()`, which aren't available for arrays in the standard Java library. For example, having an array of strings `arr`, one could use the following expression to check whether it contains the string `"Hello"`:

```
Arrays.asList(arr).contains("Hello")
```

However, the same approach doesn't work for primitive arrays. Consider the following method:

```
static boolean containsZero(int[] arr) {
    return Arrays.asList(arr).contains(0);
}
```

This method can be successfully compiled, but it always returns `false`, regardless of the content of the array. The `asList` method is declared as

```
public static <T> List<T> asList(T... a) {…}
```

As the type parameter T can only be substituted with a non-primitive type, a primitive array cannot be assigned to the T[] type. The compiler then wraps it into a one-element array, producing List<int[]> that contains the original array, which, of course, is not equal to zero (note that the number zero is automatically boxed to Integer here). The problem could be detected by the compiler if the Collection .contains() method accepted only values of the collection element type, but this method accepts any object. We will discuss this in greater detail in mistake 69 in chapter 8.

> **Static analysis**
>
> Pay attention to static analyzer warnings that report when an incompatible type is passed to collection methods accepting an Object type. IntelliJ IDEA uses the Suspicious Collections Method Calls inspection to report such problems. SonarLint features the S2175: Inappropriate Collection Calls Should Not Be Made rule.

WAYS TO AVOID THIS MISTAKE

- Avoid passing primitive arrays to the Arrays.asList() method. This is unlikely to produce the desired result.
- Create intermediate variables with explicitly declared types:

```
static boolean containsZero(int[] arr) {
  List<int[]> list = Arrays.asList(arr);
  return list.contains(0);
}
```

Now, it's immediately clear that the list variable type is wrong.

2.10 Mistake 10: Conditional operators and variable arity calls

Another source of confusion is when a conditional operator is used inside the variable arity method call. Assume we want to print the formatted string via System.out .printf() but use the default substitution parameter if it wasn't supplied:

```
static void printFormatted(String formatString,
                           Object... params) {
  if (params.length == 0) {
    System.out.printf(formatString, "user");
  } else {
    System.out.printf(formatString, params);
  }
}
```

Let's test this method:

```
printFormatted("Hello, %s%n");
printFormatted("Hello, %s%n", "administrator");
```

These two calls print the following text, as expected:

```
Hello, user
Hello, administrator
```

Now, the developer notices that the branches of the `if` statement look very similar and wants to collapse them using the conditional expression:

```
static void printFormatted(String formatString,
                           Object... params) {
  System.out.printf(formatString,
          params.length == 0 ? "user" : params);
}
```

After this refactoring, the code looks more compact, and some people may like it more. The problem is that the code semantics changed. Now, our test prints something like this:

```
Hello, user
Hello, [Ljava.lang.Object;@7291c18f
```

If we look at the original method, we'll see that the branches of the `if` statement have an important difference: the `then` branch uses a variable arity call style, and the compiler automatically wraps it into an array. On the other hand, the `else` branch passes an array explicitly, so wrapping doesn't occur.

However, when we are using the conditional expression, the compiler cannot wrap only one of its branches. It perceives the conditional expression as a whole. Because the type of the `then` branch is `String` and the type of the `else` branch is `Object[]`, the type of the whole conditional expression is a common supertype of `String` and `Object[]`, which is simply `Object`. This is not an array, so the compiler adds automatic wrapping, which means the `params` array is wrapped one more time. You can fix this if you avoid relying on the compiler and wrap the `user` string manually:

```
params.length == 0 ? new Object[]{"user"} : params
```

However, it's less confusing to avoid having a conditional expression inside a variable arity method call at all.

Static analysis

Pay attention to static analyzer warnings. IntelliJ IDEA uses a Suspicious Ternary Operator in Varargs Method Call inspection, which reports if one of the conditional operator branches has an array while the other does not.

WAYS TO AVOID THIS MISTAKE

- Be careful when using a conditional expression as a variable arity argument. Whenever possible, use an `if` statement instead.

- If you still want to keep a conditional expression, extract it to a variable using Introduce Variable or Extract Variable refactoring in your IDE:

```
Object adjustedParams = params.length == 0 ? "user" : adjustedParams;
System.out.printf(formatString, adjustedParams);
```

Now, it's visible in the code that the expression type is `Object`, and the compiler will wrap it one more time.

2.11 Mistake 11: Ignoring an important return value

Like many other programming languages, Java allows you to ignore the resulting value of a method call. Sometimes, this is convenient, such as when the resulting value is of no interest. For example, a `map.remove(key)` call returns the value that was associated with the removed key. Often, we already know it or it's not necessary for the subsequent code.

A more extreme example is `list.add(element)`. The `List.add()` method is an override of `Collection.add()`, which returns `false` if the collection does not support duplicates and the element was already there. This is useful for `Set.add()`, as you cannot add a repeating element to the set, so you can use the return value to check whether the element was already in the set before the call. However, the `List` interface supports duplicates, which implies that the `List.add()` method always returns `true`. It cannot be changed to `void` because the return value is required by a parent interface, but there's nothing useful we can do with this return value.

Unfortunately, this ability causes many mistakes: people often mistakenly ignore the return value. Probably the most common kind of mistake is assuming you are dealing with a mutable object that updates itself, while in fact, it's immutable and returns the updated value. Consider the following example:

```
String s = "Hello World!";          Attempt to remove
s.substring(6);               ⟵⎯⎯┘ "Hello " from the string

BigInteger value = BigInteger.TWO;   Attempt to increment
value.add(BigInteger.ONE);    ⟵⎯⎯┘  the value
```

In these cases, it would be more appropriate to reassign the variable or create another one:

```
String s = "Hello World!";          New string is assigned
s = s.substring(6);           ⟵⎯⎯┘ to the old variable

BigInteger value = BigInteger.TWO;            A new variable, result, is created to
BigInteger result = value.add(BigInteger.ONE);  ⟵⎯⎯┘ hold the result of the increment.
```

Note that you can ignore the return value in lambdas and method references as well. For example, here the code author mistakenly tried to trim all the strings inside the list:

```
void trimAll(List<String> list) {
  list.forEach(String::trim);
}
```

The `forEach` method allows you to use all the collection elements, but it does not allow you to update them. It accepts the `Consumer` functional interface, whose abstract method `accept()` returns `void`, so the result of the `trim()` call is silently ignored. It would be correct to use the `replaceAll()` method here:

```
void trimAll(List<String> list) {
  list.replaceAll(String::trim);
}
```

Another class of mistakes arises from using the wrong method. Well, it's possible to use the wrong method even if you use a return value, but the ability to ignore it makes this problem happen more often. For example, I have come across a mistake like this:

```
void processBitSets(BitSet s1, BitSet s2) {
  s1.intersects(s2);                           Mistake: this line
  processIntersection(s1);                      does nothing
}
```

Here, the author wanted to create an intersection of two `BitSet` objects, retaining only those bits that are set in both `s1` and `s2`. The `BitSet` object is mutable, and there is, indeed, a method that performs the desired operation: `s1.and(s2)`. However, the author mistakenly used the `intersects()` method, which just tests whether the intersection is non-empty without updating the sets. Unlike `and()`, this method returns a `boolean` value, which was ignored. A similar mistake is possible if you want to call the `interrupt()` method of the `Thread` class but you mistakenly call `interrupted()` instead, likely due to selecting the wrong item in the code-completion pop-up.

In modern Java, it's popular to design APIs in a fluent style in which you can chain several calls together. It looks nice, but sometimes people forget to make the final call that should do the actual thing. For example, consider the following unit test, which uses the AssertJ library (https://assertj.github.io/doc/):

```
@Test
public void testCreateList() {
  List<String> list = createList();
  assertThat(!list.isEmpty());
}
```

The last line may look perfectly fine to developers who are not very experienced in using AssertJ. In fact, `assertThat()` by itself asserts nothing. Instead, it returns an `Assert` object that should be checked via a successive call:

```
assertThat(!list.isEmpty()).isTrue();
```

A similar problem happens with Stream API. For example, here, the developer wants to filter the list of strings, removing empty strings:

```
stringList.stream().filter(str -> !str.isEmpty());
```

I also saw attempts to sort the list like this:

```
stringList.stream().sorted();
```

Here, filtering and sorting is not actually performed, as the terminal operation is not called, and the result is not assigned. The correct code would look like this:

```
stringList = stringList.stream().filter(str -> !str.isEmpty())
        .collect(Collectors.toList());
stringList = stringList.stream().sorted()
        .collect(Collectors.toList());
```

Alternatively, if the original list is known to be mutable, one can use the `removeIf()` and `sort()` methods to modify the list in place:

```
stringList.removeIf(String::isEmpty);
stringList.sort(null);
```

There are also methods that actually produce some side effect, and it looks like the return value is not important. Some developers may even be unaware that the method has a non-void return value. In fact, it can be quite important. For example, several old file-handling APIs in Java return `false` to indicate failure instead of throwing an `IOException`. These include methods from the `java.io.File` class: `createNewFile()`, `delete()`, `mkdir()`, `rename()`, and others. Filesystem operations may fail for a variety of reasons, including lack of drive space, insufficient access rights, inability to reach the remote filesystem due to network failure, and so on. Ignoring these errors may cause more problems later, and it will be hard to find the original cause.

The methods `InputStream.read()` and `Reader.read()`, which accept arrays, are also deceptive. For example, one might want to read the next 100 bytes of the stream and process them somehow:

```
void readPrefix(InputStream is) throws IOException {
  byte[] arr = new byte[100];
  is.read(arr);
  process(arr);
}
```

However, the `read()` method is not obliged to fill the whole array. Depending on the stream source, it may fill only part of the array, even if the stream contains more. That's because, by specification, this method blocks, at most, once. Also, if the end of the stream is reached, the method will return `-1` and not write to an array at all. Without checking the return value of the `read()` method, it's impossible to say how many bytes were actually read.

Static analysis

Static analyzers can report if the result of method is ignored when it should not be. IntelliJ IDEA uses the inspection Result of Method Call Ignored, which reports all the previously listed methods. SonarLint has separate rules to check the return value of methods without side effects (S2201: Return Values from Functions Without Side Effects Should Not Be Ignored) and the result of methods like `InputStream.read`

(continued)

(S2674: The Value Returned From a Stream Read Should Be Checked). The Error Prone analyzer has a CheckReturnValue bug pattern that also reports some of these problems.

Unfortunately, it's hard to say, in general, whether the result of a specific method should be used. The IntelliJ inspection knows about standard library methods as well as some other popular APIs, like AssertJ. However, there are thousands of Java libraries as well as your own project code, and inspection does not know in advance where it's safe to ignore the return value. You can set the inspection to report all nonlibrary calls where the return value is ignored, but be prepared for tons of false-positive reports.

You can help the static analyzer with annotations. There are annotations named `@CheckReturnValue` in different annotation packages to signal that the return value must be checked. They can be applied not only to individual methods but also to classes, interfaces, and whole packages to signal that the return value must be checked for every method declared inside. There's also the `@CanIgnoreReturn-Value` annotation in the Error Prone package, which allows you to override the effect of `@CheckReturnValue`. If you don't want to depend on these packages, IntelliJ IDEA allows you to declare an annotation named `@CheckReturnValue` in any package you want. It will also be recognized—though in this case, only if applied to the methods directly. See appendix A for more details about annotation packages.

There's another annotation in the JetBrains annotations package: `@Contract`. If you mark your method with `@Contract(pure = true)`, IntelliJ IDEA will know that the method produces no side effect and will warn if the resulting value is not used. Sometimes, IntelliJ IDEA can infer this annotation automatically. You can help the inference procedure if you explicitly declare classes as final when you do not intend to extend them.

WAYS TO AVOID THIS MISTAKE

- Avoid using old APIs that report errors via the `boolean` return type. For file operations, use the newer `java.nio.file.Files` API. The old way to create a directory `path` along with parent directories is

```
new File(path).mkdirs();
```

In Java 7 and newer, it's preferred to use

```
Files.createDirectories(Paths.get(path));
```

This way, you'll get proper exceptions if something goes wrong.

- As for the `InputStream.read()` method, since Java 11, there's an alternative: `readNBytes()`, which has better interface and may block several times until the requested number of bytes is read.

- When learning a new API, read the Javadoc and pay attention to the mutability of the objects. In both JDK and third-party libraries, modern APIs prefer immutable objects, which no method can modify, so the return result must always be used. In particular, this is a common practice in APIs that follow the functional programming style.

- Old-style Java APIs often use methods prefixed with `set-` to update the object state. Modern APIs prefer the `with-` prefix, which means a new object is returned every time this method is called. If you call a method with the `with-` prefix, it's likely you should use the result. For example, a HexFormat API, which appeared in Java 17 and allows you to present binary data in hexadecimal format, follows this convention. It's also an example of an immutable object:

```java
static void printInHex(byte[] data, boolean uppercase) {
  HexFormat format = HexFormat.ofDelimiter(":");
  if (uppercase) {
    format = format.withUpperCase();        ◁──┐ The HexFormat object is immutable;
  }                                              don't forget to reassign format
  System.out.println(format.formatHex(data));  │ when calling the with- method.
}
```

- When designing a new API, avoid returning results in both the argument and return values, like `InputStream.read(byte[])` does. This may encourage users to ignore the part of the result returned in the return value. Instead, create a new object that contains all the pieces of the result and return it.

Immutability and performance

Sometimes, writing to a mutable object passed as a method parameter is justified from a performance point of view. However, this approach makes the API harder to use. In modern Java, object allocation and garbage collection are significantly improved compared to the older versions, and now, it's preferred to create a new object instead of modifying an existing one, unless you have a good reason. This is reflected in the new API method `readNBytes()`, which was released in Java 11. In addition to the `readNBytes(byte[] array, int offset, int length)`, which repeats the signature of the older `read()` method, there's `readNBytes(int length)`, which just returns a new array. It's very convenient, and it's quite hard to misuse this method, as if you ignore the return result, you'll simply get nothing. Of course, depending on the usage scenario, this method may require additional data copying, which could be unacceptable in hot code paths. On the other hand, in many places, additional overhead is negligible, and by using this method, you can simplify your code and avoid possible errors. Don't forget about this when designing new API methods.

2.12 Mistake 12: Not using a newly created object

Java allows you to write an *object creation expression* (or `new` expression) without using its return value, like this:

```java
new Object();
```

In rare circumstances, this can be useful, such as when the object constructor produces a side effect like registering a newly created object somewhere. Sometimes, this is also used to check whether the constructor throws an exception. For example, I observed that programmers use `new java.net.URI(uriString)` to check whether `uriString` is a syntactically valid URI. The constructor throws `URISyntaxException` when the supplied string violates the URI format, as specified in RFC 2396, so by catching this exception, you may validate URIs supplied by a user.

Unfortunately, this ability also causes mistakes in the code when a programmer creates an object but forgets to assign it to the variable or return from the method. This does not cause compilation errors, and static analyzers won't always help you, as they might be unsure whether avoiding using the newly created object is intended.

One particularly common problem is creating an exception without throwing it:

```
void process(int value) {
  if (value < 0) {
    new IllegalArgumentException("Value is negative");
  }
  // use value
}
```

Here, an exception object is created and not thrown, so it will just be silently discarded, and the method will proceed with the negative `value` without validation.

> **Static analysis**
>
> Static analyzers usually report if an exception object was created and discarded. IntelliJ IDEA features the Throwable Not Thrown inspection, which reports this case. SonarLint reports S3984: Exceptions Should Not Be Created Without Being Thrown. SpotBugs reports a warning "Exception Created and Dropped Rather than Thrown."

WAYS TO AVOID THIS MISTAKE

- Avoid side effects and complex validation in constructors. This way, dangling `new` expressions will be meaningless, and you will never need to write them on purpose.
- It's a reasonable idea to enforce using a newly created object. Configure your linter or static analyzer to warn about any unused newly created object. This way, you'll need to add an explicit suppression comment to every object creation expression, which will signal that the code is intended.

2.13   *Mistake 13: Binding a method reference to the wrong method*

Method references, introduced in Java 8, provide a compact way to specify functions in Java. Unlike with lambdas, when you use method references, you don't need to think up variable names to pass them from functional interface method to a target method. Compare the following, for example:

```
IntBinaryOperator op = Integer::sum;        ◁─┤ Method reference
IntBinaryOperator op = (a, b) -> Integer.sum(a, b);      ◁─┤ Lambda
```

When you are using lambda, you need to specify a parameter list for the called method. As a result, the call often becomes longer and more verbose. It's no wonder many developers prefer the brevity of method references.

However, this brevity may also add confusion. When you have several overloads of the method or constructor, you cannot easily determine which one of them is called when looking at the method reference, even if all the overloads have a different number of parameters. If you don't remember the exact declaration of the functional interface, you may end up binding to a completely different method or constructor.

Consider the following class, where you store textual content associated with some filenames. The clients may create new files or append more lines to existing files. So, you may decide to maintain a map that associates filenames with `StringBuilder` objects. The `add()` method allows you to add a new line, and the `dump()` method writes the current content to the standard output:

```
public class Storage {
  private final Map<String, StringBuilder> contents = new TreeMap<>();

  void add(String fileName, String line) {
    contents.computeIfAbsent(fileName, StringBuilder::new)
            .append(line).append("\n");
  }

  void dump() {
    contents.forEach((fileName, content) -> {
      System.out.println("File name: " + fileName);
      System.out.println("Content:\n" + content);
    });
  }
}
```

Now, let's try to use this class:

```
Storage storage = new Storage();
storage.add("users.txt", "admin");
storage.add("users.txt", "guest");
storage.add("numbers.txt", "3.1415");
storage.dump();
```

We expect to get the following output:

```
File name: numbers.txt
Content:
3.1415

File name: users.txt
Content:
admin
guest
```

In fact, we get something different:

```
File name: numbers.txt
Content:
numbers.txt3.1415

File name: users.txt
Content:
users.txtadmin
guest
```

As you can see, the content starts with the key, which is not what we wanted. Let's take a closer look at the `add()` method:

```
contents.computeIfAbsent(fileName, StringBuilder::new)
```

Here, we create a new entry in the map if it wasn't created before. We've used a method reference as a factory for new entries. But which `StringBuilder` constructor are we calling here? If you convert the method reference to lambda (you can use an automated quick fix provided by your IDE), you'll get the following:

```
contents.computeIfAbsent(fileName, s -> new StringBuilder(s))
```

Now, it's clearer. The function passed to `computeIfAbsent()` has an argument, which is the key passed as the first parameter. It's easy to forget about this, as usually, you don't need this argument, and if you do need it, you can capture the `fileName` variable instead. In lambda, you can just ignore this argument. However, when a method reference is used, the compiler looks for a constructor that accepts a string. As there's actually such a constructor in `StringBuilder`, the compilation finishes successfully, but the newly created `StringBuilder` will not be empty.

It would be correct to use a lambda and the default constructor here. A method reference is not suitable here at all:

```
contents.computeIfAbsent(fileName, s -> new StringBuilder())
```

Aside from overloads, variable arity methods may also cause unexpected behavior. In one project, we have a utility method named `newHashSet()` that creates a `HashSet` and prepopulates it from the supplied arguments. The method is declared in the following way:

```
class Utils {
  @SafeVarargs
  public static <T> HashSet<T> newHashSet(T... elements) {
    return new HashSet<>(Arrays.asList(elements));
  }
}
```

Note that this method can be used without arguments at all. In this case, an empty `HashSet` will be created.

In another part of the code, we populated the following multimap, which contains objects of some `Item` type:

```
Map<Item, Set<Item>> map = new HashMap<>();
```

The addition of a new element looks pretty straightforward:

```
map.computeIfAbsent(key, Utils::newHashSet).add(value);
```

Here, we have the same problem: we want to add a new value to the existing set or create an empty set if it doesn't exist for a given key. However, an argument is mistakenly passed to `newHashSet()`, and as a result, the key `Item` was also always added to the set.

A similar surprise is possible with the `Arrays.setAll()` method. This method is declared in the following way:

```
public static <T> void setAll(T[] array,
                              IntFunction<? extends T> generator) {…}
```

It accepts an array and a function. The function is called for every array index, and its result is stored in the corresponding array element.

Suppose you want to create an array containing `StringBuilder` objects for subsequent filling. It may seem like a good idea to use the `setAll()` method and a method reference:

```
StringBuilder[] array = new StringBuilder[size];
Arrays.setAll(array, StringBuilder::new);
```

For small values of the size variable, this may even work as expected. But as the size grows larger, it may become unbearably slow, and it could even end up with `OutOf-MemoryError`. If you replace the method reference with a lambda, you'll see the following:

```
StringBuilder[] array = new StringBuilder[size];
Arrays.setAll(array, index -> new StringBuilder(index));
```

A function passed to `setAll()` accepts an index of the current element. It's unnecessary for our purposes, but the compiler selects a constructor that accepts an initial capacity of `StringBuilder`, which defines the amount of memory `StringBuilder` will pre-allocate to store the characters. For small indexes this may go unnoticed, but for larger ones, you will pre-allocate much more memory than necessary. Figure 2.9 provides an illustration of how the memory layout will look after the `setAll()` call. In this case, the correct code would use lambda and ignore the `index` parameter:

```
StringBuilder[] array = new StringBuilder[size];
Arrays.setAll(array, index -> new StringBuilder());
```

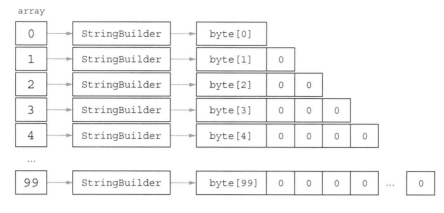

Figure 2.9   Final memory layout after invoking `Arrays.setAll()` **for** `size = 100`. **The internal** `byte[]` **buffer held by** `StringBuilder` **becomes larger and larger toward the end of the array.**

WAYS TO AVOID THIS MISTAKE

- Use method references carefully when pointing to a method or constructor that has overloads or variable arity parameters. You may accidentally link to an incorrect method or pass more arguments than intended. When in doubt, use lambda. Some developers avoid method references completely and always use lambdas. You can configure your linter or static analyzer to highlight all the method references. Unfortunately, it seems unlikely that any static analyzer can highlight only incorrectly bound method references, as analyzers cannot know whether this behavior is intended.

- In some cases, it's easy to forget that a functional argument accepts a parameter. `Map.computeIfAbsent()` and `Arrays.setAll()` are such unfortunate methods, so you should be especially careful when using method references with them.

2.14 *Mistake 14: Using the wrong method in a method reference*

It's easy to use a method reference where a functional interface is required. This ease may cause you to let your guard down and mistakenly use the completely wrong method. Probably the most amusing example I've seen involves mapping the `Integer.max()` or `Integer.min()` static methods to a `Comparator` interface. Consider the following code:

```
List<Integer> list = Arrays.asList(0, -3, -2, 3, -1, 1, 2);
list.sort(Integer::max);    ⟵⎯ Incorrect
System.out.println(list);
```

Here, the author wanted to simply sort the list of integers. As the `sort()` method requires a comparator, the author thought that `Integer::max` would work, as the method name seems to suggest it will compare two numbers and select the larger of them. This code compiles but produces a totally incorrect result:

```
[0, -1, -2, -3, 3, 1, 2]
```

The result might be different if the sorting algorithm in the standard Java library changes in the future, but the problem is that it doesn't sort anything. For `Comparator`, you need to implement a single `compare()` method that accepts two `Integer` values and returns an `int` value whose sign shows which of the input values is larger. The `Integer.max()` method accepts two `int` values (Java performs the automatic unboxing conversion for you) and returns `int`, so from the Java point of view, it fits the `Comparator` interface. However, the sign of the returned value doesn't show which of the inputs is bigger; it's just the sign of the larger number itself, so the sorting works incorrectly. To fix this code, you can specify `Comparator.naturalOrder()` or just use `list.sort(null)`, as the natural order comparator is used by default. More pitfalls related to comparators are discussed in chapter 7.

WAYS TO AVOID THIS MISTAKE

- Pay attention to static analysis messages. IntelliJ IDEA reports an Invalid Method Reference Used for `Comparator` warning when `Integer::min` or `Integer::max` is used for `Comparator`.
- Write unit tests, even if the code looks evident. Here, one may think that list sorting is a straightforward operation that cannot be broken. However, as we've seen, this is not always the case.

Summary

- Priority among mathematical operators is not always intuitive. Particularly, bitwise and logical operators can be tricky. Use parentheses every time the precedence might not be obvious to you or future code readers.
- The plus sign has different meanings when applied to numbers and to strings. In some cases, it's possible to mix them up. Try to avoid mixing addition and concatenation in single expressions, and ban unary plus in your projects.
- When creating a long string using a series of concatenations, it's possible to erroneously apply a subsequent method call only to the last fragment, instead of the whole string. Lean toward using text block syntax, which is available in newer Java versions.
- Conditional expressions have nontrivial and counterintuitive type conversion rules when their branches have expressions of different types. Use an `if` statement when in doubt.
- Avoid boxed types, like `Integer`, `Double`, or `Boolean`, as often as possible. They may cause implicit conversions, which will not only cause performance overhead but also may produce a `NullPointerException` if `null` is accidentally stored there.

- While variable arity methods are convenient to use, they add ambiguity when exactly one argument is passed at a variable arity position. Sometimes, you may have an array or collection accidentally wrapped into another array.

- Java allows you to ignore the result of a method call or `new` expression. While sometimes, this is intentional, it often causes unpleasant mistakes. Remember that many classes are immutable and produce a new object instead of modifying themselves. Also, be sure to add a `throw` word before a newly created exception.

- Method references provide neat and concise syntax to create a functional expression. Be careful when the method or constructor is overloaded, however, as the compiler may bind to the wrong method. When in doubt, use lambda syntax.

Program structure 3

This chapter covers

- Mistakes that happen when using `if–else` chains
- Problems using `while` and `for` loops
- How to avoid pitfalls around the initialization of fields and classes
- Missing a call to a superclass method
- What happens if you accidentally declare a static field instead of an instance one

Java provides a number of constructions to alter the program control flow. These include branching statements (`switch` and `if–else`), loop statements (`for` and `while`), and so on. It is common for beginners to make mistakes in control flow statements, and it is a useful skill to be able to identify them. Such mistakes may result in visiting the wrong branch, having more loop iterations than expected, and other undesirable outcomes. Another class of mistakes discussed in this chapter originates from the errors in program structure outside of the method body, like incorrect initialization order or accidental use of the `static` modifier where it should not be used.

61

3.1   *Mistake 15: A malformed if–else chain*

A common and useful pattern in Java programming is an `if–else` chain that allows you to perform different actions depending on multiple conditions, like this:

```
if (condition1) {
  ...
}
else if (condition2) {
  ...
}
else if (condition3) {
  ...
}
else if (condition4) {
  ...
}
else {
  ...
}
```

When this chain is quite long, occasionally, an intermediate `else` keyword will be missing:

```
if (condition1) {
  ...
}
else if (condition2) {
  ...
}
if (condition3) {          ⟵┐  The else is
  ...                         │  missing here.
}
else if (condition4) {
  ...
}
else {
  ...
}
```

This would be no problem if there was no final `else` block and all the conditions were mutually exclusive:

```
if (input == 1) {…}
else if (input == 2) {…}
else if (input == 3) {…}
else if (input == 4) {…}
```

In this case, two conditions cannot be equal at the same time, so the behavior of the program is not affected if we remove some or all of the `else` keywords. However, this is not always the case. Sometimes, conditions are ordered from more specific to more general, but the program logic assumes that if a more specific condition is satisfied, then a more general one should be ignored. An unconditional `else` branch at the end is the partial case of this scenario: it's the most general behavior that should be executed if no specific conditions were satisfied.

When this kind of mistake is present, two branches could be executed. In the preceding example, if `condition1` or `condition2` is true, then the final, unconditional `else` will be executed as well. This may be unnoticed during testing if only `condition3` and `condition4` were covered. Unfortunately, static analyzers cannot always report this problem because, quite often, having two independent chains of `if` statements is actually intended.

It's possible to make code less error prone if you can shape your `if` chain so that every branch does nothing except assign the same local variable (or several variables). Let's see how it can be done. Consider the following `if` chain:

```
if (condition1) {
  process(getData1());
} else if (condition2) {
  process(getData2());
} else if (condition3) {
  process(getData3());
} else if (condition4) {
  process(getData4());
} else {
  process(getDefaultData());
}
```

Here, we call the same `process` method with a different argument. It would be better to introduce the intermediate variable for the argument and move the `process()` call out of the branches:

```
Data data;
if (condition1) {
  data = getData1();
} else if (condition2) {
  data = getData2();
} else if (condition3) {
  data = getData3();
} else if (condition4) {
  data = getData4();
} else {
  data = getDefaultData();
}
process(data);
```

Now, the code has more lines, but it's more errorproof. For example, let's skip one of the `else` keywords:

```
Data data;
if (condition1) {
  data = getData1();        ◁─┐  Static analysis warnings: the result
} else if (condition2) {      │  of the assignment is unused.
  data = getData2();        ◁─┘
} if (condition3) {         ◁─┤  The else is missing here.
```

```
  data = getData3();
} else if (condition4) {
  data = getData4();
} else {
  data = getDefaultData();
}
process(data);
```

You can go further and declare the local variable as `final` to indicate that you intend to assign it only once. Now, the absence of `else` will be immediately noticed by the compiler:

```
final Data data;
if (condition1) {
  data = getData1();
} else if (condition2) {
  data = getData2();
} if (condition3) {
  data = getData3();          ⊲──┐  Compilation error: the data
} else if (condition4) {         │  variable is reassigned.
  data = getData4();
} else {
  data = getDefaultData();
}
process(data);
```

I personally don't like declaring local variables as `final` because this adds too much visual noise to the code. However, I must admit it helps with catching errors like this, and I know developers who consistently use `final` on locals for extra safety. Alternatively, you can rely on an IDE. For example, IntelliJ IDEA underlines reassigned variables by default (figure 3.1). A good rule of thumb to keep in mind is that if the variable is underlined but you didn't want to reassign it, then something is probably wrong.

```
Data data;
if (condition1) {
  data = getData1();
} else if (condition2) {
  data = getData2();
} if (condition3) {
  data = getData3();
} else if (condition4) {
  data = getData4();
} else {
  data = getDefaultData();
}
```

Figure 3.1 A chain of conditions in the IntelliJ IDEA editor with a missing `else`. Note that the data variable is underlined, which means it's assigned more than once, so it cannot be declared `final`. Additionally, the IntelliJ IDEA static analyzer highlights data in gray in the first two branches to indicate that these assignments are always overwritten.

As an alternative, you can extract the `if` chain to a separate method, assuming it has enough information to evaluate the conditions:

```
Data getData() {
  if (condition1) {
    return getData1();
  } else if (condition2) {
    return getData2();
  } else if (condition3) {
    return getData3();
  } else if (condition4) {
    return getData4();
  } else {
    return getDefaultData();
  }
}
```

Now, the original method is simplified to

```
process(getData());
```

When using `return` in branches, you are free to keep or remove `else` keywords, as they don't change the program behavior:

```
Data getData() {
  if (condition1) {
    return getData1();
  }
  if (condition2) {
    return getData2();
  }
  if (condition3) {
    return getData3();
  }
  if (condition4) {
    return getData4();
  }
  return getDefaultData();
}
```

Compared to the original code, this shape is much better. Specifically, now you have separated the side-effect code (`process()` call) and side-effect-free code (computing the data). It's much easier to test or reuse the side-effect-free method `getData()`.

WAYS TO AVOID THIS MISTAKE

- Configure code style in your IDE so that `else if` is placed on the same line as the closing brace of the previous branch. In this case, the problem will be more eye-catching after reformatting:

  ```
  if (condition1) {
    …
  } else if (condition2) {
    …
  ```

```
    }
    if (condition3) {
      ...
    } else if (condition4) {
      ...
    } else {
      ...
    }
```

- Cover all the conditional branches with unit tests.
- Try to keep `if` branches in one of two shapes: either return something or assign the same variable. In the first case, `else` is not required at all. In the second case, if you miss the `else` keyword, you will get a static analyzer warning that the result of the assignment is unused or a compilation error if the variable is declared as final.

3.2   *Mistake 16: A condition dominated by a previous condition*

Another problem that can arise from a series of `if–else` conditions occurs when the conditions are not mutually exclusive. In this case, the order of conditions affects the program behavior. If two or more conditions can be true at the same time, only the first branch will be executed, so branch order may be important.

In a more specific scenario, one condition *dominates* another one. We say that condition X dominates condition Y if Y can be true only when X is also true. In this case, `if (Y) {…} else if (X) {…}` is a reasonable code pattern, while `if (X) {…} else if (Y) {…}` is clearly a mistake—the last branch is never taken.

Simple cases of condition dominance include numeric ranges and `instanceof` checks. For example, consider the following code that determines the tariff plan based on customer age:

```
enum Plan {CHILD, FULL, FREE}
Plan getPlan(int age) {
  if (age >= 6) return Plan.CHILD;
  if (age >= 18) return Plan.FULL;    ◁——┐  This condition is
  return Plan.FREE;                        never satisfied.
}
```

The idea was to assign the CHILD plan for customers ages 6 to 17 (inclusive). However, the order of conditions is wrong: `age >= 6` dominates over `age >= 18`. As a result, `age >= 18` is never true and the FULL plan is never returned.

The following method (adapted from a real production code base) to convert an object to a `BigInteger` is an example of condition dominance involving `instanceof` checks:

```
BigInteger toBigInteger(Object obj) {
  if (obj instanceof Number)
    return BigInteger.valueOf(((Number) obj).longValue());
  if (obj instanceof BigInteger)
```

```
    return (BigInteger) obj;
  if (obj instanceof BigDecimal)
    return ((BigDecimal) obj).toBigInteger();
  return BigInteger.ZERO;
}
```

The idea was to convert any number (`Long`, `Double`, `Integer`, etc.) via the intermediate `long` value but apply a better algorithm for `BigInteger` and `BigDecimal` inputs. However, as `BigInteger` and `BigDecimal` classes extend the `Number` abstract class, such inputs also fall into the first condition, making the following branches useless. Mistakenly ordered `instanceof` checks are harder to spot, as the type hierarchy could be complex and not completely known by a code writer or reader.

Static analysis

Data-flow-based static analysis, like the Constant Values inspection in IntelliJ IDEA, is capable of detecting many dominating conditions. In both of the preceding samples, it reports that the subsequent conditions are always false. PVS-Studio has a similar warning, V6007: Expression Is Always True/False.

Some static analyzers can detect even more complex dominance conditions. For example, consider the following erroneous implementation of a classic FizzBuzz problem:

```
for (int i = 1; i < 100; i++) {
  if (i % 3 == 0) System.out.println("Fizz");
  else if (i % 5 == 0) System.out.println("Buzz");
  else if (i % 15 == 0) System.out.println("FizzBuzz");
  else System.out.println(i);
}
```

The idea is to print `FizzBuzz` when i is divisible by 15. However, the `i % 15 == 0` condition is dominated by previous ones, so it's unreachable. The IntelliJ IDEA analyzer is capable of detecting this case.

Still, even an advanced analyzer cannot detect all the cases. For example, most common Java static analyzers don't warn in the following code that parses command-line arguments:

```
for (String arg : args) {
  if (arg.startsWith("--data")) {
    setData(arg.substring("--data".length()));
  } else if (arg.startsWith("--database")) {
    setDataBase(arg.substring("--database".length()));
  } else { … }
}
```

Any string that starts with `--database` also starts with `--data`, so the second condition is unreachable. In theory, it's possible to detect this statically, but in IntelliJ IDEA, it's not implemented as of this writing, so you cannot rely on static analysis completely. In any case, it's always possible to have more complex conditions (e.g., involving custom method calls from your project) where a static analyzer cannot do anything.

(continued)

It should also be noted that even incorrect `instanceof` chains may not be reported by static analyzers, as type hierarchies do not always provide all the necessary information. For example, consider the following method, which processes collections and has optimized implementations for random access lists and other lists:

```
void process(Collection<?> data) {
  if (data instanceof List) {
    processList((List<?>) data);
  } else if (data instanceof RandomAccess) {
    processRandomAccessList((RandomAccess) data);
  } else {
    processAnyCollection(data);
  }
}
```

As the `RandomAccess` interface doesn't extend the `List` interface, you may implement it without implementing the `List`. Thus, it's theoretically possible for the second condition to be true, and generally, static analyzers will be silent here. However, as stated in the documentation, `RandomAccess` is a marker interface for `List` implementations, so correct implementations of `RandomAccess` also implement `List`, and they will never reach the `processRandomAccessList()` call. Arguably, this was a mistake in JDK implementation: `RandomAccess` should be declared as extending `List`. Do not make the same mistake in your code; always declare intended superinterfaces.

WAYS TO AVOID THIS MISTAKE

- When you have a series of `if-else` branches, check the test coverage report, and make sure that all the branches are covered with tests. If you see that a branch is not covered, write a test to cover it. If you have a condition dominance problem, you will quickly notice it.
- Since Java 21, it's been possible to use switch patterns for a series of `instanceof` checks. The body of the `toBigInteger()` method shown previously could be rewritten in the following way:

```
return switch (obj) {
  case BigInteger bigInteger -> bigInteger;
  case BigDecimal bigDecimal -> bigDecimal.toBigInteger();
  case Number number -> BigInteger.valueOf(number.longValue());
  case null, default -> BigInteger.ZERO;
};
```

The big advantage of this construct is that it checks the dominance automatically. If you put the `Number` case label at the beginning, you'll have a compilation error:

```
return switch (obj) {
  case Number number -> BigInteger.valueOf(number.longValue());
```

```
  case BigInteger bigInteger -> bigInteger;
  case BigDecimal bigDecimal -> bigDecimal.toBigInteger();
  case null, default -> BigInteger.ZERO;
};
```

Compilation error: this case label is dominated by a preceding case label.

While this doesn't help with other kinds of dominant conditions, like numeric ranges, this is already a big step forward.

- Try to keep conditions mutually exclusive. Particularly for numeric ranges, specify both range bounds. While this makes the code more verbose, it's also more explicit and more flexible, as reordering the conditions does not affect the behavior. For example, the getPlan() method could be rewritten in the following way:

```
Plan getPlan(int age) {
  if (age >= 0 && age <= 5) return Plan.FREE;
  if (age >= 6 && age <= 17) return Plan.CHILD;
  if (age >= 18) return Plan.FULL;
  throw new IllegalArgumentException("Wrong age: " + age);
}
```

We also specified the complete range for the FREE plan, which makes the code even more robust. Now, it throws an exception if a negative age is passed to the method. Also, an exception will be thrown if we mistakenly specified the wrong bounds, skipping some ages. Suppose we introduce a new tariff plan for young people, ages 18 to 24. Now, the FULL plan is applicable for ages 25+. Next, imagine we fixed the condition for the FULL plan but forgot to add a condition for a new plan:

```
Plan getPlan(int age) {
  if (age >= 0 && age <= 5) return Plan.FREE;
  if (age >= 6 && age <= 17) return Plan.CHILD;
  if (age >= 25) return Plan.FULL;
  throw new IllegalArgumentException("Wrong age: " + age);
}
```

Thanks to our throw statement, the problem will immediately show itself when the system is tested with a person between the ages of 18 and 24. The exception is much easier to spot than the wrong plan silently applied, so it's much more likely that the problem will be discovered during early testing.

- If you need a chain of conditions that are not mutually exclusive, consider adding a comment that explicitly states that the order of conditions is important and why conditions are written this way.

3.3 Mistake 17: Accidental pass through in a switch statement

This problem is tightly connected with the previous one. For unfortunate historical reasons, the switch operator in Java falls through into the next branch by default, so you have to explicitly use the break statement to exit the switch:

```
void performAction(Button button) {
  switch (button) {
    case YES:
      actOnYes();
      break;
    case NO:
      actOnNo();
      break;
    case CANCEL:
      actOnCancel();
      break;
  }
}
```

If you accidentally miss one of the break statements, two actions will be performed.

Fortunately, this problem was addressed in Java 14. Now, there's an alternative arrow syntax for switch branches, which doesn't allow pass-through behavior at all:

```
void performAction(Button button) {
  switch (button) {
    case YES -> actOnYes();
    case NO -> actOnNo();
    case CANCEL -> actOnCancel();
  }
}
```

Static analysis

Static analyzers may warn about pass-through switch branches. For example, Sonar-Lint has a rule, S128: Switch Cases Should End with an Unconditional Break Statement, which warns by default. SpotBugs has the warning Switch Statement Found Where One Case Falls Through to the Next Case. If you use IntelliJ IDEA, check the inspection Fallthrough in Switch Statement, which might be turned off. There's a convention between static analyzers to suppress the warning if the pass through is marked with a comment like // fallthrough:

```
switch (button) {
  case YES:
    actOnYes();
    // fallthrough
  case NO:
    actOnYesAndNo();
    break;
  case CANCEL:
    actOnCancel();
    break;
}
```

Here, the // fallthrough comment explicitly indicates the intent to fall into the next case. Most static analyzers recognize this comment and no longer warn when they see it. The approach to explicitly mark all the intended fall through switch branches with a comment is supported by the *Google Java Style Guide*.

WAYS TO AVOID THIS MISTAKE

- Always use the new arrow syntax if you can use Java 14 or newer.
- Try to keep switch branches in one of two shapes: either return something or assign the same variable. In the case of a return, you don't need to add a break statement at all. In the case of an assignment, you can declare the variable final, and accidental fall through will cause a compilation error, as the variable will be assigned twice:

```
final Boolean answer;
switch (ch) {
    case 'T':
    case 't':
        answer = true;        ◁──┐ Break is accidentally
    case 'F':                      omitted.
    case 'f':
        answer = false;       ◁──┐ Compilation error: the
        break;                     answer is reassigned.
    default:
        answer = null;
}
```

When migrating to Java 14 or newer, such switch statements can be easily transformed to `switch` expressions, which will make the code even more clear and robust. Modern IDEs can perform such transformations automatically. Here's how the resulting code looks:

```
final Boolean answer = switch (ch) {
    case 'T', 't' -> true;
    case 'F', 'f' -> false;
    default -> null;
};
```

3.4   Mistake 18: Malformed classic for loop

The classic `for` loop in Java was inherited from C. Although it's flexible, this construct is pretty dangerous and becomes a source of many subtle bugs. Usually, it appears in the idiomatic way, when it is necessary to iterate over the range of numbers:

```
for (int i = from; i < to; i++) {
  // body
}
```

One of the problems is that the same variable must be mentioned three times there. This makes it quite easy to mix the variables, especially if you have several nested loops. Erroneous code may look like this:

```
for (int i = 0; i < 10; i++) {
  for (int j = 0; j < 10; i++) {    ◁──┐ Typo: i++ is written
    // use i and j                        instead of j++.
  }
}
```

It might be hard to notice but the inner loop increments the variable `i` of the outer loop. As a result, the inner loop never finishes. Another example of an infinite loop looks like this:

```
for (int i = 0; i < 10; i++) {
  for (int j = 0; i < 10; j++) {        ⟵┐ Typo: i < 10 is written
    // use i and j                        │ instead of j < 10.
  }
}
```

Here, we increment the correct variable, but we have the wrong condition. While infinite loops are usually easy to detect during testing, things could be more complicated if the inner loop has the break statement on some condition:

```
for (int i = 0; i < 10; i++) {
  for (int j = 0; j < 10; i++) {
    // use i and j
    if (condition()) {
      break;
    }
  }
}
```

In this case, the loop can finish via the condition, and sometimes, the program may look like it's working correctly but still be wrong. It's also possible to have a typo in both the condition and the update clauses:

```
for (int i = 0; i < 10; i++) {
  for (int j = 0; i < 10; i++) {
    // use i and j
  }
}
```

Now, the loop finishes, but, of course, not all possible combinations of `i` and `j` are processed. Such bugs could lurk in code bases for years (e.g., in validation or normalization loops). For instance, imagine you want to replace all negative values in a square array with zero. The code may look like this:

```
void normalizeData(int[][] data) {
  int rows = data.length;
  for (int i = 0; i < rows; i++) {
    int columns = data[i].length;
    for (int j = 0; i < columns; i++) {     ⟵┐ The j variable should be
      if (data[i][j] < 0) {                   │ used in the loop condition
        data[i][j] = 0;                        │ and update statement.
      }
    }
  }
}
```

It will require very careful review to notice that the inner loop has the wrong condition and update expressions. Also, this works for some inputs. If negative numbers rarely appear, this bug could slip through quality assurance unnoticed and make it into the production code.

Static analysis

Dataflow-based static analysis tools can easily detect infinite loops, like those previously listed. For example, IntelliJ IDEA highlights loop conditions and issues warnings like Condition Is Always True if only the condition or the update expression are wrong. Unfortunately, this will not help if both of them are mistaken.

Some static analysis tools provide inspections to report nonidiomatic loops in various ways. One possibility is to report when the loop variable is modified inside the loop body. If you use this kind of inspection, the `normalizeData` example will be reported, as the inner loop modifies the loop variable of the outer loop. Unfortunately, such inspections produce many undesired warnings in legitimate cases, so to use them efficiently, you either need a very strict code style or you'll have to suppress many warnings. In IntelliJ IDEA, such an inspection is called Assignment to `for` Loop Parameter, and it's turned off by default. SonarLint provides the rule S127: `for` Loop Stop Conditions Should Be Invariant. Some malformed `for` loops can be caught by the PVS-Studio warning V6031: The Variable X Is Being Used for This Loop and for the Outer Loop.

WAYS TO AVOID THIS MISTAKE

- Use code templates provided by your IDE to type idiomatic range iteration loops. For example, IntelliJ IDEA offers the *fori* live template. When you type *fori* and press Enter, the whole loop is generated. After that, you can change the variable name, and it will be properly updated everywhere. Eclipse has a similar template to iterate over an array. Instead of typing the `for` loop manually, type *for* and press Ctrl-Space to invoke the code completion pop-up. Select the For – Use Index on Array option to generate the `for` loop automatically.
- When testing the looping code, don't forget to cover the cases in which both inner and outer loops have at least two iterations. In the `normalizeData` sample, a unit test will catch a mistake if it passes an array like `{{-1, -1}, {-1, -1}}` and ensures that it's normalized.

3.5 *Mistake 19: Not using the loop variable*

Sometimes, developers write the loop correctly but forget to use the loop variable in the body, using a constant value instead. An example of such use was discovered by the PVS-Studio team in the Apache Dubbo project. The following is a classic code pattern that maps the content of one array to another:

```
String[] types = …
Class<?>[] parameterTypes = new Class<?>[types.length];
for (int i = 0; i < types.length; i++) {
  parameterTypes[i] = ReflectUtils.forName(types[0]);
}
```

Unfortunately, `types[0]` was mistakenly written instead of `types[i]`. This code might work correctly if there's only one element in the `types` array or all the elements are the same, so it may bypass simple tests. Also, simple static analysis diagnostics, like Variable Is Not Used do not help here, as the `i` variable is, in fact, used in the loop body.

Static analysis

The PVS-Studio analyzer has a heuristic diagnostic V6016: Suspicious Access to Element by a Constant Index Inside a Loop. This may produce false positive reports, as in rare cases, using a constant index might be intended. Nevertheless, it's a good idea to check these reports.

WAYS TO AVOID THIS MISTAKE

- Consider using `Arrays.setAll()` to fill an array:

```
Arrays.setAll(parameterTypes, i -> ReflectUtils.forName(types[i]));
```

  In this case, the array index is available as a lambda parameter, so if you don't use it, it will be much more visible.

- Try to avoid using indices at all. In many cases, it's possible to rewrite code using higher-level constructs, like Stream API. For example, here one may write the following:

```
Class<?>[] parameterTypes = Arrays.stream(types)
    .map(ReflectUtils::forName)
    .toArray(Class<?>[]::new);
```

  Now, all the indices are encapsulated inside Stream API implementations and don't appear in the client code. Using Stream API might have additional costs, but in most cases, it's insignificant.

3.6   *Mistake 20: Wrong loop direction*

Sometimes, it's necessary to modify the classic `for (int i = lo; i < hi; i++)` pattern. One common example of such a modification happens when it is necessary to iterate the collection in a backward direction. The forward loop visits the numbers starting from `lo` (including `lo`) and finishing just below `hi` (excluding `hi` itself). If you want to iterate the same numbers in a backward direction, you should write

```
for (int i = hi - 1; i >= lo; i--)
```

A common mistake while writing the backward loop or changing the loop direction manually is to forget changing `i++` to `i--`:

```
for (int i = hi - 1; i >= lo; i++)
```

Luckily, this problem can be detected statically. Also, you should be careful to avoid off-by-one errors in the initial value (using `hi` instead of `hi - 1`) or bound (using `i > lo` instead of `i >= lo`). These problems may not be detected by static analyzers, as such initial values and bounds may be intentional.

Static analysis

IntelliJ IDEA has a Loop Executes Zero or Billions of Times inspection, which reports a warning if there's a mismatch between the variable update direction and bound condition, as in `i >= lo; i++`. Similarly, SonarLint reports S2251: A `for` Loop Update Clause Should Move the Counter in the Right Direction warning. It's very unlikely for such a combination to be intentional, as it will be executed either zero times, if the bound condition is false since the beginning, or billions of times, until loop variable overflow occurs.

WAYS TO AVOID THIS MISTAKE

- IDEs may provide an action to reverse the direction of an existing loop. For example, IntelliJ IDEA has a Reverse Direction of `for` Loop intention action available on the loop declaration. It could be more robust to write an ascending iteration loop and then use an IDE action to convert it to the descending one.
- If you want to iterate over an array or `List` in the reverse direction, IDEs may provide code templates to do this. For example, IntelliJ IDEA has a postfix template called *forr* to create a reverse loop over an array or `List`. Given an array named `arr`, for example, one may type `arr.forr` to generate a loop declaration:

```
for (int i = arr.length - 1; i >= 0; i--) {

}
```

- If you use Java 21 and want to iterate over a list in reverse order, consider a new `reversed()` method, which was added to the `List` interface. It returns a reverse-ordered view of the list and greatly simplifies iteration of the list in reverse order. For example, before Java 21, you should write

```
for (int i = list.size() - 1; i >= 0; i--) {
  var element = list.get(i);
  … // use element
}
```

Now, using the `reversed()` method, you can avoid indices completely:

```
for (var element : list.reversed()) {
  … // use element
}
```

3.7 Mistake 21: Loop overflow

Sometimes, it's desired to include the upper bound of a loop, and the commonly used pattern is `for (int i = lo; i <= hi; i++)`. Note the use of the less-than-or-equal operator here instead of a simple less-than in the loop condition. In most cases, this kind of

loop works fine, but you should ask yourself whether `hi` could be equal to `Integer`
`.MAX_VALUE` (or `Long.MAX_VALUE` if the loop variable has a long type). In this rare case,
the loop condition will become always true, and the loop will never terminate, as the
loop counter will silently overflow and continue with negative numbers. This case
might sound unrealistic, but I actually had this bug in production code that resulted
in an infinite loop. The problem could be fixed in several ways (e.g., by adding a
lower-bound condition):

```
for (int i = lo; lo <= i && i <= hi; i++)
```

WAYS TO AVOID THIS MISTAKE

- While the problem is extremely rare, pay attention to less-than-or-equal iteration loop conditions and ask yourself whether the bound could be `MAX_VALUE`.
  Cover this corner case with a test, if possible.
- Consider using Stream API instead of loops, like `IntStream.rangeClosed(lo,`
  `hi)`. This is much more concise, and the `MAX_VALUE` corner case is properly handled inside the `rangeClosed` implementation, so you don't need to worry about
  it. Unfortunately, using Stream API may add performance overhead, so use it
  with care in performance-critical code.

We cover more overflow-related problems in chapter 4.

3.8   *Mistake 22: Idempotent loop body*

An *idempotent operation* is an operation that may produce a side effect but doesn't
change anything if performed several times subsequently. For example, a simple
assignment is idempotent:

```
x = 0;
```

This statement has a side effect: it changes the value of the x variable. However, it
doesn't matter if you perform this operation once, twice, or a hundred times; the
result will always be the same. Conversely, the following operation is not idempotent:

```
x += 10;
```

It updates the value of x, using its previous value, so the result will vary, depending on
how many times this operation is performed.

Here's a simple rule: all the code executed during a loop iteration must not be
idempotent. By *all the code*, I am referring to the loop body, loop condition, and
update statement, if we are speaking about the `for` loop. When this rule doesn't hold,
the loop likely has a bug. To understand this, let's consider a `while` loop:

```
while (condition) {
    body;
}
```

Let's assume the condition has no side effect and the body is idempotent. In this case, we have three options:

1 *The condition is false initially.* The loop is not executed at all.

2 *The condition is true initially, but the body makes it false.* The loop is executed only once.

3 *The condition is true initially, and the body doesn't change it.* The loop is infinite, and the program hangs.

If the third option never occurs in practice, then the loop is completely redundant and could be rewritten using an `if` statement. Here's a simple example:

```
while (x < 0) {
  x = 0;
}
```

Here, if x is initially a negative number, it will be changed to 0 at the first iteration. Otherwise, x will be unchanged. In no case will the loop continue to the second iteration, so, technically, this is not a loop at all and can be replaced with a conditional statement:

```
if (x < 0) {
  x = 0;
}
```

Of course, you should be careful when fixing such an error. It's also possible that the loop was intended but something should be changed in its body.

It's more interesting when case 3 actually occurs. Let's consider the following code snippet, which is very similar to one I have actually seen in production code:

```
static String makeUniqueId(String id, Set<String> usedIds) {
  int i = 1;
  String uniqueId = id;
  while (usedIds.contains(uniqueId)) {
    uniqueId = id + "_" + i;
  }
  return uniqueId;
}
```

This method is intended to generate a unique identifier based on the proposed one (passed as an id parameter). If the proposed identifier is not used yet (is not contained in usedIds set), then we use it. Otherwise, we try to add a suffix like _1 to the identifier until we find an unused one.

If you look more closely at this code, you will realize the loop body is idempotent and the condition has no side effect, so we have a problem. The loop body assigns a variable, uniqueId, based on the values of id and i, but id and i are never changed inside the loop, so we never try suffixes like _2 or _3. Instead, we end up in an infinite loop, trying the same suffix again and again, as shown in figure 3.2.

How it was intended to work   **How it actually works**

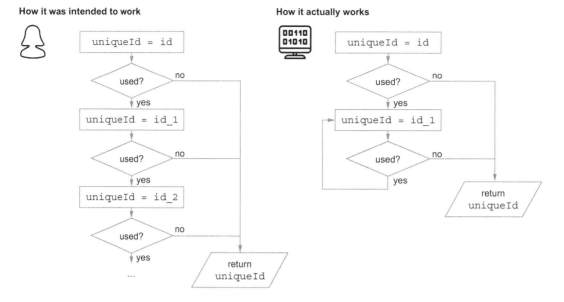

Figure 3.2   Here, the goal was to find the unused string for `id`. In fact, after the first attempt, it falls into an infinite loop.

This mistake is dangerous because it may easily slip through unit testing. The developer can test this method using the following assertions:

```
assertEquals("id", makeUniqueId("id", Set.of()));
assertEquals("id_1", makeUniqueId("id", Set.of("id")));
```

This works fine, so the developer might think the method is implemented properly. A code coverage tool will also show that these assertions cover all the instructions and branches of the method. However, the method implementation is wrong, and these tests are not enough. The following call ends up in an infinite loop:

```
makeUniqueId("id", Set.of("id", "id_1"));
```

Once the problem is identified, the fix is simple: just add `i++` to the loop body.

Static analysis

IntelliJ IDEA has Idempotent Loop Body inspection that can detect simple cases, like those shown previously. Unfortunately, it may not report if interprocedural analysis is necessary to prove the loop body idempotence.

Sometimes, a loop body becomes idempotent only under some circumstances, so more "normal" loop iterations may happen when the program state changes.

Suppose you need a method to analyze a format string similar to one passed to `printf()`. The method must return `true` if the format string contains the `"%d"` format specifier. However, you cannot simply use `str.contains("%d")`, as it's also possible to escape a `"%"` symbol itself, duplicating it. For example, for the input `"%%d"`, we should return false, but for `"%%%d"`, we should return true. One may come up with the following implementation:

```
static boolean hasPercentD(String str) {
  int pos = 0;
  while (true) {
    pos = str.indexOf('%', pos);
    if (pos == -1 || pos == str.length() - 1) {       Exit if there are no % characters
      return false;                                    anymore or only one is left at
    }                                                  the end of the string.
    char c = str.charAt(pos + 1);
    if (c == 'd') {
      return true;                    Handle %d
    }
    if (c == '%') {
      pos += 2;              Handle %%
    }
  }
}
```

Here, two-argument versions of the `indexOf()` method are used, so we can continue to search from the previous place, looking for a percent sign. If it's followed by `d`, we immediately return `true`, and if it's followed by another `%`, we skip it and continue searching. This implementation correctly handles any combination of `"%%"` and `"%d"` in the single string, so one may write quite a few successful unit tests. For example, the following tests pass:

```
assertTrue(hasPercentD("Hello %d!"));
assertFalse(hasPercentD("%%d!"));
assertFalse(hasPercentD("%%%%"));
assertFalse(hasPercentD("%%%%%"));
assertFalse(hasPercentD("%%d%d"));
assertTrue(hasPercentD("%%d%%%d"));
```

Moreover, if you count code coverage with JaCoCo, you may happily note that these tests cover 100% of the `hasPercentD()` method lines or instructions. Even mutation coverage with Pitest reports that 100% of the mutations are killed. So when looking at metrics, the developer might be confident the method works correctly and is well-tested.

Still, the code has a very unpleasant bug. If a percent character is followed by anything aside from `d` or `%`, then the loop falls into an idempotent state. The `pos` variable is not updated in this case, so the `indexOf()` call will find the same percent character again and again, and the method never finishes. You may try calling it with, for example, `"%s"` as your input.

Unfortunately, static analyzers are silent here. While it's theoretically possible to detect such a problem statically, I am not aware of static analyzers that are capable of reporting this case. The only hint you may get from testing is that test coverage reports a missing branch at the `c == '%'` condition—for the preceding test suite, this condition is never false when reached. Therefore, it's a good idea to pay attention to branch coverage, even if line or instruction coverage is reported to be 100%.

WAYS TO AVOID THIS MISTAKE

- When writing unit tests for loops, ensure more than just the 0 and 1 iterations are covered by tests. The loops are intended to iterate more than once (otherwise it's just a conditional statement), so it's a good idea to test the more-than-once scenario.
- Be careful with methods like `indexOf()` when you process the string. The pattern `pos = str.indexOf(ch, pos)` is quite common to move to the next occurrence of `ch`. However, if you don't update `pos` after that in some branch of your code, it's possible that you'll end up in an endless loop.

3.9   *Mistake 23: Incorrect initialization order*

Initialization is a complex problem in programming. When you initialize a whole program, a subsystem, or an individual object, you have to deal with the fact that some part of it is not fully initialized yet, so you cannot freely use any functions. You should carefully order initialization steps; otherwise, you may end up accessing a noninitialized field.

3.9.1   *Static fields*

Here's a simple example, which is based on a real bug fix in the Kotlin IntelliJ Plugin, though the original problem appeared in the Kotlin language, rather than Java. For brevity, let's use Java 16 records:

```
record Version(int major, int minor) {
  public static final Version CURRENT =
                parse(Application.getCurrentVersion());
  private static final Pattern REGEX =
                Pattern.compile("(\\d+)\\.(\\d+)");

  static Version parse(String version) {
    Matcher matcher = REGEX.matcher(version);
    if (!matcher.matches()) {
      throw new IllegalArgumentException();
    }
    int major = Integer.parseInt(matcher.group(1));
    int minor = Integer.parseInt(matcher.group(2));
    return new Version(major, minor);
  }
}
```

Here, we have a simple parser of application version strings. For convenience, a public field, CURRENT, is provided, which stores a version of the currently running application. We assume there's an `Application.getCurrentVersion()` static method, which returns the current version as a string.

As the parser uses a regular expression, it's a common practice to extract it as a constant. This approach improves the performance because you need to compile the regular expression only once.

Unfortunately, this class cannot be initialized at all. During the initialization of the CURRENT field, we need the parse() method to function properly, which requires the REGEX field to be initialized. However, as the REGEX field is declared after the CURRENT field, it's not initialized yet, so when parse() is called, it's still equal to null. As a result, class initialization fails with NullPointerException inside the parse() method.

This problem can be easily fixed by reordering the REGEX and CURRENT field declarations. Also, it was discovered quickly because the problem always manifests itself via exception when anybody tries to use this class. Sometimes, however, the initialization order affects only one code path. I've seen a code pattern like this:

```
class MyHandler {
  public static final MyHandler INSTANCE = new MyHandler();
  private static final Logger LOG =
          Logger.getLogger(MyHandler.class.getName());

  private MyHandler() {
    try {
      …
    }
    catch (Exception ex) {
      LOG.log(Level.SEVERE, "Initialization error", ex);
    }
  }
}
```

Here, the singleton instance of MyHandler is created during the class initialization. Usually, everything will work fine. However, if an exception happens during the MyHandler construction, it won't be logged as intended. Instead, the uninitialized LOG field will be dereferenced and class initialization will fail with NullPointerException, masking the original problem.

Static analysis

IntelliJ IDEA only has simple analysis for this purpose, yet it can catch the first problem: Nullability and Data Flow Problems inspection reports a possible NullPointer-Exception at REGEX.matcher call. This warning may look confusing, and some developers might even think that the inspection is wrong here because the REGEX field seems to be properly initialized. Check the initialization order if you see a warning like this.

Standalone static initializers, like PVS-Studio, have more advanced initialization cycle analysis. PVS-Studio reports both of the previously listed code snippets and points to the exact code locations where the fields are declared and used.

- Be careful when initializing classes or objects. Try to avoid complex calls during the initialization or move them to the initializer end. If that's not possible, make sure called methods don't expect your class or object to be fully initialized.
- Don't forget to test rarely visited code paths. Error reporting code executes rarely, but it's crucial for further investigation of the problem. If it doesn't function correctly, the error report you get from the user or server logs might be completely meaningless.

3.9.2   *Subclass fields*

Another initialization problem common in Java occurs when an overridden method is called from a superclass constructor. For example, consider a class like this that represents an entity with a numeric identifier:

```
class Entity {
  final int id;

  Entity() {
    id = generateId();
  }

  protected int generateId() {
    return 0;
  }
}
```

The constructor calls the `generateId()` method here, so subclasses can override it and provide their own strategy to generate entity identifiers. Now, suppose you have a subclass that generates identifiers using random numbers. It could be implemented like this:

```
class RandomIdEntity extends Entity {
  final Random random = new Random();

  @Override
  protected int generateId() {
    return random.nextInt();
  }
}
```

At first glance, it may look OK; however, this doesn't work, since any attempt to construct a `RandomIdEntity` instance yields to `NullPointerException`. The initialization of the `random` field is effectively a part of the `RandomIdEntity` class constructor, which is executed after a superclass constructor. Essentially, this class is equivalent to the following:

```
class RandomIdEntity extends Entity {
  final Random random;
```

```
  RandomIdEntity() {
    super();
    random = new Random();
  }

  @Override
  protected int generateId() {
    return random.nextInt();
  }
}
```

When the superclass constructor is executed, subclass fields are not initialized yet (except in rare cases when the final fields are initialized with compile-time constants). However, we are calling an overridden method `generateId()`, which assumes that the `random` field is already initialized. The initialization flow is illustrated in figure 3.3.

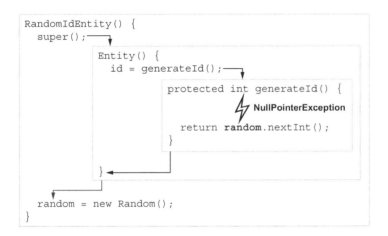

**Figure 3.3   Initialization flow of `RandomIdEntity()` class. The `random`
field was used via superclass constructor before it was initialized.**

In this sample, the problem will become clear as soon you try to instantiate the subclass; however, this is not always the case. Sometimes, accidental use of the uninitialized fields may lead to very subtle and hard-to-diagnose bugs.

Static analysis

Some static analyzers can detect possible problems like this. For example, SonarLint has the rule S1699: Constructors Should Only Call Non-overridable Methods (off by default) that reports any calls to overridable methods from constructors. Similarly, IntelliJ IDEA has the Overridable Method Called During Object Construction inspection to report this problem.

- Avoid calling non-final instance methods from constructors of non-final classes. In general, keep your constructors as simple as possible. If you need to use any helper methods, default to declaring them as static, private, or final, so subclasses cannot override them.
- Try to move nontrivial initialization logic out of the constructor. For example, you may initialize the `id` field lazily when it is first accessed (though lazy initialization has its own caveats when it comes to thread safety):

```
class Entity {
  Integer id;

  int getId() {
    if (id == null) {
      // not thread-safe
      id = generateId();
    }
    return id;
  }

  protected int generateId() {…}
}
```

- If you cannot avoid calling an overridable method in the constructor, clearly state in the method's Javadoc specification that this method might be called when the object is not fully initialized.

3.9.3   *Class initialization order*

Another kind of problem occurs when the initializers of two classes depend on each other. The class initializer includes `static {}` sections declared in the class body as well as initializers of static fields. The Java virtual machines (JVMs) ensure execution of a class initializer only once, and its execution should be finished before you use the class so that all the static fields are completely initialized when you access them.

The problems start to appear when the initializer of class A depends on class B, whose initializer depends on class A. To understand better how class initializers work, let's consider the following synthetic sample:

```
class A {
  private static final B unused = new B();        ← ─┐ Class A creates an instance
  static final String WELCOME = "Hello".toUpperCase();   │ of class B, which requires
                                                         │ the initialization of class B.

  public static void main(String[] args) {
    System.out.println(B.MSG);
  }
}
                                                   ┌ Class B refers to a field of
}                                                  │ class A, which requires the
class B {                                          │ initialization of class A.
  static final String MSG = A.WELCOME;    ← ───────┘

  public static void main(String[] args) {
```

```
    System.out.println(B.MSG);
  }
}
```

As you can see, we have two classes, A and B, and the `main()` method of each has an identical body. Does this mean the result of the execution of both classes will be the same? Also, how will the `unused` field affect the program behavior? Think about it.

Let's assume we launched the A class. You may notice that initializer of class A uses class B. Namely, it creates a new instance of type B. This will trigger the initialization of class B even if class A is not completely initialized yet. The order of initialization is the following:

1 Class A initializer starts.
2 Class B initializer starts.
3 `B.MSG = A.WELCOME;` (but `A.WELCOME` is still `null`!).
4 Class B initializer ends.
5 `A.unused = new B();`
6 `A.WELCOME = "Hello".toUpperCase();`
7 Class A initializer ends.

So when `MSG` is assigned, `WELCOME` is still not initialized, and the program will output `null`, which might be unexpected. However, if we launch the B class, the initialization order will be different, as the class B initializer will start first:

1 Class B initializer starts.
2 Class A initializer starts.
3 `A.unused = new B();` (class B is not fully initialized, but this works).
4 `A.WELCOME = "Hello".toUpperCase();`
5 Class A initializer ends.
6 `B.MSG = A.WELCOME;` (now, its value is `"HELLO"`).

This time, we will see `HELLO` in the output, which is more expected.

Field initializers are normally executed in the same order in which fields are declared in the class, so if we swap the `unused` and `WELCOME` fields, then the class launching A will output `HELLO`. There's one exception, however: if the field initializer is a compile-time constant expression of a primitive or the `String` type, then the field will be initialized during class loading, before initialization starts. If you remove the `toUpperCase()` call from our sample, you'll also see that `null` is not printed anymore, as the `WELCOME` field will be initialized during class loading.

While using a class that is not completely initialized may have unpleasant consequences, this is not the biggest problem with circular dependency in class initializers. The biggest problem occurs when you start using both of these classes from different threads. As the virtual machine guarantees that a class initializer is never executed twice, it acquires a lock during class initialization. When one class is initialized during another class initialization, two locks will be acquired. If another thread tries to acquire the same two locks in reverse order, there will be a deadlock. As a result, both threads will be completely stuck until the program is terminated. Any other thread that tries to access any of these classes later will be stuck as well. This may render the program completely unusable.

We can demonstrate this problem creating a separate class that initializes A and B in different threads:

```
public class Test {
  public static void main(String[] args) {
    Runnable[] actions = {() -> new A(), () -> new B()};
    Stream.of(actions).parallel().forEach(Runnable::run);
    System.out.println("ok");
  }
}
```

This program, when launched, may be deadlocked without printing "ok". On my machine, it gets stuck more than 50% of the time, though it may depend on the hardware, OS, and version of JVM used.

To diagnose this problem, you can run the jstack tool, specifying the process identifier of the Java process that got stuck. Here's an excerpt from the output using Java 11:

```
"main" #1 prio=5 os_prio=0 …
   java.lang.Thread.State: RUNNABLE
    at com.example.B.<clinit>(Test.java:22)
    at com.example.Test.lambda$main$1(Test.java:8)
    at com.example.Test$$Lambda$2/0x0000000800061040.run(Unknown Source)
…
"ForkJoinPool.commonPool-worker-19" #21 daemon prio=5 os_prio=0 …
   java.lang.Thread.State: RUNNABLE
    at com.example.A.<clinit>(Test.java:14)
    at com.example.Test.lambda$main$0(Test.java:8)
    at com.example.Test$$Lambda$1/0x0000000800060840.run(Unknown Source)
```

Here, you can see two threads spending their time inside the `<clinit>` method, which is a special method name to denote a class initializer. Therefore, you may guess that something is wrong with initializers of these classes. If you use Java 17 or newer, you will see an additional hint:

```
"main" #1 prio=5 os_prio=0 …
   java.lang.Thread.State: RUNNABLE
    at com.example.B.<clinit>(Test.java:22)
    - waiting on the Class initialization monitor for com.example.A
    at com.example.Test.lambda$main$1(Test.java:8)
    at com.example.Test$$Lambda$2/0x0000000800c00c18.run(Unknown Source)
…
"ForkJoinPool.commonPool-worker-1" #23 daemon prio=5 os_prio=0 …
   java.lang.Thread.State: RUNNABLE
    at com.example.A.<clinit>(Test.java:14)
    - waiting on the Class initialization monitor for com.example.B
    at com.example.Test.lambda$main$0(Test.java:8)
    at com.example.Test$$Lambda$1/0x0000000800c00a00.run(Unknown Source)
```

Now, the JVM reports `waiting on the Class initialization monitor`, so you can easily see that the class B initializer waits for the class A initializer, and vice versa.

While our sample is synthetic, such problems really happen in practice. One common case of an initialization loop happens when a superclass declares a field of a subclass type:

```
class A {
  public static final A INSTANCE = new B();
}
class B extends A {
}
```

This code may look completely harmless, but here, deadlock is also possible if one thread triggers the initialization of class A, while another thread triggers the initialization of class B. You can observe the deadlock using the same `Test` class as used previously. The most unpleasant problem here is that initially, when your application has a small number of users, you may rarely have tasks executed in parallel, and deadlock may not occur. However, as your application becomes more popular and more actively used, deadlocks may appear, freezing the application completely. At this point, it might be difficult to refactor your application to avoid cyclic dependency. For example, the `A.INSTANCE` public field may already be used by third-party plugins, so you cannot simply move it to another class without breaking other code.

> **Static analysis**
>
> The latest sample with subclass is easy to detect statically, so various static analyzers report it. SonarLint has a S2390: Classes Should Not Access Their Own Subclasses During Initialization rule, and IntelliJ IDEA has a Static Initializer References Subclass inspection that reports here. Don't ignore these reports, as they indicate a very serious problem.

WAYS TO AVOID THIS PROBLEM

- Keep class initializers as simple as possible. If you need something complex, consider lazy initialization. Instead of exposing a public static field, create a method that will perform initialization on demand.
- If you know your program has an initialization loop, do not postpone fixing it until you actually hit a deadlock. Fixing the problem at an earlier stage may be much easier.
- If your program is expected to serve many clients in parallel, be sure that your automatic tests cover this case. It's possible for your program to work fine sequentially but have serious problems when different requests are handled in parallel.
- Upgrade to newer Java versions. As you can see, monitoring tools like jstack are improved in newer versions, which helps with investigating these problems.

3.9.4   *Enum initialization loop*

The enum type in Java consists of several predefined constants. Usually, developers don't think about the initialization of these constants, assuming that when you start using the enum all the constants already exist. However, they are not magically pre-created. Instead, they are initialized as a part of the enum class initialization. If you use a custom constructor for enum constants, you can observe them uninitialized. For example, it's quite possible to have an initialization loop if you have two enums that refer to each other:

```
enum Pet {
  DOG(Voice.BARK),
  CAT(Voice.MEOW);

  final Voice voice;
  Pet(Voice voice) { this.voice = voice; }
}

enum Voice {
  BARK(Pet.DOG),
  MEOW(Pet.CAT);

  final Pet owner;
  Voice(Pet owner) { this.owner = owner; }
}
```

It may be unnoticed when this code is written, but if you stop and think, you will notice a chicken-and-egg problem here. If Pet is initialized first, Voice is not initialized yet, and vice versa. You can check this:

```
System.out.println("Dog voice is " + Pet.DOG.voice);
System.out.println("Barking pet is " + Voice.BARK.owner);
```

The first line correctly outputs BARK, but the second line outputs null. That's because when Voice.BARK was initialized, Pet.DOG was not initialized yet, so null was assigned to the owner field. To circumvent this problem, you can declare the owner field non-final and set it after the constructor invocation.

Note that during the enum constant initialization, the enum is not fully functional. In particular, the values() method doesn't work yet, as not all the values are created. This method could be called implicitly when you are using a switch statement or expression over the current enum in Java versions prior to Java 21. For example, the following enum, while appearing innocent, cannot be initialized at all if you are using Java 20 or older:

```
enum DayOfWeek {
  SUN, MON, TUE, WED, THU, FRI, SAT;

  final boolean weekend;

  DayOfWeek() {
    weekend = switch (this) {
```

```
    case SAT, SUN -> true;
    default -> false;
  };
 }
}
```

Due to implicit invocation of the `values()` method, you'll see a `NullPointer-Exception` inside the class initializer when you try to use this enum.

Why is `values()` called?

You may wonder why the `values()` method should be called in this case. The Java bytecode has no instruction for an `enum` switch, so it's necessary to desugar it to a numerical `switch` during the compilation. A simple way to do this would be to call the `ordinal()` method and replace the labels with the corresponding enum ordinal numbers:

```
weekend = switch(this.ordinal()) {
  case 6, 0 -> true;
  default -> false;
}
```

This approach has problems if the `enum` will be modified later, but the class that uses `enum` will not be recompiled. New `enum` constants may appear, or existing constants may be reordered; in this case, ordinal values may change, so you'll end up visiting the wrong `switch` branch. To fix this, an intermediate array is created, which maps the runtime ordinal values to the ordinal values that were actual during the compilation, so the compiled code looks like this:

```
weekend = switch(DayOfWeek$1.$SwitchMap$DayOfWeek[this.ordinal()]) {
  case 6, 0 -> true;
  default -> false;
}
```

The array is located in a synthetic holder class, and it's initialized when you execute the `switch` for the first time. To initialize it, you need to iterate all the `enum` constants. That's why the `values()` method is called, so the `enum` itself must be fully initialized.

On the other hand, this complication is unnecessary if your current class is the `enum` class itself because if a new constant is added, the `switch` expression will be recompiled as well. This case was handled separately in Java 21, and now, the preceding sample does not have an implicit `values()` call, so it works as expected.

WAYS TO AVOID THIS MISTAKE

- Don't forget that from the virtual machine point of view, enum is basically an ordinary class, and enum constants are initialized as static fields. If you have a nontrivial constructor, you can observe enum in noninitialized state.
- Do not use `switch` on an enum during the initialization of the same enum, unless you have migrated to Java 21. Such a `switch` cannot function properly, as

it implicitly calls the `values()` method, which doesn't work until all the constants are initialized.

3.10   *Mistake 24: A missing superclass method call*

When inheriting a class, it's desired sometimes to augment superclass method behavior with additional logic. Often, this happens in UI programming when a UI event is handled in both the subclass and the superclass. For example, suppose you are developing a user interface control using some framework and want to handle specifically when the user presses the X button on the keyboard. In some frameworks, you should override a method like `onKeyDown()` and process the corresponding event:

```
public void onKeyDown(KeyEvent event) {
  super.onKeyDown(event);
  if (event.getKeyChar() == 'x') {
    // handle key 'x'
  }
}
```

In such scenarios, it's essential to explicitly call a superclass method. Otherwise, other standard hotkeys will not be handled. However, it's easy to miss the super call or accidentally remove it during refactoring. The compiler won't warn you, and you likely won't have runtime exceptions either. However, the program behavior will be incorrect.

Sometimes, the method of a superclass is not called intentionally, even though it has nontrivial behavior. In this case, one may say that there's no mistake, but it's still a code smell, which is called *refused bequest*. In general, refused bequest means the subclass intentionally removes some functionality of its superclass. In this case, it's desired to rethink your class hierarchy. It's likely better to avoid inheritance at all, replacing it with delegation.

Static analysis

Annotation packages for static analysis may contain an annotation like `@MustBe-InvokedByOverriders` (in JetBrains annotations) or `@OverridingMethodsMust-InvokeSuper` (in Error Prone annotations). These annotations could be used to mark superclass methods that must be invoked by the corresponding subclass method. Static analysis tools that support these annotations will check and report methods in subclasses that fail to invoke the superclass method. The corresponding IntelliJ IDEA inspection is called Method Does Not Call Super Method, and Error Prone bug pattern is called MissingSuperCall.

WAYS TO AVOID THIS MISTAKE

- Avoid designing an API that requires implementation inheritance and overriding nonabstract methods in particular. Instead, prefer interfaces.

  For example, to handle UI events, it would be more robust to declare an interface like `KeyListener` and the ability to add new listeners to the UI component. In this case, you don't need to do extra steps to invoke previously registered listeners, as they will be invoked by a UI component automatically. In fact, the Java Swing toolkit is designed this way, so it's rarely required to override a nonabstract method there, as you can customize many things implementing the interfaces. In contrast, the initial version of AWT, the first Java UI framework, relied on overwriting the `Component.handleEvent()` method. This made it possible to forget calling the superclass method, which could result in ignoring some events. Later, this method was deprecated.

- If you still want to rely on implementation inheritance in your API, lean toward defining all the overridable non-abstract methods as empty. Do not forget to mark all the nontrivial methods not intended for overriding as `final`. If you call the overridable methods from final methods, the subclasses will not be able to omit the important functionality. For example, a superclass that defines a component could be implemented as follows:

```
public final void onKeyDown(KeyEvent event) {
  … // Process standard keys
  afterKeyDown(event);
}

protected void afterKeyDown(KeyEvent event) {}
```

Now, the inheritor cannot override the `onKeyDown()` method because it's final. However, it's possible to override the `afterKeyDown()` method to achieve the same behavior. In this case, it's unnecessary to call the superclass method, as it does nothing.

3.11 Mistake 25: Accidental static field declaration

Sometimes, developers accidentally declare a static field when an instance field is intended. This may happen due to refactoring or a copy-paste error. As a result, a single field instance is shared between all the objects of a given class. This kind of bug could be very annoying if it was not spotted during code review or via static analysis. That's because, depending on the class usage pattern, such code may pass simple tests and even sometimes produce correct behavior in production if object instances are typically used one after another. For example, imagine the following simple class:

```
class Person {
  private static String name;

  public void setName(String newName) {
    name = newName;
  }

  public String getName() {
    return name;
  }
}
```

It's possible that the sole purpose of this object is to be deserialized from a database, used, and thrown away. As long as two objects don't exist at the same time, the program might function properly. However, once the number of users increases, the chance for two users to have simultaneous sessions also increases.

This bug is very dangerous, as when it happens, you are unlikely to have an exception. Instead, the wrong data might leak to another place, potentially violating privacy or security.

Static analysis

IDEs might address this problem by having different highlighting for static nonfinal fields. Developers can train themselves to pay special attention to such highlighting because static nonfinal fields have limited application and should not be generally used. Also, there are static analysis inspections that report when a static field is modified from a nonstatic method. For example, IntelliJ IDEA has an Assignment to Static Field from Instance Context inspection, though it might be turned off by default. SonarLint reports S2696: Instance Methods Should Not Write to Static Fields by default.

Unfortunately, marking the field as final doesn't solve the problem completely, as you might have a mutable object stored in static final field. For example, it might be a mutable collection. In this case, you don't assign the field directly, but data is still shared between objects. Imagine that you have a tree-like structure, wherein every node can return a list of its child nodes:

```
interface TreeNode {
  List<TreeNode> getChildren();
}
```

Now, we have a `TreeWalker` class that simplifies the breadth-first traversal of this tree:

```
class TreeWalker {
  private static final Queue<TreeNode> toProcess =
    new ArrayDeque<>();

  TreeWalker(TreeNode root) {
    toProcess.add(root);
  }

  TreeNode nextNode() {
    TreeNode next = toProcess.poll();
    if (next != null) {
      toProcess.addAll(next.getChildren());
    }
    return next;
  }
}
```

It's assumed that clients create the `TreeWalker` object passing a tree root as a constructor argument. Then, clients repeatedly invoke `nextNode()` until it returns `null`. Figure 3.4 illustrates traversing a simple tree.

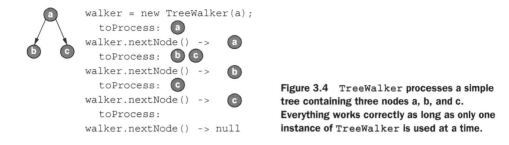

Figure 3.4 `TreeWalker` **processes a simple tree containing three nodes a, b, and c. Everything works correctly as long as only one instance of** `TreeWalker` **is used at a time.**

As you can see, the `toProcess` field was accidentally declared static. As long as we never have two `TreeWalker` objects used simultaneously and always process the whole tree till the end, we won't notice a problem. However, if two `TreeWalker` objects are created in separate threads, the nodes from different trees may go to the wrong place. Figure 3.5 shows a possible execution when two threads start processing two independent trees. In this case, nodes from the thread 2 tree, like y, may be retrieved in thread 1, and vice versa. The situation can be even more complicated, as `ArrayDeque` methods like `poll()` and `addAll()` called inside `nextNode()` are not thread safe, and you may completely break the internal structure of `ArrayDeque`. In this case, you may observe exceptions like `ArrayIndexOutOfBoundsException` popping from `ArrayDeque` internals. Having an exception is actually a happy case, as you immediately see that your program is wrong and needs to be fixed. However, the exception is not guaranteed.

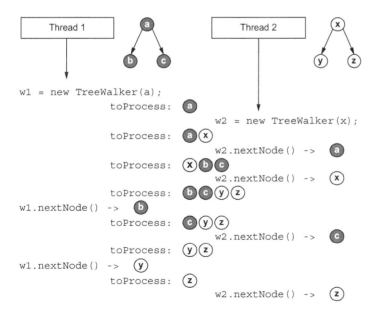

Figure 3.5 **A possible execution when using** `TreeWalker` **from two threads concurrently. As the** `toProcess` **variable is accidentally shared, nodes may leak from one thread to another.**

Once I processed the codebase of RubyMine IDE to remove usages of an obsolete `java.util.Stack` collection. This collection is a part of the old Java 1.0 collection framework, where all the modification operations are synchronized. This is rarely useful. If you actually need to access a collection from several threads, modern alternatives, like `ConcurrentLinkedDeque`, would be preferred. And if the collection is never accessed concurrently, this synchronization just adds unnecessary overhead.

I have seen a class (say, `Xyz`), where an instance field of type `Stack` was declared and used in a clearly non-thread-safe way. I concluded that as the code is not thread-safe already, it's not a problem to make it even less thread safe, so I replaced the `Stack` with `ArrayList`-based implementation. Unexpectedly, some tests started to fail sporadically with `ArrayIndexOutOfBoundsException`. Further investigation revealed that `Xyz` instance was stored in a static field of another class, which was clearly a mistake: it was not intended to share a single `Xyz` instance between all the users. This produced very subtle errors in the highlighting of Ruby source files in the IDE when two or more editors were opened at once. As synchronized collection was used before, we had no exceptions, just slightly incorrect behavior. Thanks to replacing the collection with an unsynchronized one, we revealed the problem.

> ### Mutable objects
>
> Sometimes, the object might look immutable when, in fact, it's not. There are several infamous examples in the Java standard library, notably `java.text.DateFormat` and its inheritors, like `SimpleDateFormat`. It looks like a good idea to cache a `DateFormat` object in a static field and reuse it to format many dates in the same way. However, when you call the `format()` method, it mutates the private fields in the object, so calling `format()` concurrently may produce unexpected results. Static analyzers may know about this and warn if you try to store such an object in a static field. For example, SonarLint has a rule named S2885: Non-Thread-Safe Fields Should Not Be Static that reports such problems. In modern Java, it's preferred to use a modern class to format dates named `DateTimeFormatter`, which is immutable and can be shared between threads.

WAYS TO AVOID THIS MISTAKE

- Avoid declaring static nonfinal fields. They are useful in very limited contexts. Set up your IDE to have a distinctive highlighting for such fields. The highlighting should alert you that something unusual is going on in this code.
- Set up your static analysis tool to report warnings when static fields are updated from nonstatic contexts. While this is sometimes correct, such updates are very suspicious and could be incorrect in multithread programs.
- Avoid storing mutable objects in static fields. If you are unsure whether a given object is mutable, check the class documentation. When creating mutable classes, explicitly state this in the class Javadoc.
- Avoid using thread-safe mutable objects when thread safety is unnecessary and you have a non-thread-safe alternative. Thread-safe objects may introduce

additional performance overhead and may hide problems when the object is accidentally used from several threads.

- If the object is expected to be used from several threads, consider writing integration tests that emulate this situation.

Summary

- While the `if` statement is a very simple concept, it has its pitfalls as well. One common problem is forgetting `else` in the middle of `if`–`else` chains. Another problem is the incorrect order of conditions, which may cause some branches to never be visited. Ensure that every `if` branch is covered by your tests.

- For legacy reasons, `switch` statements in Java require an explicit `break` to avoid visiting the subsequent branch. If you accidentally forget it, the program behavior may become subtly different. Prefer using `switch` with the arrow syntax available in newer Java versions, as this form of `switch` is not affected.

- Classic `for` loops that iterate over a range of numbers are surprisingly tricky and error prone. When possible, prefer generating them automatically using your IDE.

- Mistakenly written `while` and `for` loops may result in the program state not changing after the first loop iteration. This might be unnoticed if the loop is usually iterated a maximum of one time. Test your loops to ensure they work correctly when two or more iterations are necessary.

- Many mistakes happen in programming in general during initialization, as the initialization code must deal with the program, which is not fully initialized yet. In Java, these problems may appear if field initializers depend on each other or a superclass constructor calls a subclass method when the subclass is not initialized yet.

- Special care should be taken to avoid class initialization loops, as this may cause a complete program freeze due to deadlock when different classes are initialized from different threads.

- Pay attention to the difference between static fields that have one instance per program and regular fields that have one instance per object of a given class. Sometimes, a field is mistakenly declared as static, and this may result in bugs that are hard to reproduce and diagnose.

Numbers

Modern programs usually operate with very high-level abstractions. Still, numbers and primitive math is used by programmers quite often. Unfortunately, computer math differs in many ways from real math, and these differences often produce unpleasant bugs. An experienced Java programmer should be aware about many peculiarities of number processing in this language, including numeric overflow and implicit conversions.

4.1 Mistake 26: Accidental use of octal literal

For historical reasons, Java supports octal literals. An *octal literal* looks very much like a normal number, except it starts with 0. For example, 037 is an octal literal that represents a decimal number 31 (as $3 \times 8 + 7 = 31$). It's an extremely rare situation when octal literals are actually necessary. The only reasonable use of octal literals that comes to mind is representing Unix file permissions, as there are three bits of permissions (read/write/execute) for different classes of users (user, group, and others). So sometimes, it's convenient to represent them as a constant like 0644, which means the user can read and write, while group and others can only read. There is no other widely known context in which octal numbers could be useful.

Occasionally, people add an extra leading zero before the decimal literal by mistake. Some developers are simply unaware of octal numerals and may use a leading zero to align a series of numbers:

```
int n1 = 9876;
int n2 = 5432;
int n3 = 0123;    ←——  A leading zero is added to
int n4 = 4567;          align the numbers better.
```

Here, a leading zero was added to the series of constants to make it look more uniform. As the literal doesn't contain the digits 8 or 9, it's parsed as a valid octal literal, but its numeric value is completely different (83 instead of 123). Depending on further use of the constant, such a mistake might go unnoticed for a long time.

WAYS TO AVOID THIS MISTAKE

- The best solution is to ban octal literals from your project completely. Configure your style checker or static analyzer to report octal literals as errors. IntelliJ IDEA has the Octal Integer inspection, which reports every octal literal. The corresponding SonarLint rule is called S1314: Octal Values Should Not Be Used (turned off by default). If you like to align numbers in adjacent lines, use spaces instead of leading zeroes.

4.2 Mistake 27: Numeric overflow

To make computations fast, computers must allocate a fixed number of bits for every number, by default. This means you have to deal with *numeric overflow* when the result of the computation does not fit the memory chunk allocated to store the value. What happens in this case depends on the programming language and the data type used.

4.2.1 Overflow in Java

By default, numeric operations in Java overflow silently, just yielding the incorrect result. Java performs math computations on four data types: int, long, float, and double. When other numeric primitive types, like byte, short, and char, participate in computation, they are *widened* to int before the actual operation happens. The overflow behavior for integral types differs significantly from floating-point types.

For int and long, if the result of computation exceeds the type, the higher-order bits are simply discarded. We won't dig into details of *two's complement number format* representation here; instead, let's formulate the practical rules for the int type (for long, they are similar):

- If the result of addition or subtraction of two int values is larger than Integer .MAX_VALUE (which equals 2,147,483,647), then 2^{32} is subtracted from the correct result, so you'll always get the negative number instead of a positive one.
- If the result of addition or subtraction of two int values is less than Integer .MIN_VALUE (which equals −2,147,483,648), then 2^{32} is added to the correct result, so you'll always get the positive number instead of a negative one.
- If the result of multiplication of two int values overflows, you may get a completely random number that doesn't resemble the original one. Strictly speaking, this isn't random, but it's rarely practical to try to get anything useful from it.
- The result of division of two int values never overflows, except in only one case: Integer.MIN_VALUE / -1. In this case, you'll get Integer.MIN_VALUE, as the int type does not include the corresponding positive number. We'll discuss this number in mistake 29, later in this chapter.

The problem with the overflow is that it happens silently. If you don't detect it immediately, you may not notice that the result is incorrect until much later, after many additional computations, making it difficult to identify the cause of the mistake. For example, let's calculate the expression (x * x + 1_000_000) / x for different values of x (table 4.1).

Table 4.1   Step-by-step computation of the (x * x + 1_000_000) / x **expression in Java for different values of x. Incorrect results that occur due to numerical overflow are shown in *italics*.**

x	x * x	x * x + 1000000	(x * x + 1000000)/x	Correct result
10,000	100,000,000	101,000,000	10,100	10,100
46,300	2,143,690,000	2,144,690,000	46,321	46,321
46,340	2,147,395,600	*-2,146,571,696*	*-46,322*	46,361
46,350	*-2,146,644,796*	*-2,145,644,796*	*-46,292*	46,371
100,000	*1,410,065,408*	*1,411,065,408*	*14,110*	100,010

As you can see, we can get correct results for x values up to 46,300. However, as the square of x approaches Integer.MAX_VALUE, we start having trouble. First, the result of addition overflows, and we suddenly get the negative result. Very soon after that, the multiplication overflows as well. This is especially sad because the correct final result after division would fit the int type perfectly, but we cannot get it, due to intermediate overflow.

When we are just beyond the overflow, we can detect the problem, as the number becomes negative. However, when we are going further, it may become positive again. For example, when x equals 100,000, the result will be 14,110, which, although positive, is not even close to the correct result of 100,010. Unfortunately, Java does not indicate whether overflow happened.

The behavior is somewhat better for floating-point numbers, because if you have intermediate overflow, you will likely end up with special numbers, like infinity or NaN, so you can just check the result of the whole operation. Let's calculate the same expression, this time using the `double` type and assuming x $= 10^{200}$:

```
double x = 1e200;
double res = (x * x + 1_000_000) / x;
```
res is now infinite, due to intermediate overflow.

So you can check the floating-point number against infinity or NaN after the series of calculations and report the error.

When you work with floating-point numbers, you may also experience *numeric underflow*. This happens when the result of a computation using the `float` or `double` type is too close to zero. For example, let's compute the hypotenuse of a very small right triangle using the Pythagorean theorem:

```
double x = 3e-200;
double y = 4e-200;
double hypot = Math.sqrt(x * x + y * y);
```

The result will be zero instead of the expected `5e-200` because an underflow happens in the intermediate multiplication. Note that you can easily solve this particular problem by using the library method `Math.hypot(x, y)`, which is carefully written to avoid an underflow. In practice, underflow happens rarely, as you would need to be working with extremely small numbers, so in most cases it's safe to ignore it.

One famous overflow problem is average calculation. The math formula to calculate the average of two numbers is as simple as `(a + b) / 2`. However, it doesn't work if you use the Java `int` or `long` types, and the sum exceeds the type domain. The expected average always fits the type domain, as it cannot exceed both input numbers, but you may get the incorrect result:

```
int a = 1_000_000_000;
int b = 2_000_000_000;
int average = (a + b) / 2;
```
The average is -647,483,648, which is incorrect.

This bug was discovered in 2006. It appeared in the binary search procedure in standard libraries for a number of programming languages, including Java. The binary search may work incorrectly if you have an array containing more than 2^{30} elements. This bug can be fixed using an unsigned right shift, which cancels out the overflow effect:

```
int a = 1_000_000_000;
int b = 2_000_000_000;
int average = (a + b) >>> 1;
```
Now, the average is 1,500,000,000, as expected.

The *unsigned right shift* operates on the bitwise representation of a number, moving bits to the right. For positive `int` values, shifting by one bit to the right is equivalent to dividing by two. However, when the value is negative, unsigned right shift interprets it as a positive number larger than `MAX_VALUE`, as if overflow doesn't happen. Note, though, that the unsigned right shift trick doesn't work when input numbers can be negative.

Alternatively, you can switch to the `long` type when computing the intermediate sum. This solution is quite simple and does not make the algorithm much slower. Also, it works if you need to compute an average of more than two `int` numbers. While it's fixed in the standard library, the bug may still reside in other places, and the problem is that it appears only with very large inputs.

It's interesting that a similar bug still exists in the Java standard library in another place. Stream API allows you to calculate the average of long numbers, but internally, it calculates the sum in the `long` variable as well, so the result could be surprising when the input numbers are large:

```
LongStream.of(Long.MAX_VALUE, Long.MAX_VALUE)
        .average().getAsDouble()
```

Counterintuitively, this expression evaluates to -1 because `Long.MAX_VALUE + Long.MAX_VALUE` overflows to -2. Unfortunately, there's no primitive integer type in Java larger than `long`, in which you could store an intermediate sum in this case. You can use `BigInteger`, which has arbitrary length, but this would result in significant performance overhead. One possible solution to compute the average of several `long` values without possible overflow is to divide every input number independently and store the remainders in a separate variable:

```
static double average(long... values) {
  long divs = 0;
  long rems = 0;
  int n = values.length;
  for (long a : values) {
    divs += a / n;
    rems += a % n;
  }
  return divs + rems * 1.0 / n;
}
```

This algorithm uses the following fact: `a == (a / n) * n + a % n`. As no remainder exceeds the number of input values n, which does not exceed `Integer.MAX_VALUE`, the `rems` variable cannot overflow.

This approach is not suitable for Stream API, as you may not know in advance how many `long` numbers you have. Also, you need to perform many division operations, which might be undesired. Alternatively, one could emulate a 128-bit integer, using two `long` variables to hold an intermediate sum. I used this approach in the StreamEx (https://github.com/amaembo/streamex) library.

Static analysis

While static analyzers try to help here, they cannot cover most of the possible overflow cases, as almost any computation can potentially overflow. The simple thing analyzers detect is overflow in constant expressions. For example, try declaring a variable like this:

```
int microseconds = 24 * 60 * 60 * 1000 * 1000;
```

The result of this computation doesn't fit the int type, so it will silently overflow. IntelliJ IDEA reports this problem with the Numeric Overflow inspection. Note, however, that bytecode-based analyzers, like SpotBugs, cannot report such problems at all, as constants are computed during compilation. This means there's no computation inside the bytecode, and the analyzer cannot know whether it overflows. In any case, if any variables are used in the computation, the analyzer will be unlikely to help.

On the other hand, SpotBugs can report the previously described problem with average value computation with the Computation of Average Could Overflow warning. This quickly becomes annoying, as in many cases, overflow never happens. For example, it's often necessary to calculate the average for the screen coordinates to place UI elements. The assumption that screen coordinates will never exceed one billion looks quite safe, so using normal division is OK. However, the static analyzer may report every instance of such division, which will result in tons of noise warnings, so I would not recommend static analyzers here. Instead, take this general advice: be careful when working with too-big numbers.

WAYS TO AVOID THIS MISTAKE

- Always think about possible overflow when doing integer math. Multiplication is the most dangerous operation, as it may produce a result that is significantly larger than the operands. Use the following rule of thumb: if at least one of your int operands exceeds 50,000, it's better to take a closer look and check for possible multiplication overflow.

- Try to rewrite your formula using algebraic transformations or bitwise operations to avoid intermediate overflow if the final result usually fits your data type. For example, for the int type, the expression (x * x + 1_000_000) / x overflows when x exceeds 46,330. However, if you simply change it to x + (1_000_000 / x), it won't overflow anymore.

- Use library methods for complex computations when possible, as they might be carefully written to avoid intermediate overflow or underflow. For example, Math.hypot(x, y) is essentially the same as Math.sqrt(x * x + y * y), but it won't overflow, even if the intermediate expression x * x overflows.

- When you need to perform integer computations without possible overflow, you may use the BigInteger class. This may be much slower than simple operations, but it is guaranteed not to create overflow. Using the long type instead of int may also help in many practical cases without significant performance degradation. Note that at early stages of some project development, numbers above 2 billion might look unrealistic, but sometimes, the amount of data grows quickly. For example, the NuGet, which is the package manager for the .NET ecosystem, used the `int` type to track the downloads count (it is written on C#, not Java, but the idea is the same). As the service got more popular, the downloads count of one package exceeded 1 billion, with 10 million new downloads weekly, so overflow would be reached in quite a realistic timeframe. Luckily, the problem was noticed in advance, and there was enough time to fix it.

- It's possible to catch the numeric overflow if you use `Math.*Exact` methods instead of plain operators (e.g., `Math.addExact(x, y)` instead of x + y). These methods throw `ArithmeticException` in case of overflow, so you can catch it and react. These methods are called *intrinsic functions*. Instead of actually calling them, the JIT compiler replaces them via one or two CPU instructions, so when there's no overflow, the performance is expected to be comparable to simple operations.

  Unfortunately, using methods like `addExact()` may make your code difficult to read. Java doesn't provide any kind of user-defined operator overloading, so you cannot tell the compiler to treat a simple + operator as `addExact()`. However, sometimes, these methods are exactly what you need. For example, they are used in the implementation of the JDK method `str.replace(target, replacement)`, which allows you to replace all the occurrences of the string `target` within the `str` with the `replacement`. Naturally, the resulting string could become longer if the replacement is longer than the target. Before the resulting string is created, it's necessary to calculate its length. At this point, it's already known how many replacements should be made, so the length of the resulting string should be

```
bufferSize = str.length() +
  (replacement.length() - target.length()) * replacementCount;
```

As you can see, this calculation may overflow in multiplication and addition, and you may get a completely incorrect buffer size and start filling it. In this case, the desired behavior was to throw `OutOfMemoryError`. This can be easily achieved with exact operations, like this:

```
int bufferSize;
try {
  bufferSize = Math.addExact(str.length(),
      Math.multiplyExact(
          replacement.length() - target.length(),
          replacementCount));
} catch (ArithmeticException e) {
  throw new OutOfMemoryError();
}
```

This looks quite verbose, but it's OK for widely used library code.

4.2.2   *Assigning the result of int multiplication to a long variable*

One common overflow case is when the result of integer multiplication is assigned to a `long` variable or passed as a `long` parameter. This happens when you need to perform unit conversion. For example, if you have the time in seconds and want to pass it to the method accepting microseconds, you may write a code like this:

```
void process(int seconds) {
  long microseconds = seconds * 1_000_000;
  useMicroseconds(microseconds);
}
```

This will work correctly if the number of seconds doesn't exceed 2,147 (about 35 minutes). If it does, then the multiplication will silently overflow, and you may get incorrect behavior. Please note that in Java, the target variable type is not used to determine the type of mathematical expression, so even if we assign the result to the `long` variable, the multiplication is performed using the `int` type. The code can be easily fixed using the `L` suffix:

```
long microseconds = seconds * 1_000_000L;
```

> ### Static analysis
> The IntelliJ IDEA analyzer reports this error with the Integer Multiplication or Shift Implicitly Cast to `long` inspection. SpotBugs has a bug pattern named Result of Integer Multiplication Cast to Long.

WAYS TO AVOID THIS MISTAKE

- If you are about to multiply two numbers and assign the result to `long`, check that at least one of the operands is also `long`, to avoid potential overflow. You may add an explicit `(long)` cast or use the `L` suffix for literal.
- Use API methods instead of performing manual computations. In this case, you can use the `TimeUnit` enum:

  ```
  long microseconds = TimeUnit.SECONDS.toMicros(seconds);
  ```

- When possible, test your code with large numbers.

4.2.3   *File size, time, and financial computations*

In addition to time computations, pay attention to file offset computations. For example, sometimes, binary files are organized in fixed-size blocks with each block numbered, usually starting with 0. When it's desired to read or write the xth block, it's necessary to seek within the file using the `RandomAccessFile.seek()` method or similar. In this case, one should multiply x by the block size to get the offset. The problem may appear if the multiplication is performed using the `int` type. People rarely work with files of sizes exceeding 2 GB, so the size, in bytes, usually fits the `int` type, and overflow doesn't happen. However, when the file size exceeds 2 GB, calculations using the `int` type may cause unpleasant bugs, like corrupted files and data loss.

Another dangerous area is financial computations. It's usually recommended to store an amount of money, like an item price or account balance, using the `BigDecimal` type. However, this adds a significant performance overhead, which could be unacceptable. Using `float` or `double` is a bad idea, as rounding errors may negatively affect the value. Sometimes, a better alternative is to use an `int` or `long` type scaled to the minimal precision you need. For example, if you round all the values to one cent, it might seem like a good idea to store amounts of money in cents and perform all the computations in cents. However, there's also a significant risk of overflow. It's hard to predict how the quantities may scale in the future. The amount of money to process may unexpectedly increase due to inflation or business growth.

A notable example of this scenario took place in 2021, at the Nasdaq Stock Market. It stored share prices in 32-bit unsigned integer values, using ¢0.01, or $0.0001, precision, and the maximum share price that could be represented with this data type was $(2^{32} - 1) / 10,000 = \$429,496.7295$. At the time of development, this likely looked like a practical limit, as no share price was close to this number. However, Berkshire Hathaway's share price exceeded this number on May 4, 2021, causing a numerical overflow in the stock exchange's backend. Using a 64-bit data type would be much safer here.

Care should be taken if you convert any date interval or absolute date value into a single number, regardless of how you do this. A well-known year-2038 problem demonstrates why this is important: if you store the number of seconds since the Unix epoch (January 1, 1970) in a signed `int` variable, it will overflow in January 2038. Windows 95 and Windows 98 were known to crash completely after roughly 49.7 days of continuous running. These operating systems stored the number of milliseconds since the last boot in a 32-bit unsigned integer, and the overflow in this number caused the problem.

In January 2022, another date-related overflow bug occurred, this time affecting the Microsoft Exchange Server. It has a versioning scheme for Microsoft Filtering Management Service updates that contains 10 digits, like YYMMDDNNNN, where YY is the last two digits of the year, MM is the month, DD is the day, and NNNN is the update number within that day. It appeared that these version strings were parsed to 32-bit signed integer values. It worked perfectly until the end of 2021, as 2112310001 is less than 2^{31}; however, the version string for the first update in year 2022 was 2201010001, which is more than 2^{31}. This caused a severe malfunction of Microsoft Exchange Server and required manual actions for every customer to fix it. Such date-related overflows are particularly dangerous, as they may affect all your customers at once.

WAYS TO AVOID THIS MISTAKE

- Unless you have a very strong reason, always use the `long` type to store file size and offset within the file. Convert operands to the `long` type before any offset computation.

- Test your code with files that are larger than 2 GB.

- Do not underestimate the quantities your software will have to deal with in the future. Numbers that look ridiculously large today might be completely reasonable tomorrow.

- If you convert the date value or time interval into a number, calculate in advance when the overflow will happen. If it's sooner than the very distant future, it's probably better to use a wider numeric type.

4.3 Mistake 28: Rounding during integer division

Sometimes, integer division is used where floating-point division is expected. The common pattern looks like this:

```
void process(int value) {
  double half = value / 2;
  … // Use half.
}
```

Here, before the assignment, an integer division will be performed truncating the fractional part. As a result, the `half` variable will never contain the fractional part, and, for example, `process(2)` and `process(3)` will store the same number in it.

Static analysis

Such a mistake can be easily detected by many static analyzers. The corresponding IntelliJ IDEA inspection name is Integer Division in Floating Point Context, and the SonarLint rule is called S2184: Math Operands Should Be Cast before Assignment. However, this may become more dangerous if developers tend to overuse the implicit type for local variables:

```
void process(int value) {
  var half = value / 2;
  … // Use half.
}
```

Now, the type of `half` variable will be inferred to `int`. It becomes unclear whether it was intended to truncate the result of division or it's a mistake and the floating-point type was actually intended. Static analyzers are usually silent here, even if the `half` variable is used in floating-point context later (with automatic widening).

WAYS TO AVOID THIS MISTAKE

- Be careful with division. Always ask yourself whether you want the truncated result or the fractional part. Use an explicit floating-point constant or a cast operator, in the latter case:

```
double half = value / 2.0;          ◁────────────┐  Explicit double
double half = (double) value / 2;   ◁──┐          │  constant 2.0
                                        │ Explicit cast │
                                        │ operator      │
```

- Never use the implicit variable type for primitive variables. You won't save many characters, but the inferred type might differ from what you are expecting. This also confuses static analyzers, and they cannot help you anymore because they don't know your intent.

4.4   Mistake 29: Absolute value of Integer.MIN_VALUE

The `Integer.MIN_VALUE` (-2147483648) number is special—there's no positive counterpart. As integer numbers take 32 bits in the computer memory, we have 2^{32} possible numbers, which is an even number. However, as we need to represent zero, we have an uneven count of positive and negative numbers. This leads to an equation that completely violates the laws of math:

```
System.out.println(Integer.MIN_VALUE == -Integer.MIN_VALUE);    ⟵  Prints true
```

To make things worse, this also spoils the behavior of the `Math.abs()` method:

```
System.out.println(Math.abs(Integer.MIN_VALUE));    ⟵  Prints –2147483648
```

That is, the math says that the absolute value of the number is never negative. Java doesn't agree with this: the result of `Math.abs(Integer.MIN_VALUE)` is negative.

When does this matter? Some people use the `Random.nextInt()` method when they actually need a random number within some bounds. For example, to get a random number between 0 and 9, one may use the following:

```
Random random = new Random();                              ⟵  Random number between
int randomNumber = Math.abs(random.nextInt()) % 10;            0 and 9 (almost always)
```

This works in 4,294,967,295 cases out of 4,294,967,296. However, once in 2^{32} runs, `nextInt()` returns `Integer.MIN_VALUE`, and the random number will become -8, which may result in an extremely rare and difficult-to-reproduce bug in production. Table 4.2 shows how `randomNumber` is calculated for different values returned by `random.nextInt()`.

Table 4.2   The resulting `randomNumber` for different values returned by `nextInt()`

random.nextInt()	Math.abs(random.nextInt())	Math.abs(random.nextInt()) % 10
0	0	0
123	123	3
-1024	1024	4
-2147483647	2147483647	7
-2147483648	-2147483648	-8

Another scenario appears when it's necessary to distribute some objects evenly (e.g., to process them in a thread pool, put them into hash buckets, or distribute the computation to a cluster). In this case, an object hash code is often used to assign the target thread, bucket, or cluster node. The code may look similar to this snippet:

```
static final int NUMBER_OF_NODES = 10;

void processObject(Object obj) {
  int node = Math.abs(obj.hashCode()) % NUMBER_OF_NODES;
  process(node, obj);
}
```

This case is similar, though it's probably easier to reproduce. If the object hash code is `Integer.MIN_VALUE`, then the resulting node will be `-8`, and it's unclear what will happen next.

   Note that you won't have this problem if your divisor (`NUMBER_OF_NODES` in the preceding sample) is a power of 2 because, in this case, the remainder will be zero.

Static analysis

SonarLint reports these problems via rule S2676: Neither `Math.abs` nor Negation Should Be Used on Numbers That Could Be `MIN_VALUE`. Some cases, like the one previously mentioned, can be detected by SpotBugs via bug patterns Bad Attempt to Compute Absolute Value of Signed 32-bit Hashcode and Bad Attempt to Compute Absolute Value of Signed Random Integer.

WAYS TO AVOID THIS MISTAKE

- Use `Math.abs()` with care; remember that the result could be negative.
- If you use Java 15 or later, consider using `Math.absExact()` instead. Instead of returning a negative number, it will throw an `ArithmeticException` if the input is `Integer.MIN_VALUE`.
- Avoid using `Math.abs()` with a subsequent `%` operation; use `Math.floorMod()` instead. It's a variation of the remainder operation, but the resulting sign is the same as that of the divisor rather than the dividend. If the divisor is a positive number, you will always get a positive result:

  ```
  void processObject(Object obj) {
    int node = Math.floorMod(obj.hashCode(), NUMBER_OF_NODES);
    process(node, obj);
  }
  ```

- If you need a random number within a given range, do not use the remainder calculation at all. Instead, use a library method, `nextInt()`, that accepts a parameter. It works correctly and also produces a uniform distribution. In contrast, a remainder technique may produce slightly skewed results: lower numbers may appear more often.

  ```
  Random random = new Random();
  int randomNumber = random.nextInt(10);   ⟵┐
  ```
  Random number between
  0 and 9 (always)

- Create objects with an `Integer.MIN_VALUE` hash code in the tests and pass them to your code. This would allow you to catch such mistakes before they slip into production.

4.5   *Mistake 30: Oddness check and negative numbers*

Sometimes, it's necessary to check whether a given number is odd. There's no ready method to do this in the Java standard library, but it looks like it would require a simple algorithm, so programmers usually do this check manually. How would you check whether a given integral number is odd? You might come up with the following solution:

```java
public static boolean isOdd(int value) {
  return value % 2 == 1;
}
```

This approach works correctly for positive numbers. However, as we saw in the previous section, when a negative value is used with the `%` operator, the result cannot be positive. Therefore, this method never returns `true` for a negative value. Table 4.3 shows what happens inside the `isOdd()` method, depending on the input value.

Table 4.3   Computation inside the `isOdd()` method.

Value	Value % 2	Value % 2 == 1
-3	-1	false
-2	0	false
-1	-1	false
0	0	false
1	1	true
2	0	false
3	1	true

In many cases, people don't work with negative values, so the formula `value % 2 == 1` will work correctly. This may add a false sense of security that the formula is correct, so a developer may use it without considering anything might go wrong. One day, negative numbers may appear on the horizon, making the program behave incorrectly.

You may encounter the same problem with other divisors as well. For example, assume you have an angle value in degrees and want to normalize it to fit the 0°–359° interval. The first thought could be to use the simple remainder operator:

```java
int normalized = angle % 360;
```

However, if the input angle happens to be negative, then the result will be negative as well, which might be unexpected. To support both positive and negative inputs, you can use the `floorMod()` method:

```java
int normalized = Math.floorMod(angle, 360);
```

Static analysis

The `value % 2 == 1` pattern can be easily detected by static analyzers. IntelliJ IDEA has the inspection Suspicious Oddness Check to report such checks. Unfortunately, it's turned off by default. SonarLint has the rule S2197: Modulus Results Should not Be Checked for Direct Equality. SpotBugs reports this problem using the Check for Oddness That Won't Work for Negative Numbers warning.

WAYS TO AVOID THIS MISTAKE

- It's safer to compare the remainder to zero instead of a positive or negative number. Therefore, you may use the `value % 2 != 0` formula instead.
- An alternative method is to rely on bitwise arithmetic extracting the lowest bit from the number: `(value & 1) == 1`.
- If you ever need an oddness check in your program, instead of writing a formula inline, create a utility method like `isOdd`, test it thoroughly, and use it everywhere.
- If your dividend could be negative, ask yourself whether the `floorMod()` method suits your needs better than the simple remainder operator.

4.6   *Mistake 31: Widening with precision loss*

Primitive widening is a type conversion that changes the value of one primitive type to another, usually a wider one, preserving its value in most cases. The problem is that this doesn't happen in all cases. As widening occurs implicitly in arithmetic operations, assignments, method returns, and passing method arguments, the problem could go unnoticed.

Three widening conversions may result in precision loss—namely, int → `float`, `long` → `float`, and `long` → `double`. The problems occur only when numbers become too large. For `long` → `double` conversion, the number should be at least 2^{53} (~9×10^{15}). For int → `float` and `long` → `float`, the problems appear with much smaller numbers, starting from 2^{24} (close to 17 million). After that, the corresponding floating-point number cannot hold all the digits of the original int or `long` number, so rounding occurs. For example, consider the following sample:

```
long longVal = 1L << 53;
double doubleVal = longVal;
double doubleValPlusOne = longVal + 1;                          true is
System.out.println(doubleVal == doubleValPlusOne);    ◁──┘    printed.
```

It's obvious that `longVal` and `longVal + 1` are different numbers. However, when converted to `double`, they become the same, due to rounding.

WAYS TO AVOID THIS MISTAKE

- Avoid using the `float` type, unless you are absolutely sure it's justified for performance reasons. This will rule out the int → `float` and `long` → `float` conversion problems, and you will be safe until you reach 10^{15}, which is certainly enough for many domains.

- Avoid implicit widening of floating-point numbers. Add explicit type casts to show readers that the rounding is intended:

```
double doubleVal = (double) longVal;
```

- Always ask yourself whether the rounding is harmful in your case.

- If you care about precision more than performance, use the `BigDecimal` type, as it allows you to control the precision completely.

4.7   Mistake 32: Unconditional narrowing

Sometimes, you have mismatched numeric types and need to apply an explicit primitive conversion. Probably, the most dangerous conversion is from a `long` to an `int` type. For example, some standard API methods, like `Stream.count()` or `File.length()`, return a value of the `long` type, but often you have to pass it to a method that accepts the `int` type. The simplest and shortest way to do this is using the type-cast operator:

```
processFileLength((int) file.length());
```

Here, however, we have the same concerns that were listed in the Numeric Overflow mistake considered previously. The `long` numbers greater than `Integer.MAX_VALUE` or less than `Integer.MIN_VALUE` cannot be represented with the `int` type, so Java needs to deal with this somehow. As previously discussed, it simply discards the higher bits, keeping only 32 lower bits, or 8 hexadecimal digits. This behavior is quite logical from a machine point of view but might be completely confusing and unexpected for a human.

If the file length happens to exceed 2 GB, the result of the type cast will overflow to a negative number. If the file is even bigger, exceeding 4 GB, the resulting number will be positive again but much smaller than the actual file length. For example, if the file size is 5,000,000,000 bytes, its hexadecimal representation is `0x12A05F200L`. After narrowing, the first 1 gets lost, and the number becomes `0x2A05F200`, which is 705,032,704. Depending on what you will do with this length value later, this may cause an exception, incorrect behavior, or even silent data corruption.

> ### Static analysis
> Static analysis might help to identify narrowing casts. IntelliJ IDEA has the Numeric Cast That Loses Precision inspection (off by default). Unfortunately, such an inspection may report many harmless casts, which undermines its usefulness.

WAYS TO AVOID THIS MISTAKE

- When adding an explicit narrowing cast, for example, to convert a `long` value to `int`, always ask yourself whether the value never exceeds the maximum possible value of the target type. It's a good idea to add a comment explaining why the cast operation here is safe.

- If you are unsure, consider using the `Math.toIntExact()` method instead of the `(int)` cast. This method throws an `ArithmeticException` if the input `long` value cannot be exactly represented via `int` type. In this case, the exception report will point to the problematic place, and you can avoid incorrect program behavior or data corruption.

- When possible, use the `long` type for quantities like duration in milliseconds, file size, downloads count, and so on. In the modern programming world, it's not uncommon for these numbers to exceed two billion, even if it looks like an unreachable limit when you start your program.

4.8 Mistake 33: Negative hexadecimal values

In Java, numeric types are signed, so, for example, the `int` type range is –2,147,483,648 to 2,147,483,647, and you cannot have an `int` literal outside of this range. If we write this in hexadecimal notation, we will have `-0x8000_0000..0x7FFF_FFFF`; however, when you are working with hexadecimal numbers, it's often more convenient to treat them as unsigned. Java allows you to do so, and the positive literals from `0x8000_0000` to `0xFFFF_FFFF` are also legal, but they map to the corresponding so-called two's complement negative numbers. Without going into the details on two's complement representation, I'll just say that one needs to subtract 2^{32} to get the corresponding negative number. For example, `0xFFFF_FFFF` becomes –1, `0xFFFF_FFFE` becomes –2, and so on (table 4.4). This is often convenient when working with binary but may cause mistakes when the widening conversion takes place.

Table 4.4 Decimal and hexadecimal `int` numbers in Java

Decimal number	Signed hexadecimal	Unsigned hexadecimal
-2,147,483,648	-0x8000_0000	0x8000_0000
-2,147,483,647	-0x7FFF_FFFF	0x8000_0001
-2	-0x2	0xFFFF_FFFE
-1	-0x1	0xFFFF_FFFF
0	+0x0	0x0000_0000
1	+0x1	0x0000_0001
2,147,483,646	+0x7FFF_FFFE	0x7FFF_FFFE
2,147,483,647	+0x7FFF_FFFF	0x7FFF_FFFF

For example, suppose you want to apply a mask to a long number, clearing 32 higher bits. It looks like this code would do the trick:

```
long mask = 0x0000_0000_FFFF_FFFF;
long result = value & mask;
```

However, this doesn't work. The literal `0x0000_0000_FFFF_FFFF` is the `int` literal, not the `long` one (the `L` suffix is missing). Normally, you can use an `int` literal, as it will be widened to the equivalent `long` one. Here, however, the `int` literal represents −1. When it's widened to `long`, it's still −1, or `0xFFFF_FFFF_FFFF_FFFFL` (all bits set). So applying this mask does not change the value at all.

Static analysis

In some cases, static analyzers might be helpful in a scenario like this. For example, IntelliJ IDEA warns you when the `int` hexadecimal constant is used where the `long` type is expected (the inspection name is Negative `int` Hexadecimal Constant in `long` Context).

WAYS TO AVOID THIS MISTAKE

- Be careful when dealing with bitwise arithmetic. Remember that numbers are signed, which affects automatic widening.
- Always use the `L` suffix on literals when working with long values, as this will prevent an unexpected implicit type conversion. Note that it's not recommended to use lowercase `l`, as it can be mixed up with the 1 digit, depending on the font used.

4.9 *Mistake 34: Implicit type conversion in compound assignments*

A *compound assignment* is an assignment like x *= 2, in which the previous value is modified using a binary operation. Some developers assume x *= y is equivalent to x = x * y, but in fact, it's equivalent to x = (type_of_x)(x * y). So while it's not evident from the code, *implicit narrowing conversion* may be performed during compound assignment. This allows for amusing assignments, like this:

```
char c = 'a';
c *= 1.2;      ⟵┤ c is now 't'.
```

Here, the `'a'` character is implicitly widened to the `double` number `97.0`, which is multiplied by `1.2`, yielding `116.4`. This result is implicitly narrowed to the `char` type, yielding `'t'`. Luckily, this scenario occurs mostly in puzzlers, rather than real code. However, the following pattern was actually discovered in a production code base (in the Spring framework project, to be specific):

```
byte b = getByte();
if (b < 0) {            The value of b
  b += 256;     ⟵┤    is unchanged!
}
```

The author of this code wanted to convert negative byte values to positive ones (like changing -1 to 255). However, this doesn't work. In fact, the assignment inside the condition is equivalent to

```
b = (byte)((int) b + 256);
```

So we widen `b` to `int`, add `256` (producing the correct result), and then narrow it back to `byte`, which simply restores the original value of `b` to fit the `byte` type range `-128..127`. This would work correctly if the variable `b` were to be declared as `int`.

Another compound assignment example that may do nothing to bytes is unsigned right shift:

```
byte b = -1;
b >>>= 1;
```

Here, the byte value is first widened to `int` and becomes `0xFFFFFFFF`. Then, after the shift, it becomes `0x7FFFFFFF`. Finally, it's implicitly narrowed back to `byte`. At this point, higher bits are dropped, and it becomes `-1` again.

Static analysis

Both of the preceding cases are reported by the Nullability and Data Flow Problems IntelliJ inspection. The warning sounds like Variable Update Does Nothing; however, this inspection may not report more complex cases and will be silent if the result is not exactly the same. Therefore, you cannot rely too much on static analyzers here.

WAYS TO AVOID THIS MISTAKE

- Pay attention to the target variable type of a compound assignment. Ask yourself whether narrowing conversion is possible in your case.
- Avoid using the `byte` and `short` types. Instead, use `int` or `long` where possible. In many cases, this will save you from undesired overflow problems. Using `byte` fields, `short` fields, or array elements could be justified if you need to save memory. However, you won't have any performance degradation if you replace the `byte` or `short` type of local variables, method parameters, or return values with `int`.
- If you really need to use the `byte` or `short` types, test your code on negative inputs or add assertions to ensure negative inputs are not possible.
- Use library methods when possible, even for simple math operations. For example, you could convert negative byte values to positive ones by using the `Byte .toUnsignedInt` method:

  ```
  int b = Byte.toUnsignedInt(getByte());
  ```

  In this case, implicit narrowing to `byte` is impossible, and declaring the variable type as `byte` will result in a compilation error.

4.10 *Mistake 35: Division and compound assignment*

Another kind of mistake is possible if the right-hand operand of a compound multiplication assignment is a division operation. Assuming the type of `a`, `b`, and `c` is `int`, one may naively think that `a *= b / c` is equivalent to `a = a * b / c`. In fact, it's `a = a * (b / c)`, which may produce a completely different result, taking into account integral division semantics. We encountered such a problem in the Sipdroid project. Originally, the buffer size for audio recording was calculated using the following formula:

```
int min = AudioRecord.getMinBufferSize(…) * 3 / 2;
```

The idea was to increase the result of `getMinBufferSize()` method by 50%. This code worked correctly. However, later it was decided that increasing it by 50% is necessary only if the buffer is shorter than 4 KB. Therefore, the code was changed in the following way:

```
int min = AudioRecord.getMinBufferSize(…);
if (min <= 4096) min *= 3 / 2;
```

Now, `3 / 2` evaluates before the multiplication, and it always results in `1`. As a result, we always multiply the `min` by one, not changing its value at all.

> **Static analysis**
>
> In code patterns like this, IntelliJ IDEA reports Suspicious Integer Division Assignment. Additionally, another warning, Variable Update Does Nothing, is reported here, as we effectively multiply the variable by 1.

WAYS TO AVOID THIS MISTAKE

- Be careful when you have another math operation on the right side of a compound assignment. It's better to completely avoid a compound assignment if you are unsure.
- Check your math operations with simple code snippets (e.g., using JShell). Just set the input variables to some reasonable values, and then copy the math operations from your program and check whether the result is expected.

  A somewhat similar problem might occur if you use `a -= b - c`, which is equivalent to `a = a - b + c`, not `a = a - b - c`. Again, if a compound assignment looks confusing, it's better to avoid it to make the code clear.

4.11 *Mistake 36: Using the short type*

In mistake 33, we suggested to avoid using the `byte` and `short` types. We would like to additionally stress this for the latter. While the `byte` type is occasionally useful, especially when you are actually working with bytes (e.g., reading and decoding binary data), the `short` type is probably the least useful primitive type in Java. It may become especially dangerous when it leaks into an API. If you have methods that accept `short` parameters or return `short` values, sooner or later, you may produce an overflow problem when the type simply cannot fit all the values you have. In this case, refactoring the code might be hard, especially if your code is in a library with external clients.

A problem like this happened in the software package BioJava. It contained a method to align protein structure and used the `short` type to calculate alignment penalty, which is derived from the number of amino acids in the protein sequence.

While most proteins are rather short (around 300–500 amino acids), there are also a few huge proteins. The human protein *titin* may contain more than 34,000 amino acids; this causes overflow of the `short` type, which can only hold values up to 32,767. As a result, the alignment procedure worked incorrectly for such a huge protein. To fix this, it was necessary to change the signatures of public methods to migrate from the `short` to the `int` type.

A similar problem appeared in the Apache POI library, which provides a programmatic interface for Microsoft Office file formats, such as Microsoft Excel XLS files. Initially, many methods that work with Excel rows accepted `short` values. This limited the number of rows to 32,767. Later, in 2002, a big refactoring and an incompatible API change were necessary to replace the `short` type with `int`. Still, the code heavily relied on the `short` type internally, and many casts from `int` to `short` were required. It took several more iterations to get rid of the `short` type in most places.

WAYS TO AVOID THIS MISTAKE

- Do not use the `short` type, even if you are completely sure your number will never exceed 32,767. Your estimation could be wrong, or new data could appear later. Even if it's correct, it will be hard to use your API. Because Java automatically widens the `short` type to `int` in math operations, users of your API will often need to explicitly downcast their values to `short`, which could be very annoying. It's unlikely you will have any practical benefit from using the `short` type. It can be useful in extremely rare cases when you want to have a compact footprint of a long-living object to save some memory.

- If you carefully measured the memory footprint and still believe using the `short` type provides a significant benefit in terms of memory utilization, consider not exposing it to clients. Use the `short` type only for private fields and private methods.

4.12 Mistake 37: Manually writing bit-manipulating algorithms

Sometimes, programs consider numbers not as quantities but bit vectors and manipulate individual bits using operations like *bitwise and* or *bitwise shift*. Such manipulations are referred to as *bit twiddling*. One possible application is to pack several values into a single number. For example, it's quite common to have a variable for which different bits represent different Boolean values. This saves computer memory and makes the operations blazingly fast, as processors naturally work with bits. JIT compilers translate bitwise arithmetic operators in Java directly to the corresponding bitwise assembly instructions.

Bitwise operations may look simple, but this simplicity can be deceiving. Many simple algorithms have corner cases. For example, it looks like an easy task to keep the desired number of least-significant bits in a number:

```
int value;

void applyMask(int keepBits) {
  value &= (1 << keepBits) - 1;
}
```

So, if `keepBits` is 8, `1 << keepBits` evaluates to `0x100`, and after subtracting 1, we get `0xFF`. As a result, the eight least-significant bits of value are preserved, while the others are zeroed.

This works fine for `keepBits` between 0 and 31. However, one may expect that when `keepBits` is 32, the method will preserve all 32 bits of value or simply do nothing. In fact, `1 << 32` is the same as `1 << 0`, which is simply 1. That's because when performing a bitwise shift operation, Java first computes the remainder of the shift amount modulo 32 for the `int` type and modulo 64 for the `long` type. This remainder is used as the actual shift amount. As the remainder of 32 modulo 32 is simply 0, we don't shift at all. After subtracting 1 from 1, we get 0, so the method will reset the `value` to 0, instead of doing nothing. This could be unexpected in some applications.

There's one more corner case with bitwise shift operation. Its result can be either `int` or `long`, depending on the left operand type (unlike other arithmetic operations, where the resulting type is defined by both operands). This becomes problematic for left-shift operations if the result is expected to be `long`. In this case, the left operand is often 1 and it's easy to forget to add the `L` suffix. Let's consider a simple method that sets a bit inside a field of type `long`:

```
long mask;

void setBit(int k) {
  mask |= 1 << k;
}
```

Here, 1 was written erroneously instead of `1L`, so the shift operation has the `int` type. As previously noted, when you shift an `int` value by `k` bits, the actual amount of shift is determined by the remainder of `k` modulo 32, so the shift amount is always between 0 and 31. On the other hand, as our `mask` is long, users would normally expect the `setBit()` method to work for `k` between 32 and 63 as well—but this is not the case. For example, calling `setBit(40)` will actually set the 8th bit of the mask, rather than the 40th. Depending on the context, it's possible for unit tests to cover only small values of `k`, so such an error could go into production unnoticed.

Static analysis

Static analyzers may catch the latter mistake, as it's suspicious when an `int` result of a left shift is implicitly cast to `long`. The IntelliJ IDEA inspection Integer Multiplication or Shift Implicitly Cast to `long` reports this problem.

WAYS TO AVOID THIS MISTAKE

- Avoid littering your code with many bitwise operations. Instead, extract them to isolated, well-tested utility methods, and reuse those methods.
- If you use bitwise operations on `long` values, write unit tests in which higher bits are used.

- Always think about corner cases. Write unit tests for boundary inputs.
- Do not invent bitwise algorithms by yourself. Consult authoritative sources, like *Hacker's Delight* by Henry S. Warren, Jr. (O'Reilly Media, 2012).
- Think twice whether you actually need to pack several values into a single number manually. Consider using library classes. The `BitSet` class is a more convenient representation of bit strings. It provides many methods with clear semantics that work for any inputs. Also, the number of bits is not limited to 32 or 64, so if you need more bits in the future, you won't need to change your code much. The performance overhead is acceptable in many cases.
- If you want to represent a number of flags, consider declaring an enum that enumerates these flags and using `EnumSet`. This will make your code much clearer and more robust with very little additional cost.

4.13 Mistake 38: Forgetting about negative byte values

In Java, the `byte` primitive type allows you to store a number between `-128` and `127`. This could be counterintuitive, as usually, people think of bytes as values between `0` and `255`. We already saw in mistake 34 how a byte value being updated using a compound assignment may cause unexpected behavior. However, problems are possible in other code patterns as well. For example, when it's necessary to compose a number from two individual bytes, the following code may look OK at first glance:

```
int readTwoBytes() {
  byte lo = readLowByte();
  byte hi = readHighByte();
  return (hi << 8) | lo;
}
```

Unfortunately, it works as expected only if bytes are within the range of `0` to `127`. Suppose the call to `readLowByte()` returns `-1`. In this case, it's widened to the `int` type, and its hexadecimal representation will become `0xFFFFFFFF`. So the whole `readTwoBytes` method will return `-1`, regardless of the `hi` value.

Static analysis

Occasionally, static analyzers report this problem. SonarLint has the S3034: Raw Byte Values Should Not Be Used in Bitwise Operations in Combination with Shifts rule, which reports it; however, this rule only covers specific code patterns, so even with the static analyzer, it's still possible to make such a mistake.

Ways to avoid this mistake

- When performing bitwise operations in Java, remember that negative numbers are possible. If widening occurs, higher bits will become ones instead of zeroes. To cancel this effect, use a mask, like this:

```
return ((hi & 0xFF) << 8) | (lo & 0xFF);
```

- Encapsulate low-level bit manipulation operations into utility methods, and test them really well. After that, they can be reused throughout a project without introducing additional problems.

4.14   *Mistake 39: Incorrect clamping order*

The following problem appears quite often in practice: having to adjust an input number so it fits the given interval. This could be written using an `if` chain:

```
if (value < 0) value = 0;
if (value > 100) value = 100;
```
The value is now in
the 0...100 interval.

Alternatively, it could be written using a conditional expression:

```
value = value < 0 ? 0 : value > 100 ? 100 : value;
```

However, this may look too verbose. Also, it requires mentioning the lower and upper bounds twice, and sometimes, these are more complicated than simple numbers.

One may avoid the repetition using a combination of `Math.min()` and `Math.max()` calls:

```
value = Math.max(0, Math.min(value, 100));
```

This looks smart and short. However, this construct is error prone. The whole expression is not very intuitive, so it's quite easy to accidentally swap the `max` and `min` calls:

```
value = Math.min(0, Math.max(value, 100));
```

Now, the result is always `0`, which is not evident from how this expression looks. I saw a bug like this in a procedure to render a progress bar: it got stuck at 0%. A similar bug was also discovered in a Jenkins CI source code.

Static analysis

Some static analysis tools detect such errors when bounds are constant values. IntelliJ IDEA reports the warning Result of `min` Is the Same as the First Argument Making the Call Meaningless. SonarLint reports this problem via rule S3065: `min` and `max` Used in Combination Should not Always Return the Same Value. SpotBugs reports an Incorrect Combination of `Math.max` and `Math.min` bug pattern. Unfortunately, static analyzers might not help if the bounds are the result of nontrivial computation, as they need to be able to compare them without executing your program.

WAYS TO AVOID THIS MISTAKE

- Pay attention when using the `Math.min()` and `Math.max()` methods. Ask yourself which result you will get when the first operand is larger and when it's smaller. Occasionally, developers use `min()` instead of `max()`, or vice versa, in other contexts as well.

- As with every confusing code pattern, it's best to extract it to a utility method and use it everywhere. A method like this would work:

```
public static int clamp(int value, int min, int max) {
  if (min > max) {
    throw new IllegalArgumentException(min + ">" + max);
  }
  return Math.max(min, Math.min(max, value));
}
```

This also checks that the supplied min value doesn't actually exceed the max value, so you can detect cases when this invariant is violated.

- If you notice that your favorite library, or even the standard library, is missing an important method or if the existing methods are confusing, consider contributing to the library. This way, you will give back to the community, and other developers will be able to use your method, making fewer mistakes and writing more robust programs. After writing this section, I contributed the `Math.clamp()` method to the OpenJDK, so, since Java 21, it's available in the Java standard library, and you don't need to write it yourself anymore.

4.15   Mistake 40: Misusing special floating-point numbers

When working with floating-point numbers, it's important to remember there are several values that may require special handling or produce unexpected results when used.

4.15.1   Signed zero: +0.0 and –0.0

There are two floating-point zeros: `+0.0` and `–0.0`. They have distinct representation in computer memory, but they appear to be equal if you compare them via `==`. You can get `-0.0` as a result of some computations. For example, the following code prints `-0.0`:

```
System.out.println(-1 * 0.0);
```

This behavior is explicitly stated in *Java Language Specification* § 15.17.1 (https://docs.oracle.com/javase/specs/jls/se21/html/jls-15.html#jls-15.17.1), which has the following clause: "[T]he sign of the result is positive if both operands have the same sign, and negative if the operands have different signs." This behavior is not unique to Java. Any programming language that follows the IEEE 754 standard for floating-point numbers behaves this way.

It should be noted that when a `double` value gets boxed into `Double`, `+0.0` and `-0.0` become different. You can see the difference in the following code:

```
Double d = 0.0;
System.out.println(d.equals(-0.0));    ⟵┤ Prints false
System.out.println(d == -0.0);    ⟵┤ Prints true
```

`Double.equals()` considers the boxed values different, but when comparing to a primitive `-0.0`, the `Double` value is unboxed and the primitive comparison returns `true`.

This difference may show up unexpectedly. For example, assume that you have values from the following set −1.0, −0.5, 0.0, 0.5, 1.0. Now, you want to get all the possible results of multiplication of two such numbers. You may want to store them into the set like this:

```
Set<Double> multiplications = new HashSet<>();
for (double i = -1; i <= 1; i += 0.5) {
  for (double j = -1; j <= 1; j += 0.5) {
    multiplications.add(i * j);
  }
}
System.out.println(multiplications);
```

The resulting set contains eight values instead of seven, as it includes both `0.0` and `-0.0`:

```
[1.0, 0.5, -0.0, -0.5, -1.0, 0.25, -0.25, 0.0]
```

You may also try `LinkedHashSet` and `TreeSet`. The resulting set will still contain eight values, even though the order might be different.

Even if you didn't use any boxed types, like `Double`, you may run into this difference. For example, if you declare Java `record` (available since Java 16), you'll get methods like `equals()` and `hashCode()` for free; the question is how they are implemented. If you have a `double` component, the comparison rules will be the same as for boxed `Double`. Consider the following example:

```
record Length(double d) {}
Length l1 = new Length(0.0);
Length l2 = new Length(-0.0);
System.out.println(l1.equals(l2));      ◁──┤ Prints false
```

WAYS TO AVOID THIS MISTAKE

- Do not forget that Java distinguishes between `+0.0` and `-0.0` internally, and sometimes this difference shows up in your code as well. If necessary, normalize them before storing into fields or collections:

  ```
  if (d == -0.0) d = 0.0;
  ```

  This line of code is somewhat strange, as `+0.0` satisfies the condition as well, but ultimately, it does what's intended: it replaces `-0.0` with `+0.0` without changing any other values.

- Avoid comparing floating-point numbers for exact value in general. It's probably not a good idea to store them in the set as well. Even if you never have negative numbers, you may not get an exact comparison, due to the limited machine precision. Here's a classic example:

  ```
  Set<Double> set = new HashSet<>();
  set.add(0.3);
  ```

```
set.add(0.1 + 0.2);
System.out.println(set);
```

One may expect that the set will contain only one number after these operations, but in fact, it will contain two: [0.3, 0.30000000000000004]. As floating-
point numbers are converted to binary, most finite decimal fractions, like 0.1,
0.2, and 0.3, become infinite, so it's necessary to cut their binary value. As a
result, there are actually no floating-point numbers that correspond to the dec-
imals 0.1, 0.2, and 0.3 exactly. When you are summing these approximate values, errors add up as well, and you may get a different decimal value when
going back from binary.

4.15.2 *Not a number: NaN values*

NaN stands for *not a number*. Double.NaN and Float.NaN are very special values. These
are the only values in Java that aren't equal to themselves. For example, the following
code prints false twice:

```
System.out.println(Double.NaN == Double.NaN);
System.out.println(Float.NaN == Float.NaN);
```

It's recommended to use the Double.isNaN or Float.isNaN library methods to check
whether a number is NaN. Explicit comparison to Float.NaN or Double.NaN is detected
by most static analyzers (the IntelliJ IDEA inspection name is Comparison to
Double.NaN or Float.NaN, and the Error Prone bug pattern name is EqualsNaN), and
nowadays, such mistakes rarely appear in Java code. However, NaN could be implicit as
well; for example, consider the following method:

```
void process(double a, double b) {
  if (a < b) {
    … // Process the a < b case.
  } else if (a > b) {
    … // Process the a > b case.
  } else {
    … // Process the a == b case.
  }
}
```

The author of the code assumes that if a is not bigger than b and is not smaller than b,
then a is equal to b. However, it's also possible that either a or b is NaN. In this case, the
last branch will be taken, and the results could be unexpected.

WAYS TO AVOID THIS MISTAKE

- When comparing floating-point numbers, always ask yourself if it's possible to
  have NaN at this point.
- If NaN values are not expected, consider adding asserts:

  ```
  assert !Double.isNaN(a);
  assert !Double.isNaN(b);
  ```

For public APIs, use preconditions:

```
if (Double.isNaN(a) || Double.isNaN(b)) {
    throw new IllegalArgumentException();
}
```

This will allow you to catch the bug earlier if NaN values unexpectedly appear in this method.

4.15.3 *Double.MIN_VALUE is not the minimal value*

For some algorithms, it's necessary to represent the minimal and maximal possible value. There are consistent constants for all the integral types in Java. If you need the minimal and maximal int values, you can use Integer.MIN_VALUE and Integer.MAX_ VALUE, respectively. For the long type, the constants Long.MIN_VALUE and Long.MAX_ VALUE are available, and so on. However, things are different for floating-point types. While Double.MAX_VALUE is, indeed, the maximal finite double value, Double .MIN_VALUE is not the minimal one. Instead, it's the minimal positive value that can be represented with the double type, which is roughly equal to 4.9×10^{-324}. There's no explicit constant for the minimal finite double value, but you can use -Double.MAX_ VALUE if you need one.

Accidental use of Double.MIN_VALUE instead of -Double.MAX_VALUE is possible when a developer refactors the code to change from the int to the double type. In this case, Integer.MIN_VALUE could be blindly replaced with Double.MIN_VALUE, which may result in incorrect behavior if this value is later compared to zero or negative numbers.

For example, one may need to find the maximum value of a double[] array. Unfortunately, no standard method is available for this. While you can achieve a similar result via the Stream API, some programmers are concerned about the possible performance overhead and prefer to write it manually. One possible implementation is to start with the minimal possible value and then apply Math.max() in a loop:

```
static double max(double... data) {
  double max = Double.MIN_VALUE;
  for (double d : data) {
    max = Math.max(max, d);
  }
  return max;
}
```

As you can see, Double.MIN_VALUE was erroneously used as a starting value. This method works correctly if at least one positive number is available. However, if all the input numbers are negative or zero, then 4.9×10^{-324} will be returned instead of the maximum.

WAYS TO AVOID THIS MISTAKE

- When you need the minimal finite double number, use -Double.MAX_VALUE instead of Double.MIN_VALUE. Additionally, think about whether infinite values should be handled. It's probably better to use `Double.NEGATIVE_INFINITY` for the minimal value and `Double.POSITIVE_INFINITY` for the maximal value.

- Be careful when migrating an integral type to a floating-point one. Blindly replacing `int` to `double` and `Integer` to `Double` may keep the code compilable, but it may also introduce semantic mistakes. Review and test your code thoroughly after such a migration.

- Whenever possible, use libraries for standard algorithms, like calculating the maximal value of an array. In many cases, `DoubleStream.of(values).max()` is a good alternative to a hand-written `max()` function. If you are using the Google Guava library, a `Doubles.max()` utility method is available.

Summary

- Octal numerals may be used, accidentally resulting in a different numeric value. Prohibiting them completely in your codebase is a good idea.

- Numeric overflow is one of the most annoying bugs in programming. When you have numerical calculations in your program, ask yourself whether overflow is possible and how the program should behave in this case.

- There are some numbers that behave unusually. This includes `Integer .MIN_VALUE` (equal to itself when negated), `-0.0` (equals `+0.0`), and `Double.NaN` (not equal to itself). Check whether your code handles such inputs correctly.

- Compound assignment operators are tricky, as they may perform implicit narrowing conversion and change the evaluation order, producing a different result than expected.

- When speaking about bytes, developers usually imagine a number between `0` and `255`, but the `byte` type in Java ranges from `-128` to `127`.

- Avoid the `short` type in favor of `int` and the `float` type in favor of `double`. You'll rarely get the performance benefit or reduced memory usage of `short` and `float`, but they may introduce problems due to reduced precision or overflow.

- Many numeric algorithms, like oddness check, clamping values, and setting a bit in the number, are deceivingly simple, so developers prefer writing them inline. Yet it's quite possible to write them incorrectly. Isolate every algorithm in a separate, well-tested method.

Common exceptions

In this chapter, we discuss some of the most common exceptions in Java programs caused by bugs. This chapter differs somewhat from the others, as we will concentrate on the effects of the bugs, rather than their causes.

All the exception classes in Java inherit a single `Throwable` class. Any exception can be thrown explicitly via a `throw` statement. Some exceptions can be thrown by the virtual machine itself. Here, we will mainly speak about such exceptions. Figure 5.1 shows the hierarchy of exceptions covered in this chapter.

It's important to understand that exceptions are your friends, not enemies. Many programmers dislike exceptions, but they are there to help you write programs without bugs. It's much better to have an exception as early as possible

124

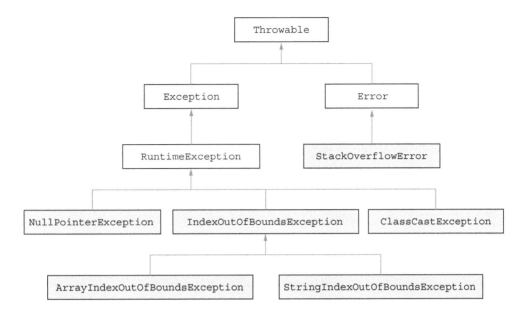

Figure 5.1   Hierarchy of exception classes. All Java exceptions inherit `Throwable`**, and many of them have** `Exception`**,** `Error`**, or** `RuntimeException` **as a superclass. Exceptions covered in this chapter are shaded.**

instead of continuing the execution of your program in an incorrect state, which may cause much more severe consequences, like data loss or a security breach. One more important exception, `ConcurrentModificationException`, will be covered separately when we will talk about collections in chapter 8.

5.1   Mistake 41: NullPointerException

`NullPointerException` constantly chases Java developers. Java language design cannot prohibit storing `null` into non-primitive variables or returning `null` from methods whose return type is non-primitive. Developers often use `null` as a sentinel value for many purposes:

- An uninitialized value during object construction or just after creation of an array
- A lazily initialized value for which a non-null value will be written the first time anybody needs this value
- An unspecified value (e.g., a `middleName` field in a `User` class for users who have no middle name or prefer not to specify it)
- A value that is not found (e.g., a `Map.get()` library method that returns `null` if the corresponding mapping is not found in the map)

- An empty collection sentinel (e.g., methods of a `Queue` interface, like `poll()` or `peek()`, that return `null` if the queue is empty)

And there are many other purposes. The problem is that the `null` value itself does not bear any semantics. So when a Java developer encounters a reference value, the following questions arise: Is it possible that `null` is stored into this value, and if yes, what exactly does it mean?

From the developer's point of view, many variables never contain `null`, and many methods never return `null`. We can call them *non-nullable variables* and *non-nullable methods*, respectively. Other variables and methods may contain or return `null` under some circumstances—let's call them *nullable*. Some programming languages, like Kotlin, encode value nullability directly in the type system. There, you can declare a variable of non-nullable type, and the compiler will prohibit storing a potentially nullable value. Also, if the type of the value is nullable, you cannot dereference it directly without a `null` check or a special safe-call operator. Thanks to this, an unexpected `NullPointerException` occurs in Kotlin programs much less often than in Java. Unfortunately, Java has nothing like this.

To reduce the risk of `NullPointerException`, there are several main approaches:

- Whenever possible, avoid `null` values in your code base.
- Use the `Optional` type where the absent value is possible.
- Use annotations to augment the Java type system with nullability information.
- Use advanced interprocedural static analysis tools that can detect many potential `NullPointerException` problems.

Let's cover these in greater detail.

5.1.1   *Avoiding nulls and defensive checks*

To avoid `null` values as often as possible, you should not return `null` from your methods, and you should never accept `null` as a parameter; however, sometimes, this is difficult to do. For example, this could be tricky if you implement an interface or extend a class declared in a standard library and, by contract, requires returning `null` under some circumstances. Think about the scenario of implementing your own `Map`. In this case, you are required to return `null` from the `Map.get()` method if the supplied key is absent in your map. Some people go even further, avoiding using APIs that require returning or accepting nulls. Unfortunately, this approach is not always practical and often involves reinventing the wheel.

Another important thing is sanitizing the input values—at least in public methods and constructors. Just add an `Objects.requireNonNull()` call for every reference parameter you receive, right at the method entry. The `requireNonNull()` method simply throws a `NullPointerException` if its argument is `null`. You can optionally specify a second argument to provide a clarifying message for the exception. If a non-null argument is supplied, this method just returns it, so by using this return value, one can conveniently initialize fields:

```
public class Person {
  private final String firstName, lastName;

  public Person(String firstName, String lastName) {
    this.firstName = Objects.requireNonNull(firstName);
    this.lastName = Objects.requireNonNull(lastName);
  }
}
```

Doing this helps you to catch a `NullPointerException` as early as possible. If you don't do this, you may accidentally store a `null` value into a field, effectively putting the program into an invalid state. As a result, the problem will occur much later when you dereference the field, and you'll have no clue how the `null` value appeared in the variable.

What if your method accepts a collection as the input? You can also traverse it at the method entry to ensure it doesn't contain nulls:

```
public void process(Collection<String> data) {
  data.forEach(Objects::requireNonNull);
  …
}
```

Unfortunately, collection traversal is not free. It costs CPU time that depends on the collection size, and this could be unacceptable, especially if you pass the same collection through many methods and every method checks all the collection elements. One possibility is using the `List.copyOf()`, `Set.copyOf()`, and `Map.copyOf()` *collection factory methods* available since Java 10:

```
public void process(Collection<String> data) {
  data = List.copyOf(data);
  …
}
```

These methods produce unmodifiable copy and disallow nulls. But, more importantly, if the input collection is already a result of the `copyOf` method, it doesn't make an extra copy and simply returns the argument. So, if you want to pass the same collection through many methods, adding `copyOf` to every method will result in, at most, one copying and `null` check.

Even if you think avoiding nulls everywhere is too restrictive and you consider `null` a valid input or output sometimes, there are certain data types for which using the `null` value is a bad practice:

- *Collections, iterables, arrays, and maps*—In these cases, the absence of data is usually designated by an empty collection, array, or map. It's a bad practice to assign different semantics to `null` and *empty* collections. Many clients won't expect `null` instead of an *empty* container, and as a result, a `NullPointer-Exception` may happen at run time.

Note that there are two separate things: nulls as collection (array and map) elements and `null` instead of collection itself. The difference is illustrated in the following sample:

```
Collection<String> collectionContainingNull() {
  return Collections.singleton(null);
}

Collection<String> nullInsteadOfCollection() {
  return null;
}
```

Returning collections containing nulls, like in the former method, is not ideal and may lead to problems (we will discuss them in Chapter 8), but sometimes, this can be justified. However, it's better to avoid returning `null` instead of collection, as in the latter method, at all costs.

Unfortunately, this problem appears in the Java standard library itself. The `java.io.File` class contains methods like `list()` and `listFiles()`, which return `null` in the case of an I/O error. It's quite convenient to iterate through the directory files using a for-each loop:

```
for (String fileName : new File("/etc").list()) {
  System.out.println(fileName);
}
```

However, if there's no `/etc` directory on the filesystem, instead of graceful error handling you will get a `NullPointerException`. Luckily, the newer NIO file API (e.g., the `Files.list` method) addresses this problem. Here, a proper `IOException` is thrown in case of error, so you will have detailed information on what happened and may handle this case:

```
try(Stream<Path> stream = Files.list(Path.of("/etc"))) {
    stream.forEach(System.out::println);
}
```

- `Stream` *or* `Optional` *type*—Again, use `Stream.empty()` or `Optional.empty()` to denote an empty result. Returning `null` is especially bad here, as `Stream` and `Optional` classes are designed for a fluent call chains style, so it's quite expected for users to immediately call something like `map()` on the result of the method that returns `Stream` or `Optional`.
- *Enum type*—This should especially be avoided if we are speaking about enum declared in the project, not in the standard library. In this case, the possibility to return `null` is just another option, so it's much better to encode this option directly as an enum constant. Doing this, you can choose a good name—NOT_ FOUND, UNSPECIFIED, UNKNOWN, UNINITIALIZED, or whatever else—and provide clear documentation. For example, the `java.math.RoundingMode` enum from the Java standard library specifies how to round the result of calculation. Sometimes, it's preferable not to round at all. In these cases, `null` could be used to

specify the absence of rounding, but the JDK authors wisely decided to create a separate constant: `RoundingMode.UNNECESSARY`. This constant declaration contains an explanation of what will happen if the computation cannot be performed without rounding (an `ArithmeticException` is thrown), so there's no need to explain this at every method that uses `RoundingMode`.

Sometimes, you may find out that different methods returning the same enum value assign a different meaning to the `null` result, so there's a chance it will be incorrectly interpreted. You can add several distinct enum constants and replace a `null` result with the appropriate one, resolving the ambiguity.

- `Boolean` *type*—In general, using primitive wrapper types, like `Boolean` or `Integer`, is suspicious, unless you are instantiating the type parameter, like `List<Integer>`. Essentially, the `Boolean` type is just an enum containing two values: `Boolean.TRUE` and `Boolean.FALSE`. If you assign a special semantics to a `null` value, you are turning it into a three-value enum. In this case, it would be much less confusing to declare an actual three-value enum.

Using enum instead of `Boolean` will also allow you to give better names for `TRUE` and `FALSE` values. For example, assume you are working on an online shop application and want to handle the case in which a user removes an item from the basket. You want to ask the user whether they would like to move the item to the wish list instead, so you decide to display a confirmation window, like the one shown in figure 5.2.

In the code, you decided to return a `boolean` value, like this:

```
boolean shouldMoveToWishList() {
  ...
  // Show dialog and return "true" if user pressed "Yes"
}
```

Later you realize that at this point the user may reconsider the removal and want to cancel the whole operation. So, you are going to add a "Cancel" button to the dialog, as shown in figure 5.3.

Figure 5.2 Confirmation window with two possible outcomes

Figure 5.3 Confirmation window with three possible outcomes

Now, the `shouldMoveToWishList()` method should return three different values, and it might be tempting to change the return type to an object `Boolean` and use `null` for `"Cancel"`:

```
Boolean shouldMoveToWishList() {
  …
  // Show a dialog and return
  // - true if the user pressed Yes;
  // - false if the user pressed No; and
  // - null if the user pressed Cancel.
}
```

People do this because it looks like the easiest approach. You don't need to change much at the call sites after that; however, this is quite dangerous. Suppose the method is used like this:

```
if (shouldMoveToWishList()) {
  addItemToWishList(item);
}
deleteItemFromBasket(item);
```

After updating to a `Boolean` type, you won't have a compilation error here, so you may easily forget to refactor this code. Now, when the user presses Cancel, automatic unboxing occurs at the `if` statement condition and you'll get a `NullPointer-Exception`.

It would be much better to introduce an enum and put all three values there. You may declare a more generic enum, which can be reused in other contexts:

```
enum UserAnswer {
  YES, NO, CANCEL
}
```

Alternatively, you may prefer a specific enum for this scenario:

```
enum ItemRemovalRequest {
  REMOVE_FROM_BASKET,
  MOVE_TO_WISH_LIST,
  CANCEL
}
```

In this case, a compilation error will force you to fix the code at the call site. With enums, you can use a `switch` statement instead of an `if` statement:

```
switch (shouldMoveToWishList()) {
  case REMOVE_FROM_BASKET -> deleteItemFromBasket(item);
  case MOVE_TO_WISH_LIST -> {
    addItemToWishList(item);
    deleteItemFromBasket(item);
  }
  case CANCEL -> { /* do nothing */ }
}
```

Now, the possible outcomes are much clearer, and readers of the code don't need to guess what `null` means in this context. Another advantage of enum is that you can add more options there in the future, if necessary.

> **Static analysis**
>
> Static analysis tools may help you avoid returning `null`. IntelliJ IDEA has the inspection Return of `null` (turned off by default), which warns if you return `null` where an array, collection, or `Optional` is expected. SonarLint reports `null`, where `Optional` is expected with the S2789: `null` Should Not Be Used with `Optional` rule. SpotBugs has the Method With `Optional` Return Type Returns Explicit `null` warning for this purpose.

WAYS TO AVOID THIS MISTAKE

- Use defensive checks via `requireNonNull()` and similar methods at your API boundaries if you don't expect nulls.
- It is also reasonable to check that input collections contain no nulls, though this may imply a performance cost.
- Avoid returning nulls when your variable type is `Collection`, `Stream`, or `Optional`. Return an empty container instead, whenever possible.
- Avoid returning arrays, collections, or maps that contain `null` elements. This is a reasonable recommendation, even if you prefer a more `null`-friendly approach. The callers of your methods usually don't expect a returned array or collection to contain nulls.
- If you encounter an error, such as the file not being found, and cannot recover from it by yourself, it's better to throw an exception containing the detailed information than to return `null`.
- If you have an enum, consider introducing a special enum constant instead of returning `null`.
- Avoid boxed primitive variables, like `Integer` or `Boolean`. It's possible to store `null` in these, but it's often unclear whether such a situation is expected and what it means. Instead of using `Boolean`, declare an enum with three constants.

5.1.2 Using Optional instead of null

Some developers who want to avoid `null` prefer to use the `Optional` type instead. I imagine the `Optional` variable as a box that could be either empty or contain a non-null value.

Note that the primary purpose of an empty `Optional` is to designate the absence of a value. For example, if you are writing a search method that could find nothing, you can wrap the result into `Optional`:

```java
public Optional<User> findUser(String name) {
  if (!userExists(name)) {
    return Optional.empty();
  }
  return Optional.of(getExistingUser(name));
}
```

This way, you're clearly signaling to the API clients that the absent value is possible and they must deal with it. The `Optional` type provides useful methods to transform the result in a fluent way. For example, assuming the `User` class has a method named `fullName()`, you can safely use a call chain like this:

```
String fullName = findUser(name).map(User::fullName)
                            .orElse("(no such user)");
```

Here, we extract a full name, replacing it with a `"(no such user)"` string if `findUser()` returned an empty `Optional`.

Using `Optional` as a return value is a good idea. Of course, you should never return `null` from a method whose return type is `Optional`. However, it's inconvenient to use `Optional` as a method parameter, as all the callers will be forced to wrap input values. If you want to accept an empty value as an input to your method and cannot encode this emptiness in another way, then it's okay to accept `null` and document what it means. There are differing opinions on whether it's okay to create fields of the `Optional` type.

There are three standard ways to get an `Optional` object:

- `Optional.empty()`—To get an empty `Optional`
- `Optional.of(value)`—To get a non-empty `Optional` throwing a `NullPointerException` if the value is `null`
- `Optional.ofNullable(value)`—To get an empty `Optional` if the value is `null` and a non-empty `Optional` containing a value otherwise.

One should be careful using the last method, as it's suitable only when the `null` value should be converted to the empty `Optional`. Some developers prefer using `ofNullable()` everywhere because it's considered safer, as it never throws an exception. However, this safety is deceiving. If you already know your value is never `null`, it's better to use `Optional.of()`. In this case, if you see an exception, you will immediately know you were wrong, and there's probably a bug in the previous code. If you have used `ofNullable()`, you will silently get an empty `Optional`, so your program will not throw an exception but will behave incorrectly, and you may not notice this until much later.

5.1.3 *Nullity annotations*

One popular approach to minimize possible `NullPointerException` problems in Java is to use nullity annotations; you can use one of the popular annotation packages listed in Appendix A. If you don't like external dependencies, it's also possible to declare such annotations right in your project. Usually, static analysis tools allow you to configure custom nullity annotations.

The two most important annotations are usually `@Nullable` and `@NotNull` (or `@Nonnull`). The `@Nullable` annotation means it should be expected that the annotated variable contains `null` or the annotated method returns `null`. In contrast, `@NotNull` means the annotated value is never `null`. These annotations document the code and provide hints for static analysis. The most common problems reported by static analysis tools are dereferencing a nullable value without a `null` check and checking a non-null value against `null`:

```
import org.jetbrains.annotations.*;

interface MyInterface {
  @NotNull String getNotNull();
  @Nullable String getNullable();

  default void test() {
    if (getNotNull() == null) {          Warning: condition
                                          is always false.
      ...
    }

    System.out.println(getNullable().trim());       Warning: trim() invocation may
  }                                                  cause NullPointerException.
}
```

While checking a non-null value against `null` might not look like a real problem, such warnings may help to remove the redundant code. Sometimes, they may even point to the actual mistake. For example, if you are working with XML DOM API and want to read a value of an XML element attribute, you can find the `getAttribute()` method inside the `org.w3c.dom.Element` interface, which accepts the attribute name and returns the attribute value. It might be quite natural to expect that `null` will be returned if the specified attribute is missing. This may lead you to believe the following code is correct:

```
String getName(Element element) {
  String name = element.getAttribute("name");
  if (name == null) {
    return "<default>";
  }
  return name;
}
```

However, this code is wrong. According to the `getAttribute()` documentation, this method returns an empty string instead of `null` if the attribute is not found. If it's desired to distinguish between an empty attribute and an absent attribute, the `hasAttribute()` method should be used. While the Java standard library is not annotated with any nullability annotations, some static analyzers, like IntelliJ IDEA, Spot-Bugs, and PVS-Studio, have so-called external annotations applied to the standard library. As a result, the analyzer knows the `getAttribute()` method never returns `null` and warns you about an always false condition: `name == null`.

Another common source of a similar type of mistakes is the Reflection API. There are many query methods, like `Class.getMethod()`, `Class.getField()`, and so on. These methods never return `null`; instead, they throw an exception, like `NoSuch-MethodException`, if the corresponding object is not found. We often saw that developers check the result of this method against `null` and ignore the exception. Static analyzers may help to identify such problems.

Some annotation packages allow you to specify default nullity for a whole class—or even a package. This could be handy if your API is completely, or mostly, `null` hostile. For example, the Eclipse JDT Annotation Package contains a `@NonNullByDefault` annotation. You can apply it to a class, interface, or package and specify the types of source code elements:

```
import org.eclipse.jdt.annotation.*;

@NonNullByDefault({DefaultLocation.PARAMETER,
                   DefaultLocation.RETURN_TYPE})
public interface MyInterface {
  String processString(String input);
}
```

Here, it's specified that all the method parameters and method return values in `MyInterface` are non-null by default. In particular, the `processString()` method does not accept `null` as a parameter and never returns a `null` value. Using such an annotation can greatly simplify nullity specification.

Sometimes, it's useful for a static analyzer to know not only whether the method accepts `null` but also what exactly will happen if `null` is passed. For example, the `Class.isInstance()` standard library method always returns `false` when a `null` argument is passed. If the analyzer knows this, it may behave better. Consider the following code example:

```
default void processObject(@Nullable Object obj,
                           @NotNull Class<?> cls) {
  if (!cls.isInstance(obj)) return;
  int hash = obj.hashCode();
  … // Process hash
}
```

As `obj` is marked as `@Nullable` and there's no explicit `null` check, a naïve analyzer might issue a warning at the `obj.hashCode()` call that it may lead to a `NullPointer-Exception`. However, this is, in fact, impossible. If `obj` is `null`, then the result of the `isInstance()` call is `false` and we don't reach the `obj.hashCode()` call. To specify this knowledge about methods behavior, IntelliJ IDEA uses the contract annotation applicable to methods. This annotation is available in the JetBrains annotations package. For the `isInstance()` method, the contract could be specified as follows:

```
@Contract("null -> false")
```

This means if the method argument is `null`, then the resulting value is `false`. IntelliJ IDEA understands such annotations and takes them into account during the analysis, so you won't see a false-positive warning in the preceding code example. As with nullity annotations, the standard library is pre-annotated with contracts. For your code, you can use the contract annotation explicitly.

Even if nullity annotations are used in the project, developers often need to deal with unannotated code. This could come in the form of legacy parts written before nullity annotations were introduced or modules imported from other projects. IntelliJ IDEA may still help in this case, as it tries to infer nullity annotation automatically. For example, you may write the following method:

```
static String processString(String input) {
  String result = input.trim();
  if (result.isEmpty()) return null;
  return result;
}
```

If you open auto-generated documentation for this method, using the Quick Documentation shortcut, you'll see the inferred annotations, which are displayed in *italics* (figure 5.4).

This means the annotations are inferred automatically: IntelliJ IDEA has checked the source code of your method and determined the nullity of the parameter and the return

```
@Nullable ↗
static String processString(
  @NotNull ↗ String input
)
```

Figure 5.4   Inferred annotations in IntelliJ IDEA are shown in italics.

value. Unfortunately, this works only in rare cases, as IntelliJ IDEA must analyze your code online while you continue editing it, so it's pretty limited in terms of the CPU time it can spend on this analysis.

IntelliJ IDEA also provides a separate Infer Nullity action (available under the Code | Analyze Code menu). This is a more advanced mechanism to annotate your project or its parts automatically. Still, it's not ideal. There are more advanced static analyzers, like Infer (https://fbinfer.com/), that can perform deep interprocedural analysis to find nontrivial potential `NullPointerException` problems.

5.2   *Mistake 42: IndexOutOfBoundsException*

A major benefit of Java over languages like C is that it performs bounds checks for you. You cannot accidentally read or write beyond the array length, as you will get an `ArrayIndexOutOfBoundsException` from the virtual machine instead of a silently malfunctioning program. The same principle is followed in the standard library. If you try to access string characters beyond the string length (e.g., via the `charAt()` or `substring()` methods) or list elements beyond the list size, you'll also get an appropriate exception, like `StringIndexOutOfBoundsException` or simply `IndexOutOfBoundsException`.

However, these exceptions are intended only to identify bugs in your program and prevent worse consequences, like data corruption, incorrect behavior, or security holes. In fact, you still need to do bounds checks by yourself. Various flavors of `IndexOutOfBoundsException` are quite a common problem in Java programs.

For example, suppose you want to check whether the first character of the string is a digit. It's easy to forget a bounds check in this code:

```
void processString(String s) {
  if (Character.isDigit(s.charAt(0))) {
```

```
    processStringStartingWithDigit(s);
  }
}
```

This code behaves well until the empty string is supplied as the input. I have encountered similar bugs with arrays and lists as well.

Sometimes a bounds check is present but implemented incorrectly. I've seen three typical problems with it:

- *The bounds check is performed after the index access, probably due to refactoring or a copy–paste error.* For example, here, it was intended to check the index before array access:

```
void processArrayElement(int[] data, int index) {
  if (data[index] >= 0 &&
      index < data.length) {          ⊲──┐ The check has no effect: if
                                          │ index is out of bounds, we
    ...                                   │ already have an exception.
  }
}
```

- *The relation is accidentally flipped.* For example, here `data.length > index` was intended:

```
void processInput(int[] data, int index) {
  if (data.length < index &&          ⊲──┐ We proceed only if the
      data[index] >= 0) {                 │ index is out of bounds.
    ...
  }
}
```

- *There is an off-by-one error.* There's a corner case in which the index is exactly equal to the array, list, or string length. Such an index is out of bounds, but sometimes, developers don't pay attention to this case. For example, here, it was intended to exit the method if the `index >= data.length`:

```
void processInput(int[] data, int index) {
  if (index > data.length) return;    ⊲──┐ If index is exactly data.length, the
  if (data[index] >= 0) {                 │ execution continues to the next
                                          │ line, resulting in an exception.
    ...
  }
}
```

Static analysis

The first two cases are detected by the IntelliJ IDEA static analyzer, unless a complex expression is used as the index. Don't forget to help the static analyzer by extracting the repeating complex expression to intermediate variables. The third problem can be detected by the PVS-Studio analyzer (the diagnostic name is V6025: Possibly Index Is Out of Bound).

Things become trickier if you need to perform a bounds check before accessing a contiguous range of indexes. A common example is filling part of an array, given a starting offset and number of elements to fill. Normally, you should check that the starting offset and count are nonnegative and the array size is at least equal to the sum of the starting offset and count.

Additional care should be taken, as the sum of offset and count may overflow. Therefore, a simple check, like `offset + count <= length`, might not be enough. For example, imagine you have an array of 1,000,000,000 elements and your method is called with an offset of 500,000,000 and an unexpectedly large count of 2,000,000,000. In this case, `offset + count` will overflow to a negative number, −1,794,967,296, which is obviously smaller than any positive length, so the check will pass, even though the input is incorrect. The overflow-proof condition may look like this:

```
length >= 0 && offset >= 0 && count >= 0 && count <= length - offset
```

Here, we replaced addition with subtraction after checking that all the values are non-negative. Subtraction of two nonnegative `int` values never overflows.

In some cases, you just need to throw an exception if the supplied offset and count are incorrect, without doing anything else. For example, you may need this if you implement a three-argument `InputStream.read()` method. In this case, it's convenient to use the `checkFromIndexSize()` method, which has been included in the `java.util.Objects` class since Java 9:

```java
class MyInputStream extends InputStream {
  @Override
  public int read(byte[] b, int off, int len) {
    Objects.checkFromIndexSize(off, len, b.length);
    …
  }
}
```

There are also the methods `checkIndex()` and `checkFromToIndex()`, which could be helpful. For example, you can use them if you implement your own `List`:

```java
class MyList<T> implements List<T> {
  public T get(int index) {
    Objects.checkIndex(index, size());
    …
  }

  public T set(int index, T element) {
    Objects.checkIndex(index, size());
    …
  }

  public List<T> subList(int fromIndex, int toIndex) {
    Objects.checkFromToIndex(fromIndex, toIndex, size());
    …
  }
  …
}
```

Note, however, that these check methods are not always suitable. For example, if you implement `List.add(index, element)`, the index is allowed to be equal to the list size (but not bigger), so by using `checkIndex(index, size())`, you'll violate the interface contract. One could consider using `checkIndex(index, size() + 1)`, but in this case, an overflow is possible if the size is `Integer.MAX_VALUE`, which could be a perfectly legal size for the list. Make sure you are aware whether such a situation is possible in your case.

Static analysis

Some static analyzers support annotations to specify the allowed range of method parameters. Sometimes, it helps to catch the problem during development, before you actually hit the exception. For example, the Checker framework annotations package contains a `@NonNegative` annotation, which denotes that the method parameter cannot be negative or `@Positive` if zero is also impossible. So if you use a method parameter as an index, you can annotate it:

```
int getValue(@NonNegative int index) {
    return myData[index];
}
```

In this case, the static analyzer may warn you if you call this method with a negative argument. The JetBrains annotation package provides a `@Range` annotation that allows you to specify explicitly the lower and upper bounds. An equivalent for `@NonNegative` for an `int` parameter would be `@Range(from = 0, to = Integer.MAX_VALUE)`.

WAYS TO AVOID THIS MISTAKE

- If you accept an index value from the clients, check its bounds immediately. The sooner the mistake is discovered the better.
- Be careful when using numeric comparisons with indexes. It's easy to mix up the `<`, `<=`, `>`, and `>=` operations. Substitute some example values in your mind, and consider which result your condition should have. For example, if the size of the array or list is 5 and the index is 4, should it be true or false? What if both index and size are equal to 5?
- Consider using range annotations to document your code better and aid static analysis tools.

5.3   *Mistake 43: ClassCastException*

There are two main sources of a `ClassCastException` in Java. The first is explicit type cast expression, and the second is an implicit cast added when a generic type is instantiated.

5.3.1   *Explicit cast*

To avoid `ClassCastException` on explicit cast, it's recommended to protect every explicit cast with the corresponding `instanceof` check:

```
if (obj instanceof MyType) {
  MyType myType = (MyType) obj;
  … // Use myType.
}
```

This code pattern is so important that since Java 16, the `instanceof` expression was enhanced, and you can simplify it:

```
if (obj instanceof MyType myType) {
  … // Use myType.
}
```

The `MyType myType` clause is called a *pattern*. You can learn more about patterns in the Java 16 language specification or various tutorials. The important thing here is that you can avoid explicit cast and protect yourself from `ClassCastException`, as the pattern-based `instanceof` expression never throws one.

Unfortunately, many projects still cannot migrate to Java 16+, and even if they can, tons of code was written in older Java versions, in which it was necessary to spell the same type in `instanceof`, cast expression, and variable type (unless you are using the `var` keyword). As usual, bugs like repetitions, so if you need to repeat something, there are several chances for things to go wrong. Sometimes, these types differ due to a typo or a mistake introduced during refactoring.

Another way to check the type before cast is calling `getClass()`. This code pattern appears often in `equals()` method implementations, especially when the class is not final:

```
public class Point {
  final int x, y;

  public boolean equals(Object o) {
    if (this == o) return true;
    if (o == null || getClass() != o.getClass()) return false;
    Point point = (Point) o;
    return x == point.x && y == point.y;
  }
}
```

Here, the cast is also safe because the `getClass()` called on `this` object is either `Point` or its subclass. In this case, a possible mistake appears when a developer copies the `equals()` method implementation from another similar class without updating the cast type. To avoid such a problem, do not copy an `equals()` method from another class, even if that class is very similar. Instead, use IDE features to automatically generate the `equals()` implementation from scratch.

However, most `ClassCastException` problems appear when the cast is performed without the previous `instanceof` or `getClass()` check, when the developer is completely sure the cast will succeed. One particularly bad case is casting the method parameter unconditionally upon the method entrance:

```
public void process(Object obj) {
  String str = (String) obj;
```

```
  … // Use str.
}
```

In this case, while the method declares the `Object` parameter type, in fact, it accepts `String` parameters only. As a result, we cannot rely on the compiler's type checks and should be extremely careful to pass a value of the proper type. It would be much better to change the method declaration:

```
public void process(String str) {
  … // Use str.
}
```

Sometimes, compatibility concerns arise. There are probably third-party clients that already call `process(Object)`, which you cannot update immediately. In this case, it's a good idea to declare a deprecated overload:

```
/**
 * @param obj object to process (must be a String)
 * @deprecated use {@link #process(String)} instead.
 */
@Deprecated
public void process(Object obj) {
  process((String) obj);
}

public void process(String str) {
  … // Use str.
}
```

Now, while older clients will work as before, you will have a deprecation warning at the call sites where non-string arguments are used. Eventually, all the clients will update and the deprecated overload can be removed. Since Java 9, you may add an intermediate stronger deprecation state using `@Deprecated(forRemoval = true)` to clearly state an intent to remove this method in the future version.

The problem becomes more complicated when your method overrides or implements the method from a superclass or interface. Sometimes, it's impossible to modify the supertype and you will have to accept a more generic type. Still, you can at least localize the cast in the intermediate method and produce a better error message in case an unexpected object is supplied, as in this example:

```
@Override
public void process(Object obj) {
  if (!(obj instanceof String)) {
    throw new IllegalArgumentException(
               "Unexpected object passed: " + obj);
  }
  process((String) obj);
}

private void process(String str) {
  … // Use str.
}
```

Here, we must accept an `Object` according to the interface we're implementing. However, we guard the cast with a condition where we can throw a custom exception. In this sample, we added a string representation of a supplied object, but in real code, you can provide more context to help debug the unexpected value and determine where it comes from.

If you can modify the supertype but it's hard to adapt all the inheritors, you might want to consider declaring a generic parameter. For example, suppose you have an interface like this:

```
interface Processor {
    void process(Object obj);
}
```

If your implementation of `StringProcessor` accepts only the `String` parameter, you can declare a type parameter on the interface:

```
interface Processor<T> {
    void process(T obj);
}
```

Of course, this would require subsequent refactoring of all inheritors and users of this interface, as raw type warnings will appear everywhere. However, this can be done incrementally, as the code will still compile even with raw types. You may declare `StringProcessor implements Processor<String>`, and other implementations implement `Processor<Object>`. It's also possible that during the refactoring, you will discover more implementations that only work with a specific subtype, so the type parameter will be useful in other places as well.

Static analysis

There's a Cast Conflicts With `instanceof` inspection in IntelliJ IDEA (turned off by default) that can detect if you have a cast under an `instanceof` check and the cast type differs from the `instanceof` type. While it occasionally produces false warnings, it may be helpful. If the cast type is obviously incompatible with the `instanceof` type, the Nullability and Data Flow Problems inspection may also warn you.

SpotBugs also has many warnings, including Impossible Cast and Impossible Downcast, for cases in which the cast is completely impossible. Other warnings, like Unchecked/Unconfirmed Cast and Unchecked/Unconfirmed Cast of Return Value from Method, report cases when a cast can fail under certain conditions. However, these warnings are noisy and may produce false positives.

Another useful inspection in IntelliJ IDEA is called Too Weak Variable Type Leads to Unnecessary Cast. It reports type casts that could be removed if you use a more concrete variable type instead. Take the following example:

```
List<String> list = List.of("a", "b", "c", "d");
for (Object s : list) {
    System.out.println(((String) s).repeat(2));
}
```

(continued)

Here, you can declare the variable s as String and remove the cast completely, and the inspection suggests you should do so. This code may not cause ClassCast-Exception in its current shape, but who knows what will happen later? If you can avoid cast, it's better to do so and rely on static type checking instead. So it's perfectly reasonable to fix all the warnings of this inspection, especially taking into account that the automated quick fix is provided.

WAYS TO AVOID THIS MISTAKE

- Since Java 16, it's been strongly encouraged to use pattern matching with instanceof syntax to blend instanceof and cast operations together whenever possible. This way, you mention the target type only once, avoiding copy-paste mistakes.
- When implementing the equals() method, don't copy the implementation from another class. Instead, use IDE capabilities to generate this method from scratch. This way, you'll avoid copy-paste mistakes, such as forgetting to update the cast type.
- Avoid unguarded casts without a previous instanceof check. If you are sure your variable always contains an object of a specific type, then you should probably update the declared variable type to that type. If it comes from the method parameter or the method return type, consider updating them as well and removing the cast. This way, an object of incompatible type could not be stored there at all, as this would cause a compilation error.
- Use code template generation mechanisms to write instanceof cast code sequences automatically. IntelliJ IDEA features the *inst* live template for this purpose. Just type *inst* in the editor, and then press Enter. It will ask you to select the variable and the target type. The rest will be generated automatically.

5.3.2   *Generic types and implicit casts*

Another common source of ClassCastException is an implicit cast when a generic type is instantiated. In this case, you have no cast expression in the source code, which could be confusing. For example, consider the following method:

```
void printFirstItem(List<String> list) {
  String s = list.get(0);
  System.out.println(s);
}
```

The List class is declared as List<E>, and the get() method returns the E type. However, in Java, generics are erased at run time. For historical reasons, generic types exist and are checked only in source code. When a Java program is executed, the type arguments of any value of generic type are not known anymore, and any occurrence of a type parameter, like E, is replaced with its upper bound (or Object, if there's no explicit upper bound declared). So, from the perspective of the virtual machine, there is no `List<E>` or `List<String>`, there's just `List`. The Java virtual machine knows nothing about the `E` type, and the `get()` method simply returns an `Object`. To convert the `Object` type to `String`, a Java compiler inserts an implicit cast, desugaring the method to the following:

```
void printFirstItem(List list) {
  String s = (String) list.get(0);
  System.out.println(s);
}
```

This is how the method looks to the virtual machine. It works with the raw type `List`, but every time you call a method that returns its type parameter (e.g., the `get()` method), the implicit cast operation is performed. This cast might fail if the original list was not actually a list of strings. A situation like this may happen if you have an unchecked cast or unchecked call somewhere at the `printFirstItem()` call site, as in the following example:

```
List<String> list = new ArrayList<>();
List<?> objects = list;
((List<Object>) objects).add(1);      ◁────  Unchecked
printFirstItem(list);                          cast
```

Here, we first assign `list` to variable `objects` of the more generic type `List<?>`, which is allowed. However, after that, we perform an unchecked cast of `objects` to `List<Object>`. The compiler issues an Unchecked Cast warning here, which means whether such a cast is actually possible won't be checked at run time. In fact, as types are erased at run time, the cast to `List<Object>` disappears in the bytecode completely. We just add an object of type `Integer` to the list, and nobody stops us. This essentially creates a time bomb: now, the list is broken, but the program continues executing as if everything is correct. The bomb explodes later, when the `printFirst-Item()` method is executed and we try to get the string.

   As you can see, an unchecked cast may produce a problem much later, so it's better to avoid it. I cannot advise to remove them completely, as in rare cases, they are inevitable. However, in many cases, you can avoid an unchecked cast. For example, imagine you have two methods like this:

```
List<String> getList() { … }
void processList(List<CharSequence> list) { … }
```

Now, you want to pass the result of `getList()` to the `processList()`. Even though `String` implements the `CharSequence` interface, as a general rule, it's not safe to pass the `List<String>` where `List<CharSequence>` is expected. That's because if `processList()` modifies the list, it may add another implementation of `CharSequence` (e.g., `StringBuilder`) to the list, so `List<String>` will not only contain strings.

   However, you may know in advance that `processList()` will not modify the list at all. In this case, you know that passing `List<String>` to `processList()` is safe. But you cannot simply call `processList(getList())`, as it will cause a compilation error. To fix the compilation error, you may consider adding an upcast to `List<?>` and then an unchecked cast:

```
processList((List<CharSequence>)(List<?>)getList());
```

But it still produces a warning. So how can you convince Java that it's safe? A good solution here is to declare the `processList()` method using a wildcard type with `?` `extends`:

```
List<String> getList() { … }
void processList(List<? extends CharSequence> list) { … }
```

Now, `processList()` says that it accepts a `List` of any particular `CharSequence`. This signature still allows for querying list elements inside the `processList()`, but now, you cannot add new elements (except nulls) without unchecked casts. This is fine, as you weren't going to add anything.

Sometimes, you cannot modify the signature of the method. It could be a library method, or the signature could be enforced by a parent interface. In this case, you can still fix the problem at the call site without an unchecked cast:

```
processList(Collections.unmodifiableList(getList()));
```

The `unmodifiableList()` library method has a nice feature. This is its declaration:

```
public static <T> List<T> unmodifiableList(List<? extends T> list)
```

Note that the parameter type is `List<? extends T>`, not just `List<T>`. As a result, aside from wrapping your list in an unmodifiable wrapper, it can also adapt the list type by accepting a list of more concrete elements and returning the list of more abstract elements. If you have custom generic types, don't hesitate to write read-only or write-only adapters.

Another way to step on `ClassCastException` is using a raw type. A raw type is a parameterized type used without any parameters, like simply `List` instead of `List<?>` or `List<String>`. Their main purpose is the ability to gradually migrate your code base from Java 1.4 to Java 1.5, something you should not have to worry about these days. However, as this syntax is allowed by Java compilers, people may use a raw type accidentally.

When a raw type is used, the compiler doesn't check anything about type parameter compatibility. It may issue warnings, but it will allow you to do anything that was allowed in Java 1.4, where no generic types existed. For example, the following code is perfectly compilable in modern Java versions, despite `List` being a parameterized class:

```
List list = new ArrayList<>();        ◁──┐  Accidental raw
list.add(123);                            │  type List
printFirstItem(list);
```

There are compiler warnings about *unchecked calls* on the second and third lines, which means the calls are potentially unsafe and the compiler cannot guarantee type safety.

WAYS TO AVOID THIS MISTAKE

- Occasionally, unchecked casts in Java can be useful, due to the imperfections of the Java type system. However, you must understand why you need an unchecked cast, why it's impossible to solve the problem in another way, and what consequences could result. It's better to encapsulate unchecked casts into well-tested utility methods or use existing methods for this purpose. If you need an unchecked cast, try to extract it into a separate small method and use `@SuppressWarnings("unchecked")` to avoid the warning.

- Sometimes, adapter methods, like `Collections.unmodifiableList()`, may help to avoid unchecked casts.

- When declaring methods, consider using more generic types in method parameters involving wildcards, like `?  extends` (if you only need to read from the object) or `?  super` (if you only need to write to the object). This approach is often called *PECS*, which stands for *producer extends consumer super*. It not only helps to avoid the unchecked casts but also documents your code better, as the user of your method will understand whether you are going to read or write.

- Avoid using arrays to store objects of generic type. Java does not allow you to create a generic array, so you will always need unchecked casts when working with such arrays. In most cases, you can replace such an array with `ArrayList`, which already encapsulates an array and hides all the unchecked casts inside its implementation.

- Avoid raw types as frequently as possible. When you use raw types, compiler checks become much weaker, and you may easily screw things up storing objects of an incorrect type somewhere. In modern Java, there are only a few places where raw types could be useful, notably if you want to create an array of generic type. But as I've just said, this is a bad idea.

- It's possible to ask the javac compiler to report raw types via the command line option: `-Xlint:rawtypes`. You can use it to find raw types in your program and try to eliminate them.

- There are wrappers in the `Collections` utility class, like `checkedList()` and `checkedMap()`, that allow you to actually control the type of elements added to the collection or map. Consider using them if you really care about the type safety of your collections. In this case, even an unchecked cast will not allow you to store an object of invalid type. For example, you can wrap the `ArrayList` from the `printFirstItem()` sample with the `checkedList()`. In this case, an attempt to add a number to a list of string will cause an exception:

```
List<String> list = Collections.checkedList(
                    new ArrayList<>(), String.class);
List<?> objects = list;
((List<Object>) objects).add(1);      ←――┐ ClassCastException
printFirstItem(list);                      └ happens at run time.
```

While using these wrappers everywhere is probably too pedantic, they are useful if you want to investigate exactly where an object of incorrect type appeared inside your collection. Just wrap the collection temporarily, run your program again, and you will see an exception at the element addition rather than at the retrieval.

5.3.3   Different class loaders

The Java Virtual machine distinguishes classes by name and class loader. Usually, if you see a `ClassCastException`, this means the class has a different name. However, it's also possible for the class to have the same name but a different class loader (figure 5.5).

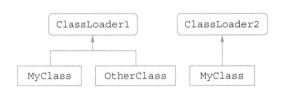

Figure 5.5   Classes with the same name can be loaded by different class loaders

This doesn't happen in simple Java programs, as such programs usually use the same class loader for all the classes. However, this may easily happen in more complex ones that have modular architecture or plugin support. In this case, it's possible that the classes from different plugins or modules are loaded using different class loaders.

To illustrate what the possible problem looks like, let's create a custom class loader. The easiest way is to use `URLClassLoader` and instruct it to load classes from the same location the classes of your application are located. This can be done in the following manner:

```
import java.net.*;

public class MyClass {
  public static void main(String[] args) throws Exception {
    URL url = MyClass.class.getResource(".");
    ClassLoader parent = System.class.getClassLoader();
    try (URLClassLoader newLoader =
           new URLClassLoader(new URL[]{url}, parent)) {
      Class<?> anotherMyClass = newLoader.loadClass("MyClass");
      Object o = anotherMyClass.getConstructor().newInstance();
      System.out.println("Class: " + o.getClass());
      System.out.println("Loader: " + o.getClass().getClassLoader());
      System.out.println("Instance of: " + (o instanceof MyClass));
      MyClass cls = (MyClass) o;
    }
  }
}
```

URL pointing to the folder where compiled MyClass.class is located

A parent class loader is necessary to resolve system classes, like java.lang.Object, which is the superclass of MyClass.

The cast never succeeds.

The instanceof check returns false.

Note that there's no package statement and we load the class with the same name, `MyClass`, from the default package. This program produces the output like this:

```
Class: class MyClass
Loader: java.net.URLClassLoader@12edcd21
```

```
Instance of: false
Exception in thread "main" java.lang.ClassCastException: class MyClass
Cannot be cast to class MyClass (MyClass is in unnamed module of loader
java.net.URLClassLoader @12edcd21; MyClass is in unnamed module of loader
'app')
    at MyClass.main(MyClass.java:13)
```

As you can see, we successfully loaded a `MyClass` class one more time, but it's a different class with the same name. The `instanceof` check returns false, and the cast fails. It might look confusing to see the message like Class `MyClass` Cannot Be Cast to Class `MyClass`, but the additional explanation in the parentheses makes it clear that the class loaders differ.

WAYS TO AVOID THIS MISTAKE

- Be careful when defining your own class loaders, like `URLClassLoader`, when you want to load some classes dynamically. In particular, pay attention to the parent class loader used. To make your class functional, it's necessary to load other classes, like superclasses and interfaces, as well, and all of them will be loaded via your class loader. However, it always tries its parent class loader first, so all classes that can be loaded by the parent will return the parent. In the preceding sample, we used `System.class.getClassLoader()` as a parent class loader, so it could load standard library classes but could not load your application classes. Replace it with `MyClass.class.getClassLoader()`, and you'll be able to load existing classes of your application as well.

- If your application has a pluggable architecture, pay attention to plugin or module boundaries and be careful when passing objects between plugins. Even if two plugins depend on the same library, it's possible that the library classes are loaded by separate class loaders—for example, to allow plugins to use different versions of the library . In this case, if you pass a library object to another plugin, you won't be able to cast it to the same type at destination.

- If you actually need to work with an object loaded by another class loader and have no clean options to resolve this, you can use the reflection. Just store that object as an `Object` type and call the methods reflectively, using API methods, like `getMethod()` and `invoke()`:

  ```
  obj.getClass().getMethod("myMethod").invoke(obj);
  ```

  Don't forget that such code is very fragile, as you don't have compile-time checks that the called method actually exists and has compatible parameters. If you use this approach, encapsulate all the reflection calls into separate methods, explain in the comments why it was done this way, and write unit tests to ensure this approach actually works.

5.4   Mistake 44: StackOverflowError

Recursion is a useful programming technique that allows you to implement many algorithms in cleaner way than loops. This comes at a cost though. The recursive calls eat the stack of the thread, and if the depth of the recursion is too big, you may get a `StackOverflowError` exception instead of the result of the computation. On popular JVM implementations, the maximum depth is not a constant: it depends on many things, like whether the executed method is interpreted or JIT compiled and which tier of JIT compilation was used. It also depends on how many parameters and local variables the recursive calls have. The same code may work correctly once but produce a `StackOverflowError` the next time, just because JIT was not fast enough to finish the compilation of the recursive method.

5.4.1   Deep but finite recursion

Some programming languages, especially functional programming languages, can automatically eliminate so-called *tail recursion* during compilation when your recursive call is the last action in the method. For example, JVM languages, like Scala and Kotlin, support this when compiling into JVM bytecode. In Scala, optimization is done automatically when possible, but you can assert it via `@tailrec` annotation, so compilation will fail if the recursion cannot be optimized. In Kotlin, you should use the `tailrec` function modifier. For example, you can write the following recursive function in Kotlin, which sums numbers from 0 to limit (I deliberately write this function in not quite idiomatic Kotlin, to make it clearer for readers who don't know this language):

```
tailrec fun sum(limit: Long, accumulator: Long = 0): Long {
  if (limit == 0L) return accumulator
  return sum(limit - 1, accumulator + limit)
}
```

Here, we have a recursive call of the `sum()` function that accepts a `limit` parameter. To make it the last call, we need to accumulate the current result in another `accumulator` parameter, which is 0 by default. If the limit is already 0, we just return the accumulator value. Otherwise, we call the same function recursively, updating the accumulator and decreasing the `limit`. Without `tailrec` modifier, this method fails with `StackOverflowError` if the limit is quite large (e.g., 1,000,000). However, the `tailrec` modifier instructs the Kotlin compiler to eliminate the tail recursion, converting it into a loop in the bytecode, and this function can work with a large input value as well. Unfortunately, there's nothing like this in the Java compiler. Some virtual machines, like IBM OpenJ9, may perform this optimization during JIT compilation, but it's not guaranteed.

On the other hand, tail recursion can always be mechanically rewritten to a loop right in the source code. IntelliJ IDEA provides a way to do this. There's an action called Replace Tail Recursion With Iteration, which is available in the context actions menu (usually activated via Alt-Enter) when staying on the tail call. While the resulting code might not be so pretty, it will not suffer from possible stack overflow. For example, here's a simple tail recursive implementation of an `indexOf` function on a string:

```
/**
 * @param s string to search in
 * @param start start offset
 * @param c symbol to search
 * @return position of symbol c inside string s
```

```
 * starting from start offset; -1 if not found
 */
static int indexOf(String s, int start, char c) {
  if (start >= s.length()) return -1;
  if (s.charAt(start) == c) return start;
  return indexOf(s, start + 1, c);
}
```

Running this method on very long strings containing, for example, 10,000 characters may produce a `StackOverflowError`. Applying the Replace Tail Recursion With Iteration action will convert it into a loop:

```
static int indexOf(String s, int start, char c) {
  while (true) {
    if (start >= s.length()) return -1;
    if (s.charAt(start) == c) return start;
    start = start + 1;
  }
}
```

This implementation may not look so nice, but now, it can process strings of arbitrary size. I recommend rewriting tail recursion with loops, either automatically or manually, unless you are completely sure the maximal depth of your recursive calls does not exceed several hundreds.

Unfortunately, not every recursive call is a tail call, so it cannot always be optimized. Still, it's always possible to rewrite it using a loop. However, to store the state of intermediate calls, you'll need to use a side collection in the program heap. Usually, `ArrayDeque` collection fits well to emulate the stack calls.

As an example, let's consider a simple recursive tree traversal search algorithm that cannot be expressed via tail recursion. Let's assume we have tree nodes that contain names and children (figure 5.6) and a method to find a node by name among the descendants, returning `null` if not found:

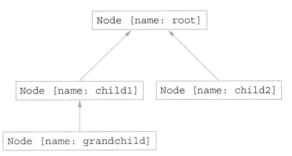

Figure 5.6   Simple tree of named nodes

```
record Node(String name, Node... children) {
  Node find(String name) {
    if (name().equals(name)) return this;
    for (Node child : children()) {
      Node node = child.find(name);
      if (node != null) return node;
    }
    return null;
  }
}
```

This method is simple and clear, and in many cases, it would be OK to use. For example, the following code creates a tree like the one shown in figure 5.6 and successfully finds the grandchild node:

```
Node root = new Node("root",
        new Node("child1", new Node("grandchild")),
        new Node("child2"));
System.out.println(root.find("grandchild"));
```

However, if you expect to have very deep trees, it would be better to get rid of recursion. All you need is to maintain a list of nodes to visit in a collection:

```
Node find(String name) {
  Deque<Node> stack = new ArrayDeque<>();
  stack.add(this);
  while (!stack.isEmpty()) {
    Node node = stack.pollLast();
    if (node.name().equals(name)) return node;
    Collections.addAll(stack, node.children());
  }
  return null;
}
```

The method becomes a little bit longer and probably harder to understand, but now, you are limited by heap size instead of the stack size, which allows you to traverse much deeper trees.

Sometimes, the state to maintain between calls may consist of several variables, so you'll need to declare an additional data structure to maintain the state. Java records could be handy in this case. Also note that it's common for recursive calls to contain many intermediate frames. For example, method A may call method B, which calls method C, which calls method A again. In this case, it could be quite nontrivial to refactor the code and avoid the recursion.

WAYS TO AVOID THIS MISTAKE

- When making recursive calls, always consider whether it's possible the stack capacity will be exceeded. Normally, the virtual machine can handle between 1,000 and 10,000 recursive calls, depending on many things, like how many parameters and local variables your methods have, whether they were interpreted or JIT compiled, and so on. So if you expect that the depth of calls will approach a thousand, it's better to play it safe and use heap instead of stack space.
- Avoid implementing standard algorithms manually. In many cases, recursion is used to implement one of a few common algorithms, like graph search or tree traversal. Use well-tested library methods instead, which already avoid recursion.

5.4.2   Infinite recursion

In the previous example, recursive calls are intended and recursion is finite, but its depth exceeds the virtual machine stack. The recursion, though, can be truly infinite—regardless of the provided stack capacity, it will run out eventually. The difference is illustrated in figure 5.7. Finite recursion changes the program state and, eventually, reaches the exit condition. On the other hand, infinite recursion does not change the program state, except by consuming more space in the stack. It's also possible for the state to be changed but the recursion termination condition never to be satisfied. In this case, rewriting the recursion

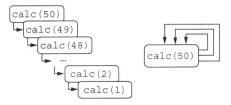

Figure 5.7 Finite recursion (left) and infinite recursion (right)

with a loop will not help, as the loop will be infinite as well. This simply means the program has a bug that should be fixed.

A simple case of accidental infinite recursion I have observed many times is when it was intended to delegate the call. For example, let's assume we have a UI button interface that handles the pressed event:

```
interface Button {
  void onPressed();
}
```

Now, we have a wrapper that can disable the button:

```
class ButtonWrapper implements Button {
  private final Button delegate;
  private boolean enabled;

  ButtonWrapper(Button delegate) {
    this.delegate = delegate;
  }

  public void setEnabled(boolean enabled) {
    this.enabled = enabled;
  }

  @Override
  public void onPressed() {
    if (!enabled) return;           delegate.onPressed()
    onPressed();                    was intended.
  }
}
```

Here, it was intended to call the `onPressed()` method on delegate, but the qualifier was mistakenly omitted. As a result, when the button is not disabled, we will have an infinite recursion.

In general, infinite recursion occurs when you call the same method with the same parameters and the program state (values of variables and fields relevant to this part of the program) is also the same. So when you make a call, the program returns to the original state, but more stack space has been used.

One example of accidental state equality is recursive traversal of tree-like data structures. It's very simple to traverse a tree or a directed acyclic graph. All you need is to process the current node then call yourself recursively for all the child nodes. However, if your data structure happens to contain a cycle, stack overflow can easily happen. There are two possible cases: either having a cycle is legal but you weren't aware of this during traversal, or the cycle is introduced due to an earlier mistake in the program. In the former case, you should track previously visited nodes to avoid visiting them twice. In the latter case, fixing the traversal is unnecessary; there's nothing wrong in recursive tree traversal, if we know in advance that cycles should be impossible. Instead, the earlier mistake should be found and fixed.

A simple example of such a recursive traversal can be found in standard library implementations of the list `hashCode()` method. If the list contains itself, its hash code cannot be calculated by specification. For example, the following code throws a `StackOverflowError`:

```
List<Object> list = new ArrayList<>();
list.add(list);
System.out.println(list.hashCode());
```

This is not a bug in the `hashCode()` implementation, as such a behavior is specified. In general, it's a bad idea to add a collection to itself.

Standard implementation of the `toString()` method has a simple protection against this, so the following code completes successfully:

```
List<Object> list = new ArrayList<>();
list.add(list);                          [(this Collection)]
System.out.println(list);            ←─┘ is printed.
```

However, the protection covers only the shortest possible cycle: when a collection is added directly to itself. If you create a longer cycle, `StackOverflowError` will still happen. For example, the following code fails:

```
List<Object> list = new ArrayList<>();
list.add(List.of(list));                 StackOverflowError
System.out.println(list);            ←─┘ happens here.
```

A classic example of a data structure a program might traverse is a filesystem. It's a common task to traverse a subtree of directories and files to perform some action on them. Don't forget filesystems may contain cycles as well. If you follow symbolic links during traversal, it's very easy to create such a link that points to a parent directory. Even if not, some operating systems, like Linux, allow mounting filesystems recursively, one into another (using the `mount --rbind` command). If you happen to traverse a directory that contains such a mount point, you may end up with stack overflow. Sometimes, it's acceptable to ignore this problem, especially if you traverse the directory that was previously created by your program automatically and you can assume nobody has interfered with the content of that directory. However, if you traverse any custom, user-specified directory, it's probably a good idea to protect yourself from potential stack overflow.

As a Java IDE developer, I stepped on this problem when traversing a superclass hierarchy in Java programs during code analysis. In correct Java programs, a superclass cannot extend its own subclass, so if you follow the chain of superclasses, you'll eventually come to `java.lang.Object`. However, it's not guaranteed that a program opened in Java IDE is a correct Java program. It may contain compilation errors, but the analysis will still be executed. A naïve analyzer that doesn't track previously visited classes may easily end up with stack overflow on the following code:

```
class A extends B {}
class B extends A {}
```

Static analysis

Simple cases of infinite recursion can be detected by static analyzers. Pay attention to the corresponding warnings (e.g., the Infinite Recursion inspection in IntelliJ IDEA or the InfiniteRecursion bug pattern in Error Prone). They rarely report, but if they do, it's almost always a real bug.

WAYS TO AVOID THIS MISTAKE

- When traversing a tree-like data structure, carefully consider whether it may contain cycles. Review how the data structure is created, and check its specification. Having cycles may be a rare corner case, but if possible, it's best to avoid them.
- Reuse library methods to traverse the graph; don't invent them by yourself. It's often tempting to write a simple recursive procedure in place; however, if you discover later that cycles are possible, this might be harder to fix. Existing library methods track the visited elements, providing automatic protection against stack overflow.

Summary

- `NullPointerException` is a big problem every Java programmer stumbles on. There are several techniques to minimize `null`-related mistakes. Some developers tend to avoid nulls completely, while others control them using annotations.
- Use defensive checks at your API boundaries (public methods) to ensure inputs are not nulls and indexes are within the expected range before saving them to fields. This will allow you to catch problems earlier.
- Casting a variable to another type without a preceding `instanceof` check is very fragile, as you are losing the benefits provided by the static type system. If you are sure the real variable type is more concrete than the declared type, then change the declared type and remove the cast.
- Unchecked casts of generic type will not cause `ClassCastException` immediately because such a cast does not exist to the virtual machine due to type erasure. However, it may cause `ClassCastException` much later, as the compiler

may insert implicit casts at the places where you use the generic type. This makes your code much harder to debug. Avoid unchecked casts when possible; wildcard types or read-only and write-only wrappers may help you.

- Be careful when your application uses several class loaders, as classes loaded by different class loaders are different classes, even though they have the same name.

- Try to avoid arbitrarily deep recursion in Java programs, as the Java stack is quite limited. Rewrite tail recursion with loops and use heap-based data-structures like `ArrayDeque` to handle non-tail recursion.

- When traversing data structures, pay attention to whether cycles are possible. If so, it's best to memorize already-visited elements to avoid infinite recursion.

Strings

This chapter covers

- Problems with characters that don't fit the Java `char` type
- Bugs caused by relying on the default system locale
- Discrepancies between format string and subsequent format arguments
- Accidental use of regular expressions
- Pitfalls associated with Java escape sequences
- Possible mistakes when using the `indexOf()` method

A variety of bugs may come up when using strings. Strings may appear deceivingly simple, but in fact, working with them correctly is quite difficult, as many common assumptions about them are incorrect.

6.1 Mistake 45: Assuming that char value is a character

Developers often assume the Java `char` type corresponds to a single displayed character. They naturally expect the `String.length()` method to return the number of displayed characters and think it's OK to process strings `char` by `char`. This is true in simple cases, but if the character Unicode code point is higher than `0xffff` (65,535), such characters lay outside of the so-called *Basic Multilingual Plane* (BMP) and are represented as *surrogate pairs*: two Java `char` values that represent a single character. Many emoji characters are located outside the BMP and require a surrogate pair to be represented.

For example, if it's necessary to split the text into fixed chunks to distribute it to several rows in the UI, a naïve approach would be to use something like this (for simplicity, let's omit bounds checking):

```
String part = string.substring(rowNumber * rowLength,
                               (rowNumber + 1) * rowLength);
```

The risks here are splitting a surrogate pair or combining characters. As a result, you may see placeholder characters at the beginning of the line and at the end of the previous line, instead of an actual character. For example, let's assume our variables have the following values:

```
String string = "Welcome! 😁";
int rowLength = 10;
int rowNumber = 0;
```

Here, an emoji character is used, whose codepoint is `0x1f601`. It is encoded via a surrogate pair of Java characters, namely `\ud83d` and `\ude01` (figure 6.1). When the string is split, only the first character of the pair remains, so you may see `Welcome! ?` or `Welcome! ◆`, depending on the font and character set of the output.

How a programmer sees the string

index	0	1	2	3	4	5	6	7	8	9
symbol	W	e	l	c	o	m	e	!		😁

How Java sees the string

index	0	1	2	3	4	5	6	7	8	9	10
char	W	e	l	c	o	m	e	!		\ud83d	\ude01

Figure 6.1   The emoji is encoded as a surrogate pair in Java, which takes two chars.

The next level of problems happens when combining characters enter the scene. For example, assume you have the following string:

```
String string = "Welcome 👋";
```

Here, you have *waving hand* symbol with a *dark skin tone* modifier. The codepoint of *waving hand* is `0x1f44b`, while the codepoint of the *dark skin tone* modifier is `0x1f3ff`. Both codepoints are outside of the BMP, so they are represented in Java via surrogate pairs. As a result, this symbol is encoded as four chars in Java. If you use Unicode escape sequences, the same string is represented like this (figure 6.2):

```
String string = "Welcome \ud83d\udc4b\ud83c\udfff";
```

How a programmer sees the string

index	0	1	2	3	4	5	6	7	8
symbol	W	e	l	c	o	m	e		👋

How Java sees the string

index	0	1	2	3	4	5	6	7	8	9	10	11
char	W	e	l	c	o	m	e		\ud83d	\udc4b	\ud83c	\udfff

Figure 6.2   An emoji with a modifier, such as a skin tone, may take four chars or more.

Fortunately, with `rowLength = 10` and `rowNumber = 0`, you split between surrogate pairs, but you still leave the modifier out. So, if you print the result, you'll see `Welcome` 👋 with the default skin tone. This might disappoint users who especially cared about specifying the proper skin tone.

Similar things happen when you want to abbreviate text that is too long using the `substring()` call:

```
String abbreviated = longText.substring(0, 100) + "...";
```

Again, this may cause a visual glitch right before the ellipsis.

The `java.lang.Character` class provides several methods, like `isDigit()` and `isLetter()`, to test whether a character belongs to a particular class. These methods are usually overloaded: one version accepts a `char` parameter, while another accepts an `int`, which is a codepoint. It's recommended to use `int` methods; as with `char` methods, you cannot correctly process characters outside of the BMP. For example, assume you want to write a method to check whether a given string starts with a digit. It can be written like this:

```
static boolean startsWithDigit(String str) {
  return !str.isEmpty() &&
        Character.isDigit(str.charAt(0));     ⟵── isDigit(char)
}                                                   is called.
```

Note that `isDigit()` returns `true` not only for the usual digits, 0 to 9, but also for digits in other writing systems as well as various graphical variants of the digits. However, there are digits outside of the BMP. For example, symbols like 𝟘, which is encoded in Java using a surrogate pair `"\ud835\udfd8"`, is outside of the BMP. Our method will incorrectly return `false` if a string starts with such a symbol. To support such digits, you should extract a codepoint from the original string, using `str.codePointAt()`. This method returns the `int` type, so now, another overload of `isDigit()` is called:

```
static boolean startsWithDigit(String str) {
  return !str.isEmpty() &&
         Character.isDigit(str.codePointAt(0));     ⟵  isDigit(int)
}                                                       is called.
```

Another notable set of characters located outside of BMP is Chinese characters. The Table of General Standard Chinese Characters contains more than 8,000 characters. Of these, almost 200 are located outside of the BMP. Some of them may be used in Chinese personal names, so they may appear in user input if your application happens to have Chinese-speaking users.

WAYS TO AVOID THIS MISTAKE

- When it's possible to have arbitrary characters in strings, prefer codepoint-centered APIs rather than `char`-centered ones. The `String` class has several methods for this, such as `codePointAt()`, `codePointBefore()`, `codePointCount()`, and `codePoints()`. When building a new string, the `appendCodePoint()` method of the `StringBuilder` class could be useful. For example, you can extract part of the string using the Stream API in the following way:

```
String part = string.codePoints().skip(rowNumber * rowLength)
       .limit(rowLength)
       .collect(StringBuilder::new,
                StringBuilder::appendCodePoint,
                StringBuilder::append)
       .toString();
```

As you can see, this API is more verbose and harder to use, compared to a simple `substring()` call. Moreover, `char`-related methods, like `charAt()` and `substring()` have constant complexity. However, to find the *n*th codepoint inside the string, you must traverse it from the beginning to detect possible surrogate pairs. Therefore, your program may start working slower if you refactor it to use codepoints. In our example, it could be reasonable to reorganize the code to extract all the string parts, traversing the input string only once.

Methods like `codePointAt()` should be used with care. It may appear as if this method finds the *n*th codepoint for you, but in fact, it returns the codepoint at the *n*th `char`. There's no readily available method in the standard Java library to get the *n*th codepoint.

- Avoid using library methods that accept the `char` type, like `isDigit (char)`, as they don't support characters outside the BMP. Use overloads that accept `int` and pass a codepoint there.
- Try to avoid using the `char` type at all, especially in public APIs of your code, like method parameters or return values. In many cases, these would be a time

bomb waiting to explode when your code encounters surrogate pairs for the first time. It could be hard to refactor your API if it was `char`-centric initially. Therefore, it's better to make it codepoint-centric from the very beginning, even if this requires more effort.

- When working with user-readable text, use special text APIs. For example, if you need to split a string at a character boundary, you can use the `BreakIterator` class and specifically its `getCharacterInstance()` method. This method is aware not only of surrogate pairs but also of combining character sequences and ligature clusters. You can extract part of the string like this:

```
BreakIterator iterator = BreakIterator.getCharacterInstance();
iterator.setText(string);
iterator.first();
int from = iterator.next(rowLength * rowNumber);
int to = iterator.next(rowLength - 1);
```

This approach will allow you to keep modifiers, like skin tone, attached to the main symbol. There are similar performance concerns with this approach as with codepoint iteration. The `iterator.next()` call cannot simply jump to the proper position inside the string; it needs to examine every character in-between.

- Try to isolate all text-processing code. Either use libraries like ICU4J (https://icu.unicode.org/home) or write your own utility methods. Text processing is tricky, and the more code you reuse, the less you will have to test and fix.

6.2 Mistake 46: Unexpected case conversions

The standard library has a few methods that depend on the default JVM locale. JVM initializes the system locale based on current user preferences specified in the OS settings (e.g., Microsoft Windows Control Panel) or environment variables like LANG. They can also be overridden using the JVM system properties. For example, if you want to use French as the default locale, you can start the JVM with the following parameter:

```
java -Duser.language=fr
```

In Java programs, the default locale can be accessed via `Locale.getDefault()`. Some methods that operate on text use this default locale implicitly. The most notable are the `toUpperCase()` and `toLowerCase()` methods in the `String` class, which accept no arguments. Case conversion is locale dependent, but the difference can be observed only in some locales. One of the most problematic is the Turkish locale (`-Duser.language=tr`). Turkish has two separate *I* letters: dotted *İ/i* and dotless *I/ı*. Therefore, the lowercase version of the usual English *I* is not *i* but *ı*. Conversely, the uppercase version of the usual English *i* is not *I* but *İ*. This may cause unexpected results when you are working with strings that are not written in the user's language. If you want to normalize the case of XML tags, YAML keys, or some kind of internal identifiers, the program might not behave correctly if it's launched with the default Turkish locale. For example,

```
String type = "point";
boolean isPoint = type.toUpperCase().equals("POINT"); ◄──┐
```
isPoint is true in most locales but false in the Turkish locale.

Azerbaijani, which is close to Turkish, is affected in the same way. So, if your application is expected to be launched by customers from different countries, it may behave incorrectly.

Another tricky thing about case conversions is that this operation may change the length of the string. A widely known case is the German letter *ß*, which is replaced with *SS* when converted to uppercase. As a result, for example, the word *Straße* (*street*) is six characters long, while `"Straße".toUpperCase(Locale.GERMAN)` is *STRASSE*, which is seven characters long. If your code assumes the length of user input will stay the same after case conversion, it may pass many tests until a failure in production.

Static analysis

You can find existing `toLowerCase()` and `toUpperCase()` calls without a locale argument using the static analysis tools. The corresponding IntelliJ IDEA inspection name is Call to `String.toUpperCase()` or `toLowerCase()` Without a Locale. SonarLint has a rule named S1449: String Operations Should Not Rely on the Default System Locale (turned off by default).

WAYS TO AVOID THIS MISTAKE

- Avoid using `toLowerCase()` and `toUpperCase()` methods without an argument. If you don't want to stick to a particular natural language, specify the so-called root locale `type.toUpperCase(Locale.ROOT)`, which is a special locale for language- or country-neutral code, whenever possible. If you actually want to use the default user locale specified in the OS settings or environment variables, it's better to specify it explicitly, as in `type.toUpperCase(Locale.getDefault())`. In this case, it will be clear to readers of the code that the default locale is actually intended, not used by mistake.
- Test your application with different default locale settings, including the Turkish locale. Continuous integration tools support so-called matrix jobs or matrix builds when you run the same tests in different environments. Adding another test run with the `-Duser.language=tr` option could be a good idea.

6.3   *Mistake 47: Using String.format with the default locale*

Another common method that uses the default language locale is `String.format()`. The most common problem with this method is formatting floating-point numbers. The decimal separator character is . in the US locale but could be , in many other locales, like German. For example,

```
double d = 1.234;
String formattedNumber = String.format("%.2f", d);
System.out.println(formattedNumber);
```
**Prints 1.23 in US locale
but 1,23 in German locale**

As of Java 15, another flavor of this method, which is called `formatted()`, is available, so you can use `"%.2f".formatted(d)` instead of `String.format("%.2f", d)`. The new method also uses the default locale, so you will get the same result.

It's usually fine if you just print this number to the user. However, sometimes, programs try to parse back the number. Let's consider the following trivial Swing program, which asks for a number and calculates the square root:

```
import javax.swing.*;

class CalculateSquareRoot {
  public static void main(String[] args) {
    String def = String.format("%.2f", Math.PI);
    String result = JOptionPane.showInputDialog(
                "Enter the number", def);
    String message;
    try {
      message = String.format("Square root is %.2f",
        Math.sqrt(Double.parseDouble(result)));
    } catch (NumberFormatException e) {
      message = "Incorrect number!";
    }
    JOptionPane.showMessageDialog(null, message);
  }
}
```
**Use π as a
default value.**

This program provides a default value for user input. It works perfectly when launched under the US locale. However, in the German locale, the input prompt is shown in figure 6.3.

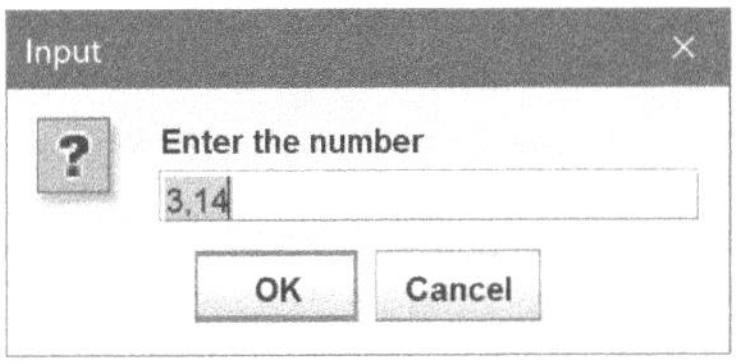

As you can see, a comma is used here as the decimal separator. If the user agrees with the default and just presses Enter, the program immediately complains that the entered number is invalid, even though the value was suggested

**Figure 6.3   A simple application that
prompts a number**

by the program in the first place. That's because the `Double.parseDouble()` method is not locale specific and it always expects `.` as a decimal separator.

Things may become more complicated if you are using a grouping separator when formatting numbers. It can be a comma, period, space, or other character, depending on the locale. The `DecimalFormat` class uses it by default. You may try the following:

```
var english = NumberFormat.getInstance(Locale.ENGLISH);
System.out.println(english.format(12345));
var german = NumberFormat.getInstance(Locale.GERMAN);
System.out.println(german.format(12345));
```
**The output is 12,345 (comma is
used as a grouping separator).**

**The output is 12.345 (period is
used as a grouping separator).**

Imagine you are using the default locale to format numbers calling getNumber-Instance() without a locale argument, but subsequent code tries to parse the resulting string assuming that . is a decimal separator. In this case, you'll get no exception, but the number will be incorrectly reinterpreted as a thousandth fraction of the original number.

WAYS TO AVOID THIS MISTAKE

- Do not use locale-independent methods, like parseDouble(), together with locale-aware methods, like String.format(). If you want to support parsing numbers in different locales, consider using the same NumberFormat object for both formatting and parsing:

```
NumberFormat format = NumberFormat.getInstance(locale);
double input = 12345.67;
String str = format.format(input);
double output = format.parse(str).doubleValue();  ⟵  The output is equal to
                                                      the input in any locale.
```

- When using methods like String.format() or NumberFormat.getInstance(), always consider the context in which the resulting string will be used. You can explicitly specify the desired locale as the first argument when necessary.

- Remember that often, the default locale is not the best option. This is especially true if you are developing a backend application. The default locale of the server may differ from the user's locale.

6.4   *Mistake 48: Mismatched format arguments*

The String.format() method and its friends, like PrintStream.printf(), accept a format string and additional arguments. The additional arguments can be referenced via format specifiers inside the format string. A common mistake occurs when the additional arguments do not match the format string. Such a mistake usually occurs when a developer updates the format string and forgets to update the additional arguments correspondingly by adding new arguments or removing or reordering existing ones. Of course, the Java compiler will not warn about such a problem, and you will have incorrectly formatted string or runtime exceptions:

```
System.out.printf("Length is %d", "123");  ⟵  IllegalFormatConversionException:
                                               d != java.lang.String

System.out.printf("Hello, %s");  ⟵  MissingFormatArgumentException:
                                     Format specifier '%s'
```

Mismatched format arguments may not cause a runtime exception at all. Particularly, all the unused format arguments will be simply ignored. For example, consider the following code:

```
int x = 10;
int y = 20;
System.out.printf("Point is: %d\n", x, y);
```

This was likely intended to print `Point is: 10, 20`. The author of this code was probably distracted and did not write the format string correctly. In any case, this code produces no exception, but the output is simply `Point is: 10`, which might be unexpected.

Another case in which an exception is not produced is the `%b` specifier. It works as expected (appends `true` or `false`) when applied to a Boolean value. However, it can also be applied to any other object. In this case, it appends `true` for a non-null value and `false` for a `null` value. The `%s` specifier can be applied to any type, calling the `String.valueOf()` on the supplied value. So if you mix arguments for `%s` and `%b` specifiers, you'll get no exception but an incorrect output:

```
DayOfWeek dw = DayOfWeek.FRIDAY;
boolean isWeekend = dw == DayOfWeek.SATURDAY || dw == DayOfWeek.SUNDAY;
System.out.printf("Day: %s; isWeekend = %b\n",
                  isWeekend, dw);   ◁──┐  Printed: Day: false;
                                        isWeekend = true
```

Figure 6.4 illustrates how the format string is processed in this case.

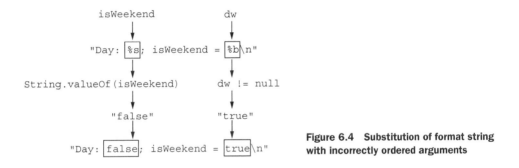

Figure 6.4   Substitution of format string with incorrectly ordered arguments

To get the correct output, you should reorder the arguments, as shown in figure 6.5:

```
System.out.printf("Day: %s; isWeekend = %b\n",
                  dw, isWeekend);   ◁──  Printed: Day: FRIDAY;
                                         isWeekend = false
```

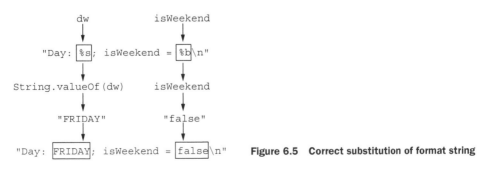

Figure 6.5   Correct substitution of format string

Static analysis

Static analyzers can usually warn when additional arguments do not correspond to the format string. IntelliJ IDEA has a Malformed Format String inspection to check this. It reports unused arguments and format strings that may cause exceptions but doesn't report, for example, using `%b` with a non-Boolean value. SonarLint reports such problems via the rules S2275: Printf-Style Format Strings Should Not Lead to Unexpected Behavior at Runtime and S3457: Printf-Style Format Strings Should Be Used Correctly (the latter can report the `%b` problem). The Error Prone analyzer has a FormatString bug pattern.

You should remember that static analyzers check format strings only if they're explicitly specified. Some analyzers may support compile-time constants, like static final fields, but will still remain silent if you construct a format string in a complex way. So you should help the static analyzer if you want the static analyzer to help you. Avoid nontrivial computation of format strings when possible.

Your project may have custom methods that have the same formatting behavior and delegate to `String.format()`. It's unlikely that static analyzers will be able to recognize them automatically. In this case, learn how to mark these methods for static analysis. For example, the Error Prone analyzer recognizes `@FormatString` and `@FormatMethod` annotations to mark the custom format method:

```
@FormatMethod void log(@FormatString String format,
                       Object... args) { … }
```

Similarly, IntelliJ IDEA recognizes the `@PrintFormat` annotation from the JetBrains annotation package (see appendix A).

WAYS TO AVOID THIS MISTAKE

- Separate string construction and actual output logic, so you can easily write unit tests to assert the output string content. For example, suppose you want to greet the user of your command-line application and you have the following method:

```
void greetUser(String userName) {
  System.out.printf("Hello, %s!%n", userName);
}
```

It's better to extract the string construction using the `String.format()` method:

```
void greetUser(String userName) {
  System.out.print(getGreeting(userName));
}

String getGreeting(String userName) {
  return String.format("Hello, %s!%n", userName);
}
```

Now, it's much simpler to write a unit-test for the `getGreeting()` method, so if you make a mistake there, you'll see a failing unit test.

- You can refer to the explicit position inside the format specifiers, as in the following example:

```
System.out.printf("Hello, %2$s! Today is %1$tD.",
                    LocalDate.now(), "John");
```

Here, `%2$s` means *use the second additional argument*. Consider using this syntax, as it's more robust. For example, you can rephrase the format string reordering the specifiers as you want without the need to reorder the additional arguments correspondingly. This is especially important if you build the format string dynamically or plan to externalize the strings for localization.

6.5   Mistake 49: Using plain strings instead of regular expressions

Some methods of the `String` class accept a regular expression string as an argument. This includes the `matches()`, `replaceFirst()`, `replaceAll()`, and `split()` methods. Occasionally, people forget about this and think that the corresponding method accepts a literal, rather than a regular expression. Mistakes mostly appear with the `split()` and `replaceAll()` methods. Consider the following example using the `split()` method:

```
String javaPackage = "java.util.concurrent";
String[] parts = javaPackage.split(".");
```

It was intended to split the `"java.util.concurrent"` string into three parts, like `["java", "util", "concurrent"]`. However, the dot character is interpreted as a regular expression that means *any character*. Now, every character of the input string will act as a delimiter, and as the length of the `javaPackage` string is 20 characters, the result of the split should be an array of 21 empty strings.

Well, in fact, this is not the case, due to another sometimes surprising property of the `split()` method. By default, it removes trailing empty strings. There's an overload of `split()` method that accepts the additional, and somewhat confusing, `int limit` parameter. Positive values of `limit` indicate how many parts to extract at most, so you can use it if you need to stop splitting at some point. The zero value of `limit` is the default and can be omitted. This means the matching is unlimited, but the trailing empty matches are removed. For example, the following code will produce an array of three elements, a, b, and c, without trailing empty strings:

```
String[] strings = "a,b,c,,,".split(",", 0);
```

If you actually need the trailing empty matches, you should explicitly pass –1 as a limit instead of 0.

Returning to our original sample, the `split(".")` call will ignore empty matches and produce an empty array, regardless of the input. If you actually want to split by a dot character, you must escape the dot with a backslash. Don't forget, though, that the backslash is handled as an escape character by Java itself. To pass it to the `split()` method as is, you need to type it twice:

```
String[] parts = javaPackage.split("\\.");
```

Alternatively, you can use the `Pattern.quote()` static method:

```
String[] parts = javaPackage.split(Pattern.quote("."));
```

This method quotes any sequence of symbols, so when using it, you need not worry about whether a given character has a special meaning inside regular expressions.

Aside from the dot pattern, the pipe pattern | is often mistakenly used in a split without escaping. In this case, the pattern matches an empty string, so the input string will be split to an array of one-character substrings.

Another potential caveat is using `split()` with the `File.separator` constant. For example, imagine you want to split the file path to the separate elements:

```
String path = new File(".").getAbsolutePath();
String[] parts = path.split(File.separator);
```

On Unix and Mac machines, `File.separator` is /, which has no special treatment in regular expression, so this code works as expected. However, if you launch the same program on Windows, `File.separator` will be a backslash, which is a meta character. Now, the regular expression compiler fails with `PatternSyntaxException` because one more character is expected after the backslash.

Static analysis

Static analyzers may warn you about the previously mentioned suspicious regular expressions. IntelliJ IDEA has an inspection named Suspicious Regex Expression Argument, which reports these problems. Error Prone reports regular expressions consisting of single dot via the BareDotMetacharacter pattern. SpotBugs reports these problems using the bug patterns . or | Used for Regular Expression and `File.separator` Used for Regular Expression. Unfortunately, static analyzers may not help if the delimiter is not a constant (e.g., passed as a method parameter). Also, it's possible that a more complex delimiter is used, which may not be recognized by a static analyzer as suspicious.

WAYS TO AVOID THIS MISTAKE

- Avoid using `String.split()`, unless you actually need to split by regular expression. If you are limited to Java standard library, you may use

```
String[] parts = Pattern.compile(delimiter, Pattern.LITERAL)
  .split(stringToSplit);
```

This snippet could be extracted into a utility method. Here, we explicitly say that `delimiter` is a plain literal. If you can use third-party libraries, there are many alternatives to split the string. For example, Guava library (https://github.com/google/guava) has a Splitter API:

```
List<String> parts = Splitter.on(delimiter)
                             .splitToList(stringToSplit);
```

Another popular utility library, Apache Commons Lang, features the `String-Utils` class, which provides various ways to split the string:

```
String[] parts = StringUtils.splitByWholeSeparator(
                     stringToSplit, delimiter);
```

- Do not use string operations like `split()` to manipulate file paths. The `Path` class provides all the necessary methods to do this in safe and OS-independent way. In particular, you may simply iterate the `Path` variable to get the components:

```
Path absolutePath = Path.of(".").toAbsolutePath();
for (Path path : absolutePath) {
    System.out.println(path);
}
```

6.6   *Mistake 50: Accidental use of replaceAll*

Sometimes, people mistakenly use the `replaceAll()` method instead of `replace()`. The `String` class API is, indeed, somewhat confusing. When you see two methods named `replace()` and `replaceAll()`, both accepting two parameters, it's quite natural to assume the former makes only one replacement, while the latter replaces all the occurrences. However, both of them actually replace all the occurrences, and the real difference is that `replace()` accepts a plain literal, while `replaceAll()` accepts a regular expression pattern. If you really need to replace only the first occurrence, there's one more method, `replaceFirst()`, which also accepts a regular expression.

Using `replaceAll()` instead of `replace()` is harmless if both the search and replacement strings are constant and don't contain any special characters. In this case, you will only have a performance degradation, as in modern Java versions `replace()` is significantly faster than `replaceAll()`. However, the search string is not always a constant. Sometimes, it comes from an external source, like user input. It may pass simple tests but fail on more sophisticated queries used in production.

Do not forget that the replacement string in `replaceAll()` is not just plain text either. If special character sequences, like *$0*, *$1*, and so on, appear there, they will be replaced with the corresponding matching groups from the regular expression. For example, consider the following method:

```
static void greetUser(String user) {
    String template = "Hello USER_NAME!";
    String greeting = template.replaceAll("USER_NAME", user);
    System.out.println(greeting);
}
```

This is a common way to create a poor man's template: just replace some special character sequences with your variables. There is nothing particularly wrong with this approach, but here, `replaceAll()` was used instead of `replace()` by mistake. It may look safe, as the search text is a constant literal that does not contain any special regular expression characters. However, if your service allows symbols like $ in the username, you can get unexpected results. For example, if a username is *$0ccerman*, it will be printed as `Hello USER_NAMEccerman!` because `$0` is replaced with the whole search pattern. Even worse, if the username is *$1lverG1rl*, you'll get an `IndexOutOfBounds-Exception` because there's no matching $1 group.

> **Static analysis**
>
> The SonarLint static analyzer recognizes and reports when `replaceAll()` is used with a constant regular expression argument that does not contain any special characters. The rule name is S5361: `String#replace` Should Be Preferred to `String#replaceAll`. Its description says this is a performance problem, as an unnecessary regular expression is compiled. However, as we can see, this could be a correctness problem as well, so don't ignore these reports, even if you think your program doesn't require top performance.

WAYS TO AVOID THIS MISTAKE

- Remember that you need the `replace()` method, unless you have a regular expression.
- Modern IDEs provide parameter hints and may highlight regular expressions differently. Pay attention to these hints and highlighting. Figure 6.6 shows what the example looks like in popular IDEs with default settings.

```
// IntelliJ IDEA
String template = "Hello USER_NAME!";
String greeting = template.replaceAll( regex: "USER_NAME",  replacement: user);

// Eclipse
String template = "Hello USER_NAME!";
String greeting = template.replaceAll(regex: "USER_NAME", replacement: user);
```

Figure 6.6   Parameter hints `regex` and `replacement`, shown in IntelliJ IDEA and Eclipse

Note that there are hints like `regex` and `replacement`. The `regex` hint is a sign that you are using the wrong method. Also, the `"USER_NAME"` literal in IntelliJ IDEA has a background color, which means there's another language (regular expression) injected there. This may also help to avoid the mistake.

6.7   *Mistake 51: Accidental use of escape sequences*

There are several escape sequences supported in Java literals. All of them start with a backslash. You may readily remember `'\n'` (line break), `'\t'` (tab character), `'\''`

(single quote), or '\"' (double quote). Others are probably less used: '\r' (carriage return), '\b' (backspace), and '\f' (form feed). Since Java 15 introduced text blocks, a new escape character, '\s', was added to designate a single space. If you want to add a backslash character to the string, you should escape it as well, using '\\'.

Sometimes, when developers want to enter a backslash, they forget to escape it. In most cases, this will lead to a compilation error, as only a limited subset of symbols is allowed after a backslash. However, it's still possible for the next symbol to be accepted by a compiler and the developer to get a completely different string instead of an error.

Such a problem is possible in rare cases when you work with Windows file paths, where a backslash is used as a separator symbol. For example,

```
String archiverPath = installationPath + "\bin\tar.exe";
```

This declaration is compiled without errors, but the resulting string will unexpectedly contain a backspace and tab symbol, instead of 'b', 't', and the directory separators.

Fortunately, raw Windows file paths rarely occur in Java programs, and it's even more unlikely that all the symbols after backslashes happen to be valid escape characters. It becomes more problematic when you use regular expressions.

Regular expressions have their own interpretation of symbols that follow a backslash. For most Java escape sequences, including '\n', '\t', '\r', and '\f', the corresponding regular expression escape sequence means the same. Therefore, it doesn't matter whether you escape the initial backslash or not. For example, in Java programs, the regular expressions "\t" and "\\t" mean the same thing: a single tab character. In the former case, it's unescaped by the Java compiler, while in the latter case, a double backslash is unescaped by the Java compiler to a single backslash, and the resulting "\t" is unescaped by the regular expression engine.

However, '\b' is a notable exception. While Java interprets it as a backspace, for the regular expression engine, it's a word boundary. This is where confusion appears. For example, you want to replace all the occurrences of the conjunction *and* with *or* without mangling words like *hand* or *android*. Using a word-boundary matcher seems like a good idea; however, it's quite easy to make a mistake and write

```
String result = s.replaceAll("\band\b", "or");
```

This code can be compiled, but the regular expression engine will look for *and* surrounded by two backspace characters, so it will be unlikely to find any instances. The correct code would be

```
String result = s.replaceAll("\\band\\b", "or");
```

The new '\s' escape sequence, which simply represents a space, is another source of mistakes. Although its main purpose is to avoid unwanted trimming of spaces at the end of a text block line, this sequence can be used in classic string literals as well. However, in regular expressions, '\s' means any whitespace character, including tab, new line, and so on. This difference may lead to subtle mistakes. For example, if you need to split an input line into fragments, using any white-space character as a separator, you may want to use a regular expression. In this case, it's easy to introduce a small mistake:

```
String[] parts = str.split("\s+");        ⟵┤ \\s+ was intended.
```

This regular expression is equivalent to " +", which matches only spaces. The bad thing is that this code not only compiles but also works correctly sometimes when other whitespace symbols, like tab, are not used in the input string. So it's quite possible for the mistake to be overlooked and to slip into production.

> ## Static analysis
>
> IntelliJ IDEA reports suspicious uses of `'\s'` with the Non-terminal Use of `'\s'` Escape Sequence inspection. The `"\band\b"` case is not reported by IntelliJ IDEA. However, SonarLint produces a performance warning here, suggesting to use `replace()` instead of `replaceAll()`, as from the regular expression point of view, `"\band\b"` does not contain any special characters. This could be also a hint, though it won't work if you use any other regular expression meta characters aside from `'\b'`.

WAYS TO AVOID THIS MISTAKE

- Be careful when using backslash in Java string literals. Remember that it always should be escaped. Pay attention to the IDE highlighting. Escape sequences are usually highlighted in a different way from normal text. For example, figure 6.7 shows how escape sequences are highlighted in IntelliJ IDEA. Unlike normal characters, escape sequences can be displayed using different font weight and color, depending on the color scheme used.

```
String archiverPath = installationPath + "\bin\tar.exe";
```

Figure 6.7   Highlighting of escape sequences '\b' and '\t' in IntelliJ IDEA

- Avoid using Windows file paths as raw strings in Java code. If possible, construct paths using the appropriate API methods, like `Path.of`:

```
Path archiverPath =
        Path.of(installationPath, "bin", "tar.exe");
```

This way, you not only avoid problems with backslashes but also make your program more portable and get some postprocessing for free. For example, here, the result will be the same, regardless of whether `installationPath` ends with a backslash.

- Be especially careful when using `'\b'` and `'\s'` within a regular expression. Always test whether a regular expression actually matches what is expected. For the `'\s'` pattern, ensure that not only space but also other whitespace characters, like tabs, are properly matched.

6.8   *Mistake 52: Comparing strings in different case*

Sometimes, developers use the `toLowerCase()` or `toUpperCase()` methods to normalize a string value, so it can be compared with something in a case-insensitive manner. Unfortunately, this operation may lead to bugs, especially if the case conversion was not there initially. A bug like this was discovered in the XMage game engine. At some point, the code looked like this:

```
if (filterMessage.startsWith("Each ")) {
  …
}
```

After a while, a case normalization was added, and the condition was changed to the following:

```
if (filterMessage.toLowerCase(Locale.ENGLISH)
              .startsWith("Each ")) {
  …
}
```

Unfortunately, the case normalization was not applied to the constant on the right. As a result, this condition cannot be true, as a lowercase-only string cannot start with E. It was unnoticed for 5 years, until it was caught by the PVS-Studio static analyzer.

Static analysis

Static analyzers can help in simple cases, like this example. IntelliJ IDEA has the Mismatched Case in `String` Operation inspection, which may be helpful. PVS-Studio reports this mistake as a part of the V6007: Expression Is Always True/False warning. Unfortunately, the check could be more complex (e.g., the prefix might come from another method), and the inspection might not catch the bug.

WAYS TO AVOID THIS MISTAKE

- Be careful when adding case normalization before comparison, as this could be a source of errors. Add a unit test to ensure the condition actually works.
- When the string to search is not constant, consider adding an assertion or precondition as a defensive measure. For example, consider a method that checks whether a given string starts with one of the prefixes from the given set. The implementation looks like this:

```
boolean hasOneOfPrefixes(String str, Set<String> prefixes) {
  String lowercased = str.toLowerCase(Locale.ROOT);
  for (String prefix : prefixes) {
    assert prefix.equals(prefix.toLowerCase(Locale.ROOT));
    if (lowercased.startsWith(prefix)) {
```

```
            return true;
          }
      }
    return false;
}
```

Here, it's expected that the prefixes in the set are already lowercase. If this is not the case, the prefix might be silently ignored. An assert statement helps to signal such a situation.

- There's a `regionMatches()` method in the `String` class that can be used to match the string prefix or suffix in a case-insensitive manner. For example, the `filterMessage` example mentioned previously could be rewritten this way:

```
String prefix = "Each ";
int len = prefix.length();
if (filterMessage.length() >= len &&
    filterMessage.regionMatches(true, 0, prefix, 0, len)) {
    …
}
```

This method is not very convenient to use directly, but if you need case-insensitive prefix matching in your project, you can create a utility method like this:

```
public static boolean startsWithIgnoreCase
        (String str, String prefix) {
  int strLen = str.length();
  int prefixLen = prefix.length();
  return strLen >= prefixLen &&
        str.regionMatches(true, 0, prefix, 0, prefixLen);
}
```

Using it instead of the `toLowerCase().startsWith()` sequence is not only more robust but also more performant, as unlike `toLowerCase()`, `region-Matches()` does not allocate a new string.

6.9   *Mistake 53: Not checking the result of indexOf method*

There are several search methods in the `String` class named `indexOf()` and `last-IndexOf()`. All of them return the position of the found occurrence or −1 if an occurrence is not found. One of the common mistakes I have observed is failure to handle the not-found case.

Usually, the found index is used for a subsequent `substring()` call or something similar. Often, this immediately leads to an exception, as `substring()` does not accept negative numbers as input. For example, here, it's intended to parse a line like `key = value` into an entry:

```
static Entry<String, String> parseEntry(String entry) {
  int pos = entry.indexOf('=');
  return Map.entry(
    entry.substring(0, pos).trim(),
```

```
    entry.substring(pos + 1).trim());
}
```

Passing a line that does not contain an equal sign will cause a `StringIndexOutOf-BoundsException`, as `pos = -1` is passed as a substring argument. While such code may slip into production due to lack of testing, having an exception is a fortunate case, as it immediately manifests the error. It's possible that the exception is actually the desired behavior and the only problem is that the exception message is unclear, so the proper fix would be to throw another exception, like this:

```
if (pos == -1) {
  throw new IllegalArgumentException(
    "Entry must have key and value, separated by '='");
}
```

However, in some cases, code execution will continue silently. For example, here, it was intended to return a substring after the dot position:

```
static String getExtension(String fileName) {
  return fileName.substring(fileName.lastIndexOf('.') + 1);
}
```

It works nicely if the filename actually contains a dot character. However, it's also possible that there's no dot at all. In this case, `lastIndexOf` returns −1, and the method will compute `fileName.substring(0)`, which is simply the whole filename. It's unclear whether this is an intended behavior, but likely, it's not. At least, I would not assume the file named png (without an extension) is an image file.

Things may become worse if the search string is longer than one character. For example, here, we assume the line contains a Java-like end-of-line comment starting with // and we want to extract its contents:

```
static String getCommentContent(String lineWithComment) {
  int pos = lineWithComment.indexOf("//") + 2;
  return lineWithComment.substring(pos).trim();
}
```

Again, it works nicely if we already know for certain that the line contains the comment. However, if it doesn't, we will just get the whole line except the very first symbol. One can only guess what will happen next if we interpret this substring as the content of a comment. It will also fail with an exception if the input line is an empty string.

Sometimes, people check for a −1 special value but only after adjusting the offset. For example, a developer may want to fix the previous method and add a condition like this:

```
static String getCommentContent(String lineWithComment) {
  int pos = lineWithComment.indexOf("//") + 2;
  if (pos == -1) {
    throw new IllegalArgumentException("Line has no comment");
  }
```

```
    return lineWithComment.substring(pos).trim();
}
```

It may look like the code is fixed, but in fact, it isn't. If the `indexOf()` call returns −1, we add 2 immediately, so we will store +1 in `pos`. As a result, this condition is never satisfied.

> **Static analysis**
>
> Static analysis tools will sometimes help with this. For example, the IntelliJ IDEA Constant Values inspection can infer that the `pos == -1` condition in the previous code sample is always `false`. However, it doesn't help in the other cases.
>
> Some people prefer comparing the `indexOf()` result with 0. It's perfectly fine to write `indexOf(subString) >= 0` or `indexOf(subString) < 0` instead of comparing to −1 exactly. However, I have also observed a typo like `indexOf(subString) > 0`. In this case, you cannot tell whether the substring is not found or it's found at zero offset. SonarLint has a rule named S2692: `indexOf` Checks Should Not Be for Positive Numbers, which reports comparisons like this.

WAYS TO AVOID THIS MISTAKE

- Always check the result of `indexOf()` and `lastIndexOf()` for −1 immediately, before performing any computation or passing this value anywhere else.
- If you look for a particular substring in a string, consider what will happen if this substring is absent. Add such scenarios to unit tests.
- Consider using libraries that provide higher-level methods for string processing. For example, the Apache Commons Lang library has a method called `StringUtils.substringAfter()` that returns a substring after a given delimiter, effectively combining `substring()` and `indexOf()` calls. However, in this case, it's also possible for the delimiter to be absent, so it's important to read the method documentation to determine how the method behaves in this case. The `substringAfter()` method returns an empty string if the delimiter is missing. Such behavior might not always be appropriate.
- When designing your own API, avoid using special numeric values, like −1, to depict the absence of a result. Instead, use special data types, like `OptionalInt`. This way, users of your API will be forced to handle the absence case and an accidental math operation before the special value check will be impossible.

6.10 *Mistake 54: Mixing arguments of indexOf*

Sometimes, it's necessary to search for a character in a string from an intermediate position instead of from the beginning. The `String.indexOf()` method accepts two arguments: the character to search for and the starting index. The problem is that it accepts the character as an `int` number that represents the Unicode codepoint. So we have two `int` arguments, and it's quite possible to mix them up. For example, imagine we are writing a method to extract a substring that starts with [and ends with]. It may look like this:

```
static String getBracketedSubstring(String s) {
  int start = s.indexOf('[');
  if (start == -1) return null;
  int end = s.indexOf(start, ']');          Attempt to find the closing
  if (end == -1) return null;               bracket after the start position
  return s.substring(start, end + 1);
}
```

Here, the order of arguments in the second `indexOf()` call is incorrect. Unfortunately, the compiler will not reject this code, and we will see no exceptions at run time. However, it doesn't work. For most strings, it will find nothing, but in rare cases, it may return a non-null but incorrect string (as a funny exercise, you can try to construct such an input when non-null is returned).

Static analysis

The Error Prone static analyzer reports this problem with the bug pattern IndexOfChar.

WAYS TO AVOID THIS MISTAKE

- While mixing argument order here may not produce an exception, the program behavior will be clearly incorrect, so even a single simple unit test will likely reveal the problem. Write tests for all your string-processing code. Testing string-processing functions is quite easy, and it pays back.
- Pay attention to parameter hints in your IDE. We already mentioned them when we discussed accidental use of `replaceAll()` instead of `replace()`, but they may also be helpful to spot misplaced arguments if the method is correct. Figure 6.8 shows how parameter hints look in IntelliJ IDEA and Eclipse for an erroneous call.

```
// IntelliJ IDEA
int end = s.indexOf( ch: start,   fromIndex: ']');

// Eclipse
int end = s.indexOf(ch: start, fromIndex: ']');
```

**Figure 6.8   Parameter hints in IntelliJ IDEA and Eclipse for the
`indexOf()` method**

As you can see, the hint says the last parameter name is `fromIndex`, and it looks strange that the character is specified there.

Summary

- The Java `char` type does not always correspond to an actual character. A character represented by two `char` values is known as a *surrogate pair*. To support emojis and other unusual characters, your code should be able to process them correctly.

- The default system locale may cause surprises. For example, the Turkish locale has an unexpected rule for uppercase and lowercase conversion. Many other locales use a comma instead of a dot as the decimal separator. Be careful when using methods, like `toUpperCase()` or `format()`, that rely on the default system locale.

- String formatting methods contain the format string and several format arguments. The Java compiler won't warn you if the arguments don't match the format string. Static analysis may help here but only if the format string is a constant.

- Some string-processing library methods, like `replaceAll()` or `split()`, accept a regular expression. It's easy to forget about this and assume that a simple literal should be passed there. Don't forget that the `replace()` method replaces the substring, while `replaceAll()` replaces the regular expression.

- Java string literals support several escape sequences, like `'\b'` and `'\t'`. In rare cases, it's possible to use them accidentally, creating a completely incorrect literal. Special care should be taken with regular expressions in which the backslash character has its own meaning.

- The `indexOf()` method returns −1 if the character or substring is not found. It's important to handle this case before doing anything else with the return value.

- Sometimes, it's easy to use the wrong method or accidentally swap the method parameters. Pay attention to parameter hints in your IDE to avoid this problem.

Comparing objects

This chapter covers

- Why you should not use reference equality for boxed types
- Standard classes for which the `equals()` method behaves unexpectedly or is not defined at all
- How to properly implement `equals()`, `hashCode()`, `compare()`, and `compareTo()`
- What can happen if you use a malformed comparison method

Object comparison is exceptionally important in Java. There are several methods associated with object comparison: `equals()`, `hashCode()`, `Comparable` `.compareTo()`, and `Comparator.compare()`. They are used implicitly by many algorithms (e.g., `Arrays.sort()`) and data structures (e.g., `HashMap`). Failure to implement them correctly may lead to annoying, difficult-to-debug problems.

If you are going to implement any of these methods, there's good news and bad news. The good news is that the contracts for these methods are perfectly specified in the Java documentation. The algorithms will function correctly, as long as you strictly follow the contracts. The bad news is that the contracts are somewhat tricky to implement, and there are many ways to screw things up.

Even if you don't implement these methods by yourself, you should be careful when using them. For some classes, `equals()` behaves in an unexpected way. There's also the reference equality operator `==`, which adds confusion, as sometimes, people mistakenly use `==` instead of `equals()`, or vice versa.

7.1   Mistake 55: Use of reference equality instead of the equals method

Java provides two common ways to compare objects. One of them is the `==` operator, which compares references to the objects and returns `true` if both references point to the same object. Another is the `equals()` method called on one of the objects. You can implement this method in the way you like, but it's commonly agreed that `equals()` is used to compare objects by content, so it will return `true` if the objects are equivalent and one of them can be used instead of other. The contract requires `a.equals(b)` to return `true` if `a == b`, but it may return true in other cases as well.

Sometimes, programmers accidentally use `==` instead of `equals()`, probably because it's easier to type or they forget about the difference between these ways to compare objects. This may cause subtle errors, as sometimes, the program may still work correctly.

One common case is using `==` to compare primitive wrapper classes, like `Boolean`, `Integer`, or `Long`. Unfortunately, sometimes, reference equality works for these objects due to caching implemented in autoboxing:

```
Integer i1 = 100;
Integer i2 = 100;                    Prints
System.out.println(i1 == i2);   ◁─┘  true
```

That's because, according to the specification, `Integer` values between −128 and 127 are always cached. During the virtual machine startup, Java creates `Integer` objects between −128 and 127 and stores them in an internal array in the `IntegerCache` private class. When you assign a primitive number, like 100, to an `Integer` object, an `Integer.valueOf()` method is called implicitly, which uses the value from the cache if the number is small enough (figure 7.1).

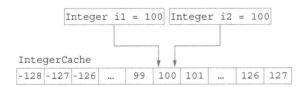

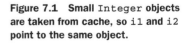

Figure 7.1 Small `Integer` objects are taken from cache, so `i1` and `i2` point to the same object.

So, if you use `==` but all your numbers are small and created only via autoboxing, then it may work. However, if larger values appear someday, they might not be available in the cache. In this case, a new object is created every time you assign a primitive number to an `Integer` variable (figure 7.2).

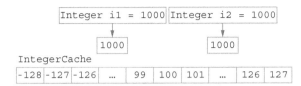

Figure 7.2   Larger `Integer` objects may not appear in the cache, so a new separate object is created every time.

As a result, your program may stop working:

```
Integer i1 = 1000;
Integer i2 = 1000;
System.out.println(i1 == i2);
```
Usually prints false

In fact, the behavior in this case is not specified. If you launch HotSpot JVM with the undocumented `-XX:AutoBoxCacheMax=1000` command line option, the preceding code will print `true`, as Java will cache more numbers. `Boolean` and `Byte` values are always cached during the autoboxing, but it's still possible to create new instances of these objects using a constructor, like `new Boolean(true)`:

```
Boolean b1 = true;
Boolean b2 = true;
Boolean b3 = new Boolean(true);
System.out.println(b1 == b2);
System.out.println(b1 == b3);
```
Prints true

Prints false

Public constructors for primitive wrappers are deprecated for removal in recent Java versions, so this possibility may disappear in the future. As of Java 21, however, you can still encounter different instances of `Boolean` and `Byte` wrappers. Note that you may step on this, even if you don't invoke the `Boolean` constructor explicitly. One notable example is a return value from the methods called reflectively. Consider the following sample:

```
import java.lang.reflect.Method;

public class Test {
  public static void main(String[] args) throws Exception {
    Method test = Test.class.getMethod("test");
    System.out.println(test.invoke(null) == Boolean.TRUE);
  }

  public static boolean test() {
    return true;
  }
}
```
May print false, depending on Java version and number of invocations

Here, you have a trivial method called `test()` that simply returns a primitive `true` value. This method is invoked via the Reflection API. As `invoke()` returns `Object`, the primitive value should be wrapped into the `Boolean` object somewhere inside the reflection implementation. The actual result depends on the Java version. Up to Java 17, the newly created object is returned, so this code prints `false`. However, if you call the same method reflectively more than 16 times, optimized implementation will be used instead, which uses a cached `Boolean` object, so if you wrap the `main()` method into a loop, it will start printing `true` eventually. Starting with Java 18, the Reflection API has been reimplemented in a more modern way, using method handles. As a side effect, now, new instances of `Boolean` are never created, and this code always prints `true`. Still, if you call the method returning a primitive value reflectively on Java 17, you may observe new instances of the `Boolean` object.

Another common mistake is comparing `String` objects using `==`. `String` objects that appear as compile-time constants in the source code are deduplicated or interned by the virtual machine automatically, so in some cases, == may work correctly. However, once you get a string that was non-trivially created, the comparison will not be successful, as separate string objects will be created:

```
String greeting = "Hello";
System.out.println(greeting == "Hello");      ⟵┤ Prints true
String greeting2 = greeting + "!";
System.out.println(greeting2 == "Hello!");    ⟵┤ Prints false
```

Here, the first comparison prints `true`, as both instances of `"Hello"` refer to the same object. On the other hand, the `greeting2` string is not a compile-time constant. It's evaluated at run time, so this is a new instance of `"Hello!"` string, which is not the same as the constant `"Hello!"` string you are comparing it with. Of course, if you use the `equals()` method instead of `==`, you'll get `true` in both cases.

Static analysis

Comparison of numbers via == is reported by the IntelliJ IDEA inspection Number Comparison Using ==, Instead of `equals()`. Similarly, comparisons of strings are reported by String Comparison Using ==, Instead of `equals()`. SonarLint reports comparisons of all boxed types and strings with rule S4973: Strings and Boxed Types Should Be Compared Using `equals()`. Unfortunately, neither one reports on comparisons of `Boolean` objects.

WAYS TO AVOID THIS MISTAKE

- Never use reference equality for any of the primitive wrapper types. Similarly, do not use it for strings. In exceptionally rare cases, it might be justified for performance reasons, but it should be proven by carefully profiling. Remember that if you are using reference equality for strings, you are stepping on slippery ground and the code may stop working after innocent-looking changes like using a string concatenation expression.

- Avoid using primitive wrapper types in general. If they are necessary, unwrap them as soon as possible.

7.2 Mistake 56: Assuming equals() compares content

It's usually assumed that if you need to compare objects by content, rather than references, you should use the `equals()` method instead of the `==` operator. Unfortunately, this doesn't always work as expected because the `equals()` method itself is not always defined, and when it's not defined, the default implementation from `java.lang.Object` is used, which silently works as `==` (*identity* `equals`). Likely the most famous object type that lacks specialized `equals()` implementation is Java array. To compare arrays by content, one must use the `Arrays.equals()` or `Arrays.deepEquals()` static methods. There are also lesser-known classes in JDK that unexpectedly don't define `equals()`:

- `StringBuilder` *and* `StringBuffer`—One may expect `StringBuilder.equals()` to compare the content of two `StringBuilder` instances. Since Java 11, you have been able to use `builder1.compareTo(builder2) == 0` to check whether the content of two builders is the same. Alternatively, `builder1.toString().contentEquals(builder2)` could be used, though it requires additional memory to convert the content of one of the builders to string. Finally, you can compare manually by using a series of `StringBuilder.charAt()` calls.
- *Atomic variables, like* `AtomicInteger` *or* `AtomicReference`—It's quite expected that two `AtomicInteger` variables would compare their payload inside `equals()`, but it doesn't work; you should explicitly read their content via `get()`:

```
var v1 = new AtomicInteger(1);
var v2 = new AtomicInteger(1);                    Prints
System.out.println(v1.equals(v2));        ◁─┘     false
System.out.println(v1.get() == v2.get()); ◁─┤ Prints true
```

  Also, you should ask yourself whether comparison of atomic variables makes any sense in your case. Atomic variables are intended for concurrent updates, so if such an update is possible at this point, even if two variables happen to equal, this may not be the case anymore right after the comparison. Such a comparison may be useful only after all the updates are finished.
- `WeakReference` *and* `SoftReference`—These don't have `equals()` implemented, so different references are not equal, even if they refer to the same object.
- *Cryptographic keys* (`java.security.Key`)—Sometimes, you may want to determine whether two keys are equal. However, many `Key` interface implementations do not provide `equals()` method implementation, so you cannot robustly compare arbitrary keys.
- `Stream`—As Java Stream can be consumed only once and the `equals()` implementation that compares two streams by content would require stream consumption, you won't be able to call `equals()` twice, which violates the consistency rule

required for the `equals()` method. Moreover, if the `Stream.equals()` were defined, you wouldn't be able to perform any operation on the stream after using `equals()`, as it's already consumed. If you need to compare the contents of two streams, it's usually better to collect them into lists and compare. If you anticipate the streams may be long but likely differ, you may alternatively use `Stream .iterator()` on both streams and compare them element by element.

- `ArrayDeque`, `PriorityQueue`, *and others*—Usually, collections have an `equals()` method that allows comparing them by content. However, the specification requires this only for `List` and `Set` implementation. Care should be taken when you work with collections that are neither lists nor sets (in particular, queues).
- *Result of* `Collections.unmodifiableCollection()`, *even if applied to* `List` *or* `Set`—One may expect that it just delegates to the `equals()` method of the original collection, but it doesn't.

You might wonder why `unmodifiableCollection()` was implemented this way: to avoid breaking the `equals()` symmetry. To illustrate, let's create two identical collections:

```
List<Integer> list1 = Arrays.asList(1, 2, 3);
List<Integer> list2 = Arrays.asList(1, 2, 3);
System.out.println(list1.equals(list2));      ⊲─┤ Prints true
```

Now, what about `list1.equals(unmodifiableCollection(list2))`? `List.equals()` is specified to return `true` only if another object also implements `List` and has equal elements in the same order. However, the `unmodifiableCollection` wrapper doesn't implement `List` (even if it wraps the `List`), so in this case, `false` must be returned. And as `equals()` must be symmetric, `unmodifiableCollection(list2).equals(list1)` must also return `false`. Note that the `unmodifiableList()` and `unmodifiableSet()` methods return the collections whose `equals()` method properly compares the content.

Another mistake that occasionally happens is when `List` is compared to `Set`. Such comparisons always return `false` by specification, even if the elements in the collections are the same.

Static analysis

Some of the cases discussed in this subsection are reported by static analyzers. For example, IntelliJ IDEA has an `equals()` Called on `StringBuilder` inspection, and SonarLint has the rule S2204: `.equals()` Should Not Be Used to Test the Values of Atomic Classes. Also, IntelliJ IDEA may warn you if you try to compare `List` and `Set` with `equals()`. The corresponding inspection is named `equals()` Between Objects of Inconvertible Types. Unfortunately, I don't know a static analyzer that will report all the cases listed here.

- Learn the cases listed in this subsection. These are the classes from the standard library most likely to cause confusion.
- If you are working with an API that's new to you and want to compare objects by `equals()`, it's best to double check the API documentation or implementation to ensure `equals()` behavior is expected.
- You should be careful with the `Collection` type. When creating a new method, one may think that list-specific behavior is not necessary, so it's OK to accept any collection as a parameter. At this point, it is worth thinking about whether you need `equals()`. While `equals()` is present in every object, comparing by content is also list-specific behavior.
- Prefer using `unmodifiableList()` or `unmodifiableSet()` over `unmodifiable-Collection()` when possible.

7.3   *Mistake 57: Using URL.equals()*

Even when the `equals()` method compares objects by content, it's not always evident what the content is exactly. Sometimes, the behavior of the `equals()` method can be quite unexpected.

One infamous case is the `java.net.URL` class, which is used to represent URLs in Java. As a URL is basically a string, it's quite natural to expect that two URLs are equal if the corresponding strings are equal. However, the `equals` method of this class does an unusual thing: it considers two hosts equal if they resolve to the same IP address. To do this, it performs a network request, which may take a very long time. Similarly, the `hashCode()` method also resolves host to IP address to be consistent with `equals()`. So it's a bad idea to store URLs to a collection that heavily relies on `equals()` or `hash-Code()`, like `HashSet`. Another problem is that this approach is simply incorrect in the modern world, where virtual hosting is used and many completely unrelated websites share the same IP address.

Static analysis

Static analyzers may help you to detect suspicious usages of the URL class. IntelliJ IDEA has two inspections for this purpose: `equals()` or `hashCode()` Called on `java.net.URL` Object and `Map` or `Set` May Contain URL Objects. Make sure they are turned on. SonarLint reports these problems via a rule named S2112: `URL.hashCode` and `URL.equals` Should Be Avoided. The Error Prone analyzer has a bug pattern named URLEqualsHashCode, and SpotBugs reports this problem using The `equals` and `hashCode` Methods of URL Are Blocking and Maps and Sets of URLs Can Be Performance Hogs rules.

Note that static analyzers may not report indirect uses of `equals()` or `hashCode()`. For example,

```
List<URL> urlList = List.of(…);
URL urlToFind = new URL("https://example.com");
```

(continued)
```
if (urlList.contains(urlToFind)) {
  System.out.println("Found");
}
```

Here, you create a list of URLs that is considered acceptable, as `equals()` and `hashCode()` are not used to create the list. However, later you call the `contains()` method, which invokes `equals()` inside. As of this writing, neither IntelliJ IDEA nor SonarLint report this `contains()` call as problematic.

WAYS TO AVOID THIS MISTAKE

- Do not use `URL` objects as map keys or set elements, and don't invoke `equals()` or `hashCode()` on URLs directly. Also, be careful when storing URLs in lists or arrays, as some operations may call `equals()` indirectly.
- It's better to avoid using `java.net.URL` completely, unless it's absolutely necessary, like passing a `URL` object to a library method that you cannot change. In most cases, `java.net.URI` is a good alternative, as it does not perform any network requests in `equals()` and `hashCode()`. Still, it does not simply compare URIs as strings. It uses case-insensitive comparison for some URI parts, like schema and host, so, for example, `HTTPS://EXAMPLE.COM` and `https://example.com` would be considered equal URIs. It's always a good idea to read the class documentation to understand how exactly equality is defined.

7.4   *Mistake 58: Comparing BigDecimals with different scales*

Another class with unusual equals implementation is `BigDecimal`. It's used to represent floating-point numbers with arbitrary precision. Luckily, it doesn't do any network requests. Still, the behavior of `equals()` is also unexpected here. `BigDecimal` instances contain an unscaled value (`BigInteger`) and a scale (`int`), which is the 10-based exponent. For example, for `BigDecimal` 0.1234, the unscaled value is 1,234 and the scale is 4 ($0.1234 = 1234 \times 10^{-4}$). However, the same number could be reproduced in a different way. For example, if your unscaled value is 12,340 and the scale is 5, you'll get the same number, as $0.1234 = 12{,}340 \times 10^{-5}$. The thing is, the `equals()` method compares the unscaled value and the scale instead of numerical values, so you may get a false result for two numerically equivalent values. Depending on how the numbers were created, you can get a different scale. Here's a simple illustration:

```
BigDecimal zero1 = new BigDecimal("0");
BigDecimal zero2 = new BigDecimal("0.0");
System.out.println(zero1.scale());          ⟵─┤ Prints 0
System.out.println(zero2.scale());      ⟵─┤ Prints 1
System.out.println(zero1.equals(zero2));     ⟵─┤ Prints false
```

As you can see, two `BigDecimal` values, constructed from `0` and `0.0` strings, have different scales. As a result, they are not equal, even though their numerical value is the same.

Static analysis

Direct calls of the `equals()` method can be found via the IntelliJ IDEA inspection `equals()` Called on `java.math.BigDecimal` (turned off by default). Note, however, that `equals()` is often called indirectly (e.g., inside `List.contains()`, as you saw in the previous mistake), so this inspection may not find every problematic place.

WAYS TO AVOID THIS MISTAKE

- To compare `BigDecimal` values, you can use the `compareTo()` method. It compares numerical values, regardless of scale, and returns 0 if numerical values are equal.
- If you still need to use `equals()`, you can normalize the values using the `stripTrailingZeros()` method. It creates a new `BigDecimal` object, changing the scale to the minimum possible without losing the precision:

```
BigDecimal zero1 = new BigDecimal("0").stripTrailingZeros();
BigDecimal zero2 = new BigDecimal("0.0").stripTrailingZeros();
System.out.println(zero1.scale());              ⊲─┤ Prints 0
System.out.println(zero2.scale());   ⊲─┤ Prints 0
System.out.println(zero1.equals(zero2));        ⊲─┤ Prints true
```

7.5 Mistake 59: Using equals() on unrelated types

When you use the `==` operator on obviously incompatible types, like `Integer` and `String`, the Java compiler will help you by issuing a compilation error. Unfortunately, you get no help from the compiler when comparing the objects with `equals()`. The `equals()` method accepts an object of any type as a parameter. If the supplied object is unrelated to this object, then, by contract, `equals()` must return `false`. This becomes a source of very unpleasant errors if you accidentally pass an unrelated object to `equals()`. As you won't get any compilation error or exception, this mistake can remain unnoticed for a long time.

One example I've seen in production code compared a collection to an item like this:

```
interface Item {}

Collection<Item> find(String name) {…}

void process(String name, Item specialItem) {
    if (find(name).equals(specialItem)) {
        … // Special case
    }
}
```

Here, the mistake is not easily visible, as the collection is the result of the method call and the method name does not immediately suggest its return type is `Collection`. Sometimes, when business requirements evolve, people refactor an existing method to return a collection instead of a single element. Imagine that a while ago, the `find()`

method returned a single item, but then, it became possible to have several items with the same name. A commonly used refactoring approach is to update the return type and then fix all the compilation errors. However, you won't have a compilation error in this sample, as it's possible to call `equals()` right on the method call result, regardless of the method return type (as long as it's not `void` or primitive). So this approach may silently break the code.

   Another piece of code initially looked like the following:

```
void fetchNameAndProcess(User user) {
  String name;
  if (user == null) {
    name = generateName();
  } else {
    name = user.fetchName();
  }
  if ("anonymous".equals(name)) {
    return;
  }
  process(name);
}
```

After a while, it became desired to fetch the name under a certain lock. There was a helper API method declared as `void withLock(Runnable r)`, so it was used:

```
String name;
withLock(() -> {
  if (user == null) {
    name = generateName();
  } else {
    name = user.fetchName();
  }
});
```

However, this code cannot be compiled, as it's not allowed to modify a local variable from inside the lambda. The developer fixed this quickly, replacing the `name` variable with a one-element array and fixing the compilation errors after that:

```
String[] name = new String[1];
withLock(() -> {
  if (user == null) {
    name[0] = generateName();
  } else {
    name[0] = user.fetchName();
  }
});
if ("anonymous".equals(name)) {
  return;
}
process(name[0]);
```

Unfortunately, the `if` statement was overlooked, as checking equality between a string and an array is a perfectly valid operation from a compiler's point of view. However, now, the condition is never satisfied, and the program will not behave as expected.

Static analysis

Static analyzers may report problems like this. For example, IntelliJ IDEA has an inspection named `equals()` Between Objects of Inconvertible Types. SonarLint reports with the S2159: Silly Equality Checks Should Not Be Made warning. This doesn't always work, though. The second sample is obviously wrong, as a string cannot be equal to an array. The first sample is less obvious. As `Item` is an interface, it's theoretically possible that some implementation also implements the `Collection` interface, and the `equals()` method may, in fact, compare objects of the same class. The IntelliJ IDEA inspection tries to analyze class hierarchy and reports if no class that is a subclass of both types on the left and right side of `equals()` exists. However, performing the search of subclasses on the fly could be slow, so it may stop searching in some cases.

WAYS TO AVOID THIS MISTAKE

- When changing the method return type, examine all the call sites using IDE features, like Call Hierarchy. If you check only those call sites that produced a compilation error, you may overlook silent changes of semantics. Many developers look for new static analysis warnings in changed files only. Imagine the refactoring described in the first example: you replaced the return type of `find()` from `Item` to `Collection<Item>`, and then you fixed all the compilation errors. However, if no change was made in the file that contains the `process()` method, you won't notice that a new static analysis warning appears at the `equals()` call. You can notice it if you explicitly examine all the call sites. This also shows the importance of running whole project static analysis on a continuous integration server. In this case, it will produce an alert if a new warning appears in an unchanged source file.

- Paying attention to code coverage may help here. If you have a test that visits the `equals()` condition, even if the test doesn't fail, the coverage will decrease when the condition becomes always `false`. If your continuous integration server is configured to send alerts when coverage has decreased, you may notice something is broken there.

7.6   *Mistake 60: Malformed equals() implementation*

Implementing the `equals()` method in Java can be error prone. It doesn't look hard to compare all the fields, but it's easy to make a mistake due to repetitive code patterns. One problem I have seen several times is comparing a field to itself instead of using the field from another object supplied as a parameter. For example, a bug like this was discovered and fixed in the Elasticsearch project:

```
class MyEntity {
  private String name;
  private List<String> attributes;
  private Object data;
  private long timeStamp;
```

```
  public boolean equals(Object o) {
    if (this == o) return true;
    if (o == null || getClass() != o.getClass()) return false;
    MyEntity other = (MyEntity) o;
    return timeStamp == other.timeStamp &&
           name.equals(other.name) &&
           attributes.equals(attributes) &&
           data.equals(other.data);
  }
}
```

It's probably hard to spot this mistake without the help of an IDE or static analyzer, especially if you don't know there's a mistake. Here, the `attributes` field is compared to itself instead of `other.attributes`. Usually, an IDE provides a facility to generate `equals()` method implementation. However, if a new field is added later, people often add new checks manually, causing mistakes like this to happen.

Another possible mistake occurs when you add several fields. In this case, it's tempting to copy and paste the line of code containing the `equals()` call and update the qualifier and argument. Typos are also possible here:

```
class User {
  String firstName, middleName, lastName;
  Gender gender;
  int age;

  public boolean equals(Object o) {
    if (this == o) return true;
    if (o == null || getClass() != o.getClass()) return false;
    User user = (User) o;
    return Objects.equals(firstName, user.firstName) &&
           Objects.equals(middleName, user.firstName) &&
           Objects.equals(lastName, user.lastName) &&
           gender == user.gender &&
           age == user.age;
  }
}
```

Again, it's not so easy to spot that `middleName` is compared to `user.firstName`. In this case, two objects with identical fields could be equal only in the unlikely situation that `firstName` is the same as `middleName`.

The most common problem with `equals()` implementation is likely caused by a forgotten field. It's very easy to forget to update `equals()` when adding a new field to the object.

Mistakes like this are quite hard to find during testing because they rarely cause an evident malfunction. For example, if you have a mistake in the comparison of one field, it only becomes important if you have two objects that differ at this field exclusively. Depending on the object semantics, this could be a rare case, so the program behavior might look correct at first glance—and even pass some tests. Also, even if the user of your program actually has two objects for which `equals()` returns the wrong result, it may be hardly noticeable. You'll be lucky if you see an exception, but more often, the result will be silent data loss, like some entry missing in the list or two items incorrectly deduplicated in the `HashMap`.

It's also quite hard to debug such mistakes. Often, incorrect `equals()` implementation leads to strange behavior of standard collection classes, like `ArrayList` or `HashSet`, so if you use a step-by-step debugger, you may end up stepping through the library class implementation, which could be complicated.

If a field can be `null`, you should take care of it. I've seen this done incorrectly many times, and the flavors of this mistake often differ. For example, it may look like this:

```
class Box {
  final Object data;

  Box(Object data) { this.data = data; }

  @Override
  public boolean equals(Object obj) {
    if (this == obj) return true;
    if (obj == null || obj.getClass() != Box.class) return false;
    Box that = (Box) obj;
    return data != null && data.equals(that.data);
  }
}
```

Here, the objects would be considered unequal if both `data` and `that.data` is `null`, which is likely a mistake. For example, `new Box(null).equals(new Box(null))` will be `false`. The solution is simple: use the `Objects.equals()` library method, as it handles `null` equality properly, so you don't need to remember how to do it correctly and efficiently.

Another typo I spotted several times in `equals()` implementations is using `this` instead of a parameter for an `instanceof` check:

```
class MyClass {
  …

  @Override
  public boolean equals(Object obj) {
    if (obj == this) return true;
    if (!(this instanceof MyClass)) return false;
    MyClass that = (MyClass) obj;
    … // compare fields
  }
}
```

It can be difficult to spot this problem without help from tools like static analyzers. The correct condition would be

```
if (!(obj instanceof MyClass)) return false;
```

A problem like this existed for quite a long time in the `Date` class of the SquirrelJME project, until it was fixed thanks to a static analysis warning. It's clearly a typo, but it could stay in the code unnoticed for a long time, as a runtime exception will happen only if `obj` happens to not be an instance of `MyClass`. In some programs, this typo could be harmless, as objects of another class are never compared to this class. However, this makes the code very fragile, and future modifications may easily break it.

Static analysis

Static analyzers can help you to spot some errors. For example, IntelliJ IDEA has an `equals()` Called on Itself inspection that produces a warning on the previously shown problem with `attributes.equals(attributes)`. SonarLint has a more general warning: S1764: Identical Expressions Should Not Be Used on Both Sides of a Binary Operator, which also reports when an `equals()` method argument is the same as the qualifier.

The `this instanceof MyClass` problem is reported by the Constant Values IntelliJ IDEA inspection because it's always true. SonarLint does not report this particular line, but it has another warning here: S2097: `equals(Object obj)` Should Test Argument Type. A developer might think SonarLint is wrong and suppress the warning because the `instanceof` condition is present in the `equals()` implementation. Be careful here. If you see a seemingly wrong static analysis warning, examine the code thoroughly and ask a colleague to take a second look if you don't see the problem.

WAYS TO AVOID THIS MISTAKE

- When possible, use IDE functions to generate `equals()` and `hashCode()` instead of implementing them manually. This is also important when you add new fields. Adjusting existing implementation manually may introduce new errors. It could be more robust to remove existing `equals()` and `hashCode()`, and then generate them again from scratch. Use the Code > Generate > `equals()` and `hashCode()` menu item in IntelliJ IDEA and Source > Generate `hashCode()` and `equals()` in Eclipse. You'll be able to select fields that participate in the equality contract and specify other options (figure 7.3).
- Since Java 16, record classes have been able to be used to store data. These classes feature `equals()` and `hashCode()` implementations generated automatically by the compiler. Use them when possible.
- When checking nullable fields for equality, use the `Objects.equals()` static method over handling `null` manually whenever possible. This is shorter, more readable, and less error prone.
- To test the `equals()` method implementation, use a special library like Equals-Verifier (https://jqno.nl/equalsverifier/). There are many ways to implement `equals()` incorrectly, and it's hard to cover all the possible problems manually. The EqualsVerifier library tries its best to test your `equals()` methods completely. In particular, it can catch the previously listed problems.

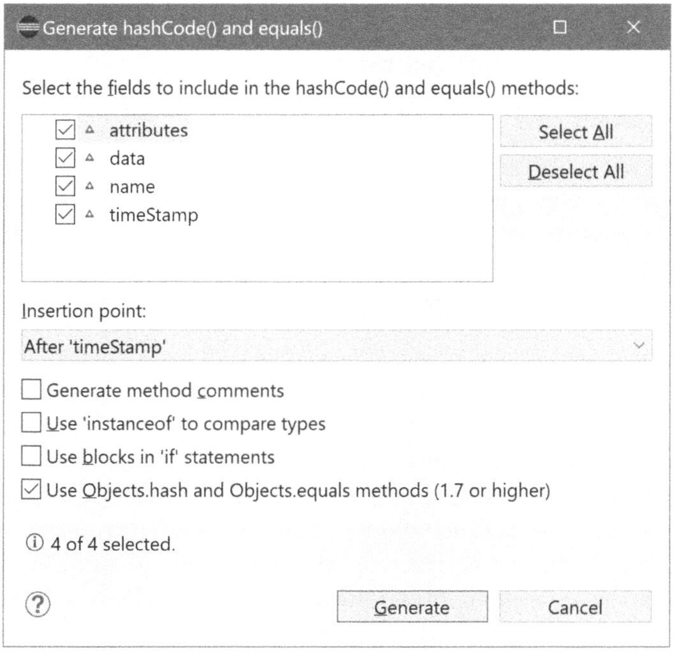

Figure 7.3   Generate `hashCode()` and `equals()` dialog in Eclipse IDE.

7.7　*Mistake 61: Wrong hashCode() with array fields*

When implementing the `hashCode()` method, you should be careful to fulfill the contract. Particularly, two objects that are equal to each other according to `equals()` must have the same hash code. Failure to fulfill this contract may lead to buggy behavior when you put the object into a collection that relies on a hash code, such as `HashSet` or `HashMap`. For example, it's possible for the two equal objects with incorrect `hashCode()` implementation to be added to the `HashSet`.

Before Java 7, implementing the `hashCode()` method manually was more challenging and error prone. You needed to get the hash codes of individual fields and mix them using a sequence of multiplications (usually, by 31) and additions. Special care should be taken to process nullable fields. This is how `hashCode()` implementation might look for a class having three fields:

```
class Person {
  String name;
  int age;
  Occupation occupation;

  public boolean equals(Object o) { … }

  public int hashCode() {
    int result = name != null ? name.hashCode() : 0;
```

```
    result = 31 * result + age;
    result = 31 * result +
      (occupation != null ? occupation.hashCode() : 0);
    return result;
  }
}
```

Java 7 introduced an `Objects.hash()` method, which improved things drastically. Now, you just need to pass all the fields that participate in the equality contract:

```
public int hashCode() {
  return Objects.hash(name, age, occupation);
}
```

Thanks to boxing, this approach works for primitive fields as well as object fields. You may have a performance cost if the JVM fails to optimize the boxing, but in many cases, it's tolerable. However, sometimes, the simplicity of `Objects.hash()` causes problems. This method always delegates to the `hashCode()` method of the corresponding field, so if `hashCode()` in the field type is not implemented, then the result of `Objects.hash()` will be wrong as well. One important case to consider is arrays. The `hashCode()` for arrays does not consider the array contents, so you may have a different hash code for arrays with the same content.

For example, assume you have a class with two array fields. It might be tempting to use `Objects.hash()` to simplify the `hashCode()` implementation:

```
class DataHolder {
  final int[] intData;
  final String[] stringData;

  DataHolder(int[] intData, String[] stringData) {
    this.intData = intData;
    this.stringData = stringData;
  }

  public boolean equals(Object o) {
    if (this == o) return true;
    if (o == null || getClass() != o.getClass()) return false;
    DataHolder dh = (DataHolder) o;
    return Arrays.equals(intData, dh.intData) &&
           Arrays.equals(stringData, dh.stringData);
  }

  public int hashCode() {
    return Objects.hash(intData, stringData);
  }
}
```

However, this implementation returns different hash codes for equal objects. You can observe this in the following code:

```
var h1 = new DataHolder(new int[0], new String[0]);
var h2 = new DataHolder(new int[0], new String[0]);
System.out.println(h1.equals(h2));                    ⟵  Prints true
```

```
var set = new HashSet<>();
set.add(h1);
set.add(h2);
System.out.println(set.size());     ⊲─┤ Prints 2
```

Here, you create two equal objects. However, if you add both to the same `HashSet`, they won't be deduplicated. This may cause confusing and difficult-to-debug problems.

If you still want to use `Objects.hash()`, you can wrap arrays into an `Arrays.hashCode()` call:

```
public int hashCode() {
  return Objects.hash(
          Arrays.hashCode(intData),
          Arrays.hashCode(stringData));
}
```

In this case, you can still use `Objects.hash` to mix array and non-array fields without coding the math manually. Note that you need to use `Arrays.deepHashCode()` and `Arrays.deepEquals()` if your array is multidimensional.

You should also be careful when using Java records. Their `hashCode()` and `equals()` methods are implemented automatically by default. However, the default implementation does not perform any special processing of arrays, so if you have array record components, they will be compared by reference rather than content. In this case, you'll probably need to implement `hashCode()` and `equals()` manually.

> **Static analysis**
>
> IntelliJ IDEA reports when you pass an array to the `Objects.hash()` method. The inspection name is `hashCode()` Called on Array.

WAYS TO AVOID THIS MISTAKE

- As with `equals()`, avoid implementing `hashCode()` manually. Use IDE capabilities to implement this method. IDEs know arrays should be handled specially, so they won't simply wrap into `Objects.hash()`.
- Be careful when using array components in Java records. Whenever possible, use `List` instead, as `List` implementations compute hash codes based on the contents of the list. Unfortunately, it's not yet possible in Java to use `List<int>`, and if you use `List<Integer>`, you will have significant performance and memory overhead. If you need a primitive array as a record component, it may be reasonable to implement `equals()` and `hashCode()` explicitly.

7.8 *Mistake 62: Mismatch between equals() and hashCode()*

As discussed previously, it's a good idea to generate `equals()` and `hashCode()` automatically using IDE functionality. However, in rare cases, you need to do something different in the `equals()` implementation. In this case, you should take care to properly implement `hashCode()` as well. In some cases, it could be tricky.

For example, sometimes, objects are considered equal if two fields are equal in any order, like this:

```
class TwoFields {
  int f1, f2;

  public boolean equals(Object o) {
    if (this == o) return true;
    if (o == null || getClass() != o.getClass()) return false;
    TwoFields twoFields = (TwoFields) o;
    return f1 == twoFields.f1 && f2 == twoFields.f2 ||
           f1 == twoFields.f2 && f2 == twoFields.f1;
  }
}
```

In this case, automatic generation of `equals()` and `hashCode()` will not produce the desired result. One may try to use `Objects.hash(f1, f2)`, but this would be an incorrect `hashCode()` implementation. You need a symmetric function that yields the same result if you swap `f1` and `f2`, but `Objects.hash()` is not symmetric. For example, `Objects.hash(1, 2)` is 994, while `Objects.hash(2, 1)` is 1,024. The simplest solution is to use addition:

```
public int hashCode() {
  return f1 + f2;
}
```

A similar approach is used in `java.util.Set` implementations, as set equality doesn't depend on the order of the elements.

Another solution is to normalize your object on construction and every modification. This is much simpler if the object is immutable. For example, you can preserve the `f1 <= f2` invariant:

```
class TwoFields {
  final int f1, f2;

  TwoFields(int f1, int f2) {
    if (f1 <= f2) {
      this.f1 = f1;
      this.f2 = f2;
    } else {
      this.f2 = f1;
      this.f1 = f2;
    }
  }
}
```

In this case, you don't need any custom logic in `equals()` and `hashCode()`. The auto-generated versions will work just fine. You can also use this approach with Java records.

Another example of nonstandard comparison in `equals()` is using `equalsIgnore-Case()` on a string field. For simplicity, assume you have only one field and want to preserve the original case, meaning you cannot normalize in the constructor:

```
final class CaseInsensitiveString {
  private final String string;

  CaseInsensitiveString(String string) {
    this.string = Objects.requireNonNull(string);
  }

  public boolean equals(Object o) {
    if (this == o) return true;
    if (!(o instanceof CaseInsensitiveString)) return false;
    CaseInsensitiveString that = (CaseInsensitiveString) o;
    return string.equalsIgnoreCase(that.string);
  }
}
```

What should the correct `hashCode()` implementation be for this class? Usually, developers try to normalize the case using `toLowerCase()` or `toUpperCase()` (remember to specify the locale explicitly):

```
public int hashCode() {
  return string.toLowerCase(Locale.ROOT).hashCode();
}
```

Unfortunately, this `hashCode()` implementation violates the contract. There are strings that have different `toLowerCase()` results, yet they are equal when compared using `equalsIgnoreCase()`. That's because `equalsIgnoreCase()` compares strings character by character and the character pair satisfies if it has either `toUpperCase()` or `toLowerCase()` equal. There are some characters that may produce the same `toUpperCase` but a different `toLowerCase` result, or vice versa. For example, the Greek Σ (sigma) character has two lowercase variants: σ and ς (with the latter used at the end of words). Let's test them:

```
System.out.println("σ".toLowerCase(Locale.ROOT));      ⟵─┤ σ
System.out.println("ς".toLowerCase(Locale.ROOT));        ⟵─┤ ς
System.out.println("σ".toUpperCase(Locale.ROOT));      ⟵─┤ Σ
System.out.println("ς".toUpperCase(Locale.ROOT));        ⟵──┤ Σ
System.out.println("σ".equalsIgnoreCase("ς"));      ⟵─┤ true
```

So `toLowerCase()` returns the original letter, either σ or ς, but `toUpperCase()` returns the same letter, Σ. As a result, `equalsIgnoreCase()` returns `true`. This means your object will return a different hash code for equal objects, so sets and maps may not work correctly with these objects. How bad can it be? For example, let's create immutable sets containing the `CaseInsensitiveString` object:

```
var s1 = new CaseInsensitiveString("ς");
var s2 = new CaseInsensitiveString("σ");
System.out.println(s1.equals(s2));         ⟵─┤ Prints true
System.out.println(Set.of(s1).contains(s2));        ⟵─┤ Prints true
System.out.println(Set.of(s1, "a").contains(s2));        ⟵──┤ Prints true
System.out.println(Set.of(s1, "a", "b").contains(s2));   ⟵─┤ Prints false
```

You can observe that a set of one or two elements correctly reports that it contains s2, while a set of three elements suddenly returns `false`. That's because `Set.of()` implementation starts relying on `hashCode()` only when you have at least three elements. Note that this result is not specified and may change in a future Java version. The thing is, if you have a `hashCode()` implementation that returns different values for equal objects, all kinds of weird things can happen.

You can fix the support of Greek sigma by replacing `toLowerCase()` with `toUpperCase()` in the `hashCode()` implementation. However, this will make `CaseInsensitiveString` fail on some other symbols.

WAYS TO AVOID THIS MISTAKE

- You will have consistent `equals`/`hashCode` implementations if you represent your object as a sequence of the same keys in both methods. If you use the hash code of `string.toLowerCase(Locale.ROOT)` in the `hashCode()` implementation, then your sequence contains a single key, namely the result of `toLowerCase()`. This means consistent implementation should compare the same value in `equals()` as well:

```
public boolean equals(Object o) {
  if (this == o) return true;
  if (!(o instanceof CaseInsensitiveString)) return false;
  CaseInsensitiveString that = (CaseInsensitiveString) o;
  return string.toLowerCase(Locale.ROOT)
      .equals(that.string.toLowerCase(Locale.ROOT));
}
```

  This is more verbose and might be less performant, as you need to create new strings. However, such an approach will always produce a consistent result (see mistake 67 for greater detail on the sequence of keys approach). Note that this implementation works differently. Specifically, `CaseInsensitiveString` objects containing σ and ς will no longer be equal to each other.

- If you want to preserve `equalsIgnoreCase()` semantics in the `equals()` method, you can use both `toUpperCase()` and `toLowerCase()` in the `hashCode()` implementation (in any order):

```
public int hashCode() {
  return string.toUpperCase(Locale.ROOT)
      .toLowerCase(Locale.ROOT).hashCode();
}
```

7.9   *Mistake 63: Relying on a particular return value of compare()*

There are two standard ways to define an order for Java objects: either implement the `Comparable` interface (producing a so-called *natural order*) or provide a custom `Comparator`. The methods `Comparator.compare()` and `Comparable.compareTo()` have a similar contract, so bug patterns connected with their uses are also similar.

Here, I refer to both these methods as *comparison methods*. One possible mistake is to compare the result of these methods to a specific non-zero constant:

```
if (comparator.compare(a, b) == 1) {
  …
}
```

Many implementations of the `compare` method, indeed, return only –1, 0, or 1. However, the contract of these methods allows them to return any positive number instead of 1 and any negative number instead of –1. So, code like this may work for a long time but suddenly stop working if the comparator implementation is changed. Cases in which something else is returned are not very rare. In particular, the standard JDK `String.compareTo()` method is known to return other numbers. If the custom comparator happens to delegate to `String.compareTo()` (probably only under certain conditions), it will return other numbers as well. For example, let's make a comparable record that contains two fields:

```
record User(String name, int age) implements Comparable<User> {
  @Override
  public int compareTo(User o) {
    int res = name.compareTo(o.name);
    return res != 0 ? res : Integer.compare(age, o.age);
  }
}
```

Here, you order users first by name and then by age if the name is equal. Let's create three sample users:

```
User u1 = new User("Mary", 30);
User u2 = new User("Mary", 20);
User u3 = new User("Joe", 30);
```

If you check `u1.compareTo(u2)`, you get 1, as here, names are equal and you delegate to `Integer.compare()`, which always returns –1, 0, or 1. However, when you compare `u1` and `u3`, the result will be 3, as now you return the result of `String.compareTo()`.

It's important to stress that the implementation of `compareTo()` shown previously is perfectly fine and follows the contract. The problem appears only if you use the `compareTo()` result incorrectly, comparing it with a specific positive number.

A bug like this might be quite hard to debug because it rarely produces exceptions. Instead, the data are processed in the incorrect order, which may produce an incorrect computation result (e.g., the wrong element is considered a maximum), and it could be nontrivial to spot the incorrect result and understand why it appeared.

Arguably, it would be better to have an enum like this in the standard library:

```
enum ComparisonResult {
  LESS, EQUAL, GREATER
}
```

You could then use it as the return value of the comparison methods because, essentially, you need to return only three different values. However, this was not possible historically, as enums appeared in Java much later than comparison methods. Also, performance considerations were probably more important at that time. Having an opportunity to return any positive or negative number sometimes allows reducing the number of conditional branches inside comparison method implementations.

Static analysis

Static analyzers will warn if you check the result of a comparison method against a specific constant directly. The IntelliJ IDEA inspection is named Suspicious Usage of Compare Method, SonarLint has a S2200: `compareTo` Results Should Not Be Checked for Specific Values rule, and SpotBugs reports with the Code Checks for Specific Values Returned by `compareTo` warning. However, most static analyzers will be silent if the expected return value is somehow calculated, like this:

```
void check(User u1, User u2, boolean reverse) {
  int expected = reverse ? 1 : -1;
  if (u1.compareTo(u2) != expected) {
    throw new IllegalArgumentException("Order is incorrect");
  }
}
```

Remember that static analysis has its limits, so don't assume it will find all the problems of a specific type.

WAYS TO AVOID THIS MISTAKE

- Do not compare the result of `compare()` or `compareTo()` calls to a specific nonzero constant, like 1 or −1, either directly or indirectly.
- Avoid manually writing algorithms involving comparators. Most useful algorithms are already available either in the standard JDK library or well-known third-party libraries. For example, I've often seen people manually write an algorithm to find the maximal or minimal element in a collection, even though the methods `Collections.max/min` and `Stream.max/min` are available in the standard JDK library. Standard methods are well-tested, and it's highly unlikely they contain bugs.

7.10   *Mistake 64: Failing to return 0 when comparing equal objects*

To make objects comparable, one needs to implement the `compareTo()` method. There are still many `Comparable` objects in the world that violate the interface contract. Let's recap the contract rules:

- *Antisymmetry*—The sign of `x.compareTo(y)` and `y.compareTo(x)` must be opposite. This also implies that `x.compareTo(x)` must be 0.

- *Transitivity*—If x.compareTo(y) > 0 and y.compareTo(z) > 0, then the result of x.compare-To(z) must also be greater than zero.
- If x.compareTo(y) == 0, then for any z, x.compareTo(z) and y.compareTo(z) must have an equal sign.

If you want to order objects without modifying their original class or are not satisfied with the natural order provided by the compareTo() method, you can define a Comparator. Its compare() method has a very similar contract. Assuming cmp is a Comparator capable of comparing objects x and y, the following rules must be satisfied:

- *Antisymmetry*—The sign of cmp.compare(x, y) and cmp.compare(y, x) must be opposite. This also implies that cmp.compare(x, x) must be 0.
- *Transitivity*—If cmp.compare(x, y) > 0 and cmp.compare(y, z) > 0, then the result of cmp.compare(x, z) must also be greater than zero.
- If cmp.compare(x, y) == 0, then for any z, cmp.compare(x, z) and cmp.compare (y, z) must have an equal sign.

One important difference between compare() and compareTo() is that while there's no natural order for null, an external comparator can (but does not have to) compare null with non-null objects (usually placing null either before or after any non-null objects). There are even static utility methods, nullsFirst() and nullsLast(), in the Comparator class which allow you to make any comparator null friendly.

It's surprisingly easy to violate the contract rules if you try to implement everything manually. In particular, developers sometimes forget that 0 must be returned for equal objects. For example, assume your comparable objects contain only one boolean field and you want to make objects that wrap true bigger than objects that wrap false. You might be tempted to write something like this:

```
class BoolObj implements Comparable<BoolObj> {
  final boolean b;

  BoolObj(boolean b) { this.b = b; }

  @Override
  public int compareTo(BoolObj o) {
    return b && !o.b ? 1 : -1;
  }
}
```

Quick tests show that this works:

```
BoolObj b1 = new BoolObj(true);
BoolObj b2 = new BoolObj(false);
System.out.println(b1.compareTo(b2));    ⊲─┤ Prints 1
System.out.println(b2.compareTo(b1));         ⊲─┤ Prints –1
```

However, if you compare two objects wrapping the same boolean value, you will also get –1, which is wrong (figure 7.4). You should process equal objects as well:

```
return b == o.b ? 0 : b ? 1 : -1;
```

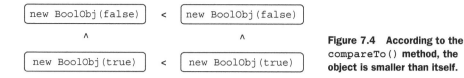

Figure 7.4   According to the compareTo() **method, the object is smaller than itself.**

It's much more robust to use the library method `Boolean.compare()` that does the same:

```
return Boolean.compare(b, o.b);
```

I saw a comparator aimed at comparing files, putting the directories first, and then comparing files by name. The comparator looked like this:

```
Comparator<File> comparator = (file1, file2) -> {
  if (file1.isDirectory()) {
    return -1;
  } else if (file2.isDirectory()) {
    return 1;
  }
  return file1.getName().compareTo(file2.getName());
};
```

As an exercise, try to understand what's wrong with this comparator, and then rewrite it in a correct way.

Static analysis

Simple cases where a comparison method does not return 0 for equal elements are reported by the IntelliJ IDEA inspection Suspicious `Comparator.compare()` Implementation.

WAYS TO AVOID THIS MISTAKE

- When implementing a comparison method, always consider that equal elements may be compared. Even if right now, this is not the case (e.g., you are going to sort the list of definitely nonrepeating objects), the same comparison method might be reused later in another context. The bugs caused by an incorrect return value for equal elements could be hard to reproduce, as they may appear only for specific datasets.
- Add a unit test for comparison method when the object is compared with itself or an equal object. Ensure the result is 0.
- When comparing `boolean` fields inside the comparison method, use `Boolean.compare()`. You may swap the arguments, depending on whether you want the `true` or `false` value to be greater.

7.11 *Mistake 65: Using subtraction when comparing numbers*

If you compare numbers, sometimes, it's tempting to use subtraction for comparison. For example, here, we compare objects with a single `int` field:

```
class IntObj implements Comparable<IntObj> {
  final int i;

  IntObj(int i) { this.i = i; }

  @Override
  public int compareTo(IntObj o) {
    return i - o.i;
  }
}
```

The `compareTo()` contract allows us to return any positive or negative number, not just 1 or –1, so this is short and looks as if it's working. However, this subtraction may overflow if you work with big numbers. For example, if you create two objects, `new IntObj(2_000_000_000)` and `new IntObj(-2_000_000_000)`, the latter will be bigger (figure 7.5). This violates the transitivity rule:

```
IntObj x = new IntObj(2_000_000_000);
IntObj y = new IntObj(0);
IntObj z = new IntObj(-2_000_000_000);
System.out.println(x.compareTo(y) > 0);    │ Both lines print true
System.out.println(y.compareTo(z) > 0);    │
System.out.println(x.compareTo(z) > 0);       ◁─┤ Prints false
```

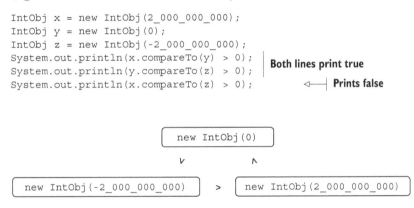

Figure 7.5   Using subtraction inside `compareTo()` leads to an incorrect result when comparing large numbers of the opposite sign.

Correct `compareTo()` implementation should simply compare numbers instead of using subtraction:

```
return i == o.i ? 0 : i < o.i ? -1 : 1;
```

As with a `boolean` field, it's much better to use the library method that does the same:

```
return Integer.compare(i, o.i);
```

This might seem to be a very rare problem. If the numbers compared are never negative, like string length, you won't run into this. Also, you are safe if the absolute value of the numbers never exceeds one billion, even if they can be negative. However, as often happens with rare problems, it can easily slip through testing and land in production code. In November 2021, it was discovered that, in rare circumstances, Android phones fail to dial emergency services, like 911. You can read more details about this story in a blog post "How a Bug in Android and Microsoft Teams Could Have Caused This User's 911 Call to Fail" by Mishaal Rahman (https://mng.bz/eElw). One can imagine possible severe consequences of a bug like this. Further investigation showed that the root cause of the problem was exactly the matter described here. Prior to the emergency call, the `PhoneAccount` objects were sorted using a comparator to determine the preferred object to use for a call. After a series of comparisons, the last comparator line looked like this:

```
// then by hashcode
return account1.hashCode() - account2.hashCode();
```

As hash codes can have any possible `int` value, overflow actually occurred, causing the sorting procedure to fail. The problem was fixed by replacing subtraction with an `Integer.compare()` call.

One may wonder why it's so important to fulfill the comparison method contract completely. After all, it's probably not a big deal if sorting goes in a slightly wrong order. Sometimes, incorrect comparators even pass simple tests and yield quite satisfactory results. Still, they may produce bigger problems on bigger inputs.

One important reason is that the TimSort algorithm, which has been the default sorting algorithm in OpenJDK since version 7, may check the comparator invariants under some conditions and may throw the exception if these invariants are violated.

For example, let's populate an array of 32 values with randomly initialized `IntObj` objects introduced previously and then sort it:

```
Random random = new Random(209);
IntObj[] objects = new IntObj[32];
Arrays.setAll(objects, i -> new IntObj(random.nextInt()));
Arrays.sort(objects);
```

This program fails with the following exception:

```
java.lang.IllegalArgumentException: Comparison method violates its general
    contract!
```

However, when I prepared this sample, I noticed that any random seed value between 0 and 208 does not cause this exception because comparison method invariants are not always checked. The first nonnegative seed that causes the exception is 209. Of course, this may change in different versions of Java if the sorting algorithm is further optimized. In any case, it's quite possible incorrect comparator implementation will pass simple tests but fail when deployed into production.

Another "gotcha" with invariant checking is the size of the array or collection to be sorted. When the number of elements is less than 32, TimSort switches to a simpler algorithm that never checks the invariants. So if you only test on small collection sizes you will never get this exception.

Comparison methods are not only used for sorting lists of arrays. Another common use is sorted collections, like `TreeSet`. Here, a contract violation may cause much more dramatic consequences than just an exception. For example, let's try to create a `TreeSet` containing our `IntObj` objects:

```
IntObj o1 = new IntObj(-2_000_000_000);
IntObj o2 = new IntObj(2_000_000_000);
IntObj o3 = new IntObj(0);
Set<IntObj> set = new TreeSet<>(Arrays.asList(o1, o2, o3));
System.out.println(set.contains(o2));                    ⟵┤ Prints true
```

So far so good: we added three objects, and the set reports it contains the second one. Now, let's remove `o1`:

```
set.remove(o1);
System.out.println(set.contains(o2));    ⟵┤ Prints false
```

When you remove `o1`, the set magically forgets it contains `o2`. If you try to iterate over this set, you'll see that `o2` is still there. However, the `contains()` method returns `false`, and the `remove()` method does not remove `o2`. That's because when `TreeSet` builds the underlying red–black tree, it relies on comparator invariants. Now the tree is broken, and it's impossible to find all the elements during its traversal.

The same problem is possible even with `HashSet` or `HashMap`. Since Java 8, these classes build a red–black tree inside buckets with too many collisions and start relying on the user-provided `compareTo()` method. It's unlikely to hit this problem on random data, but if a malicious user can control the inputs, they could prepare a hand-crafted dataset containing hash collisions and force the "treeification." The following example illustrates this:

```
record Point(int x, int y) implements Comparable<Point> {
  @Override
  public int compareTo(Point o) {
    if (x != o.x) {
      return x - o.x;
    }
    return y - o.y;
  }
}
```

The Java compiler automatically generates fields, a constructor, `equals()`, `hashCode()`, and `toString()` for us. While the behavior of `hashCode()` is not specified, so far, it's stable and known, so it's not that hard to generate hash collisions. The author decided to make the points comparable, first by the `x` coordinate and then by the `y` coordinate. As you already know, using subtraction in `compareTo()` is a bad idea. Let's illustrate this:

```
Point[] points = new Point[20];
Arrays.setAll(points, idx -> {
    int x = idx * 500_000_000;
```

```
    int y = -new Point(x, 0).hashCode();
    return new Point(x, y);
});
Set<Point> set = new HashSet<>(Arrays.asList(points));
set.remove(points[1]);
System.out.println(set.contains(points[14]));    ⟵  Prints false
```

Here, we generate 20 points with the same `hashCode()` equal to 0. We rely on the implementation detail that the hash code is calculated as `f(x) + y`, for some function `f`. It doesn't matter how exactly x is used, but y is simply added to the result, so we are just setting y to `-f(x)` for every point. Now we have many collisions, and `HashSet` switches to a red–black tree. As x values are large enough, subtraction inside the `compareTo()` method overflows sometimes. As a result, after removing one of the points, `HashSet` forgets about another one, which is completely unrelated to the removed point. That point is still inside the set and can be found when iterating over it. For example, the following expression returns `true`:

```
set.stream().anyMatch(points[14]::equals)
```

Note that the behavior of this example may change in future Java versions, as it relies on both unspecified record `hashCode()` and `HashSet` implementation details. Yet the problem will persist: invalid `compareTo()` implementation may break your sets and maps.

Static analysis

IntelliJ IDEA reports subtractions inside comparison methods with the Subtraction in `compareTo()` inspection. This inspection does not report if the subtraction is known to cause no overflow. For example, subtracting lengths of two strings never overflows, as string lengths are nonnegative.

WAYS TO AVOID THIS MISTAKE

- When doing math, don't forget that operations like addition or subtraction may overflow (see mistake 27, in chapter 4).
- Use the `Integer.compare()` library method to compare `int` fields. When implementing the `Comparator`, the `Comparator.comparingInt()` method may also be helpful.
- If very large (close to `MAX_VALUE`) or negative numbers are acceptable as inputs to your code, make sure you have unit tests that cover these cases.
- When testing code that involves sorting, be sure to prepare test data that contains at least 32 elements, or even more if possible. The more elements you add, the more likely TimSort will be able to catch an invariant violation.

7.12   Mistake 66: Ignoring possible NaN values in comparison methods

Manual comparison implementation also may not work correctly for floating-point numbers. For example, imagine the following class:

```
class DoubleObj implements Comparable<DoubleObj> {
  final double d;

  DoubleObj(double d) { this.d = d; }

  @Override
  public int compareTo(DoubleObj o) {
    return d == o.d ? 0 : d < o.d ? -1 : 1;
  }
}
```

Now, if d happens to be NaN, the contract will be violated:

```
DoubleObj x = new DoubleObj(Double.NaN);
DoubleObj y = new DoubleObj(0);
System.out.println(x.compareTo(y) > 0);   │  Each line
System.out.println(y.compareTo(x) > 0);   │  prints true
System.out.println(x.compareTo(x) > 0);   │
```

You might already have guessed how to fix this. Don't do this manually; instead, use a library method:

```
return Double.compare(d, o.d);
```

This makes the NaN value consistently larger than every other value. Additionally, this implementation orders 0.0 and –0.0, making 0.0 larger.

Static analysis

IntelliJ IDEA suggests using `Double.compare()` instead of manual implementation with the `compare()` Method Can Be Used to Compare Numbers inspection. The warning does not explain the problems with NaN comparison, so it may look like a code style matter, but in fact accepting the fix will likely make the code more correct.

WAYS TO AVOID THIS MISTAKE

- When comparing floating-point numbers, don't forget to deal with possible NaN values. The problems with NaN were discussed in greater detail in mistake 40, in chapter 4.
- If a NaN value could theoretically end up in your field, write a unit test to check whether it's handled correctly. If this should not happen, protect field assignments with preconditions. For example, the constructor in the preceding sample could be written like this:

```
DoubleObj(double d) {
  if (Double.isNaN(d))
```

```
      throw new IllegalArgumentException();
    this.d = d;
  }
```

This way, you'll know immediately if something goes wrong.

- `Double.compare()` takes care of handling the special numbers, like −0.0 and `NaN`. It's usually better to use library methods than manual implementation, as they are better tested and cover more corner cases.
- When implementing the `Comparator`, consider using the `comparingDouble()` static method.

7.13   *Mistake 67: Failing to represent an object as a sequence of keys in a comparison method*

If you need to compare several fields, the usual approach is to compare them one after another, stopping once you get a difference:

```
class Person implements Comparable<Person> {
  String name;
  int age;

  @Override
  public int compareTo(Person o) {
    int res = name.compareTo(o.name);
    if (res != 0) return res;
    return Integer.compare(age, o.age);
  }
}
```

The Guava library provides a handy `ComparisonChain` utility, which allows you to write this in a fluent style:

```
public int compareTo(Person o) {
  return ComparisonChain.start()
      .compare(name, o.name)
      .compare(age, o.age)
      .result();
}
```

If you are writing a custom comparator, rather than implementing a `Comparable` interface, there are helper combinator methods right in the JDK that will simplify things for you:

```
Comparator<Person> PERSON_COMPARATOR =
    Comparator.comparing((Person p) -> p.name)
              .thenComparing(p -> p.age);
```

While these combinators may add some performance overhead to comparison, they greatly reduce the number of possible mistakes. Unfortunately, it doesn't look very natural to use comparator combinators inside `compareTo()` methods, though it's possible to delegate to a comparator:

```
class Person implements Comparable<Person> {
  private static final Comparator<Person> MY_COMPARATOR =
      Comparator.comparing((Person p) -> p.name)
          .thenComparing(p -> p.age);

  String name;
  int age;

  @Override
  public int compareTo(Person o) {
    return MY_COMPARATOR.compare(this, o);
  }
}
```

This approach could be used if Guava or a similar library is not available and the code is not performance critical.

It's always best to represent an object as a sequence of keys and compare them one after another. In the previous example, the sequence consisted of two keys: the fields name and age. If you do something else in your compareTo() method, it will be much more error prone. A simple problem I have encountered several times is handling the special case before the main comparison. The following example illustrates this:

```
class Connection implements Comparable<Connection> {
  final String url;

  Connection(String url) { this.url = url; }

  @Override
  public int compareTo(Connection that) {
    if (this instanceof SecureConnection) return -1;
    if (that instanceof SecureConnection) return 1;
    return this.url.compareTo(that.url);
  }
}
class SecureConnection extends Connection {
  SecureConnection(String url) { super(url); }
}
```

Here, you want to compare collections by URLs but put the secure connections on top. The intention is clear, but what will happen if both this and that are secure connections? In this case, you will return –1, which violates the comparison method contract, as swapping this and that will not change the return value to the positive number. If you think of your object as a sequence of keys, you will see that it consists of two elements. The first is a boolean value, which is calculated as this instanceof SecureConnection and should be inverted, and the second is the url field (string value). So the compareTo implementation should follow the common scheme:

```
public int compareTo(Connection that) {
  int res = Boolean.compare(
      that instanceof SecureConnection,
      this instanceof SecureConnection);
```

```
    if (res != 0) return res;
    return this.url.compareTo(that.url);
}
```

Or it would look like this when using Guava:

```
public int compareTo(Connection that) {
  return ComparisonChain.start()
      .compareTrueFirst(this instanceof SecureConnection,
                        that instanceof SecureConnection)
      .compare(this.url, that.url)
      .result();
}
```

A similar problem, which happens quite often, is the failure to process nulls properly. For example, imagine you have an object with a single nullable field. I have seen implementations like this in the IntelliJ IDEA project (there were more fields to compare, but for simplicity, you can assume there's only one field):

```
record User(String name) implements Comparable<User> {
  public int compareTo(User o) {
    if (name != null && o.name != null) {
      return name.compareTo(o.name);
    }
    return 0;
  }
}
```

This comparison method is incorrect, as it returns 0 when either of the names is null. This comparator might look acceptable at first glance; however, it violates the third rule of the comparison method contract discussed in mistake 64. It can be easily illustrated if you create three objects like this:

```
User u1 = new User(null);
User u2 = new User("Mary");
User u3 = new User("Bill");
```

Now, comparing u1 with either u2 or u3 will produce 0, as u1.name is null. However, u2 is clearly not equal to u3 (figure 7.6).

Figure 7.6   Incorrect comparator implementation makes equal objects unequal.

Here, to compare correctly, you can imagine a sequence of two values: 1) nullity of name (Boolean value) and 2) the name itself. You also need to decide whether to put an object with `name == null` before or after other objects. The implementation may look like this (it puts `null` at the end):

```
public int compareTo(User o) {
  int res = Boolean.compare(name == null, o.name == null);
  if (res != 0) return res;
  return name != null ? name.compareTo(o.name) : 0;
}
```

Alternatively, you can use the `nullsFirst()` or `nullsLast()` comparator combinators, which might be more readable (though somewhat less performant):

```
import static java.util.Comparator.*;

record User(String name) implements Comparable<User> {
  static final Comparator<User> USER_ORDER =
          comparing(User::name, nullsLast(naturalOrder()));

  public int compareTo(User o) {
    return USER_ORDER.compare(this, o);
  }
}
```

I encountered similar noncanonical comparison of two fields in the BioJava project. The idea was to sort by field *y* if *x* was the same without considering order if *x* was different. So the comparator was implemented like this:

```
record MyObject(String x, String y) {}

Comparator<MyObject> cmp = (obj1, obj2) -> {
  if (obj1.x().equals(obj2.x())) {
    return obj1.y().compareTo(obj2.y());
  }
  return 0;
};
```

Such a comparator violates the same rule. Imagine the following objects are declared:

```
var obj1 = new MyObject("a", "1");
var obj2 = new MyObject("b", "2");
var obj3 = new MyObject("a", "3");
```

Now, `cmp.compare(obj1, obj2)` is zero, so `cmp.compare(obj1, obj3)` and `cmp .compare(obj2, obj3)` must have the same sign, which is not true: the former is negative, while the latter is zero. A possible fix would be to provide an order for the *x* field, like this:

```
Comparator<MyObject> cmp = (obj1, obj2) -> {
  if (obj1.x().equals(obj2.x())) {
    return obj1.y().compareTo(obj2.y());
  }
  return obj1.x().compareTo(obj2.x());
};
```

This way, the problem is fixed in BioJava. The order for field *x* could be arbitrary but consistent with `equals()`. Alternatively, one can just create a sequence of keys *x* and *y*:

```
Comparator<MyObject> cmp =
  Comparator.comparing(MyObject::x).thenComparing(MyObject::y);
```

Another possibility is to avoid comparing *x* altogether. If you don't care about the order of elements when *x* is different and you want to order them by *y* if *x* is the same, then ordering them by *y* in any case could be suitable as well:

```
Comparator<MyObject> cmp = Comparator.comparing(MyObject::y);
```

WAYS TO AVOID THIS MISTAKE

- When implementing a comparison method, always try to represent your object as a sequence of keys that should be compared one after another.
- Use comparator combinator methods (like `Comparator.comparing()`) or Guava `ComparisonChain` when possible. By the way, even if Guava is not available in your project, it's not too difficult to implement a similar API yourself.
- Use randomized property tests generating random input objects, and check that their comparator contract rules are fulfilled. If you are sorting in tests, make sure your datasets are large enough (at least more than 31 elements), so the TimSort algorithm can report contract violation.
- The "in this case, I don't care about order" thought is dangerous when writing a comparator and may lead to a contract violation. Even if, in some cases, it doesn't matter how two unequal elements are ordered, you should still define an order between them, instead of just returning 0.

7.14   *Mistake 68: Returning random numbers from the comparator*

The Java Stream API does not provide a method to shuffle the stream content. However, it's possible to sort it using the `sorted()` method. One may think it would be a good idea to use the `sorted()` method for shuffling. You just need to use a custom comparator returning random values, like this:

```
List<Integer> input = IntStream.range(0, 20)
    .boxed().collect(Collectors.toList());
List<Integer> shuffled = input.stream()
    .sorted((a, b) -> Math.random() > 0.5 ? 1 : -1)
    .collect(Collectors.toList());
```

If you try this code, you may conclude that it works. The `input` list contains all numbers between 0 and 19 in ascending order, and the `shuffled` list contains the same numbers shuffled. However, if you change 20 to 32 or higher, you will occasionally get the `IllegalArgumentException` we saw before. Of course, this is an abuse of the sorting method.

If you are wondering whether it's still possible to use sorting for shuffling without a contract violation, one possibility is to assign random ranks to the input objects and memorize them in a map, like this:

```
Map<Object, Double> ranks = new HashMap<>();
List<Integer> shuffled = input.stream()
    .sorted(Comparator.comparingDouble(
        val -> ranks.computeIfAbsent(val, v -> Math.random())))
    .collect(Collectors.toList());
```

However, this is completely inefficient. Instead, just collect your stream into `List` and use the `Collections.shuffle()` library method.

WAYS TO AVOID THIS MISTAKE

- Never try to use sorting to randomize the order of objects. Sorting and shuffling are two different algorithms, and one cannot be expressed in terms of the other. Use a proper method, like `Collections.shuffle()`.
- Do not misuse sorting operations to achieve something else. I have seen comparators like `(a, b) -> -1` used to reverse the order of elements. This may work in the current Java version, but this behavior is not guaranteed in the future, as sorting implementation may be changed someday. For example, arguments to the comparator call might be swapped. In this case, such code will stop working after the Java version update.

Summary

- Don't compare primitive wrappers, like `Integer` or `Double`, with `==`. Occasionally, this comparison may return `true`, but this works unreliably. Use the `equals()` method instead.
- Some classes don't implement the `equals()` method in the expected way. Many classes, like `AtomicInteger` and `StringBuilder`, don't implement it at all, so `equals()` behaves like `==`. If you need to compare objects' content, you should use other methods.
- The `java.net.URL` class has an unexpected implementation for `equals()` and `hashCode()`. Namely, it makes an actual network request to resolve host names to IP addresses and compares them. This is almost never expected. When in doubt, use the `java.net.URI` class instead.
- The `BigDecimal.equals()` method compares not only numeric values but also the scale, so it may return `false` for numerically equal values. If you don't need to compare scale, use `BigDecimal.compareTo()` instead.
- It's possible to call `equals()`, mistakenly passing an argument of unrelated type. Such code will compile and run without exceptions, simply returning `false`.
- There are many ways to implement the `equals()` and `hashCode()` methods incorrectly. When possible, rely on automatic generation provided by your IDE. Alternatively, use Java records in which `equals()` and `hashCode()` are provided.

- While many instances of comparison methods, like `compareTo()`, return only 1, 0, and −1, the specifications allow them to return any positive or negative number. Avoid comparing the result of these methods with a specific nonzero value.
- Implementation of comparison methods can be tricky. Use predefined methods, like `Integer.compare()` or `Boolean.compare()`, to compare primitives. When possible, use comparator methods, like `comparing()`, `thenComparing()`, `nullFirst()`, and so on. This way, it will be possible to create a more robust and easy-to-understand comparator.
- Do not misuse sorting to shuffle elements or reverse a list by providing a special comparator that violates the contract. This approach may stop working if you use more data or update to a new JDK version later. Use dedicated methods, like `Collections.shuffle()`, to achieve the same result.

Collections and maps

This chapter covers

- Common mistakes when adding or looking for an element of unrelated type in a collection
- Handling nulls in collections and maps
- Modifiable and unmodifiable collections
- Concurrent modification of collections
- Problems using the `List.remove()` method
- How to implement iterators properly

The Java Collection API appeared long ago in Java 1.2. The world was quite different then: Java had no parameterized types (generics), mutable objects were in favor, and nulls were generally accepted values. Over time, the language and the way people write programs has changed significantly. Yet with all that change, the old collection API remains ubiquitous in modern programs. Some outdated design decisions negatively affect the programming style today and may be the source of bugs.

8.1 *Mistake 69: Searching the object of unrelated type*

Before parameterized types were introduced to Java, collection and map elements could not be typed as anything more specific than `Object`, so you could easily add a string to a list of numbers. When generics were introduced, all methods that add elements to collections were restricted to accept only the collection element type. However, most of the methods that search and remove elements weren't restricted. This includes the following methods, which operate on individual elements:

- `Collection` *interface*—`contains(Object)` and `remove(Object)`
- `List` *interface*—`indexOf(Object)` and `lastIndexOf(Object)`
- `Map` *interface*—`containsKey(Object)`, `containsValue(Object)`, `get(Object)`, `getOrDefault(Object, V)`, `remove(Object)`, and `remove(Object, Object)`

Additionally, there are three methods in the `Collection` interface that accept collections containing unrestricted elements, namely `containsAll()`, `removeAll()`, and `retainAll()`.

So even if your collection is typed, you can easily call one of these methods and pass as an argument an object of unrelated type or a collection containing unrelated elements. The worst thing is that with most of the commonly used collection and map types, you won't have an immediate runtime error. Instead, the search methods will return a not-found result (e.g., `contains()` will return `false` or `indexOf()` will return −1), and the removal methods will remove nothing (or retain nothing in the case of the `retainAll()` method). So it may take a while for the error to be detected, and such errors may easily slip into production. The problem is similar to the example of calling `equals()` on unrelated types in mistake 59 in chapter 7, and the problems that can occur after refactoring described there are possible with collection methods as well. This often happens if you have different data types with similar semantics. For example,

```
Set<File> allowedFiles = new HashSet<>();

boolean isAllowed(Path filePath) {
  return allowedFiles.contains(filePath);
}
```

Here, the code was partially migrated to a newer `java.nio.file.Path` class to represent a file path. However, the collection still contains old `java.io.File` objects, and, naturally, a `contains()` call will always return `false`. It's also common to mix a `File` object and a file path stored in a `String` object.

The same problem may appear when your collection contains numbers. Primitive numbers can be converted implicitly, but a collection may contain only boxed numbers. Care should be taken in this case, as boxed numbers of different types are not equal to each other. For example,

```
void processList(List<Short> values, short pivot) {
  if (values.contains(pivot)) {                    ◁──┤ Possible
    ...
  } else if (values.contains(pivot + 1)) {    ◁──┤ Impossible
```

```
      ...
    }
}
```

Here, a list of `Short` values is checked to see if it contains `pivot` or `pivot + 1`. When compiling addition, a widening conversion is performed, so the type of `pivot + 1` becomes `int`. As the `contains()` method accepts `Object`, the result of `pivot + 1` is automatically boxed to `Integer`. Naturally, the collection of `Short` values cannot contain an `Integer` value, so the second condition is never `true`.

You might be curious why it was decided to continue to allow search methods to accept the `Object` type rather than a collection element type. One of the reasons is to be able to implement `Set.equals()` in a type-safe manner. Due to erasure, you won't be able to determine the type parameter of the set passed as an argument, so you need to cast the parameter to `Set<?>` or `Collection<?>`. After that, you should check whether this set contains all the elements of the supplied set, so you must call `contains()` on unknown objects. If the `contains()` arguments were limited to the collection element type, you would need to use an unchecked cast, which may cause `ClassCastException`, as we learned in mistake 43.

Static analysis

Many static analyzers report a warning when you query a collection for an object of obviously unrelated type. SonarLint reports with the warning S2175: Inappropriate `Collection` Calls Should Not Be Made, Error Prone has the CollectionIncompatible-Type bug pattern, and IntelliJ IDEA has the Suspicious Collections Method Calls inspection. Unfortunately, false positives and negatives are possible here. For example, consider that you have a `List<CharSequence>` list and a `Number` variable:

```
void check(List<CharSequence> list, Number num) {
  if (list.contains(num)) {
    System.out.println("contains");
  }
}
```

Can the condition be fulfilled? Theoretically, it can, as a class may exist that extends the `Number` abstract class and implements the `CharSequence` interface at the same time. An object of such class may appear in the list and be stored in the `num` variable at the same time. Therefore, such a call may not be erroneous. Still, it looks suspicious. SonarLint reports it, and IntelliJ IDEA inspection has a Report Suspicious but Possibly Correct Method Calls option, which allows you to report such cases.

WAYS TO AVOID THIS MISTAKE

- Write unit tests to cover paths when a collection or map search method should find something and when removal methods should remove something.
- Avoid collections of boxed primitive types. Instead, use libraries that provide primitive equivalents, like FastUtil (https://fastutil.di.unimi.it/). They are

much faster, use less memory, and provide methods that accept primitive values without boxing, so you won't end up in a situation in which `Integer` is compared to `Short`. Even if you cannot use third-party libraries for some reason, avoid collections of `Byte` and `Short` types at all costs. It's unlikely you'll save memory or have better performance compared to an `Integer` collection.

8.2   *Mistake 70: Mixing up single object and collection*

Some methods in the collection API accept a single object, while others accept a whole collection. Because they have similar names, it's easy to confuse one with another. For example, if you need to add a single object into the list, you should use `list.add()`, but if you need to add all the elements of another collection, you need to use `list.addAll()`. Similarly, it's easy to confuse pairs of methods like `contains/containsAll` and `remove/removeAll`. It's also worth noting the collection factory methods: `List.of()` methods create a new immutable collection from a single element or array of elements, while `List.copyOf()` creates an immutable copy from another collection. Finally, if you need to create a stream from a single element or array, you should use the `Stream.of()` static methods, but to create a stream from a collection, you need to call `collection.stream()`, which is also easy to mix up. Table 8.1 summarizes these pairs.

Table 8.1   Methods operating on a single object and collections

Single-object method	Collection method
`list.add(object)`	`list.addAll(collection)`
`list.contains(object)`	`list.containsAll(collection)`
`list.remove(object)`	`list.removeAll(collection)`
`List.of(object)`	`List.copyOf(collection)`
`Stream.of(object)`	`collection.stream()`

Usually, the compiler won't allow you to use a collection method instead of a single-object method because you will have an incompatible type; however, the opposite mistake is often possible. As we have seen in the previous section, `contains()` and `remove()` methods simply accept the `Object`-typed parameter, so the compiler will allow you to pass a collection there. Other pairs may cause problems if you actually use the `List<Object>` or raw `List` type.

Sometimes, programmers like to store into the same list elements that have no particular supertype. For example, one may want to store `Integer` and `String` objects together. Well, these classes implement some common interfaces like `Comparable` or `Serializable`, but creating `List<Comparable<?>>` or `List<Serializable>` sounds strange if you are not going to compare or serialize these objects. This leads to many developers using `List<Object>` as a collection type. Such a collection is quite dangerous, as it does not protect you from storing unrelated objects. In particular, it's possible to put another collection as an element. Consider, for example, the following code:

```
List<Object> createList() {
  List<Object> result = new ArrayList<>();
  result.add(getInitialValue());
  result.add(getPredefinedValues());
  result.add(getUserSpecifiedValues());
  return result;
}

private Object getInitialValue() { … }
private List<Object> getPredefinedValues() { … }
private List<Object> getUserSpecifiedValues() { … }
```

addAll was
intended.

addAll was
intended.

Here, the `result` collection was filled with values from three different sources: the single initial value, lists of predefined values, and user-specified values. The mistake was using the `add()` method instead of `addAll()`. The compiler says nothing here, as it's completely legal. As a result, you'll have a collection of three elements: a single object and two lists (figure 8.1).

What the developer intended

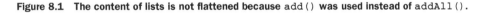

What the developer got

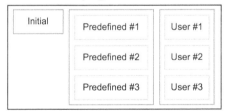

Figure 8.1 The content of lists is not flattened because `add()` **was used instead of** `addAll()`.

A similar problem can happen if you want to make an immutable copy but mistakenly call `List.of()` instead of `List.copyOf()`:

```
List<Object> createList(boolean userSpecifiedOnly) {
  if (userSpecifiedOnly) {
    return List.of(getUserSpecifiedValues());
  }
  …
}
```

**List.copyOf was intended to
make a defensive copy.**

What happens later depends on how exactly you query the collection after that. For example, if you check element types like this, then the invalid elements will be completely ignored:

```
void processList(List<Object> list) {
  for (Object element : list) {
    if (element instanceof Integer number) {
      processNumber(number);
    }
    if (element instanceof String string) {
      processString(string);
    }
  }
}
```

If you expect only a limited set of types inside the collection, it's better to throw an exception when you encounter an invalid element:

```
void processList(List<Object> list) {
  for (Object element : list) {
    if (element instanceof Integer number) {
      processNumber(number);
    } else if (element instanceof String string) {
      processString(string);
    } else {
      throw new IllegalArgumentException(
        "Unexpected element: " + element);
    }
  }
}
```

This way, you will at least see the exception, which increases the chance the problem will be discovered during testing.

Even if you created the list correctly, you may have a problem when processing it using the Stream API. For example, the following mistake can happen if you want to stream the list but used `Stream.of(list)` instead of `list.stream()`:

```
void processNumbersOnly(List<Object> list) {          list.stream()
  Stream.of(list)                              ⟵┘      was intended.
        .filter(e -> e instanceof Number)
        .forEach(num -> processNumber((Number) num));
}
```

Here, the author wanted to extract only numbers from the list and pass them to the `processNumber()` method. However, instead of streaming the list elements, this code creates a stream of one element, which is a list. The inferred type of the `e` parameter is not `Object` but `List<Object>`. It's unlikely that the `List` implementation extends the `Number` class, so this code does nothing. It's equivalent to the following:

```
if (list instanceof Number number) {
  processNumber(number);
}
```

WAYS TO AVOID THIS MISTAKE

- Do not use raw types. If you simply declare `List` without a type argument, you'll lose all the strong typing benefits and make your code much more error prone.
- Avoid using the `Object` type in general but especially as a collection element. If you need to store elements of several unrelated types together, consider wrapping them. For example, if you need to process both integer numbers and strings, you can define the following hierarchy (using the Java 16 records for brevity):

```
interface Entry {}
record IntEntry(int value) implements Entry {}
record StringEntry(String value) implements Entry {}
```

  Now, you can safely use `List<Entry>`, and the compiler will check that you are not placing irrelevant data there. If you are using Java 17 or higher, you can make the code more robust by declaring the interface as `sealed`, which would disallow external implementations.
- If you want to uniformly process several unrelated types defined in your project, consider declaring a common interface and implementing it. This not only allows you to avoid the `Object` type, but it will also improve your code in general. Even if such an interface is initially empty, it's quite possible that you'll later find it convenient for pulling some methods up from the implementation classes. This will reduce the amount of `instanceof` checks at use sites, making the code shorter and easier to read.
- If you have a chain of `instanceof` checks that should cover all possible cases, add an explicit `else` branch that throws an exception. This will greatly help to investigate mistakes if an unrelated object suddenly appears inside the variable. Note that since Java 21, exhaustive switch statements and expressions over `sealed` type hierarchies can be used to check this automatically during compilation. Together with deconstruction patterns for records, this allows you to process lists in a very clean way:

```
sealed interface Entry {}
record IntEntry(int value) implements Entry {}
record StringEntry(String value) implements Entry {}

void processList(List<Entry> list) {
  for (Entry element : list) {
    switch (element) {
      case IntEntry(int number) -> processNumber(number);
      case StringEntry(String string) -> processString(string);
    }
  }
}
```

  This way, the compiler will check automatically whether the switch statement covers all possible inheritors of the `Entry` interface. If a new inheritor appears later, the compilation error will occur at the `switch` statement, forcing you to handle the new case.

8.3   *Mistake 71: Searching for null in a null-hostile collection*

As you have seen before, Java programmers encounter `NullPointerException` bugs quite often. Many of these bugs are connected to the collections framework; standard collections and maps have at least three dispositions toward nulls:

- `null` *elements are possible in the collection.* Examples: `ArrayList`, `HashSet`, `Collections.singleton()`, and others.
- `null` *elements are not possible, yet search methods like* `contains()` *accept nulls and return a not-found result.* Examples: `ConcurrentLinkedQueue`, `EnumSet`, and `ArrayDeque`.
- `null` *elements are not possible, and search methods don't accept nulls.* Examples: collections returned from factory methods, like `List.of()`, `Set.of()`, `Map.of()`; `ConcurrentHashMap`, and `ConcurrentHashMap.newKeySet()`.

Many style guides recommend using interfaces like `Set`, `Map`, `List`, or `Collection` instead of concrete classes, like `ArrayList` or `HashSet`. In some cases, such as when using the factory methods `List.of()` or `Collections.singletonList()`, the implementation classes are not visible at all, so you have no other option than to use the interface. As a result, the declared variable type provides no hint about whether it's safe to call `contains(null)` or not.

These problems are not theoretical if you migrate a codebase beyond Java 8. The new collection factories introduced in Java 9 are attractive to use, but you may have legacy unmodifiable collections, like this:

```
Set<String> PLATFORMS = Collections.unmodifiableSet(
    new HashSet<>(Arrays.asList("PC", "Mac", "Mobile")));
```

It's tempting to replace this declaration using the new API:

```
Set<String> PLATFORMS = Set.of("PC", "Mac", "Mobile");
```

As all the elements are non-null string literals, the replacement might look safe. However, if `PLATFORMS.contains(str)` is used and `str` happens to be `null`, the call will fail with `NullPointerException`, instead of returning `false`.

WAYS TO AVOID THIS MISTAKE

- Do not blindly replace old, unmodifiable collections with collection factories, especially if the test coverage of your codebase is not very high.
- Avoid using `collection.contains(obj)` if `obj` can be `null`. Use a longer but safer condition, like `obj != null && collection.contains(obj)`.

8.4   Mistake 72: Using null values in maps

As discussed in the last mistake subsection, collections and maps have different dispositions toward `null`. However, even if you explicitly use a map implementation that
fully supports nulls (like `HashMap`), you still should be accurate, especially when it
comes to `null` values. Some methods in the `Map` interface assume mapping containing
the `null` value (let's call it `null` *mapping*) is like the absence of a value. Other methods
properly process a `null` value as a present value. There are also methods that appear
in-between. I can name five categories of methods:

- The methods `containsKey()`, `getOrDefault()`, and `put()` support `null` values,
  as shown in the following code:

```
var map = new HashMap<String, String>();
map.put("x", null);
assert map.containsKey("x");
assert map.getOrDefault("x", "default") == null;
```

  The `put()` method properly puts a `null` value, the `containsKey()` returns `true`,
  and `getOrDefault()` returns the existing `null` value instead of the supplied
  default. Note, though, that by examining the return value of `put()`, one cannot
  say whether `null` mapping or no mapping at all was recorded prior to update.

- Methods like `computeIfPresent()` and `compute()` do not distinguish between
  `null` mapping and an absent value. For example, if a remapping function
  returns `null`, then the existing mapping is removed. If a `null` mapping existed
  before the method call, then `computeIfPresent()` does not call the remapping
  function at all. In a sense, the `get()` method also falls into this category: if it
  returns `null`, you cannot determine whether it's a `null` mapping or an absent
  mapping.

- The `merge()` method allows you to insert a new entry into the map or combine
  a new value with an existing one using the provided function. Its signature
  looks like this:

```
V merge(K key, V value,
        BiFunction<? super V, ? super V, ? extends V> remappingFunction)
```

  Like `compute()`, it does not distinguish existing `null` mapping from an absent
  value either and removes the mapping if the remapping function returns `null`.
  However, it doesn't tolerate `null` as a value argument, which puts this method
  into a separate category, as exemplified in the following code:

```
var map = new HashMap<String, String>();        │ null mapping is replaced with 1;
map.put("x", null);                             │ a merge function is not called.
map.merge("x", "1", (x, y) -> null);      ⟵────┘
System.out.println(map);            ⟵──┤ Prints {x=1}    ┐ A merge function is called,
map.merge("x", "1", (x, y) -> null);      ⟵────────────── │ and mapping is removed.
System.out.println(map);            ⟵──┤ Prints {}
map.merge("x", null, (x, y) -> null);          ⟵──┤ Throws NullPointerException
```

On the first merge() call, the null mapping is replaced with "1" and the merge function is not called. On the subsequent merge() call, the merge function is called, and it returns null, so the mapping is deleted. The third call tries to write the null value via a value argument. You might expect either the null mapping to be written or nothing to happen if the method considers null absent. However, the real outcome is a NullPointerException.

- The putIfAbsent() method replaces the existing null mapping, so it appears to consider null mapping as an absent mapping; however, it can create a new null mapping if null is passed as a value. You might expect that if you call putIfAbsent() twice with the same key, the second call never has any effect. However, in fact, it can change the map:

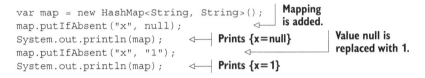

- Finally, the computeIfAbsent() method replaces existing null mapping. However, unlike compute(), it does not remove the existing null mapping if the function returns null. Instead, it doesn't do anything:

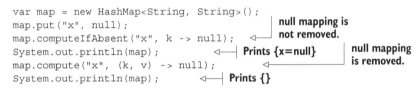

As you can see, the computeIfAbsent() call does not remove existing null mapping (but the lambda is actually called!), while the apparently similar compute() call actually removes the mapping.

Table 8.2 summarizes the behavior of different methods. These rules are quite complex—not only for beginners but also for experienced developers.

Table 8.2 Behavior of `java.util.Map` interface methods with respect to `null`

java.util.Map interface method	Distinguishes between existing null mapping and no mapping at all?	Puts null mapping if the value parameter is null?	Removes existing mapping if lambda returns null?
containsKey	yes	—	—
getOrDefault	yes	—	—
get	no	—	—
put	no	yes	—
putIfAbsent	no	yes	—

Table 8.2   Behavior of `java.util.Map` interface methods with respect to `null` *(continued)*

java.util.Map interface method	Distinguishes between existing null mapping and no mapping at all?	Puts null mapping if the value parameter is null?	Removes existing mapping if lambda returns null?
compute	no	—	yes
computeIfPresent	no	—	yes
computeIfAbsent	no	—	no
merge	no	no	yes

When Java 15 was under development, I contributed to the OpenJDK project an optimized version of `computeIfAbsent()` for `TreeMap`. The optimized code contained a mistake: `TreeMap.computeIfAbsent()` did not overwrite existing `null` mapping. This mistake slipped through code review and testing and was only noticed by an external user about a year later; it was finally fixed in Java 17. The behavior of `TreeMap.compute-IfAbsent()` in Java 15 and Java 16 remains subtly incorrect. So when it comes to `null` values, it's very easy to make mistakes, both when implementing and using the `Map` interface.

WAYS TO AVOID THIS MISTAKE

- The best way to avoid this mistake is to avoid `null` values in all maps. If you really need them, consider using some wrapper like `Optional`. For example, use `Map<String, Optional<String>>` instead of `Map<String, String>` and store `Optional.empty()` instead of a `null` value.
- If you really need `null` values (e.g., to interoperate with legacy code that is out of your control), try to stick with the simplest methods that properly support `null` values, like `containsKey()`, `getOrDefault()`, and `put()`. The code might become longer than necessary, but it will be clearer and more robust.
- When implementing your own maps, consider disallowing `null` values completely.

8.5   *Mistake 73: Trying to modify an unmodifiable Collection*

Some Java collections are mutable, and some are not. In some cases, only a subset of mutation operations works, as in the following examples:

- A collection created via `Arrays.asList()` allows you to modify existing elements (e.g., via the `List.set()` method) but does not allow you to add or remove elements.
- A set created via `Map.keySet()` allows you to remove elements but does not allow you to add new ones.
- Lists of zero or one elements returned via `Collections.emptyList()` and `Collections.singletonList()` are unmodifiable, but the `sort()` method does

not throw an exception—in fact, it does nothing because sorting zero or one elements does not require any modifications. On the other hand, the `sort()` method throws an `UnsupportedOperationException` when called for `List .of()`, even for zero or one elements.

An incomplete classification of mutable and immutable collections in the standard library is shown in figure 8.2.

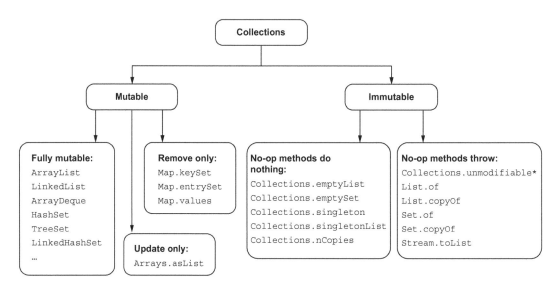

Figure 8.2   Standard Java collections categorized by mutability

Mutability is not encoded in the Java type system, so it's impossible to determine whether a collection is mutable just by looking at the collection type. This occasionally causes unexpected problems when a developer tries to modify the unmodifiable collection, resulting in runtime exceptions. It's not a big problem if the collection is always unmodifiable at a specific code location, as it's likely that testing will catch the bug. However, I have encountered cases in which a collection is sometimes modifiable and sometimes not. For example, consider the following utility method, which trims strings and removes empty ones from an input array:

```
static List<String> sanitize(String[] input) {
  if (input.length == 0) {
    return Collections.emptyList();
  }
  List<String> list = new ArrayList<>();
  for (String s : input) {
    s = s.trim();
    if (!s.isEmpty()) list.add(s);
  }
  return list;
}
```

This method returns a mutable `ArrayList` unless the input array is empty. In this case, an optimization was added to return a shared `emptyList()` instance instead of allocating a new list. You might imagine that a caller tries to modify the returned list:

```
List<String> strings = sanitize(input);
strings.add("Custom...");
```

This code works, unless `input` is an empty array, so there is a chance this problem could slip into production.

Static analysis

Static analysis may help here but only to an extent, as complex interprocedural analysis may be necessary to find out how the particular collection was created. The IntelliJ IDEA Nullability and Data Flow Problems inspection reports with the Immutable Collection Is Modified warning in simple cases. There are also annotations in the JetBrains annotations package, namely `@Unmodifiable` and `@UnmodifiableView`. They can be used to mark fields or the method return type. The `@UnmodifiableView` annotation can be used to mark collections whose modification methods are not implemented but have content that could be modified by someone else. Both annotations can be used to indicate that mutation methods should not be called on these collections, and a static analyzer will warn you if you try to call them. In some cases, these annotations may be inferred automatically.

WAYS TO AVOID THIS MISTAKE

- Assume any collection returned from called methods is unmodifiable by default. Do not try to modify it. If necessary, make a copy. If the collection returned from the method is mutable, it should be explicitly stated in the API documentation.
- Return unmodifiable collections from your methods by wrapping them with `Collections.unmodifiableXYZ()` methods or using collection factories, like `List.of()` or `List.copyOf()`. Avoid returning both modifiable and unmodifiable collections on different code paths of your method. When using the Stream API, use collectors that produce unmodifiable collections (available since Java 10) whenever possible. The `Stream.collect(Collectors.toList())` call produces a de-facto modifiable collection, even though it's not guaranteed by the specification. Use the `toUnmodifiableList()` collector to explicitly produce an unmodifiable list. Also, since Java 16, the `toList()` method is available directly in the Stream interface, which produces an unmodifiable list.
- Assume every collection passed to your method as a parameter is unmodifiable unless your method explicitly requires modifiable collection as the input. In general, modification of passed collections should be avoided in public APIs. The only place it may look natural is in collection utility methods (e.g., `Collections.shuffle()`). Sometimes, it's OK to modify a collection passed as a parameter in nonpublic methods to achieve better performance. However, this

should be justified by proper profiling. In other words, you can fill the collection in this way:

```
public List<String> getData() {
    List<String> data = new ArrayList<>();
    fillPredefinedData(data);
    fillDataFromPlugins(data);
    fillUserSpecificData(data);
    return data;
}

private void fillPredefinedData(List<String> target) { … }
private void fillDataFromPlugins(List<String> target) { … }
private void fillUserSpecificData(List<String> target) { … }
```

However, it's much better to return the result from helper methods instead of modifying the parameter:

```
private List<String> getPredefinedData() { … }
private List<String> getDataFromPlugins() { … }
private List<String> getUserSpecificData() { … }
```

In this case, the `getData()` method can use `addAll()` calls:

```
List<String> data = new ArrayList<>();
data.addAll(getPredefinedData());
data.addAll(getDataFromPlugins());
data.addAll(getUserSpecificData());          Make an
return List.copyOf(data);         ←──┘       unmodifiable copy.
```

Or even Stream API:

```
return Stream.of(getPredefinedData(),
                 getDataFromPlugins(),
                 getUserSpecificData())
          .flatMap(List::stream)
          .collect(Collectors.toUnmodifiableList());
```

This comes at some performance cost, as more intermediate objects are being created. However, this cost is rarely visible in profiles, so there is no need for premature optimization. On the other hand, now, the helper methods don't modify anything, so it's much easier to reuse and to test them.

- Modify only those collections you have created yourself. Usually, they are stored in local variables or private fields of your classes.
- The Guava library addresses this problem with the additional type hierarchy of immutable collections. For example, there are abstract classes, such as `ImmutableCollection`, `ImmutableSet`, and `ImmutableList`, that implement `Collection`, `Set`, and `List` interfaces, respectively. The implementations of these abstract classes are never modifiable, and their mutation methods are marked as deprecated, so you'll get a compilation warning and IDE highlighting if you accidentally use them. It's recommended to use these types when

declaring fields or methods. This doesn't fix the problem completely, as many other libraries you are using may not be Guava dependent and will still use standard JDK collection types. It's also possible your project has legacy components that don't use Guava collections and cannot be migrated easily or some of the developers in your project don't like depending on a third-party library. Still, using Guava collections may reduce the number of bugs related to modifying an unmodifiable collection.

8.6 Mistake 74: Using mutable objects as keys

Changing objects previously stored as map keys or set elements may break a collection. In particular, you might not be able to find or remove the object that was previously added to the collection. For example,

```
Set<List<String>> set = new HashSet<>();
List<String> list = new ArrayList<>();
set.add(list);
list.add("Value");
System.out.println(set.contains(list));    ◁── Prints false
```

As the list's content was changed after the list was added to the set, the hash code of the list was changed as well. However, the bucket index where the object is stored is based on the hash code the object had when it was added to the hash table. When `set.contains(list)` is executed, it uses the updated hash code and finds the wrong bucket, where no object is present.

I once stumbled upon a very tricky bug in which `BitSet` objects were used as map keys deep inside the IntelliJ IDEA static analyzer. New keys were derived from existing ones in a complex piece of code. We tried to copy the `BitSet` object prior to any changes, but apparently, we forgot to copy it in one case. This caused some items to mysteriously disappear from the map, and as a final result, users could receive incorrect static analysis warnings in very specific situations. It took several hours of debugging to find the problem. Unfortunately, there's no immutable `BitSet` in the standard library.

Legacy classes that process date and time, like `java.util.Date` and `Calendar`, are known to be a source of problems as well. They are mutable, so it's quite possible to accidentally change them after they are used as map keys or set elements. There are modern immutable alternatives, like `LocalDateTime`, but old classes may still be used in legacy code.

Note that there are objects that have a content-based `compareTo()` method but identity-based `equals()` and `hashCode()` methods. For example, `StringBuilder` was updated in Java 11 to implement the `Comparable` interface. This means it has inconsistent `equals()` and `compareTo()` implementations: `equals()` is always `false` for different objects, while `compareTo()` actually compares the objects' content. Can we use `StringBuilder` objects as `HashMap` keys or `HashSet` elements while modifying them? We are on slippery ground here. Since Java 8 (see JEP 180, https://openjdk.org/jeps/180), `HashMap` and `HashSet` implementation may switch to a red–black tree in a particular bucket and rely on the behavior of `compareTo()` if we have many hash colli-sions. On one hand, the default `hashCode()` in the HotSpot JVM is well distributed, and it's very unlikely to have many collisions. On the other hand, the JVM specifica-tion does not guarantee any particular kind of identity-based hash code distribution. Also, to make `HashSet` and `HashMap` rely on `compareTo()`, you need only one exact hash collision, along with a number of similar (but not exactly equal) hash codes. The following code provides a demonstration:

```
public static void main(String[] args) {
  Set<StringBuilder> set = new HashSet<>();

  for (int count = 0; count < 40; count++) {          Create 40 StringBuilder objects
    set.add(firstBucketStringBuilder());              with similar hashCode to force
  }                                                    HashSet to use a red–black tree.
  int[] hashCodes = set.stream()
      .mapToInt(Object::hashCode)
      .sorted().toArray();                             Create one more StringBuilder whose
  StringBuilder sb =                                   hashCode exactly matches the
    Stream.generate(StringBuilder::new)                hashCode of one existing object.
      .filter(b -> Arrays.binarySearch(
          hashCodes, b.hashCode()) >= 0)
      .findFirst().get();
  set.add(sb);                        ◄───────────     Add it to the HashSet, so the object
  System.out.println(set.contains(sb));                placement will be based on the compareTo()
  sb.append("b");                     ◄───────────     result rather than hashCode().
  System.out.println(set.contains(sb));
}                                                      Update StringBuilder; now, the
                                                       compareTo() result is different.

static StringBuilder firstBucketStringBuilder() {
  while (true) {
    StringBuilder sb = new StringBuilder("a");
    int hc = sb.hashCode();                            Check whether HashSet will put this
    if (((hc ^ (hc >>> 16)) & 0x3F) == 0) {            StringBuilder in bucket #0. This
      return sb;                                       code heavily relies on the current
    }                                                  OpenJDK implementation of HashSet.
  }
}
```

Prints true ─▷ (marginal note pointing to `System.out.println(set.contains(sb));`)

Prints false ─▷ (marginal note pointing to second `System.out.println(set.contains(sb));`)

The `firstBucketStringBuilder()` relies on the OpenJDK `HashMap` implementation (which is used inside the `HashSet`) and produces `StringBuilder` objects that go to the first hash table bucket when the hash table is small enough. So we create 40 `String-Builder` objects like this and then add them to the `HashSet`, forcing it to switch to red–black tree implementation. Next, we generate a single `StringBuilder` object that has exactly the same hash code as the one we already have (to speed the things up, this example uses a sorted array of hash codes and a binary search algorithm). This `StringBuilder` is stored into the variable `sb`. When we add this `StringBuilder` object to the `HashSet` and change it afterward, the `HashSet` cannot find it anymore: the `contains` method returns `false`.

Of course, this example is manually crafted. It's highly unlikely that you will have colliding hash codes like this if you don't create collisions on purpose. However, if this were to actually happen, it would be a kind of bug that is nearly impossible to reproduce.

WAYS TO AVOID THIS MISTAKE

- Avoid using mutable objects as map keys or set elements, or at least, avoid the mutations during the corresponding map or set lifetime.
- Remove legacy mutable objects, like `java.util.Date`, from your codebase when modern immutable alternatives are available.
- If you need to use mutable objects as map keys or set elements, the `java.util.IdentityHashMap` map implementation will probably serve your needs. It always compares stored objects by reference identity, regardless of the `equals()` and `hashCode()` implementation, so changes to object content won't affect the map behavior. If you need a set with the same semantics, use `Collections.newSetFromMap(new IdentityHashMap<>())`.
- You can safely use `HashSet` and `HashMap` if the mutable object does not define content-based `equals()`, `hashCode()`, and `compareTo()` methods.
- When using objects as `HashMap` keys or `HashSet` elements, check that their `compareTo()` implementation is consistent with their `equals()` implementation. Otherwise, you may have very rare bugs that occur only when hash collisions are present.
- The HotSpot JVM allows overriding the default hash code algorithm, though this feature is unspecified. In particular, the following command-line option forces an identity-based hash code to be always equal to constant value 1:

```
java -XX:+UnlockExperimentalVMOptions -XX:hashCode=2
```

Using the same identity hash code conforms to the JVM specification, although it may have an effect on performance. Consider testing your application with this option. This may help reveal the code that relies on identity hash code distribution.

8.7 Mistake 75: Relying on HashMap and HashSet encounter order

You can get the complete content of collection in many ways: by iterating it in a `for–each` loop, calling a `stream()` method, converting it to an array, or even calling `toString()`. In many collections, the order of elements is specified. In `TreeSet`, the order is either natural or it is specified by a comparator, and in `LinkedHashSet`, it is either insertion order or access order. However, in some collections, like `HashSet` or keys of `HashMap`, the order is deliberately not specified, as this allowed the authors of the Java standard library to implement the collection in more efficient ways.

Sometimes, developers forget this or simply don't think about it. The elements of `HashSet` could be printed in a user interface, and users will have a hard time finding the item they're looking for, as they will be displayed in a completely random order. If such a program was tested with only a small amount of data and the order of three or four elements looked somehow logical, the problem might not be noticed. It's also interesting that if you have a `HashSet` of small `Integer` numbers, they may appear sorted. You can try to create a set of all numbers from 0 to 99 and print it:

```
HashSet<Integer> set = IntStream.range(0, 100).boxed()
        .collect(Collectors.toCollection(HashSet::new));
System.out.println(set);    ⟵⌐  Prints
                              └  [0, 1, 2, 3, 4, 5, 6, 7, 8, …]
```

Using the standard OpenJDK implementation of `HashSet`, you may observe that the numbers come in order and continue increasing. Observing this, a developer might be convinced that the data is already sorted and no additional steps are necessary. However, this is just a coincidence, deriving from the implementation details. There is no guarantee it will be sorted if you slightly change the data. For example, if you multiply every number by 10, the numbers won't appear sorted anymore:

```
HashSet<Integer> set = IntStream.range(0, 100).mapToObj(x -> x * 10)
        .collect(Collectors.toCollection(HashSet::new));
System.out.println(set);    ⟵⌐  Prints
                              └  [0, 770, 260, 520, 10, …]
```

Sometimes, developers rely on the `HashSet` encounter order in tests. For example, let's assume that you want to test a method `getSeasons()` that returns `Set<String>`. To simplify the comparison, some developers may convert the output of the method to string, run it once, and record the result into the expected string:

```
@Test
public void testGetSeasons() {
  String result = getSeasons().toString();
  assertEquals("[Winter, Autumn, Summer, Spring]", result);
}
```

If `getSeasons()` happens to return the `HashSet`, the test becomes fragile, as it depends on the particular implementation of `HashSet`. While a change of the iteration order rarely occurs, it is certainly still possible. Such a change was introduced in Java 8, and many developers were forced to rewrite their tests when they upgraded.

Things become even more interesting if the `getSeasons()` method uses `Set.of()` immutable collection factory methods. This collection also does not guarantee any order, and to prevent developers from relying on a non-guaranteed order, it's randomized every time you restart the virtual machine. So if you run it once and record the result, the test will likely fail the next time, as the order will be different. The same happens with the order of entries in the maps returned from `Map.of()` methods.

WAYS TO AVOID THIS MISTAKE

- When iterating over a collection, ask yourself whether the collection has an order and whether its order matters. It definitely matters if you are displaying the items in a user interface. In this case, sort the elements.

- If you are asserting set or map equality in tests, compare the maps or sets directly. In this case, the order will be ignored. For example, the previously discussed test could be rewritten as

```
@Test
public void testGetSeasons() {
  assertEquals(Set.of("Winter", "Spring", "Summer", "Autumn"),
               getSeasons());
}
```

8.8 Mistake 76: Concurrent modification during the iteration

As a rule, non-concurrent Java collections forbid concurrent modification during iteration, except modifications performed via the iterator used for the iteration. This is usually enforced at run time by throwing a ConcurrentModificationException when such an illegal modification is detected. For example, the following code throws an exception:

```
List<String> list = new ArrayList<>(List.of("a", "b", "c"));
for (String s : list) {
  System.out.println(s);
  if (s.equals("b")) {
    list.add("x");
  }
}
```

How does this work? First, it should be noted that the enhanced for–each loop is syntactic sugar for the iterator loop. The previous code is equivalent to the following:

```
List<String> list = new ArrayList<>(List.of("a", "b", "c"));
Iterator<String> iterator = list.iterator();
while (iterator.hasNext()) {
  String s = iterator.next();
  System.out.println(s);
  if (s.equals("b")) {
    list.add("x");
  }
}
```

To detect concurrent modification, standard Java collections keep the modCount integer field, which is incremented every time a collection modification is performed. When an iterator is created, the current value of modCount is copied into the iterator instance. Every next() call checks whether the modCount copy inside the iterator is still equal to the modCount value in the original collection and throws an exception if a difference is detected. In this case, you successfully iterate over "a" and "b", but when a new value "x" is added to the list, the list modCount changes, while the iterator modCount stays the same. The next iterator.next() call sees the difference and throws an exception (figure 8.3).

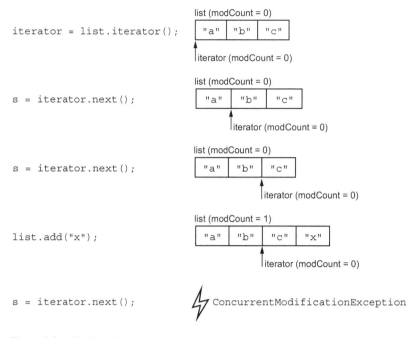

```
iterator = list.iterator();
```
list (modCount = 0)

| "a" | "b" | "c" |

iterator (modCount = 0)

```
s = iterator.next();
```
list (modCount = 0)

| "a" | "b" | "c" |

iterator (modCount = 0)

```
s = iterator.next();
```
list (modCount = 0)

| "a" | "b" | "c" |

iterator (modCount = 0)

```
list.add("x");
```
list (modCount = 1)

| "a" | "b" | "c" | "x" |

iterator (modCount = 0)

```
s = iterator.next();
```
ConcurrentModificationException

Figure 8.3   Iterator throws `ConcurrentModificationException` when `modCount` differs.

Such an approach is called *fail-fast behavior.* The approach gets its name from the fact that the iterator fails as soon as it detects the concurrent modification, rather than continuing the iteration without any guarantee the subsequent changes will be visible.

Note that an indexed loop over the list does not throw an exception, as there's no iterator. For example, the following loop terminates successfully, printing `"a"`, `"b"`, `"c"`, and `"x"`:

```
List<String> list = new ArrayList<>(List.of("a", "b", "c"));
for (int i = 0; i < list.size(); i++) {
  String s = list.get(i);
  System.out.println(s);
  if (s.equals("b")) {
    list.add("x");
  }
}
```

As discussed in mistake 18, in chapter 3, the classic `for` loop is a pretty fragile construct, and there are many ways to use it incorrectly. So, it's usually recommended to use a `for-each` loop whenever possible. However, in this case, the indexed loop terminates successfully, while the `for-each` loop will throw an exception. Here, the concurrent modification is evident, but the real code might be more sophisticated. For example, the collection could be modified inside another method called within the loop. Blindly replacing all the indexed loops with `for-each` loops might break your program.

Under some circumstances, `ConcurrentModificationException` is not thrown even if you use the iterator. For example, the following code doesn't throw an exception:

```
List<String> list = new ArrayList<>(List.of("a", "b", "c"));
for (String s : list) {
  System.out.println(s);
  if (s.equals("b")) {
    list.remove("a");
  }
}
```

Instead, it prints `"a"` and `"b"` and finishes without printing `"c"`. The reason will be clearer if you look at the desugared loop again:

```
List<String> list = new ArrayList<>(List.of("a", "b", "c"));
Iterator<String> iterator = list.iterator();
while (iterator.hasNext()) {
  String s = iterator.next();
  System.out.println(s);
  if (s.equals("b")) {
    list.remove("a");
  }
}
```

As you can see, if `hasNext()` returns `false`, you will exit the loop without calling `next()`. On the other hand, only `next()` checks the `modCount` equality. The `hasNext()` method simply checks whether the number of processed elements reaches the list size. When you remove the element after the second iteration, the list size reduces to 2, becoming equal to the iteration number, so the loop happily finishes (figure 8.4). This behavior is not specified exactly, so it's possible the exception will be thrown in future versions of Java or if you use another collection implementation. Nevertheless, you cannot always rely on `ConcurrentModificationException` being thrown.

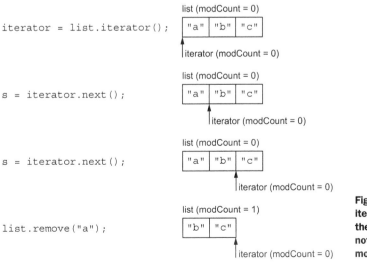

Figure 8.4   When the iterator points at the end of the `ArrayList`, it does not detect the concurrent modification.

WAYS TO AVOID THIS MISTAKE

- Treat `ConcurrentModificationException` as your friend, not an enemy. If it happens, it is trying to tell you there's a bug in your program. You should address the problem, rather than ignore the warning. Never catch `Concurrent-ModificationException` specifically. There's no legal way to handle this exception, aside from reporting it and terminating the whole task that caused it.

- Note that using the `forEach()` method or traversing the collection via a stream API is also a kind of iteration, so you should not modify a collection inside a `forEach()` lambda or stream operation.

- Replace indexed loops with for–each loops with care, even if your IDE suggests you do so. If the loop modifies the collection it loops over, then such a replacement may break your program.

- If you expect collection modifications during the iteration, you must decide whether the iteration needs to see the subsequent changes. If not, then it's reasonable to copy the original collection just for the iteration:

```
for (String element : new ArrayList<>(collection)) {
  … // Use the element; modify the collection.
}
```

- If the modifications are expected to be rare, you may use `CopyOnWriteArray-List`. The primary purpose of this collection is to provide thread-safe access, but it can be useful even if you have only one thread. This collection allows concurrent modifications, and its iterator will always see the state of the collection at the point when the iterator was created. The collection copies the internal array at every modification but does not copy it when the iterator is created. As a result, this might be faster than copying the collection for iteration, though proper benchmarking is necessary to decide which solution is better for your workload.

8.9   *Mistake 77: Mixing List.remove() overloads*

In the standard library, the `Collection.remove(Object)` method allows you to remove a given element from a collection. The `List` interface adds another method, `List.remove(int)`, which allows you to remove an element at a given index position. Unfortunately, if you have `List<Integer>`, these overloads add confusion and may result in binding the unintended method, as in the following example:

```
List<Integer> offsets = getOffsets();
offsets.remove(0);
```

Here, the element at index 0 will be removed unconditionally. However, the code author probably wanted to remove a value 0 that was stored in any position in the list. Unfortunately, it's hard to detect such mistakes with static analysis, as there's nothing suspicious about this code; it's also possible that removal by index was intended.

WAYS TO AVOID THIS MISTAKE

- Modern IDEs may display parameter name hints—pay attention to them. For the preceding code snippet, the hint tells us the argument is interpreted as `index` (figure 8.5).

```
List<Integer> offsets = getOffsets();
offsets.remove( index: 0);
```

Figure 8.5   Parameter hint displayed for the `List.remove()` method in IntelliJ IDEA

- As previously mentioned, avoid collections over boxed primitives, in favor of third-party libraries, like FastUtil. They are much faster, use less memory, and provide methods with separate names for removal by value and by index.
- The `remove(Object)` method returns a `boolean` value indicating whether the removal was successful. If you use it, you will immediately notice you are calling the wrong method. For example, you may add an assert if you expect the element 0 to appear in the list:

```
boolean success = offsets.remove(0);        ◁── Incorrect and leads to
assert success : "Element 0 wasn't found";       a compilation error
```

This will not only make your code more robust by throwing an exception if the assertion fails, but you will also immediately have a compilation error signaling that the called method is wrong.

```
boolean success = offsets.remove((Integer) 0);   ◁── Correct
assert success : "Element 0 wasn't found";
```

8.10 Mistake 78: Jumping over the next element after List.remove()

There's another bug pattern when using the `List.remove(index)` method. It appears when you loop over the list indices (e.g., to remove the list tail):

```
void trimHistory(List<?> history, int maxElements) {
  for (int i = maxElements; i < history.size(); i++) {
    history.remove(i);
  }
}
```

This method attempts to remove the tail of the `history` list if its size is greater than `maxElements`. However, it doesn't take into account that after removing a single element, the subsequent elements are shifted backward, so when you go to the next loop iteration, you skip one element. Suppose `maxElements` is 5 and the history list has 10 elements, with indexes from 0 to 9. In this case, the method will remove only elements at indices 5, 7, and 9, leaving the elements at indices 6 and 8 as is (figure 8.6).

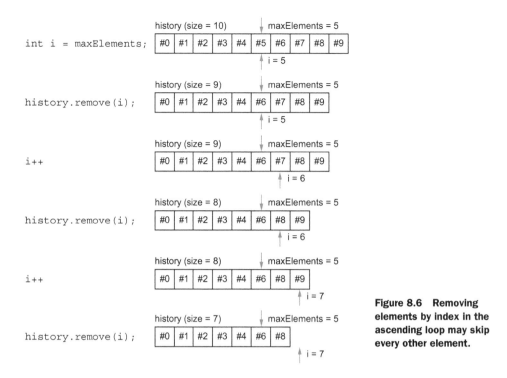

```
int i = maxElements;
```
history (size = 10)   maxElements = 5
#0 #1 #2 #3 #4 #5 #6 #7 #8 #9
i = 5

```
history.remove(i);
```
history (size = 9)   maxElements = 5
#0 #1 #2 #3 #4 #6 #7 #8 #9
i = 5

```
i++
```
history (size = 9)   maxElements = 5
#0 #1 #2 #3 #4 #6 #7 #8 #9
i = 6

```
history.remove(i);
```
history (size = 8)   maxElements = 5
#0 #1 #2 #3 #4 #6 #8 #9
i = 6

```
i++
```
history (size = 8)   maxElements = 5
#0 #1 #2 #3 #4 #6 #8 #9
i = 7

```
history.remove(i);
```
history (size = 7)   maxElements = 5
#0 #1 #2 #3 #4 #6 #8
i = 7

Figure 8.6   Removing elements by index in the ascending loop may skip every other element.

The problem may become more subtle if you remove the element under a condition:

```
for (int i = 0; i < data.size(); i++) {
  if (condition(data.get(i), i)) {
    data.remove(i);
  }
}
```

In this case, if the condition is met for some element, you don't check the condition for the following one. If the condition is rarely true, then it's much rarer for it to be true for two subsequent elements. In this case, the problem could go unnoticed during testing and slip into production.

A bug like this appeared in the IntelliJ IDEA Debugger and was reported by an external user. The debugger has a feature to preview JVM thread dumps and merge threads that have identical stack traces. This was implemented in a similar `for` loop: if a thread with an identical stack trace was encountered, it was removed from the list by index. The bug prevented the next thread from being checked, so some threads with identical stack traces were not actually merged.

To fix this problem, you can decrement a loop variable right after every `remove()` call:

```
for (int i = 0; i < data.size(); i++) {
  if (condition(data.get(i), i)) {
```

```
    data.remove(i);
    i--;
  }
}
```

Alternatively, you can only increment the loop variable if removal did not happen:

```
for (int i = 0; i < data.size();) {
  if (condition(data.get(i), i)) {
    data.remove(i);
  } else {
    ++i;
  }
}
```

> **Static analysis**
>
> Some static analyzers can detect this particular pattern, at least in simple cases. IntelliJ IDEA has a Suspicious `List.remove()` in the Loop inspection, which warns on the preceding samples. SonarLint reports this problem via its rule S5413: `List.remove()` Should Not Be Used in Ascending for Loops. This may not work if the loop is more complex though.

WAYS TO AVOID THIS MISTAKE

- Be careful when removing list elements by index in the loop. Remember that the tail will shift backward, so you may skip one element.
- If you want to remove part of your collection unconditionally, consider using `subList()` and `clear()`:

  ```
  if (history.size() > maxElements) {
    history.subList(maxElements, history.size()).clear();
  }
  ```

  Don't forget to guard the `subList()` call with a bounds check to avoid an `IndexOutOfBoundsException`. For collections like `ArrayList`, such an approach is faster than removing elements one by one in a loop, as all the elements are removed at once.

- If the semantics of your code permits, you can reverse the loop direction like this:

  ```
  for (int i = data.size() - 1; i >= 0; i--) {
    if (condition(data.get(i), i)) {
      data.remove(i);
    }
  }
  ```

  The reversed loop is not affected by this problem, as you don't traverse the shifted tail.

- Use the `removeIf()` method if the condition doesn't depend on the index:

```
data.removeIf(this::condition);
```

- If your loop is less trivial and does more than just removing elements, consider using an iterator instead of indexed access. If you remove elements via the iterator itself, it will not skip the subsequent element:

```
Iterator<Object> it = data.iterator();
while (it.hasNext()) {
  Object next = it.next();
  … // Do something else using the next element.
  if (condition(next)) {
    it.remove();
  }
}
```

- You can also use a `ListIterator` that keeps the index inside and properly updates it. Also, this allows other list modifications, like adding or replacing elements:

```
ListIterator<Object> iterator = list.listIterator();
while (iterator.hasNext()) {
  int index = iterator.nextIndex();
  Object next = iterator.next();
  … // Use index and next.
  if (condition(next, index)) {
    iterator.remove();
  }
}
```

Unfortunately, this makes the code much more verbose and harder to understand. In general, developers tend to avoid `ListIterator`.

8.11   Mistake 79: Reading the collection inside Collection.removeIf()

The `removeIf()` method was added to the `java.util.Collection` class in Java 8. It allows the removal of some collection elements by a predicate. Naturally, it would be a bad idea to modify the same collection from inside the predicate. Usually, `removeIf()` implementations detect such modifications and throw `ConcurrentModification-Exception`.

However, there's another potential pitfall associated with this method, which might at first appear harmless: querying the original collection. Since in which order predicate calls and list modifications are performed is unspecified, you may get an unexpected result; depending on the collection, it may or may not have already been modified.

Imagine you have a collection of numbers for which the order of the elements doesn't matter and you want to replace every series of adjacent numbers with the lowest number from the series. For example, a collection 1, 2, 3, 8, 9, 10, 13, 14 contains three series of adjacent numbers, namely (1, 2, 3); (8, 9, 10); and (13, 14). So you want to keep only 1, 8, and 13 and remove all the rest. It might seem like a good idea to use `removeIf()` in this scenario:

```
static void process(Collection<Integer> c) {
  c.removeIf(x -> c.contains(x - 1));
  System.out.println(c);
}
```

Here, you remove every number if its predecessor is also in the collection. Sounds good. Let's test this solution:

```
List<Integer> numbers =
    Arrays.asList(1, 2, 3, 8, 9, 10, 13, 14);
process(new ArrayList<>(numbers));
```

It works correctly and prints `[1, 8, 13]`. However, now, use another collection type—for example, `TreeSet`:

```
process(new TreeSet<>(numbers));
```

It prints `[1, 3, 8, 10, 13]`, which is not what was intended. The difference here can be explained if you look at the `removeIf()` implementation in `ArrayList` and `Tree-Set`. The `ArrayList` implementation calls the predicate for every collection element before any changes to the collection are applied. It gathers the results and then applies them all at once. This greatly optimizes the performance if you need to delete many elements, as they are moved inside the underlying array once at most.

Conversely, `TreeSet` would not gain much from such an optimization, so the default implementation is used, which just iterates over the collection and uses `iterator.remove()` every time the predicate returns `true`. As a result, for `ArrayList`, the predicate sees the original collection state, while for `TreeSet`, the predicate does not see the elements removed at previous iterations.

The result might depend not only on the kind of collection but also on the Java version. For example, let's use an `ArrayDeque`:

```
process(new ArrayDeque<>(numbers));
```

Now, you get `[1, 3, 8, 10, 13]` in Java 8 but `[1, 8, 13]` in Java 9 or higher. That's because a similar optimization was first implemented for the `ArrayDeque` class in Java 9. It's not specified whether the predicate should see the changes from previous iterations, so it's better to avoid relying on this.

WAYS TO AVOID THIS MISTAKE

- Do not query the original collection from inside the `removeIf()` predicate, as it's not specified whether the previous changes are visible. Note that `ConcurrentModificationException` will not help to detect this problem, as you are not performing the concurrent modification.

- If possible, avoid modifying the original collection and create a new collection instead. For example, you may return the new collection from the `process()` method:

```
static List<Integer> process(Collection<Integer> c) {
  return c.stream().filter(x -> !c.contains(x - 1)).toList();
}
```

In this case, you always observe the original state of the input collection, as you don't change it at all.

8.12   *Mistake 80: Concurrent modification in Map.computeIfAbsent()*

Java 8 introduced several new methods to the `Map` interface, allowing programmers to update mapping based on the previous value and whether it previously existed. These methods are `computeIfAbsent()`, `computeIfPresent()`, `compute()`, and `merge()`. The updated value is computed using a user-provided function.

For example, here's how adding a new element to a multimap looked prior to Java 8:

```
static void addToMultiMap(Map<String, List<String>> map,
                          String key,
                          String value) {
  List<String> list = map.get(key);
  if (list == null) {
    list = new ArrayList<>();
    map.put(key, list);
  }
  list.add(value);
}
```

Now, thanks to `computeIfAbsent()`, it could be a one-liner:

```
static void addToMultiMap(Map<String, List<String>> map,
                          String key,
                          String value) {
  map.computeIfAbsent(key, k -> new ArrayList<>()).add(value);
}
```

These methods are not only API shortcuts. When you call `get()` and `put()` separately, you need to find the key twice inside the map data structure, whether it's a hash table or binary tree. With a single `computeIfAbsent()` method, the search is performed only once, and if the key is absent, `computeIfAbsent()` already knows where it should be added. So using new methods could be more performant if there's an optimized implementation. `HashMap` has featured the optimized implementation since Java 8, and `TreeMap` has had it since Java 15.

This optimization has a cost. Remember that a user-specified function is called between finding a place for the new key and inserting it. If the function happens to modify the map as well, then the location found for the key may no longer be correct.

This problem was noticed only after Java 8 was released, so such a concurrent modification may cause a corrupted `HashMap` in Java 8. Since Java 9, concurrent modification in `HashMap` has been detected and `ConcurrentModificationException` could be thrown from `computeIfAbsent()` and similar methods.

Sometimes, concurrent modifications occur if a map is used to cache the results of a computation that depends on other values that appear in the same cache. If it always happens, you will easily detect the problem during testing. However, if dependency on other values happens rarely, the problem might not be detected until after the code is released.

For example, assume you want to create an engine that processes expressions like `"$b$ + $c$"` or `"$d$ * 2"`, where `$b$`, `$c$`, and `$d$` are variable references. For this engine, you need to find all the references used in a given expression. To make the example simpler, instead of writing a full-fledged parser, we will just extract substrings between odd and even occurrences of `$`:

```
static Set<String> immediateRefs(String expression) {
  String[] parts = expression.split("\\$");
  return IntStream.range(0, parts.length / 2)
               .mapToObj(pos -> parts[pos * 2 + 1])
               .collect(Collectors.toSet());
}
```

When the `"$b$ + $c$"` argument is passed here, the `parts` array will contain four strings: `""`, `"b"`, `" + "`, and `"c"`. The stream will select those with odd indices, namely `"b"` and `"c"`, and store them in the set.

Now, let's assume every variable represents an expression that may refer to other variables. For example, let's use the following set of expressions:

```
Map<String, String> map = Map.of("a", "$b$ + $c$",
                                 "b", "1",
                                 "c", "$d$ * 2",
                                 "d", "3");
```

The dependencies between them are illustrated in figure 8.7.

Now, you are interested in all the variables on which the given variable depends, either directly or transitively. For example, for the variable a, you want to return b, c, and d because a depends on b and c directly and c depends on d. You may write something like this:

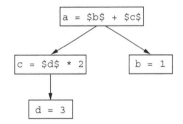

Figure 8.7   Expressions dependencies

```
Set<String> transitiveRefs(String variable) {
  Set<String> result = new HashSet<>();
  String expression = map.getOrDefault(variable, "");
  for (String ref : immediateRefs(expression)) {
    result.add(ref);
    result.addAll(transitiveRefs(ref));
```

```
  }
  return result;
}
```

Again, to simplify the example, let's assume cyclic dependencies are impossible, so you won't get into the stack overflow problem discussed in chapter 5. If there are many variables and long expressions, this method may become unacceptably slow. So it could be reasonable to use a cache:

```
final Map<String, Set<String>> refCache = new HashMap<>();

Set<String> transitiveRefs(String variable) {
  return refCache.computeIfAbsent(variable, this::calc);
}

private Set<String> calc(String variable) {
  Set<String> result = new HashSet<>();
  String expression = map.getOrDefault(variable, "");
  for (String ref : immediateRefs(expression)) {
    result.add(ref);
    result.addAll(transitiveRefs(ref));
  }
  return result;
}
```

We move the calculation code to a helper method `calc()` and call it when its result is absent in the cache. It looks smart, but it doesn't work. That's because the `calc()` method calls `transitiveRefs()` inside, which may again modify the same `refCache` map. So now, calling `transitiveRefs("a")` results in a `ConcurrentModification-Exception`. On the other hand, `transitiveRefs("b")` and `transitiveRefs("d")` will finish successfully. Moreover, if we call `transitiveRefs("c")` and `transitive-Refs("a")` after that, these calls will be successful as well:

```
@Test
public void bottomUp() {                                    ⟵──┐ This test
    assertEquals(Set.of(), transitiveRefs("d"));                │ passes.
    assertEquals(Set.of("d"), transitiveRefs("c"));         ──┘
    assertEquals(Set.of(), transitiveRefs("b"));
    assertEquals(Set.of("b", "c", "d"), transitiveRefs("a"));
}

@Test                          This test fails with
public void topDown() {    ⟵── ConcurrentModificationException.
    assertEquals(Set.of("b", "c", "d"), transitiveRefs("a"));
    assertEquals(Set.of(), transitiveRefs("b"));
    assertEquals(Set.of("d"), transitiveRefs("c"));
    assertEquals(Set.of(), transitiveRefs("d"));
}
```

The `transitiveRefs("a")` call in the former test is successful because other values are already cached, and concurrent modification doesn't happen. So the behavior depends on the call order, and if a unit test happens to have the same call order, it will pass, and the bug might go unnoticed.

To solve the problem, you should avoid using `computeIfAbsent()` and fall back on using the good old `get`/`put` sequence:

```
Set<String> transitiveReferences(String variable) {
  Set<String> result = refCache.get(variable);
  if (result == null) {
    result = calc(variable);
    refCache.put(variable, result);
  }
  return result;
}
```

WAYS TO AVOID THIS MISTAKE

- When using `computeIfAbsent()` and similar methods, always confirm the function does not modify the same map as the method, directly or indirectly.
- When in doubt, use the `get`/`put` sequence.
- Recheck your `computeIfAbsent()` calls when updating to a newer Java version. For example, if you update to Java 15 or newer, `TreeMap.computeIfAbsent()` starts throwing `ConcurrentModificationException`, so the code that worked before may stop working. Note that, even if a particular `Map` implementation does not detect concurrent modification, it's still a misuse of the `computeIfAbsent()` method, as its documentation explicitly forbids concurrent modifications.
- Be careful when writing tests that assert several things. Normally, the Arrange, Act, Assert pattern is used for writing good tests, which assumes you should not modify anything during the assertion phase. The preceding tests violate this rule, as the `transitiveRefs()` method changes the cache state, which may affect the subsequent asserts. We will discuss the Arrange, Act, Assert pattern in more detail in chapter 10.

8.13 *Mistake 81: Violating Iterator contracts*

To make your own `Collection`, `Map`, or `Iterable`, you may need to create a custom `Iterator` implementation. The problem with iterators is that, while they have quite strict contracts, in 99% of cases, they're used in a very specific way. As long as your iterator behaves correctly when used in this way, you may not notice that it's implemented incorrectly. However, your program may easily break if somebody needs to use the iterator in an unusual way.

The very specific way I am referring to is the way it's used by an enhanced `for` statement, or `for-each` statement. The enhanced `for` statement takes the `Iterable` instance, requests a new `Iterator` via an `iterator()` call, and then goes through the following steps:

1 Checks `iterator.hasNext()`. If it returns false, then the iteration finishes
2 Gets the next element via `iterator.next()` and assigns the result to the loop parameter

3 Executes the loop body

4 Returns to step 1

That's it. So if your iterator supports this scenario, it will work in any enhanced `for` loop. In particular, such a loop never does any of these things:

- Call `iterator.hasNext()` twice in a row without `iterator.next()` in-between
- Call `iterator.next()` twice in a row without `iterator.hasNext()` in-between
- Call `iterator.next()` before `iterator.hasNext()`
- Catch and handle a `NoSuchElementException` thrown by `iterator.next()` when there are no elements left

While an enhanced `for`-loop never does any of these, they are perfectly valid operations to perform on the iterator. Some utility methods that work on collections actually do these things, including standard methods like `Collections.min()` and `Collections.max()`, which find minimal and maximal collection elements. These methods start with `iterator.next()` without a prior `hasNext()` call, throwing `NoSuchElementException` directly from the iterator if the input collection is empty.

Some iterator implementations rely on the fact that `hasNext()` will be called before `next()` and prepare the next value inside the `hasNext()`. For example, assume you want to create a `Collection` that generates numbers from 0 to `max` (exclusive). One possibility is to inherit `AbstractCollection` and provide an iterator. Imagine this is implemented in the following way:

```
static Collection<Integer> range(int max) {
  if (max < 0) throw new IllegalArgumentException();
  return new AbstractCollection<>() {
    public int size() { return max; }

    public Iterator<Integer> iterator() {
      return new Iterator<>() {
        int cur = -1;

        public boolean hasNext() {
          return ++cur < max;
        }

        public Integer next() { return cur; }
      };
    }
  };
}
```

This implementation obviously violates the `Iterator` contract in several ways. For example, `hasNext()` changes its state, and `next()` never throws `NoSuchElement-Exception`. Still, it works when used in an enhanced `for` loop:

```
for (int value : range(10)) {
  System.out.println(value);
}
```

This loop will print numbers from 0 to 9, as expected. As such canonical uses work, it's possible to overlook the incorrect iterator implementation. That's why similar poorly written iterators appear in production code. However, calling `Collections.min()` reveals the problem:

```
System.out.println(Collections.min(range(10)));    ◁─── −1 is printed.
```

In this example, the problem is quite evident and could be fixed in a rather straightforward way:

```
public Iterator<Integer> iterator() {
  return new Iterator<>() {
    int cur = 0;

    public boolean hasNext() {
      return cur < max;
    }

    public Integer next() {
      if (!hasNext()) {
        throw new NoSuchElementException();
      }
      return cur++;
    }
  };
}
```

However, more complex iterators exist, including those that cannot know whether the next element is available without producing a side effect. For example, suppose you want to adapt a `BufferedReader` to iterate over its lines. Without reading the next line from the source, you may not know if it exists. Again, a naïve implementation might look like this:

```
static Iterator<String> asIterator(BufferedReader reader) {
  return new Iterator<>() {
    String next;

    public boolean hasNext() {
      try {
        next = reader.readLine();
      } catch (IOException e) {
        throw new UncheckedIOException(e);
      }
      return next != null;
    }

    public String next() { return next; }
  };
}
```

Here, you delegate to the `readLine()` method, which returns `null` if there are no more lines. As you have seen previously, this implementation is incorrect. Calling `hasNext()`

twice in a row or calling `next()` without `hasNext()` will produce an unexpected result. While it's necessary to read the next line inside the `hasNext()`, you should be careful to avoid reading two lines if `hasNext()` is called repeatedly and to ensure the next line was read when calling `next()`. So the `hasNext()` method should check whether it was already called after the last `next()` method:

```java
return new Iterator<>() {
  String next;

  public boolean hasNext() {
    if (next != null) return true;
    try {
      next = reader.readLine();
    } catch (IOException e) {
      throw new UncheckedIOException(e);
    }
    return next != null;
  }

  public String next() {
    if (!hasNext()) {
      throw new NoSuchElementException();
    }
    String cur = next;
    next = null;
    return cur;
  }
};
```

Here, the `null` value in the `next` field means either that the next value has not been read yet or you've reached the end of the input. Luckily, this iterator never returns `null`, and it's possible to call `readLine()` repeatedly at the end of the input. In other cases, you may need to introduce `boolean` fields to track whether you need to fetch the next value and whether the iteration is finished.

Static analysis

Static analyzers can perform basic checks for your iterators. IntelliJ IDEA has inspections like `Iterator.hasNext()`, Which Calls `next()` and `Iterator.next()`, Which Can't Throw `NoSuchElementException`. SonarLint has the S2272: `Iterator.next()` Methods Should Throw `NoSuchElementException` rule. Unfortunately, they don't cover all the possible problems with iterator implementations and also may produce false positives.

WAYS TO AVOID THIS MISTAKE

- Test your custom iterators thoroughly. It's not very hard to write a common utility to test the iterator contract, given an iterator (or a supplier capable of producing identical iterators) and a set of expected values. The utility should be able to call `hasNext()` without `next()` several times, and vice versa. It should also ensure the correct behavior when the iteration finishes. If `hasNext()` returns `false`, all subsequent calls to `hasNext()` must also return `false` and subsequent calls to `next()` must throw `NoSuchElementException`.

- Unless it's really necessary, do not change the iterator internal state inside the `hasNext()` method. Doing this makes the implementation more complex and fragile.
- Try to avoid manual iterator implementation as much as possible. Check the JDK and popular libraries; they may have the iterator you need. Note that you can create an `Iterator` from Java `Stream` (though this may add some overhead). If you need an iterator over integer numbers, you can use

```
return IntStream.range(0, max).iterator();
```

Similarly, you don't need to manually implement an iterator to iterate over `BufferedReader` lines. Instead, you can use

```
return reader.lines().iterator();
```

In general, reusing existing code is a great way to reduce the number of potential bugs in your program.

Summary

- When looking for a specific element in a collection, it's possible to mistakenly specify an element of unrelated type. In this case, instead of an exception, you'll just get a not-found result, so the program may silently work incorrectly.
- Avoid using types like `List<Object>`, as the compiler won't protect you from storing irrelevant elements in such collections.
- Collections have inconsistent rules about handling `null` elements. It's better to avoid storing and querying nulls at all.
- Some Java collections are mutable, while others are not. Mutable collections may not support all mutation operations. The standard Java library does not provide explicit types to designate whether a collection is mutable, so it's possible to accidentally call the mutation method on an immutable collection, causing an exception at run time.
- Sets and maps may rely on the fact that the `hashCode()` and `compareTo()` methods produce a stable result for the keys. If the key is modified while it's stored inside the collection, you may not be able to find this key again.
- Some sets and maps may not guarantee any iteration order. It's important to avoid exposing the internal order to a user interface and to not rely on it in tests.
- The `List.remove()` method has two overloads: it can remove a given element or remove by index. It's possible to accidentally call the wrong method, especially if you have `List<Integer>`. Care should also be taken if you remove several elements by index in a loop, as you may accidentally skip some elements.

- When iterating over a mutable collection or using collection methods that accept a lambda function, it's usually not allowed to modify the collection from within the iteration or the lambda function. If you try to, you may get `Concurrent-ModificationException`.
- When you implement a custom iterator, it's essential to fulfill its contract. The standard `for-each` loop utilizes only one iterator-usage scenario, so it may work correctly even with a broken iterator. However, other scenarios in which the mistake will show up are possible as well.

Library methods

9

This chapter covers

- Problems with `StringBuilder` constructor invocation
- Stream API misuse patterns
- `getClass()` method pitfalls
- `String`-to-`boolean` conversion problems
- Common mistakes in date and time formatting
- Non-atomic call sequences

In previous chapters, we discussed the pitfalls of using library methods related to numbers, strings, collections, and maps. These are most of the essential parts of the standard library; however, there are other library methods that could be misused but did not fit the previous chapters. We consider these in this chapter.

9.1 Mistake 82: Passing char to StringBuilder constructor

If you use `StringBuilder`, you can either provide the initial content or create it empty and append the initial content later:

```
StringBuilder sb = new StringBuilder("Hello");
```

The preceding code line is equivalent to

```
StringBuilder sb = new StringBuilder();
sb.append("Hello");
```

Well, it's not strictly equivalent, as the constructor parameter affects the initial size of the inner buffer, so the performance could be slightly different. Still, behaviorally, it's the same, and many people assume one can safely merge the first `append()` into the constructor to save the keystrokes. This may go badly if you start the `append`-chain with a `char`:

```
StringBuilder sb = new StringBuilder('[');    Incorrect: '[' is implicitly
sb.append(value);                             converted to int.
sb.append(']');
```

This `StringBuilder` will not start with an opening bracket. Here, the `String-Builder(int capacity)` constructor overload is linked instead, and `'['` is just widened to the `int` value 91, which is used as the initial capacity (figure 9.1). Such a bug existed for years in the profiling code of the GraalVM compiler project and was fixed in 2018, thanks to the Error Prone static analyzer.

How a programmer sees the expression

    `new StringBuilder('[')`

How the compiler sees the expression

`new StringBuilder(91)`   **Figure 9.1   The char argument in the StringBuilder constructor is widened to int.**

> **Static analysis**
>
> Static analysis tools easily detect this pattern. IntelliJ IDEA reports a `StringBuilder` Constructor Call with `char` Argument warning. SonarLint has a rule S1317: `String-Builder` and `StringBuffer` Should Not Be Instantiated with a Character to report this. Error Prone has a bug pattern named StringBuilderInitWithChar.

WAYS TO AVOID THIS MISTAKE

- Avoid using character literals in favor of string literals whenever possible. For example, here, use `"["` instead of `'['`. String literals are never implicitly converted to numbers, so similar problems are impossible with them. The performance penalty is marginal in most cases.
- Cover UI messages with unit tests. This way, you will quickly detect such problems.

9.2   *Mistake 83: Producing side effects in a Stream API chain*

Stream API was introduced in Java 8 to process data sequences in a fluent style. It's mostly intuitive and rarely causes correctness bugs. Still, there are few things developers should know to avoid undesired effects.

A Stream API call consists of creating a stream from the source, any count of intermediate operations, and a single terminal operation. There are many ways to create a stream. Probably the most common is to create it from a collection using the `collection.stream()` method. An intermediate operation, like `map()` or `filter()`, updates the content of the stream, producing another stream. Finally, a terminal operation creates a final result from the stream. Examples of terminal operations include `count()`, `toArray()`, and `collect()`. It's important to understand that the stream doesn't process anything until you call the final operation. Intermediate operations are just memorized, like a recipe for the final dish, but the baking won't start until you call the terminal operation.

Most of the intermediate operations accepting functions assume the functions do not produce any side effects. This means the only outcome of the function is its return value, and the program state doesn't change, regardless of how many times you call the function—or whether you are calling it at all. Here's an example of a `filter()` operation with a side effect:

```
List<String> containNoNeedle = new ArrayList<>();
List<String> containNeedle = list.stream()
  .filter(str -> {
    if (str.contains("needle")) {
      return true;
    }
    containNoNeedle.add(str);
    return false;
  })
  .toList();
```

In this sample, the functional parameter of the `filter()` operation doesn't only return `true` or `false` based on the string content; it may also modify another collection, which is a side effect. Therefore, it becomes crucial to call this function exactly once per input element. Otherwise, the content of `containNoNeedle` may be unexpected. Moreover, the order of calls matters: if the function is called for elements in backward order, it may also affect the result. Calling the function concurrently from several threads (which will happen if you replace `stream()` with `parallelStream()`) may produce an exception or loss of data. This is not an idiomatic use of Stream API. In fact, if you need to partition the input stream based on condition, there's a canonical way to do this, using the `partitioningBy()` collector:

```
Map<Boolean, List<String>> partitions = list.stream()
  .collect(Collectors.partitioningBy(str -> str.contains("needle")));
List<String> containNoNeedle = partitions.get(false);
List<String> containNeedle = partitions.get(true);
```

So, producing a side effect from the function passed into an intermediate operation is not recommended. A notable exception is the `Stream.peek()` operation, which has the sole purpose of producing a side effect, as its functional parameter returns `void`. However, the method documentation explicitly states that this method exists mainly to support debugging and the supplied function is not guaranteed to be executed if the stream implementation is able to optimize away the production of some or all the elements.

Sometimes, the restriction to avoid side effects appears too limiting, and it's tempting to produce a side effect. For example, assume you have a list of strings, and you want to trim all of them and select those trimmed strings that are longer than 10 characters. Some developers might want to perform both operations in a single stream:

```
void trimAndFilter(List<String> strings) {
  List<String> trimmed = new ArrayList<>();
  List<String> trimmedLong = strings.stream()
    .map(String::trim)
    .peek(trimmed::add)
    .filter(s -> s.length() > 10)
    .toList();
  … // Use trimmed and trimmedLong.
}
```

Here, `peek()` fills the `trimmed` collection, which is used after. While this code works, it's fragile, as the content of `trimmed` may depend on a subsequent operation. For example, let's say you decided later that you need, at most, five long strings. It's natural to add a `limit()` operation downstream:

```
List<String> trimmed = new ArrayList<>();
List<String> trimmedLong = strings.stream()
  .map(String::trim)
  .peek(trimmed::add)
  .filter(s -> s.length() > 10)      ┌─ We need no more
  .limit(5)                      ◁───┘  than 5 strings.
  .toList();
```

Now, `trimmedLong` has no more than five entries, which is expected. However, Stream API is smart enough to cancel the operation as soon as the fifth element is added to `trimmedLong`. As a result, `trimmed` won't contain the subsequent elements, which might be undesired. This is especially dangerous if the limit is reached rarely, so the program works correctly most of the time. It would be better to create separate streams for every resulting collection:

```
List<String> trimmed = strings.stream()
  .map(String::trim).toList();
List<String> trimmedLong = trimmed.stream()
  .filter(s -> s.length() > 10).limit(5).toList();
```

In this case, no changes to the `trimmedLong` construction affect the `trimmed` contents.

It should be noted that Stream API does not always stay the same. Sometimes, the internals are optimized to perform fewer operations when possible. For example, in Java 8, the `count()` operation always consumed the stream elements, while in Java 9, it can skip the iteration altogether, if the number of elements doesn't change. The following code fills the `trimmed` collection in Java 8 but keeps it empty in Java 9 or higher:

```
List<String> trimmed = new ArrayList<>();
long count = strings.stream()
  .map(String::trim)
  .peek(trimmed::add)
  .count();
… // Use trimmed and count.
```

Since Java 9, the `count()` operation can see that the stream source is a `List` and a `map()` and `peek()` operations never change the number of elements in the stream. So it just returns `strings.size()` without performing any intermediate operations.

Let's assume that you want to skip the first string of the original list. You can add the `skip(1)` step:

```
List<String> trimmed = new ArrayList<>();
long count = strings.stream()
  .skip(1)                      ⟵──┐  Skip the first
  .map(String::trim)               │  input string.
  .peek(trimmed::add)
  .count();
```

Now, you have `trimmed` filled if you run this code on Java versions up to 16. However, since the release of Java 17, Stream API has become even smarter. Now, the stream sees it can just return `strings.size() - 1` (or 0, if the list was empty). So, in newer versions of Java, stream elements are not actually processed and `trimmed` is empty again.

Static analysis

Some static analysis tools discourage use of the Stream `peek()` method completely. In particular, SonarLint reports a warning S3864: `Stream.peek` Should Be Used with Caution. Unfortunately, I've seen developers replace it with even worse alternatives, just to make the static analyzer happy. For example, it's possible to replace `peek()` with `map()` in the previous sample:

```
List<String> trimmed = new ArrayList<>();
long count = strings.stream()
        .map(String::trim)
        .map(str -> {
            trimmed.add(str);
            return str;
        })
        .count();
```

(continued)

In my opinion, this is much worse, as now, we have a `map()` operation with a side-effect. In fact, now SonarLint is happy, but IntelliJ IDEA complains about this code and suggests using `peek()` instead. While using `peek()` is discouraged, at least it's clear that the side effect is intended. If you need a side effect, it's probably better to rewrite the stream as a loop.

WAYS TO AVOID THIS MISTAKE

- You don't have to remember which Stream API optimization appeared in which Java version. Instead, avoid relying on side-effects from the Stream API intermediate operations at all.
- If it's not possible to express the necessary semantics via a Stream API operation without a side effect, consider using a `for` loop. While Stream API may look like a shiny new alternative, and many developers tend to use these as often as possible, there's nothing wrong with using loops, especially when a Stream API chain looks unnatural.
- Another alternative is to look for third-party libraries that extend the Stream API. For example, there's a free and open source StreamEx library (https://github.com/amaembo/streamex) I created that extends Java streams and allows you to perform more operations in a convenient way, without side effects.

9.3   *Mistake 84: Consuming the stream twice*

Another common caveat with the Stream API is that streams cannot be consumed twice. You will not run into this if you use Stream API as a call chain without storing the `Stream` object to a variable. However, you should take care if you do this. One common scenario is adding conditional steps to the stream. For example, assume you want to skip the first stream element based on a condition:

```
void process(List<String> strings, boolean skipHeader) {
  Stream<String> stream = strings.stream();
  if (skipHeader) {                        Incorrect: stream can
    stream.skip(1);            ◁────────── not be used after that.
  }
  List<String> trimmed = stream.map(String::trim).toList();
  … // Use trimmed
}
```

Here, under the `if` condition, the intermediate operation `skip(1)` is applied to the `stream` object. In rare cases, intermediate operations modify the existing object and return it back. More often, they create a new object and mark the original one as "consumed." As a result, if `skipHeader` is true, you try to consume the `stream` twice, which results in `IllegalStateException` at run time. To fix this problem, you can reassign the `stream` variable inside the `if` statement:

```
Stream<String> stream = strings.stream();
if (skipHeader) {
  stream = stream.skip(1);
}
List<String> trimmed = stream.map(String::trim).toList();
```

> Correct: a new stream is assigned to a variable.

Another possibility in this particular case is to conditionally skip zero lines:

```
List<String> trimmed = strings.stream()
  .skip(skipHeader ? 1 : 0)
  .map(String::trim)
  .toList();
```

I also have seen attempts to reuse streams that looked like this:

```
Stream<String> stream = …;
if (stream.count() == 0 || stream.anyMatch(String::isEmpty)) {
  …
  // Do something when the stream is empty
  // or contains an empty string.
}
```

Unfortunately, this doesn't work either. When `anyMatch()` is about to be executed, another terminal operation `count()` had already been invoked, so the stream was already consumed. This is an example of a problem that cannot be easily solved using plain Stream API, so it's better to use other approaches, like collecting the elements of this stream into an intermediate collection, using a loop, or using a third-party library.

> ### Solving this problem using the StreamEx library
> The StreamEx library allows you to solve this problem in quite an elegant way:
> `StreamEx.of(input).ifEmpty("").anyMatch(String::isEmpty)`. Here, the `ifEmpty()` intermediate operation is used, which allows you to replace the content of an empty stream without modifying it if it's non-empty.

Another dangerous scenario is reusing the stream inside a loop. For example, assume you have a list of strings and another of substrings. For each of the substrings, you want to print the strings that contain a given substring, trimming the whitespaces. One might come up with the following code:

```
static void print(List<String> list, List<String> substrings) {
  Stream<String> strings = list.stream().map(String::trim);
  for (String substring : substrings) {
    String text = "Strings that contain '" + substring + "': "
         + strings.filter(s -> s.contains(substring))
         .collect(Collectors.joining(", "));
    System.out.println(text);
  }
}
```

> Incorrect: stream is reused between loop iterations.

Here, the author of the code reused the same stream between loop iterations. It was probably intended to lift the repeated computation out of the loop. However, this doesn't work because after the first iteration, the stream will be consumed and can't be used anymore. This could go unnoticed if the `substrings` list often contains only one entry. For example, the following test passes:

```
print(List.of("Java", " Stream", " API"), List.of("a"));
```

Prints: Strings that contain 'a': Java, Stream

However, the call fails with `IllegalStateException` if you pass `List.of("a", "b")` as the `substrings` parameter.

> **Static analysis**
>
> SonarLint has a rule named S3959: Consumed Stream Pipelines Should Not Be Reused, which reports the latter case. The IntelliJ IDEA inspection Nullability and Data Flow Problems reports a Stream Has Already Been Linked or Consumed warning for both of the preceding samples.

WAYS TO AVOID THIS MISTAKE

- Don't store the stream in a variable. Try to express the whole stream operation as a single call chain instead.
- If you need to store a stream in a variable and use it in different code branches, remember that it cannot be consumed twice. Ensure all your branches are covered by unit tests and the loops are iterated in tests at least twice.

9.4   *Mistake 85: Using null values in a stream where it's not allowed*

You should be very careful if you have `null` values inside a stream. While nulls in a stream are supported in general, many terminal operations may prohibit them. For example, `findFirst()` will throw a `NullPointerException` if the first element happens to be `null`. That's because `findFirst()` returns an `Optional`, and the `Optional` cannot contain a `null` value. An absent `Optional` is used to designate that the stream is empty. Other terminal operations that return `Optional`, including `max()`, `min()`, and `reduce(accumulator)`, demonstrate similar behavior. They happily consume `null` as an intermediate stream value but will throw an exception if `null` is the final result.

It's interesting that the standard collectors, like `maxBy()` and `minBy()`, differ in behavior from the terminal operations `max()` and `min()`. If the final result is `null`, they don't throw an exception; instead, they return an empty `Optional`:

```
List<Integer> list = Arrays.asList(null, 1, 2);
var comparator =
    Comparator.<Integer>nullsLast(Comparator.naturalOrder());
```

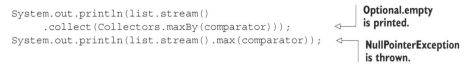

```
System.out.println(list.stream()
     .collect(Collectors.maxBy(comparator)));
System.out.println(list.stream().max(comparator));
```

Optional.empty is printed.

NullPointerException is thrown.

Not all collectors are `null` friendly, though. You can use `toList()` or `toSet()` if your stream contains nulls. However, `toMap()` collectors don't tolerate `null` values (only `null` keys), so your value-mapping function should not return `null`. The `groupingBy()` collector does not allow `null` keys. As you can see, there are many pitfalls to using `null` values in streams.

WAYS TO AVOID THIS MISTAKE

- Avoid having nulls in a stream, especially right before the terminal operation. The most common pattern when nulls may appear in a stream is to filter them out immediately with `filter(Objects::nonNull)`.
- If you still need to pass nulls to the terminal operation, read the operation or collector documentation carefully. If you are not sure, test the terminal operation behavior in a small separate program or JShell console to find out how it reacts to nulls. For example, assume you are not sure what will happen when `findFirst()` is used, and the first stream element happens to be `null`. In this case, simply type the following in the JShell console:

```
Stream.of((Object)null).findFirst()
```

You'll immediately see that the result is `NullPointerException` rather than an empty optional.

9.5   Mistake 86: Violating the contract of Stream API operations

The Stream API imposes quite strict limitations on stream operation arguments. For example, consider the `Stream.reduce(identity, accumulator)` method. The *identity* is a value of the same type as the stream elements, and the *accumulator* is a function that takes two elements and produces one. The method specification requires the accumulator operation to be associative and to return the operand unchanged when another operand is the identity. In other words, the following must hold for any values of x, y, and z:

- $x \oplus i = x$
- $i \oplus x = x$
- $x \oplus (y \oplus z) = (x \oplus y) \oplus z$

Here, i is identity and $x \oplus y$ means `accumulator.apply(x, y)`.

However, if you start using the Stream API, you may quickly notice it works even if these conditions are violated. For example, consider the case in which you want to reimplement the `hashCode()` calculation for `List`. As the `List.hashCode()` specification says, it must be calculated using the following algorithm:

```
int hashCode = 1;
for (E e : list)
    hashCode = 31*hashCode + (e==null ? 0 : e.hashCode());
```

You can try to implement it via `Stream.reduce()`, and it will work:

```
List<String> list = List.of("a", "b", "c", "d");
System.out.println(list.hashCode());              ←—| Prints 3910595
System.out.println(list.stream()
  .mapToInt(Objects::hashCode)                     | Also prints
  .reduce(1, (x, y) -> x * 31 + y));               ←—| 3910595
```

Here, though, the accumulation operation is clearly not associative and does not have an identity. For example, according to the method contract, if you apply the accumulator to (1, 10), it should yield 10 unchanged, as 1 is the identity element. However, it yields 41 instead. Nevertheless, the code produces a correct answer.

It appears that, in practice, many of the requirements for Stream API arguments are only required for parallel streams. If you replace `stream()` with `parallelStream()` in the previous example, you'll get a completely wrong answer. This is because the order of computation differs. Figure 9.2 shows how the result of this

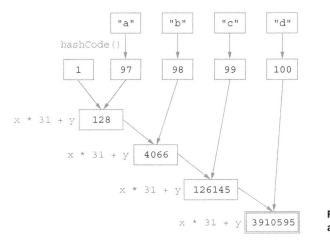

Figure 9.2   Order of computation for a sequential stream

stream is computed in sequential case, and figure 9.3 shows how it is usually computed in parallel. Using simple algebra, one can show that the result of these computations should be the same, if the associative and identity properties are fulfilled. However, in our case they are not fulfilled.

This creates an interesting situation. Many Stream API calls that can be discovered in the real world violate the Stream API specification. Still, they work correctly because they are never executed in parallel.

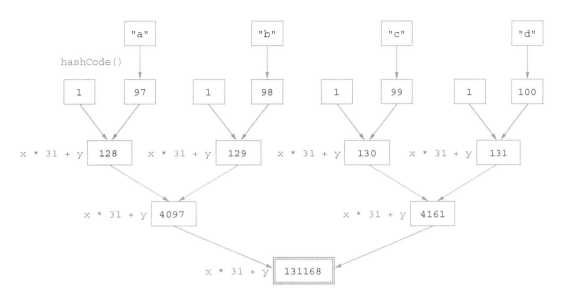

Figure 9.3   Possible order of computation for a parallel stream

This may become more dangerous if the stream chain spans several method calls. For example, you may return the stream from the method or accept the stream as a parameter. Suppose you want to calculate a hash code for the contents of an arbitrary stream:

```
static int hashCodeOf(Stream<?> stream) {
  return stream.mapToInt(Objects::hashCode)
            .reduce(1, (x, y) -> x * 31 + y);
}
```

This method will return a different value if the input stream is parallel. Moreover, the result may change, depending on the number of processor cores. By the way, the JVM option `-Djava.util.concurrent.ForkJoinPool.common.parallelism=X` (where X is the number of parallel threads) allows you to experiment with this without changing the hardware. When the input stream is large enough (e.g., `IntStream.range(0, 1000).boxed().parallel()`), the `ForkJoinPool` parallelism affects the number of chunks created. As a result, the accumulator function could be applied in a different order.

If you really want to solve this problem via Stream API, you should process stream elements strictly from left to right. This can be done using the `forEachOrdered()` operation, though it looks ugly:

```
static int hashCodeOf(Stream<?> stream) {
  var op = new IntConsumer() {
    int acc = 1;
```

```
    public void accept(int value) {
      acc = acc * 31 + value;
    }
  };
  stream.mapToInt(Objects::hashCode).forEachOrdered(op);
  return op.acc;
}
```

Now, it will work for any input stream, parallel or sequential. Well, when using `forEachOrdered()`, for most streams, the parallelization won't produce any benefit. But it's still possible a parallel stream will be faster if there are heavy upstream operations.

Sometimes, developers violate the Stream API contract to enhance the intermediate operation capabilities. One such enhancement is the ability to process overlapping pairs of adjacent stream elements. For example, with a stream of "a", "b", "c", and "d" strings, it's desired to get a stream of "a->b", "b->c", and "c->d". Let's try to write a generic utility method, which takes an input stream and a function that maps two adjacent elements to the resulting element and produces a new stream. A naïve implementation might look like this:

```
static <T, R> Stream<R> pairMap(                          ◁──┐  T is the type of input stream
    Stream<T> input, BiFunction<T, T, R> mapper) {           │  elements; R is the type of the
  var op = new Function<T, R>() {                              │  resulting stream elements.
    boolean started = false;
    T prev = null;                                         Return null for the first element (it
                                                            will be skipped) and the result of
    public R apply(T t) {                                                   mapping otherwise.
      R result = started ? mapper.apply(prev, t) : null;                          ◁──────────
      started = true;
      prev = t;           ◁──┐  Store the current element into the
      return result;         │  prev variable to be able to pass it to
    }                        │  the mapper function next time.
  };
  return input.map(op).skip(1);
}
```

Here, we create a stateful mapping operation, which stores the previous stream element and applies the user-provided `BiFunction` to the previous and current ones. We also need to remove the first element from the resulting stream via `skip(1)`. This utility method can be used in the following manner:

```
Stream<String> input = Stream.of("a", "b", "c", "d");
pairMap(input, (left, right) -> left + "->" + right)
        .forEach(System.out::println);
```

Unfortunately, this utility method also violates the Stream API contract, as functions used in `map()` are required to be stateless. Here, we rely on the assumption that stream elements are processed left to right, one after another. This works for sequential streams (though even this is not guaranteed by the specification). However, this method is completely broken for parallel streams. You cannot even disable the parallelization by adding a `sequential()` call inside `pairMap()`, as clients may call `parallel()` on the resulting stream. In fact, implementing a `pairMap()` that works correctly for parallel and sequential streams is far from trivial. This operation is implemented in my StreamEx library, so if you need such an operation and your project allows third-party library dependencies, you could consider using it. Otherwise, it's better to avoid solving this problem with Stream API at all. Some developers may hope that methods like `pairMap()` will never be used with parallel streams. It's up to you to estimate the risks of having such utility methods in your project.

WAYS TO AVOID THIS MISTAKE

- Carefully follow the Stream API contract, especially if you don't control all the stream operations.
- If you are writing a utility method that consumes or produces a stream, don't forget to test it with a `parallel()` operation.
- Don't try to solve every single problem with Stream API. While Stream API is good for solving a wide variety of data-processing problems, there are still many problems that cannot be solved in an idiomatic way, like the previous list hash code example. In this case, it's better to use a third-party library or write a good-old `for` loop.

9.6   *Mistake 87: Using getClass() instead of instanceof*

The `getClass()` method is available on any Java object and returns its runtime class mirror represented as `java.lang.Class`. Obtaining the object class at run time could be useful for diagnostics, reflection, `equals()` method implementation, and other purposes. Comparing a `getClass()` result to a class literal is similar to the `instanceof` operator. However, one should not forget that `instanceof` returns `true` for any subclass, while `getClass()` checks for the exact class:

```
if (object.getClass() == ArrayList.class) {          true if object is
    …                                                 exactly ArrayList
}
if (object instanceof ArrayList) {          true if object is ArrayList
    …                                       or any of its subclasses
}
```

There's no difference (except `null` handling) if the class you check is a final class. However, care should be taken if it's not. I encountered the following method:

```
static Object convert(Object date) {
  Class<?> cls = date.getClass();
  if (cls == java.util.Date.class) {
    return new java.sql.Date(
          ((java.util.Date) date).getTime());
  }
  if (cls == java.util.Calendar.class) {
    return new java.sql.Date(
          ((java.util.Calendar) date).getTime().getTime());
```

```
    }
    return date;
}
```

The idea behind this method is to convert different objects representing the date to `java.sql.Date`. It should be noted that `java.sql.Date` is a subclass of `java.util.Date`. Therefore, a `getClass()` comparison is used instead of `instanceof` `java.util.Date`: if the input is already `java.sql.Date`, the author of this code wants to keep it as is. However, the same approach was mistakenly used in the second `if` statement as well, probably to make the code look more uniform. This statement is visited only if the object class is exactly `java.util.Calendar`. However, it's completely impossible, as `Calendar` is an abstract class. Every instance of `Calendar` is, in fact, some subclass—usually `GregorianCalendar`:

```
Calendar obj = Calendar.getInstance();              Prints
System.out.println(obj.getClass());           ◁──┘  class java.util.GregorianCalendar
```

As a result, the second `if` statement is never executed and `Calendar` instances are not converted to `java.sql.Date`, as was intended.

> **Static analysis**
>
> Static analysis can help you in simple cases. IntelliJ IDEA warns that the second condition is always `false` in this code, as it's capable of tracking that the `cls` variable was assigned from the result of `getClass()`. Unfortunately, some developers looking at this code will still think it is correct and the static analysis is producing a false-positive warning. If you suspect a static analyzer has incorrectly marked a condition as Always True or Always False, consider confirming your hypothesis with a unit test that evaluates the condition to the opposite result.

WAYS TO AVOID THIS MISTAKE

- Use `getClass()` with care. Always ask yourself, "Is it possible to have a subclass here, and what is the desired behavior in that case?" It's reasonable to add an explanatory comment every time you use `getClass()` instead of `instanceof`.
- If you want to check whether an object is an instance of class `cls`, which is unknown at compile time, consider using `cls.isInstance(object)` rather than `cls.equals(object.getClass())`.
- Declare your classes as `final` by default, unless you explicitly want them to be inherited. In this case, you won't need to worry about whether a subclass instance could arrive in your code and how it should behave in this case.

9.7   *Mistake 88: Using getClass() on enums, annotations, or classes*

There are two known cases in which `getClass()` may return an unexpected result and another method is typically preferred: calling `getClass()` on an enum constant and on an annotation object. Developers usually perceive an enum class as final because you cannot extend an enum, so people naturally expect that `getClass()` will return the enum class itself. This often works. For example, consider the following simple enum:

```
enum MyEnum {
  A, B
}
```

Calling `MyEnum.A.getClass()` will, as you would expect, yield the `MyEnum` class. However, it's possible to declare a class body for a specific enum constant. In this case, an anonymous class will be implicitly created by the compiler:

```
enum MyEnum {
  A {
    public String toString() {
      return "Customized";
    }
  }, B
}
```

Now, `MyEnum` is not final anymore; the implicit anonymous class extends it. As a result, `MyEnum.A.getClass()` returns something like `MyEnum$1` now. This might become a problem if you use classes as map keys or compare them to each other. To work around this problem, every enum has a `getDeclaringClass()` method that always returns the declaring enum class, even if a particular constant declares a class body.

Calling `getClass()` on annotation objects is a more exotic problem, but it's still good to know about. For example, let's declare a simple annotation:

```
import java.lang.annotation.*;

@Retention(RetentionPolicy.RUNTIME)
@interface MyAnno {}
```

Now, let's try to obtain it reflectively:

```
@MyAnno
public class Test {
  public static void main(String[] args) {
    MyAnno annotation =
      Test.class.getAnnotation(MyAnno.class);
    System.out.println(annotation.getClass());
  }
}
```

If you print the annotation class, you'll see something like `$Proxy1`, a proxy class used internally by the reflection mechanism to represent the annotation. It's unlikely that you need it. To get the annotation interface type from an annotation object, use the `annotationType()` method declared in every annotation.

As `java.lang.Class` is also a Java object, it's possible to call `getClass()` on it as well, and it will always return the `java.lang.Class` object that represents a java.lang.Class class. If `getClass()` is called on the `java.lang.Class` object, it's usually a mistake, but the compiler will not warn about it. Such mistakes were observed several times in error-reporting code like this:

```
<T> T getData(String key, Class<T> expectedClass) {
  Object data = storage.get(key);
  Class<?> actual = data.getClass();
  if (actual != expectedClass) {
    throw new IllegalStateException(
        "Wrong type of data for key='" + key + "': " +
        actual.getClass());        ◁──┐ The getClass() method
  }                                    │ is called mistakenly.
  return expectedClass.cast(data);
}
```

Here, if an exception is thrown, the message will always say `class java.lang.Class` instead of the actual class of the `data` object, which will not help to investigate the problem. Obviously, it was intended to simply use `actual` instead of `actual.getClass()`.

> ### Static analysis
> Error Prone has GetClassOnEnum, GetClassOnAnnotation, and GetClassOnClass bug patterns that report all the problems listed here. IntelliJ IDEA can report the last problem with the Suspicious `Class.getClass()` Call inspection.

WAYS TO AVOID THIS MISTAKE

- Remember that `getClass()` does not always return `Cls.class` for instances of a class `Cls`, as the object you have could be a subclass of `Cls`. This could be unexpected in certain cases, particularly if `Cls` is an enum.
- When possible, use the `instanceof` operator instead of a `getClass()` call.
- Write unit tests that test the error-reporting paths; use assertions to check the actual message content, not just the exception type.

9.8   *Mistake 89: Incorrect conversion of string to boolean*

It's often necessary to convert the contents of a string to primitive types, like `int` or `boolean`. In Java, this is performed by static methods located inside the primitive wrapper classes. The methods are named uniformly and always start with *parse*: `Integer` `.parseInt()`, `Double.parseDouble()`, `Boolean.parseBoolean()`, and so on. Methods that return a number are quite strict; they throw a `NumberFormatException` if the input string does not contain a well-formed number.

The `Boolean.parseBoolean()` method is more permissive. It simply compares the input string with `"true"`, ignoring the case, so it returns `false` for any other input. For example, the following code prints `false` five times:

```
System.out.println(Boolean.parseBoolean(" true "));
System.out.println(Boolean.parseBoolean("Yes"));
```

```
System.out.println(Boolean.parseBoolean("Y"));
System.out.println(Boolean.parseBoolean("T"));
System.out.println(Boolean.parseBoolean(null));
```

Exercise caution when using this method, as any unexpected input (e.g., padded with spaces) will be silently converted to `false`, and the mistake may not be noticed. If you are processing text input, it's probably better to create your own method to parse Booleans, which will throw an exception on the unexpected input.

There's another method with a very similar signature: `Boolean.getBoolean()`. This method also accepts a string and returns a value of `boolean` type, so it's easy to mistakenly use it instead of `parseBoolean()`. This method, however, does something different: it reads the system property using a given name and then parses it using `parseBoolean()`. If you mistakenly call `Boolean.getBoolean()` instead of `Boolean.parseBoolean()`, you'll likely get a `false` result because it will return `true` only if the input string happens to be the name of an actually existing property whose value is `true`. This could go unnoticed, as you'll get no exception. The program will simply be indifferent to the input string.

There are also methods like `Integer.getInteger()` and `Long.getLong()`, which, like `Boolean.getBoolean()`, query a system property instead of parsing a string argument. However, their return type is a boxed number, like `Integer`, and they return `null` when a system property is absent, so it's easier to spot that something is wrong.

WAYS TO AVOID THIS MISTAKE

- When converting a string to a Boolean value, think in advance about which strings you want to be interpreted as `true`, which should be converted to `false`, and which should result in an exception for invalid input. It's easy to use the `parseBoolean()` library method, but it may not fit your situation. It could be better to write your own utility method.
- Don't mix `getBoolean()` and `parseBoolean()`. While their signatures are very similar, they do different things.

9.9   *Mistake 90: Incorrect format specifiers in date formatting*

Java provides a special pattern language to format dates and times of day. This language is used in the `java.text.SimpleDateFormat` constructor and newer Java date-time APIs, in the `java.time.format.DateTimeFormatter.ofPattern()` method. For example, you can format the current time as *hours:minutes:seconds*, using the following pattern:

```
String time = DateTimeFormatter.ofPattern("HH:mm:ss")
    .format(LocalDateTime.now());
```

The problem with these patterns is that sometimes, lowercase and uppercase letters mean different things, but it can be hard to remember which one you need. For example,

- Uppercase `M` is *month*, while lowercase `m` is *minutes*.
- Uppercase `D` is *day of year*, while lowercase `d` is *day of month*.

- Uppercase S is *fractions of a second*, while lowercase s is *whole seconds*.
- Uppercase Y is *week-numbering year*, while lowercase y is *normal year*.

Sometimes, it's hard to notice there's a problem. For example, imagine you mistakenly used HH:mm:SS in the preceding example. In this case, you would get hundredths of a second instead of seconds, which often looks correct. On the other hand, fractions can exceed 60, so you may see something like 18:26:93. You might also mistakenly use HH:MM:ss or even HH:MM:SS (everything in uppercase looks pretty, right?) and see a number of months instead of minutes, which also might go unnoticed.

The most unpleasant mistake is using uppercase Y instead of lowercase y. The week-numbering year (also known as *ISO year*) is almost always the same as the normal year, except for several days around the new year. Week-numbering year always has a round number of weeks (52 or 53) and always starts with Monday, so if the calendar year does not start with Monday, the next week-numbering year starts several days earlier or later. For example, week-numbering year 2021 started on January 4th. As a result, the following code could have surprising behavior:

```
String date = DateTimeFormatter.ofPattern("YYYY-MM-dd")
    .format(LocalDate.of(2021, 1, 3));
System.out.println(date);          ⟵─┤ Prints 2020-01-03.
```

However, for most dates, the YYYY and yyyy formats produce the same result. This often makes the problem invisible during testing.

Static analysis

Static analyzers may help you detect mistakes in these patterns. IntelliJ IDEA has the Suspicious Date Format Pattern inspection for this purpose. SonarLint reports the S3986: Week Year (YYYY) Should Not Be Used for Date Formatting warning. However, it only detects the problem if the pattern literal is passed directly to a formatting method like ofPattern(). Currently, it doesn't work if the pattern is extracted to a variable or constant.

WAYS TO AVOID THIS MISTAKE

- Always test date- and time-formatting patterns with specific inputs to ensure they work as expected. Add test input where the ISO week-numbering year differs from the calendar year.
- Use only a few different date and time formatting patterns, extract them to constants, and reuse the same constants everywhere. The fewer pattern literals you have, the fewer opportunities there are to make a mistake.

9.10   *Mistake 91: Accidental invalidation of weak or soft references*

When you store an object to a variable in Java, you are, in fact, storing a reference to that object. This kind of reference is called a *strong reference*. As long as there's at least one strong reference to an object, the object will be alive and the garbage collector will not destroy it. In addition to strong references, the Java virtual machine supports *weak* and *soft references*. If you create this kind of reference to an object, you explicitly tell the virtual machine you don't mind if this object will be garbage collected when there's not enough heap memory, as long as there are no strong references to the same object. Such an object is called *weakly reachable* or *softly reachable*, depending on the kind of reference pointing to it. The typical application for these references is caching objects, which are nice to have in memory, but you can always recompute or deserialize from the disk if they are not there. This helps the virtual machine use heap memory more efficiently.

Softly reachable and weakly reachable objects

An object is weakly reachable if only weak references point at it. If at least one soft reference points at the object, it becomes softly reachable, and if at least one strong reference points at it, it becomes strongly reachable. Weakly reachable objects are cleared by the garbage collector as soon as it discovers them, so they usually disappear during the next garbage collection cycle, though this may depend on such factors as garbage collection implementation and the heap generation at which the object resides. Often, weak references are used as map keys. There's even a standard `WeakHashMap` class that implements such a map. The mappings disappear automatically when no other code references them.

Softly reachable objects may survive several garbage collection cycles. There's an unspecified algorithm to decide whether to collect a softly reachable object. It's based on how much time has passed since the object was created or accessed. Still, it's guaranteed that all the softly reachable objects will be collected before the virtual machine throws `OutOfMemoryError`.

One problem with these references is that garbage collection may occur at any point of program execution, and if the object becomes weakly reachable or softly reachable, it can be collected, even if it was alive just a few moments before. Even this simple code may fail with `NullPointerException`:

```
Object obj = new Object();
WeakReference<Object> ref = new WeakReference<>(obj);      obj is not used
                                                           directly anymore.
System.out.println(ref.get().hashCode());
```

If the local variable `obj` is not used after creation of the weak reference, the created object becomes weakly reachable. As a result, it could be collected after `ref` is created but before `ref.get()` is called, so `ref.get()` may return `null`. This problem was discovered in the OpenJDK `ResourceBundle` class. The problem with bugs like this is that they can live for years without anyone noticing, as the error will occur only when GC happens at very specific times. It also may depend on how the code is executed by the JVM. For example, the HotSpot JVM interpreter may not mark local variables as not used anymore, so if the preceding sample is executed in the interpreter, `ref.get()` will never return `null`. However, JIT compilers are smarter, and they release the variable after the last actual use, so GC may collect the object even if the variable is still in the scope.

WAYS TO AVOID THIS MISTAKE

- Unless you have a strong reference to the object, never assume the `get()` method of `WeakReference` or `SoftReference` will return a non-null value, even if you just created the reference or already called `get()` on the previous line. Always check the `get()` result for `null` and avoid calling it several times. Instead, store it in a local variable.

- Do not assume a variable's lifetime lasts until the execution leaves the variable scope. In fact, compilers can forget about variables after their last use. If the variable holds the last strong reference to the object, then it could be collected right after the last use. If it's really necessary, you may explicitly prolong a variable's life by using the `reachabilityFence()` method (added in Java 9):

```
Object obj = new Object();
WeakReference<Object> ref = new WeakReference<>(obj);
System.out.println(ref.get().hashCode());    ◁──┐  ref.get() is guaranteed to
Reference.reachabilityFence(obj);                │  return obj, as we have a
                                                 │  reachabilityFence() call.
```

The sole purpose of the `reachabilityFence()` call is to guarantee the object passed as a parameter will remain strongly reachable and, thus, alive at least until this call.

9.11   *Mistake 92: Assuming the world is stable*

Java has very convenient property: local variables and method parameters are completely controlled by the method's code. Their values cannot be altered, unless you explicitly change them in the same method via assignment, increment, or decrement expression. If you read a local variable and found that its value was 5, it will remain 5 until you explicitly change it, no matter how much time has passed and regardless of what may have changed in another part of the program.

Most of the time, you can be relatively sure about the stability of your own object fields. If the fields are private and you control all modifications, you can be confident nobody will modify your fields intermittently. Well, field stability is not 100% guaranteed, like the stability of local variables and parameters is. Sometimes, you may discover that another part of your program deliberately breaks encapsulation using the reflection method `Field.setAccessible(true)` and modifies a field unexpectedly. However, this is considered bad practice, and usually, if this breaks the program, it's the responsibility of the coder who broke the encapsulation. By the way, you can further protect your code against such hacks if you declare a Java module, using module-info.java file.

It's important to remember, however, that the wider world can change at any moment, so if you read any property of the world external to your program, you can't be sure how long that property will stay the same. For example,

- If you check that a particular file exists, you cannot be sure it will still exist the next second. Another process could delete it at any moment. It's also possible the file is located on a network device and will become inaccessible due to a network failure.

- If you check the file size and then allocate a buffer of that size and read the file into that buffer, be prepared for the file to be larger or smaller because another process might be writing to that file at the moment.

- If you check the current date, you cannot be sure it will stay the same after some time. You may assume your computation is very quick and it's unlikely it will be done around midnight, but it's also possible, for example, for your computer to be put to sleep, suspending the computation for an indefinite period of time (probably several days).

- If you check the number of processors available using `Runtime.getRuntime()` `.availableProcessors()`, this number might change during program execution. For example, the thread affinity mask of your current process might be changed, which could affect the result of the `availableProcessors()` call.

My team once discovered a rare failure of a unit test that checked whether backup folders were being generated correctly. It looked roughly like this:

```
@Test
public void testBackupFolder() throws IOException {
  Path tempDir = Files.createTempDirectory("test");
  Path backupFolder = createBackupFolder(tempDir);      ⟵  The createBackupFolder() is
  var nameFormat = DateTimeFormatter.ofPattern(             the method we are testing.
    "'Backup'-yyyy-MM-dd-HH-mm");
  String expectedName = nameFormat.format(LocalDateTime.now());
  assertEquals(backupFolder.getFileName().toString(),
    expectedName);
}
```

The backup folders were named based on the current date and time (hours and minutes). To check whether the name matched the expected pattern, the test method queried the current time again, via `LocalDateTime.now()`, and then formatted the expected folder name. Of course, the time queried inside the `createBackupFolder()` method as well as inside the test method could differ. However, the difference is usually no more than a few milliseconds, so hours and minutes aren't changed. As a result, the test passed for many months until the first failure, when the number of minutes appeared to be different.

Tests that fail sporadically are called *flaky tests*. A flaky test is generally not as harmful as a bug in production code. Yet it prevents smooth continuous integration, and an automatic merge of an unrelated change could fail due to this problem, wasting other developers' time.

When working with a filesystem, it's preferred to reduce the number of I/O queries to avoid possible changes between them. For example, there are several filesystem query methods in the `java.nio.file.Files` class: `isDirectory()`, `isRegularFile()`, `isSymbolicLink()`, `getLastModifiedTime()`, `size()`, and so on. If you need to call several of these methods at once, it's best to use the `Files.readAttributes()` method, which performs a single filesystem query and returns the structure containing all of the information at once. For example, assume you want to get the size of the file if it's a regular file, and return –1 otherwise. The following code snippet is simple and will work in most cases:

```
static long getFileSize(Path path) throws IOException {
  if (!Files.isRegularFile(path)) return -1;

  return Files.size(path);          File can be replaced with
}                                    a directory at this place.
```

However, it's also possible for another process to remove the regular file and create a directory with the same name instead. A directory size could be a system-dependent number, like 8,192, depending on the number of files in a directory, so in such a rare case, this method could return any unrelated number. The following implementation is more robust, as it performs a single atomic query to the filesystem:

```
static long getFileSize(Path path) throws IOException {
  BasicFileAttributes attributes = Files.readAttributes(
      path, BasicFileAttributes.class);
  if (!attributes.isRegularFile()) return -1;        The attributes are read atomically and
  return attributes.size();                          cannot change between subsequent
}                                                    isRegularFile() and size() calls.
```

This problem is a corner case and can be ignored for many applications. However, the following problem happens more often. Sometimes, developers check the file size and then open the file and read it, incorrectly assuming the size is still the same. For example, some routine might need to load file in the memory, but it does this only for small files to avoid consuming too much memory. This can be implemented in the following way:

```
static byte[] readFileIfItsNotTooLarge(Path path) throws IOException {
    long size = Files.size(path);
    if (size > 1024 * 1024) {
        throw new UnsupportedOperationException("File is too large");
    }
    return Files.readAllBytes(path);
}
```

Unfortunately, such an implementation does not guarantee you won't read more than one megabyte of data. It's possible the file has been opened for writing by another process (or even by the same process). Even if there are no active writes taking place at the moment, the filesystem may not immediately update the file size in the directory entry, so `Files.size()` might return the outdated value. You should never assume the result of `Files.size()`, `File.length()`, or similar methods really matches the file content. One possibility for fixing this is to try to read, at the most, the desired number of bytes and then check whether the end of the file is reached:

```
static byte[] readFileIfItsNotTooLarge(Path path) throws IOException {
  final int maxSize = 1024 * 1024;
  try (InputStream is = Files.newInputStream(path)) {
    byte[] bytes = is.readNBytes(maxSize);
    if (bytes.length == maxSize && is.read() != -1) {
      throw new UnsupportedOperationException("File is too large");
    }
    return bytes;
  }
}
```

WAYS TO AVOID THIS MISTAKE

- Remember that subsequent requests to the current time and date may return different results. If you need a stable result, query the time and date once and store it in the variable for further reuse.
- Do not assume a filesystem is stable. Changes may occur any time, between any two queries from your application. When possible, use atomic operations.
- Sometimes, it's OK to ignore such problems and assume a particular part of the filesystem is stable. If your application creates its own data folder, it's usually fine to assume nobody else has touched it. However, be careful when working with user-specified folders.

9.12 Mistake 93: Non-atomic access to concurrently updated data structures

Similar problems appear when you are working with data that is shared between several threads. Such shared data might be stored in a volatile variable or concurrent collection. For example, I have seen many times code like this run on a concurrent queue:

```
void takeAndProcess(Queue<String> queue) {
  if (!queue.isEmpty()) {
    String element = queue.remove();
    … // Process element
  }
}
```

Here, we effectively check whether the queue is empty twice: the first time inside the isEmpty() method, and the second time inside the remove() method, so the interaction with the queue is not atomic. If another consumer that takes elements out of this queue exists, it's quite possible for the queue to be cleared between these calls. A more appropriate way to do this is to use a single method, like poll():

```
void takeAndProcess(Queue<String> queue) {
  String element = queue.poll();
  if (element != null) {
    … // Process element
  }
}
```

Unlike `remove()`, the `poll()` method just returns `null` if the queue is empty, instead of throwing an exception, so it's possible to add a `null` check on a local variable that can't be affected by another thread.

Another common error associated with concurrent collections is the old-style "get-and-put" sequences on concurrent maps. For example, here, we maintain occurrence counts for every key:

```
void addValue(ConcurrentMap<String, Integer> map, String key) {
  Integer value = map.get(key);
  if (value == null) {
    value = 1;
  } else {
    value++;
  }
  map.put(key, value);
}
```

This is also non-atomic code, and we may get the incorrect value if another thread updates the same entry concurrently. Luckily, since the releasee of Java 8, several help-ful methods have been available in the `Map` interface, namely `putIfAbsent()`, `compute()`, `computeIfAbsent()`, `computeIfPresent()`, and `merge()`. These help implement most get-and-put scenarios in an atomic way, so they are clean and error proof. Our example could be fixed with the help of `merge()`:

```
void addValue(ConcurrentMap<String, Integer> map, String key) {
  map.merge(key, 1, Integer::sum);
}
```

Now, as long as the concurrent map implementation is correct, we will increment the value atomically.

A similar problem can happen if you work with atomic variables like `Atomic-Integer`. Imagine you want to double the value inside the `AtomicInteger`. A naïve approach would be to read it, multiply by 2, and store the result:

```
atomic.set(atomic.get() * 2);
```

However, this solution is not thread safe, as the operation is not atomic. So if two con-current threads execute this code, it's possible for the multiplication to be performed only once. The correct solution would be to use the `updateAndGet()` method:

```
atomic.updateAndGet(value -> value * 2);
```

WAYS TO AVOID THIS MISTAKE

- When working with concurrent collections, it's important to understand that any sequence of calls is non-atomic, as a collection might be modified from another thread between calls. Read the collection documentation carefully to find the atomic operations suitable for your task.
- Writing correct concurrent programs is a complex topic that requires study. The mistake mentioned here is a common one, but there are many other subtle

problems you might encounter. If you write concurrent code, spend time learning the underlying concepts. Reading *Java Concurrency in Practice* by Brian Goetz et al. (Addison-Wesley Professional, 2006) would be a good starting point.

Summary

- The Stream API may optimize out parts of the computation, as the intermediate operations are not intended to produce important side effects. Avoid having side effects in the Stream API pipeline.
- A Java stream cannot be consumed twice. Be careful when you assign a stream to a variable, as you can mistakenly use it more than once.
- While it's okay to have nulls in the stream, not every terminal operation is friendly toward `null` values. If you really need to pass nulls to the terminal operation, check whether it supports them.
- Use the `getClass()` method with care. Don't forget that its result is the exact runtime class of the object, which might be a subclass of your expected class.
- If you need to convert string to a Boolean value, you may accidentally call the `Boolean.getBoolean()` method, which does something completely different.
- Date formatting specifiers are very confusing, and it's easy to use an incorrect specifier. Pay especial attention to YYYY, which is a *week-numbering year*, rather than a normal year.
- Be careful when you make two subsequent requests to something that can change in-between. It could be the system time, file metadata, a weak reference, or a concurrent collection. Use atomic requests whenever possible.

Unit testing

While unit testing is aimed at reducing the number of bugs in a program, the unit test itself is a program, so it's natural that it may contain bugs, too. Some developers assume it's not a big problem because if a unit test has a bug, then it will likely fail. However, I have seen many buggy unit tests that actually don't test anything, so if the bug appears in the program, then the test won't do its job of detecting the regression. In this chapter, we explore some bugs that can occur in unit tests.

Throughout this book, I've only discussed mistakes related to the Java language itself and its standard library. Here, I'll make an exception and discuss a few mistakes one can make using testing frameworks, such as JUnit or TestNG. I believe this is an important part of the book. First, every Java program, be it a backend Spring application, a microservice, an Android project, a desktop game, or a general-purpose library, needs unit tests. Another point is that throughout the book, I often recommend writing unit tests to avoid or quickly identify certain mistakes. This advice only works if your unit tests are correctly written and actually executed during the test run.

10.1 Mistake 94: Side effect in assert statement

Before talking about actual unit tests, let's consider `assert` statements. These statements are used to perform invariant checks in Java code. They are usually executed in testing or staging environments (JVM is launched with the -ea parameter, which is short for *enable assertions*) and ignored in production environments. Their most common problem is when the expression under assert produces a side effect. For example, the following `assert` statement is likely incorrect:

```
assert set.add(value) : "set already contains " + value;
```

When assertions are turned off, the element won't be added to the set at all because the expression under the `assert` statement will not be evaluated. Essentially, this statement is equivalent to the following:

```
if (assertionsEnabled) {
  if (!set.add(value)) {
    throw new AssertionError("set already contains " + value);
  }
}
```

The bug could be fixed by extracting the expression to a separate local variable:

```
boolean added = set.add(value);
assert added : "set already contains " + value;
```

The following is another sample that actually happened in production code:

```
static int extractNumber(String message) {
  Pattern pattern = Pattern.compile("\\((\\d+)\\)");
  Matcher matcher = pattern.matcher(message);
  assert matcher.find();
  return Integer.parseInt(matcher.group(1));
}
```

Here, the author of this code wants to find in the input string a number in the parentheses and expects that this number will always be found. However, `matcher.find()` has a side effect: it fills in the groups. If we run this code without -ea, the following `matcher.group(1)` call will fail.

The unpleasant thing about assertions is that they are usually turned on when you run tests, so even if you have 100% test coverage, you may not spot this kind of problem, but the program will be broken in production.

> **Static analysis**
>
> Static analysis tools may detect such problems. IntelliJ IDEA has an `assert` State-ment with Side Effects inspection that reports here. Unfortunately, such analysis is not robust, as it's generally difficult to determine statically whether a given method has side effects.

WAYS TO AVOID THIS MISTAKE

- Configure your CI to run tests with disabled assertions once in a while to ensure the program behavior with disabled asserts is the same as it is with them enabled.
- Do not overuse `assert` statements. For example, in the preceding matcher sample, if the number is not found, it's more likely a failed precondition than invariant. So it looks like a good idea to replace `assert` with `if`:

```
if (!matcher.find()) {
  throw new IllegalArgumentException(
            message + " must contain (number)");
}
```

10.2 *Mistake 95: Malformed assertion method calls*

To write unit tests, programmers need to plug in some testing framework, like JUnit or TestNG. After that, the classes and methods for tests should be created according to the framework convention. These methods normally contain three parts:

1 *Arrange*—Preparatory code to set up the environment in which the test should be performed, like creating and configuring helper objects. In some simple tests, this is unnecessary.
2 *Act*—Executing the function you want to test.
3 *Assert*—Ensuring the function result is what you expect.

These steps are commonly known as the *Arrange, Act, Assert* (AAA) pattern. Simply following them may save you from many pitfalls, so avoid writing tests that have a different structure.

Nevertheless, as the test is also code, it's possible to make mistakes at every stage. It's usually not a big problem if your test starts failing due to a mistake in the test code, as you will quickly notice this and discovering the cause is usually not very difficult. It's much more problematic when, due to a mistake, a test stops testing anything and always reports success, even if the function you are trying to test behaves incorrectly.

Many such mistakes happen at the *Assert* stage. Usually, to assert something, it's necessary to call one of many methods starting with the `assert` prefix. For example, in JUnit, `assertTrue()` checks that the argument is `true`, and `assertEquals()` checks that two arguments are equal to each other. As the names of these methods are similar, it's quite possible to mistakenly call the wrong one.

For example, I have observed that some developers mistakenly use `assertNot-Null()` instead of `assertTrue()` or `assertFalse()`:

```
assertNotNull(data.isEmpty());
```
⟵ **assertTrue was intended.**

As the `isEmpty()` method returns a `boolean` value, it's automatically boxed to a `Boolean` object, which, of course, can never be `null`; thus, the test will always pass, regardless of the actual result of the `isEmpty()` method. Due to autoboxing, the compiler is silent here.

Another problem may appear if you forget the parameter to the assertion method. Many assertion methods in JUnit or similar libraries accept an optional message parameter. For example, the `assertNotNull(object)` method and `assertNotNull (message, object)` are available in JUnit 4. Unfortunately, this means that if you supply only a message and forget to supply the object, it will still compile, but the message will be interpreted as an object. Of course, a message is almost never `null`, so such an assertion will never fail:

```
assertNotNull("Check that we have a content");
```

Here, the developer wanted to write

```
assertNotNull("Check that we have a content",
              storage.getContent());
```

However, the second parameter was omitted by mistake. As a result, the assertion tests nothing. I discovered and reported a problem like this in the OpenJ9 project.

A similar problem may appear with the `assertNotEquals()` method:

```
String oldContent = storage.getContent();
assertEquals(expectedContent, oldContent);
storage.modifyContent();
assertNotEquals("Check that content was modified",
                storage.getContent());
```

This assertion will always pass, unless the content is equal to the string parameter supplied. The last line was intended to be

```
assertNotEquals("Check that content was modified",
                oldContent, storage.getContent());
```

Static analysis

Sometimes, problems like this can be detected by static analyzers. For example, IntelliJ IDEA has the Null-Check Method Is Called with Obviously Non-null Argument inspection, which reports when `assertNotNull()` is called with a constant string argument or a boxed `boolean` value.

- Do not rely solely on methods like `assertNotNull()` and `assertNotEquals()`. This advice is helpful not only for avoiding the aforementioned problem. In general, these methods assert only a very weak fact about your value: it's not equal to something. Try to add a more rigid assertion that ensures what your value *is* rather than something it *is not.*

- Always make sure you see your test fail. A software development practice known as *test-driven development* (TDD) requires writing tests before actual code. If you strictly follow the TDD rules, you should not write any production code before you see your test fail. In this case, it's easy to spot the malformed assertion call, as there will be no failure, even if your code actually produces an incorrect result.

10.3   *Mistake 96: Malformed exception test*

Sometimes, you may want to assert that a particular exception is thrown in a unit test. Historically, there was no easy way to do this, and this resulted in the following code pattern:

```
@Test
public void ensureException() {
  try {
    doSomething();
    fail("No exception was thrown");
  }
  catch (MyException ex) {
    assertEquals("Expected exception message",
               ex.getMessage());
  }
}
```

Here, we expect that the `doSomething()` call will fail with `MyException`, and its message is `Expected exception message`. If this is not the case, the test must fail. The problem is that this pattern is quite verbose, and it's easy to get it wrong. The most common mistake is forgetting the `fail()` call:

```
@Test
public void ensureException() {
  try {
    doSomething();
  }
  catch (MyException ex) {
    assertEquals("Expected exception message",
               ex.getMessage());
  }
}
```

In this case, the test looks correct: it will properly fail if the exception message or exception type doesn't match. However, if `doSomething()` starts returning normally without throwing an exception at all, the test will not report this problem.

JUnit 4 has a parameter for the `@Test` annotation to expect a particular exception, so it can be used, which would make the test more concise and less error prone:

```
@Test(expected = MyException.class)
public void ensureException() {
  doSomething();
}
```

However, this approach doesn't allow you to assert the particular message of the exception. JUnit 5 has an `assertThrows()` method that adds more flexibility. A similar method was added to JUnit 4.13 as well, so you can simply write the following:

```
@Test
public void ensureException() {
  MyException ex = assertThrows(MyException.class,
                               () -> doSomething());
  assertEquals("Expected exception message", ex.getMessage());
}
```

Here, `assertThrows()` ensures an exception of a given type was thrown and returns that exception, so you can make further asserts, like checking the exception message.

WAYS TO AVOID THIS MISTAKE

- Use modern versions of testing frameworks, and utilize new methods, like `assertThrows()`.
- In case you can't update the testing framework or the provided methods don't have the desired flexibility, write your own `assertThrows()`-like helper method and use it everywhere. In this case, you only need to write it correctly once.

10.4   Mistake 97: Premature exit from test method

In most cases, unit test method bodies have a straightforward linear sequence of statements without any complex control flow. However, sometimes, a developer introduces control flow instructions, such as a `return` statement that terminates the test either on a condition or due to an exception. This complicates reading and understanding the test method. It's possible for someone to add more assertions at the end of the method, but they may become unreachable if the `return` statement is executed. When you add unreachable statements to production code, you can write a test and see that the statements are not executed. However, this won't work if you add unreachable statements to the test code.

I saw such a test in the Morphia project. Here's how it looked:

```
public void testMapping() throws Exception {
  E e = new E();
  e.mymap.put("a.b", "a");
  e.mymap.put("c.e.g", "b");

  try {
    getDs().save(e);
```

```
  } catch (Exception ex) {
    return;          ←┐  Successful test
  }                   │  ends here.

  Assert.assertFalse("Should have got rejection…", true);
  e = getDs().get(e);
  Assert.assertEquals("a", e.mymap.get("a.b"));     These assertions are
  Assert.assertEquals("b", e.mymap.get("c.e.g"));   never executed.
}
```

The intention was to test two things. First, it tests whether the `save()` method throws an exception, and second, it tests whether we can read the expected values using `get()` methods. However, if the exception is expectedly thrown by the `save()` method, the test terminates right inside the catch block. As a result, the two `assert-Equals()` calls at the end of the method are never executed.

WAYS TO AVOID THIS MISTAKE

- Avoid early returns from unit test methods. This might be confusing and may cause some assertions not to be executed. In the previous example, using `assertThrows()` would solve the problem perfectly:

```
public void testMapping() {
  E e = new E();
  e.mymap.put("a.b", "a");          A new variable is
  e.mymap.put("c.e.g", "b");        needed here, as e is
                                    captured in lambda.
  assertThrows(Exception.class, () -> getDs().save(e));
  E restoredE = getDs().get(e);     ←─────────
  Assert.assertEquals("a", restoredE.mymap.get("a.b"));
  Assert.assertEquals("b", restoredE.mymap.get("c.e.g"));
}
```

- Avoid testing several things in a single unit test. If you want to add more assertions, create a new unit test.

10.5 *Mistake 98: Ignoring the AssertionError in unit tests*

The mechanics of unit tests is simple: if something unexpected happens, an `AssertionError` is thrown, which is caught by the testing framework and handled to display a failing test. This has an important consequence: it's not enough to throw an `AssertionError` from methods like `assertEquals()`. It's also necessary to pass this exception to your test method caller. One potential mistake here is to catch an overly broad exception inside the test. For example, one might want to check the computation result but assume it's not a big problem if computation fails with an exception:

```
public void testFileProcessing() {
  try {
    List<String> input = Files.readAllLines(Path.of("input.txt"));
    List<String> expected = Files.readAllLines(Path.of("output.txt"));
    assertEquals(expected, processInput(input));
```

```
  } catch (Throwable ignored) {
    // Some I/O error, ignore
  }
}
```

Yes, it's a poorly written unit test in general, but the most problematic aspect is that if `assertEquals()` fails, then the thrown `AssertionError` will be ignored and the test framework will not detect the test failure.

Another possible mistake is to use assertion methods in a separate thread without transferring the exceptions to the original thread, like this:

```
public void testComputation() throws InterruptedException {
  Thread thread = new Thread(() -> {
    assertEquals("Expected", computeSomething());
  });
  thread.start();
  thread.join();
}
```

Here, if the assertion fails, the `AssertionError` is thrown in a separate thread. It will be caught by a default *uncaught exception handler*, which prints the exception stack trace to the standard error stream. However, it won't be passed to the original thread at which the test started. As a result, the testing framework will mark this test as successful, and the failure could go unnoticed unless somebody looks into the output.

I've seen similar mistakes several times, but they are difficult to illustrate because they usually involve a large amount of code to set up the threads and gather the results. One relatively simple sample was found in the OkHttp project, although the test was disabled and likely incomplete. The test case method looks like this:

```
ExecutorService executor = Executors.newCachedThreadPool();
CountDownLatch latch = new CountDownLatch(2);
executor.execute(new AsyncRequest("/r1", latch));
executor.execute(new AsyncRequest("/r2", latch));
countDownLatch.await();
… // further asserts
```

Here, we create two asynchronous requests and execute them in a newly created thread pool, assuming every request decrements the count of the latch. Then, we check that the result of the requests is correct.

A simplified `AsyncRequest` class looks like this (stripped of all the network request logic and using Java record syntax for brevity):

```
private record AsyncRequest(String path, CountDownLatch latch)
             implements Runnable {
  public void run() {
    try {
      String actual = performRequest();
      assertEquals("Result", actual);
      latch.countDown();
    } catch (Exception e) {
```

```
      throw new RuntimeException(e);
    }
  }

  private static String performRequest() {
    return "Result";
  }
}
```

At first glance, it looks like it actually asserts the return value of the `performRequest()` method. However, let's change the `performRequest()` body to return something different (e.g., `"Result1"` instead of `"Result"`). Now, `assertEquals()` fails, which causes the background process to throw `AssertionError` and terminate without updating the count in the latch. The original test method starts waiting for the latch indefinitely, so the whole test suite may hang if this test fails. This may result in a big waste of time, as builds on the continuous integration server could also hang and it might not be immediately clear which test is causing the problem.

One may try to fix this by moving the `countDown()` call to the `finally` section, so it executes no matter what, and the waiting always succeeds:

```
try {
  String actual = performRequest();
  assertEquals("Result", actual);
} catch (Exception e) {
  throw new RuntimeException(e);
} finally {
  latch.countDown();
}
```

Now, the test doesn't hang anymore, but it also won't fail if the assertion inside `Async-Request` fails. A better solution would be to transfer the exception into the original thread, using the `Future` object:

```
Future<?> f1 = executor.submit(new AsyncRequest("/r1"));
Future<?> f2 = executor.submit(new AsyncRequest("/r2"));
f1.get();
f2.get();
```

In this case, the `CountDownLatch` becomes unnecessary, and the exception happening in the thread pool is properly transferred to the testing framework.

Static analysis

Static analyzers may catch the first problem in simple cases, when the assertion and try-catch statement are located in the same method. SonarLint has rule S5779: Assertion Methods Should Not Be Used within the Try Block of a Try-Catch Catching an Error, and IntelliJ IDEA has an inspection called Assertion Is Suppressed by `catch`. Both produce a warning in the previous `testFileProcessing` example.

WAYS TO AVOID THIS MISTAKE

- Avoid catching overly broad exceptions, like `Throwable`, not only in unit tests but in general. This often leads to ignoring the important problems and makes their investigation much harder when they appear in deployed production code. If you really need to ignore an exception, catch it precisely.
- Be cautious when placing assertion calls inside `try` blocks.
- If you would like to perform some computations in parallel, avoid using raw threads. Use `java.util.concurrent` APIs, like `ExecutorService` or `ForkJoinPool`. Also, join your parallel computation using `Future` or `CompletableFuture`, instead of using a side synchronization mechanism, like `CountDownLatch`. Futures will properly transfer the exceptions.
- Consider keeping all the assertion calls in the original thread. Follow the *Arrange, Act, Assert* pattern. This pattern assumes all the assertions are performed after the action. Try to collect all the parallel computation results in the original thread, and then assert all of them.

10.6   Mistake 99: Using *assertNotEquals()* to check the equality contract

The `assertNotEquals()` method exists in various test frameworks and provides a way to assert that two values are not equal. The problem with this method is the vague definition of "not equal." For example, consider the following method call:

```
assertNotEquals(obj1, obj2);
```

What do we mean by saying that `obj1` is not equal to `obj2`? There are four options:

- `obj1.equals(obj2)` returns `false`;
- `obj2.equals(obj1)` returns `false`;
- Both `obj1.equals(obj2)` and `obj2.equals(obj1)` return `false`;
- At least one of `obj1.equals(obj2)` and `obj2.equals(obj1)` returns `false`;

Well-implemented `equals()` methods must be symmetric: the `obj1.equals(obj2)` and `obj2.equals(obj1)` results must be the same, and symmetric `equals()` implementation implies these four options to be identical. However, the purpose of tests is to catch bugs, and bugs could be anywhere, including the behavior of the `equals()` method itself.

Unfortunately, some popular testing frameworks don't specify exactly how their `assertNotEquals()` behaves—and sometimes, the behavior is quite surprising. For example, in the TestNG (https://testng.org/) framework (at least, in version 7.4.0) `assertNotEquals()` is exactly the opposite of `assertEquals()`. The `assertEquals()` implementation is very strict: it checks both `obj1.equals(obj2)` and `obj2.equals(obj1)`. Also, it fails if either `obj1` or `obj2` are `null` (but not both) without calling the `equals()` method at all. This is great, but at the same time, it makes `assertNotEquals()` very loose. It succeeds if either `obj1.equals(obj2)` or `obj2.equals(obj1)` return `false` or if one of the objects is `null` (in this case, `equals()` is not called at all).

Suppose you are implementing your class, `MyCustomClass`, with a custom `equals()` method. To check the `equals()` implementation, you may want to write some asserts, like this:

```
assertNotEquals(new MyCustomClass(), null);
assertNotEquals(new MyCustomClass(), 1);
assertNotEquals(new MyCustomClass(), "");

assertEquals(new MyCustomClass(), new MyCustomClass());
```

It looks like we tested something. However, even this trivial implementation passes these tests:

```
class MyCustomClass {
  @Override
  public boolean equals(Object obj) {
    return true;
  }
}
```

That's because in the first test, the `equals()` method is not called at all, and in the subsequent two tests, the `equals()` method is called in both ways. So even if `new MyCustomClass().equals("")` erroneously returns `true`, the opposite call, `"".equals(new MyCustomClass())`, returns `false`, as it's the `equals()` method defined in the `String` class, which is implemented correctly (figure 10.1). So these tests say nothing about the implementation of `equals`.

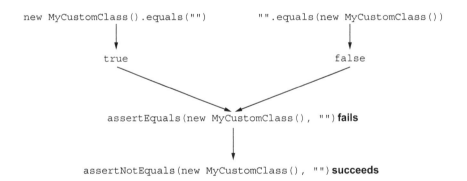

Figure 10.1 `assertNotEquals()` **behavior in TestNG is opposite to** `assertEquals()`**.**

WAYS TO AVOID THIS MISTAKE

- Try to avoid `assertNotEquals()`, especially if you aren't sure whether your `equals()` method is always symmetric. If you really need to assert that equals returns `false`, use the more explicit `assertFalse(obj1.equals(obj2))`.
- As mentioned in chapter 7, to test the `equals()` method implementation, use the EqualsVerifier library (https://jqno.nl/equalsverifier/).

10.7 Mistake 100: Malformed test methods

Sometimes, a unit test is well written but is not executed at all because it's not well formed. Depending on the testing framework and its configuration, such a problem could be any of the following:

- The `@Test` annotation is missing.
- The method is not public.
- The method is static.
- The method returns a non-void value.
- The method is declared in a nonpublic nested class.
- The method is declared in an inner class that has no `@Nested` annotation.
- An annotation from the wrong testing framework is used. For example, when both JUnit and TestNG frameworks are available in the classpath, it's quite easy to import the wrong class and annotate, for example, via `@org.junit.Test` instead of `@org.testng.annotations.Test`. In this case, the test won't be launched via the TestNG runner.
- The data provider did not provide any data for parameterized tests.
- The test method name is not well formed (in JUnit 3, test methods should start with the `test` prefix).

As a result, you may be confident you are actually testing something, while, in fact, you are not. This is especially dangerous if you have a large test suite with dozens of methods. In this case, it's hard to notice if some of them are missing.

Such problems are discovered sporadically, even in big projects like OpenJDK. When single-file Java programs were implemented in Java 12, a unit test was added. However, the corresponding `@Test` annotation was missing. As a result, the test was never launched, and the corresponding functionality was not tested for more than three years until the problem was discovered.

> **Static analysis**
>
> Some static analyzers may detect malformed tests. For example, IntelliJ IDEA has a JUnit Malformed Declaration inspection that catches some of the problems listed in this subsection. SonarLint has rules named S5790: JUnit5 Inner Test Classes Should Be Annotated with `@Nested` and S5810: JUnit5 Test Classes and Methods Should Not Be Silently Ignored.

WAYS TO AVOID THIS MISTAKE

- As previously mentioned, following TDD principles can help you to spot malformed tests, as there will be no failure. Not every developer likes to follow TDD strictly, but even if you wrote the production code before writing the test, it's a good idea to intentionally break your code to see if the test fails. This approach also allows you to detect many other problems in tests.

- Many malformed test methods are not recognized as valid entry points in IntelliJ IDEA, and thus, there's no Run icon in the gutter, as shown in figure 10.2. As you can see, this icon is absent next to the `malformedTest()` method, while it is present next to the `properTest()`.

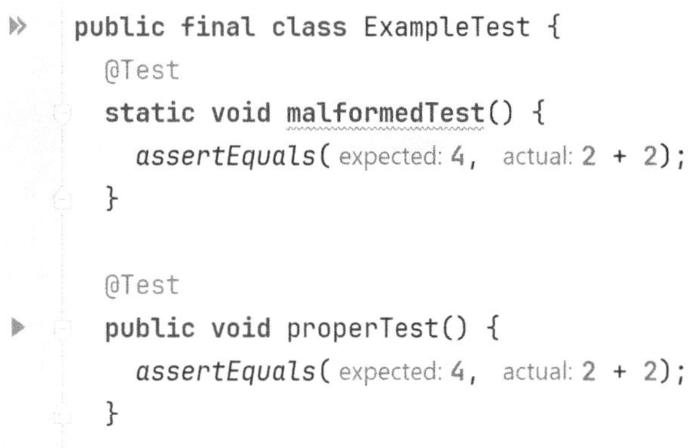

```
public final class ExampleTest {
  @Test
  static void malformedTest() {
    assertEquals( expected: 4,  actual: 2 + 2);
  }

  @Test
  public void properTest() {
    assertEquals( expected: 4,  actual: 2 + 2);
  }
```

Figure 10.2   Malformed test methods have no Run gutter icon.

Summary

- Avoid side effects inside `assert` statements, as expressions inside them are not evaluated at all when assertions are turned off.
- Try not to rely on weak assertion methods, like `assertNotNull()` and `assert-NotEquals()`. If such assertions pass, it doesn't mean much, as there could easily be a mistake in the test itself.
- Ensuring in tests that a given method throws an exception was tricky in older versions of test frameworks. This is no longer a problem with new methods, like `assertThrows()`. Use modern API methods to write more robust tests.
- Returning from the test method prematurely on some condition is a bad sign. If more assertions will be added at the end of the method later, they might be not checked when preliminary return takes place.
- Test frameworks require some extra attention to detail to make tests work, like adding `@Test` annotation or declaring the test method public. Make sure you fulfill all the requirements; otherwise, your test will not be executed at all.

appendix A
Static analysis
annotations

To make static analysis more efficient, it's useful to augment your Java program with additional hints. This is usually done via a special set of annotations distributed as a separate package. Throughout the book, we mentioned some of them. Notably, we discussed many nullity annotations, like `@Nullable`, in chapter 5. Here, I'd like to provide an overview of popular annotation packages and describe some commonly used annotations, so you may have a better idea about how they can help to reduce mistakes in your application.

Note that even some standard Java annotations may allow you to tailor static analysis to your API to some extent. The simplest is the `@Deprecated` annotation, available in JDK, which discourages users from using a particular API at all. In this case, the Java compiler itself plays the role of static analyzer and warns you. In Java 9, this annotation was extended; now, it's possible to make the warning stronger by specifying the `@Deprecated(forRemoval = true)` parameter, which should encourage clients to migrate to something else.

A.1 Annotation packages

Most static analyzers either provide their own packages or understand annotations declared in other packages. Here's a list of some popular packages used in Java projects:

- *Error Prone annotations*—This package is provided with the Error Prone static analyzer developed by Google. It declares a number of annotations recognized by the Error Prone analyzer. Some of these annotations might be recognized by other static analysis tools as well. This package does not contain nullity annotations.

- *Project page*—https://errorprone.info/
- *Package name*—com.google.errorprone.annotations
- *Maven coordinates*—com.google.errorprone:error_prone_annotations

- *The Checker Framework annotations*—This package contains hundreds of annotations to augment the Java type system. The Checker Framework can use these annotations and report errors when augmented types are incompatible.
  - *Project page*—https://checkerframework.org/
  - *Package name*—org.checkerframework
  - *Maven coordinates*—org.checkerframework:checker-qual

- *JetBrains annotations*—This annotation package is supported by JetBrains and recognized by the IntelliJ IDEA static analyzer. In addition to static analysis annotations, this package contains annotations that can aid in debugging (e.g., `@Debug.Renderer`).
  - *Project page*—https://github.com/JetBrains/java-annotations
  - *Package names*—org.jetbrains.annotations and org.intellij.lang.annotations
  - *Maven coordinates*—org.jetbrains:annotations

- *Android annotations*—Annotation package created by Google to aid Android application developers. Aside from usual offerings, like `@Nullable`, it contains Android-specific annotations, like `@RequiresPermission`. These annotations are recognized by Android Studio IDE.
  - *Project page*—https://developer.android.com/jetpack/androidx/releases/annotation
  - *Package name*—androidx.annotation
  - *Maven coordinates*—androidx.annotation:annotation (in Google repository)

- *JDT Annotations for Enhanced Null Analysis*—This package contains nullity annotations recognized by the Eclipse compiler for Java and the Eclipse IDE by default.
  - *Project page*—https://eclipse.dev/jdt/
  - *Package name*—org.eclipse.jdt.annotation
  - *Maven coordinates*—org.eclipse.jdt:org.eclipse.jdt.annotation

- *Java Concurrency in Practice annotations*—This package contains annotations discussed in the book *Java Concurrency in Practice* by Brian Goetz et al. (Addison-Wesley Professional, 2006) to aid static analysis for concurrent programs. It includes four annotations: `@GuardedBy`, `@Immutable`, `@ThreadSafe`, and `@NotThreadSafe`. Some static analyzers, like SpotBugs, recognize them and may produce specific warnings. This package has not been updated since the book's publication.
  - *Project page*—https://jcip.net/
  - *Package name*—net.jcip
  - *Maven coordinates*—net.jcip:jcip-annotations

- *JSR 305: Annotations for Software Defect Detection*—JSR stands for Java Specification Request. JSRs are formal documents that describe proposed specifications and technologies programmers can add to the Java platform within the Java Community Process (JCP). JSR 305 is an abandoned initiative to standardize static analysis annotations. The package was published to Maven Central by the FindBugs static analyzer developers. It never had an official status, and it has been unsupported for quite some time. Nevertheless, you may still see these annotations in old projects and libraries. Even new projects occasionally depend on these annotations, likely because the package name (`javax.annotation`) looks somewhat official. The same package name is used in another artifact, namely JSR 250 Common Annotations, which serves another purpose, not related to static analysis. If you use both JSR 250 and JSR 305 packages in the same project you won't be able to use Java Platform Module System, as it forbids using the same package name in more than one module (so-called split packages). I advise to avoid using JSR 305.

- *FindBugs/SpotBugs annotations*—These annotations are recognized by the FindBugs static analyzer and its successor, SpotBugs. This package essentially repeats JSR 305, using a different package name to solve the previously mentioned problem. However, it still depends on meta-annotations declared in the JSR 305 package, so you'll still have JSR 305 as a transitive dependency. This is probably not a big issue, but you should be careful to avoid accidental import of wrong annotation. For example, the annotation `javax.annotation.Nonnull` will be available in the project, along with `edu.umd.cs.findbugs.annotations.NonNull`, and it's possible to mistakenly use the wrong one via code completion.
  - *Project page*—https://spotbugs.github.io/
  - *Package name*—edu.umd.cs.findbugs.annotations
  - *Maven coordinates*—com.github.spotbugs:spotbugs-annotations

A.2 Kinds of annotations

Here are some examples of what semantics static analysis annotations may convey:

- *Nullity annotations*—This is the most popular kind of static analysis annotation in Java, as the inability to express nullity in the Java type system is the cause of many bugs. We discuss them in detail in mistake 41 on `NullPointerException`.

- *Annotations to indicate the return value of a method should not be ignored*—The static analyzer will warn you if you don't use the result of the annotated method (see mistake 11). This annotation is usually named `@CheckReturnValue`, and you can find it in the JetBrains, Error Prone, and FindBugs/SpotBugs packages. The Error Prone `@CheckReturnValue` annotation can be applied to the whole class or package. In this case, you can cancel its meaning on the individual members inside the annotated scope with the opposite `@CanIgnoreReturnValue` annotation.

- *Annotations to indicate a method does not produce any side effects*—The Checker Framework has the `@SideEffectFree` annotation for this purpose as well as `@Pure` annotation, which provides an additional guarantee that the result of the method is always the same for the same input. Similar semantics can be expressed with the JetBrains annotation `@Contract(pure = true)`. Such annotations usually imply the result value of the method should be checked. The only case in which ignoring the result of a side-effect-free method might be desired is when you want to check whether an exception is thrown from the method (it's debatable whether the exception should be considered a side effect).

  Thanks to this annotation, the static analyzer knows your mutable fields or array elements cannot be changed by a method call, so it can trust their values. For example, consider the following method:

```
void checkArray(int[] data) {
    if (data[0] > 0) {
        System.out.println("All numbers are positive");
        return;
    }                                                     binarySearch()
    int index = Arrays.binarySearch(data, 0);  ◀────┘    is a pure call.
    if (index >= 0) {
        System.out.println("0 is found at " + index);
    } else if (data[0] <= 0) {                       ◀───┐ "Condition is always
        System.out.println("First number is negative");  │ true" is reported by
    }                                                     │ IntelliJ IDEA.
}
```

  Here, you check whether the value of the first array element is positive, and at the end of the method, you check this again. Between the checks, you call the `binarySearch()` library method. In the general case, the called method may modify the array, so the first array element may change. However, the `binary-Search()` method is pre-annotated as pure. IntelliJ IDEA's built-in static analyzer trusts this annotation, so it assumes the first element is still non-positive after the call. Thanks to this, it can emit a useful warning at the last `if` statement, which is redundant or erroneous.

- *Annotations to indicate ranges of numeric values*—These are usually applied to a method result value to indicate that the method returns not any possible number but a number within a limited range. They are also applied to fields or method parameters. Here are a few examples:
  - `@Nonnegative` in the JSR 305 package and `@NonNegative` in the Checker Framework annotations indicate the value is always a non-negative number. For example, library methods like `String.length()` or `Collection.size()` always return non-negative numbers.
  - `@GTENegativeOne` in the Checker Framework annotations indicates the value is either positive, 0, or –1. For example, library methods like `String.indexOf()` can return a positive index or –1, if nothing was found.

– `@IntRange` in the Checker Framework annotations and Android annotations and `@Range` in the JetBrains annotations allow you to specify any custom integral range of values.

Such information can be used to validate method inputs or report when method outputs are tested against impossible values. For example, the following method checks the result of the `LocalDateTime.getHour()` method against 24:

```
void processDate(LocalDateTime date) {
    if (date.getHour() == 24) {                         ←┐  Warning: condition
        System.out.println("It's too late");             │  is always false.
    }
}
```

This is impossible, as `getHour()` can only return values between 0 and 23. This method is pre-annotated as `@Range(from = 0, to = 23)`, so IntelliJ IDEA knows about its range and produces a warning. Among other problems, range annotations on method parameters can help prevent mistake 42: `IndexOutOfBounds-Exception`.

- *Annotations to indicate that a method returns an unmodifiable collection or map*—The JetBrains annotations package provides `@Unmodifiable` to mark truly unmodifiable collections and `@UnmodifiableView` to mark a collection that could be modified by someone else, so the analyzer cannot assume its size or content will remain the same. Annotate return values of your methods with one of these annotations, and the static analyzer may report if the caller tries to modify the return value (see mistake 73 for details).
- *Annotations that require overriding methods in subclasses to call this method*—Such an annotation is named `@OverridingMethodsMustInvokeSuper` in Error Prone and in the JSR 305 annotation package. Android annotation is called `@CallSuper`, and the JetBrains one is named `@MustBeInvokedByOverriders`. If you annotate an overridable method, the static analyzer will ensure that the overriding methods actually call a superclass method (see mistake 24 for details).
- *Annotations on string parameters or variables indicating a string is interpreted as a regular expression*—There's a `@RegEx` annotation in the JSR 305 package, `@Regex` in the Checker framework package, and `@RegExp` in JetBrains annotations. When a static analyzer sees such an annotation, it may turn on regular-expression-specific checks for this particular string, like checking the regular expression for syntax errors. This annotation helps prevent problems like mistake 49 (using plain strings instead of regular expressions).
- *Annotations on methods or string parameters indicating the method works like* `String .format()` *or* `System.out.printf()` *(the format string parameter is passed, followed by format arguments)*—The Error Prone and Checker Framework packages provide `@FormatMethod` annotation, which should be applied to a method or constructor. On the other hand, JetBrains annotation `@PrintFormat` should be

applied to a string parameter. Annotating your own format-like methods may help to avoid mismatched format arguments (see mistake 48).

There are other less-common annotations as well. In addition to providing a hint for the static analyzer, these annotations serve the purpose of additional code documentation. For example, if you see a method is annotated with `@Nonnegative`, you immediately know negative values are never returned by this method.

Unfortunately, it looks like there's no standard package recognized by a majority of static analysis tools, and similar annotations from different tools might have slightly different semantics. As a result, it is often difficult to migrate from one static analysis tool to another if you already extensively use annotations recognized by the original tool. IntelliJ IDEA tries to understand annotations from different packages, but it's not implemented in a consistent way, so some annotations are recognized, while others are not.

appendix B
Extending static analysis tools

As we have seen throughout this book, many bugs in our programs can be detected by static analyzers. However, even the best static analyzer cannot find all the problems in your code that could be potentially found statically. That's because your project likely uses your own APIs and has your own patterns and antipatterns. In many projects and libraries, there are methods that should not be called with specific arguments in a specific sequence or under specific conditions. Surely, it's possible to describe all the caveats in the API documentation, but it would be naïve to expect every developer to read the documentation and remember it when using the API.

In appendix A, we discussed how annotation packages could be used to help the static analyzer learn something about your project. Sometimes, static analyzers support configuration options that can also help adapt the analyzer to your project. For example, the IntelliJ IDEA inspection Result of Method Call Ignored allows you to specify a list of methods that should be reported if their return value is ignored. You can add methods from your project there. In this case, you should take care to share the inspection configuration profile with other team members, preferably by committing it into version control, so other people may benefit from your configuration.

However, sometimes, it's desired to have completely custom static analysis rules, ideally with quick-fix actions that allow modifying code to make it compliant. Most static analyzers provide ways to do this, usually via plugins.

In this appendix, I'll describe how to extend Error Prone, SpotBugs, and IntelliJ IDEA to create custom warnings. For illustration purposes, I present a very simple example. Suppose you don't like when people in your project compute the hypotenuse length manually using the formula `Math.sqrt(x * x + y * y)`. As noted in mistake 27, this computation may undergo an intermediate numeric overflow or underflow, causing the final result to be incorrect. There's a library method called `Math.hypot(x, y)`, which produces more precise results and does not overflow or underflow when the result of intermediate calculations is out of the `double` type domain. Our goal in this example is to issue a warning when the explicit `Math.sqrt(x * x + y * y)` formula appears in the source code.

By no means can this appendix serve as a full reference for extending static analyzers. Here, I just want to illustrate how to start developing your own plugins and writing the simplest ones. Please refer to the corresponding plugin API documentation for details on more advanced uses.

The source code for the projects described in this appendix is available in the following GitHub repository: https://github.com/amaembo/100_java_mistakes_appendix.

B.1   *Error Prone plugins*

The Error Prone static analyzer allows you to write plugins with custom inspections or bug checkers. You can find the description on how to write your own plugins in the Error Prone documentation at https://errorprone.info/docs/plugins. To get a better understanding of how to create your own checker, you may consult the Error Prone source code. For a simple checker, you may need about 100 lines of Java code.

Let's write a simple bug checker plugin for the Error Prone analyzer. You can find this project in the error_prone_custom_check directory. You can create it as a Maven project with a dependency to the `com.google.errorprone:error_prone_check_api` artifact. It's also recommended in Error Prone documentation to use the Google AutoService generator (https://github.com/google/auto/tree/master/service) to register a plugin automatically.

An Error Prone bug checker is a class that extends the `com.google.errorprone.bugpatterns.BugChecker` abstract class. It also needs to implement one of the *tree-matcher* interfaces, depending on what kind of source elements we want to report. Many are declared inside the `BugChecker` class. For example, if you wanted to inspect the `instanceof` expressions, you would need to implement the `InstanceOfTreeMatcher` interface. As we want to report `Math.sqrt()` method invocations, the `MethodInvocationTreeMatcher` should be implemented. We also need to specify some metadata in the `@BugPattern` annotation, like the warning message and severity level:

```
@AutoService(BugChecker.class)
@BugPattern(name = "MathHypotCanBeUsed",
        summary = "Math.hypot() can be used instead",
        severity = BugPattern.SeverityLevel.WARNING)
public class HypotChecker extends BugChecker
  implements BugChecker.MethodInvocationTreeMatcher {
  …
}
```

Now, let's define some matchers to match subexpressions of the syntax tree. The first matcher matches multiplication expressions, where both operands refer to the same variable:

```
// Matches expressions like x * x
static final Matcher<ExpressionTree> SQUARE_MATCHER =
  Matchers.ignoreParens(Matchers.allOf(
    Matchers.kindIs(Tree.Kind.MULTIPLY),
    (expr, state) -> ASTHelpers.sameVariable(
        ((BinaryTree) expr).getLeftOperand(),
        ((BinaryTree) expr).getRightOperand())));
```

Next, you'll need to define a matcher to match a sum of squares:

```
// Matches expressions like x * x + y * y
static final Matcher<ExpressionTree> SUM_OF_SQUARES_MATCHER =
  Matchers.ignoreParens(Matchers.allOf(
    Matchers.kindIs(Tree.Kind.PLUS),
    (expr, state) -> SQUARE_MATCHER.matches(
      ((BinaryTree) expr).getLeftOperand(), state),
    (expr, state) -> SQUARE_MATCHER.matches(
      ((BinaryTree) expr).getRightOperand(), state)));
```

Finally, let's define a matcher to match a `Math.sqrt()` call whose argument is a sum of squares:

```
// Matches expressions like Math.sqrt(x * x + y * y)
static final Matcher<MethodInvocationTree> SQRT_MATCHER =
  Matchers.allOf(
    Matchers.staticMethod()
      .onClass("java.lang.Math").named("sqrt"),
  Matchers.argument(0, SUM_OF_SQUARES_MATCHER));
```

Now, you just need a method to call this final matcher:

```
@Override
public Description matchMethodInvocation(
    MethodInvocationTree tree, VisitorState state) {
  return SQRT_MATCHER.matches(tree, state) ?
         describeMatch(tree) :
         Description.NO_MATCH;
}
```

That's basically it. Assuming our plugin has `org.example:hypotchecker` Maven coordinates, you can install it via `mvn install` and use it in your own projects with the following Maven compiler plugin configuration:

```
<plugin>
  <groupId>org.apache.maven.plugins</groupId>
  <artifactId>maven-compiler-plugin</artifactId>
  <version>3.11.0</version>
  <configuration>
    <encoding>UTF-8</encoding>
    <showWarnings>true</showWarnings>
    <compilerArgs>
      <arg>-XDcompilePolicy=simple</arg>
      <arg>-Xplugin:ErrorProne</arg>
    </compilerArgs>
```

```
    <annotationProcessorPaths>
      <path>
        <groupId>com.google.errorprone</groupId>
        <artifactId>error_prone_core</artifactId>
        <version>2.15.0</version>
      </path>
      <path>
        <groupId>org.example</groupId>
        <artifactId>hypotchecker</artifactId>
        <version>1.0.0</version>
      </path>
    </annotationProcessorPaths>
  </configuration>
</plugin>
```

> Plug in the Error Prone analyzer itself.

> Plug in our checker.

This sample project can be found in the staticanalysis_sample directory. Let's create a test class to check how the plugin works:

```
package com.example;

public class Test {
  public static void main(String[] args) {
    double x = Double.parseDouble(args[0]);
    double y = Double.parseDouble(args[1]);
    System.out.println(Math.sqrt(x * x + y * y));
  }
}
```

Now, when building the project, you will have a compilation warning like this:

```
[WARNING] Test.java:[7,33] [MathHypotCanBeUsed] Math.hypot() can be used instead
```

For more information about developing Error Prone bug checkers, you can consult the "Writing a check" tutorial in the Error Prone documentation: https://github .com/google/error-prone/wiki/Writing-a-check.

B.2   *SpotBugs plugins*

Writing SpotBugs plugins is significantly more challenging, as it works on the Java byte-code level, so you have to find the specific bytecode patterns. Unfortunately, we cannot provide a full excursion into the exciting world of Java bytecode, as this topic would require a whole separate book. If you are interested in Java bytecode, I recommend reading chapter 4, "Class Files and Bytecode," of *The Well-Grounded Java Developer*, by Benjamin Evans, Jason Clark, and Martijn Verburg (Manning, 2nd edition, 2022).

Still, let's take a small peek inside. The easy way to learn the Java bytecode is to write some Java code, compile it, and then disassemble it with the `javap` tool. Let's do this to understand how the root of the sum of squares sample looks inside the class file. The simple program that includes your sample expression may look like this:

```
class Test {
  void test(double x, double y) {
```

```
    Math.sqrt(x * x + y * y);
  }
}
```

First, compile it with the `javac Test.java` command. After that, launch `javap -c Test`. You need the `-c` command line option to actually disassemble the method code. Now, check the output. It starts from the default constructor generated by the compiler. This part is not interesting for us. After that, you can see the disassembled body of the `test()` method:

```
void test(double, double);
Code:
  0: dload_1
  1: dload_1
  2: dmul
  3: dload_3
  4: dload_3
  5: dmul
  6: dadd
  7: invokestatic  #7  // Method java/lang/Math.sqrt:(D)D
  10: pop2
  11: return
```

This is the bytecode of your method. The Java Virtual Machine is basically a stack machine, so instructions typically take arguments from the stack, perform the computation, and put the result back onto the stack. All the instructions of Java bytecode are listed in Java Virtual Machine specification § 6.5 (https://mng.bz/5oB4). Without going into too much detail, here, you see the following instructions:

- `dload`—Push the double value from the local variable or method parameter to the stack.
- `dmul`—Take two double values from the stack, multiply them, and push the result back.
- `dadd`—Take two double values from the stack, add them together, and push the result back.
- `invokestatic`—Pop arguments from the stack, invoke a static method with these arguments, and push the result back.

The `pop2` instruction pops the result of `Math.sqrt()` from the stack, as you are not using it. The `return` instruction says the method execution should stop here. These instructions are not part of your expression, so they are not interesting to us.

Now, let's create a SpotBugs plugin project. You can find it in the spotbugs_ custom_check directory. The easiest method is to create it from a Maven archetype. You can do this with the following command:

```
$ mvn archetype:generate \
      -DarchetypeArtifactId=spotbugs-archetype \
      -DarchetypeGroupId=com.github.spotbugs \
      -DarchetypeVersion=LATEST
```

Alternatively, you can use an IDE wizard to create a new project from the archetype. For example, in IntelliJ IDEA, you can select the Maven Archetype generator in the new project wizard and then specify com.github.spotbugs:spotbugs-archetype in the Archetype field and LATEST in the Version field, as shown in figure B.1.

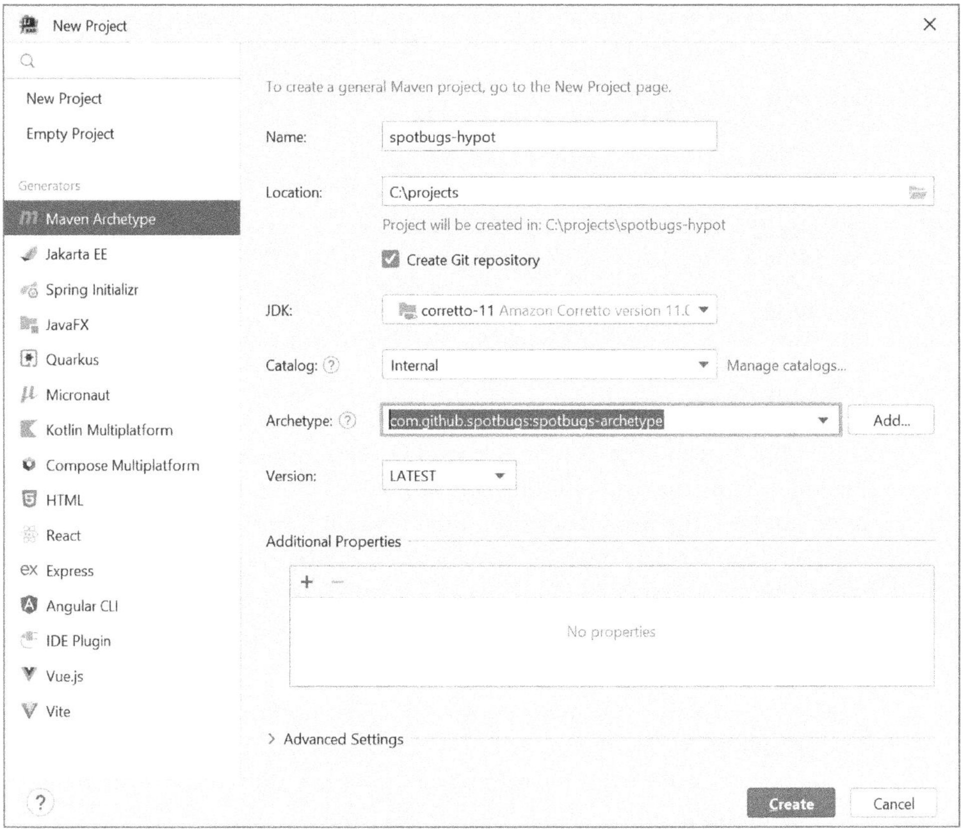

Figure B.1 Creating a SpotBugs plugin with Maven Archetype

After the project is initialized, you'll have a sample bug detector class called My-Detector. It extends the OpcodeStackDetector class. OpcodeStackDetector is a helper abstract class that maintains the JVM stack state automatically. Thanks to this, you don't need to worry about the dload instruction. At any moment, you can use getStack().getStackItem(0) to retrieve the information about topmost stack value, getStack().getStackItem(1) to retrieve the information about second stack value, and so on. For example, you can use the following code to ensure that two values on the stack are loaded from the same register, which means it's the same local variable or parameter:

```
OpcodeStack.Item item1 = stack.getStackItem(0);
OpcodeStack.Item item2 = stack.getStackItem(1);
int reg1 = item1.getRegisterNumber();
int reg2 = item2.getRegisterNumber();
if (reg1 == reg2 && reg1 != -1) { ... }
```

The `OpcodeStack.Item` type represents the value stored on the stack and contains many pieces of useful information about that value, like whether it was loaded from a register or a field, whether it's a result of a method call, and so on. Here, for the sake of simplicity, let's support only values loaded from local variables and parameters. Values originated from other places (e.g., loaded from a field or returned from a method call) have register number −1, and they are excluded.

Some values also have a *special kind*, which is a sort of tag. You can create your own tags and attach them to values you find interesting. For this problem, we need two additional tags, which can be defined as constants:

```
import static edu.umd.cs.findbugs.OpcodeStack.Item.*;

...

/**
 * Value is a square of local variable or parameter
 */
private static final @SpecialKind int SQUARE = 100;
/**
 * Value is a sum of two squares
 */
private static final @SpecialKind int SUM_SQUARES = 101;
```

The `MyDetector` class contains the implementation of the `sawOpcode()` method, which is called for every bytecode instruction. The instruction is passed as a parameter. While it's required to implement this method, sometimes, it's more convenient to override the `afterOpcode()` method. By default, `afterOpcode()` does all the bookkeeping to maintain the stack state, so we need to attach our new special values there. It's convenient to add some code before and after the supermethod call. Before the call, the stack contains the arguments of current instruction, so we can examine them. After the supermethod call, the stack contains the result, and we can update its special kind, if necessary. We need to track `dmul` and `dadd` instructions. For `dmul`, we should check that the two arguments are the same variables, as previously shown. For `dadd`, we should check that both arguments are squares. Putting this all together, we can write the following:

```
public void afterOpcode(int seen) {
  @SpecialKind int kind = NOT_SPECIAL;
  OpcodeStack stack = getStack();                    Check if we are about to
  if (seen == Const.DMUL) {                          multiply two identical values.
    OpcodeStack.Item item1 = stack.getStackItem(0);
    OpcodeStack.Item item2 = stack.getStackItem(1);
    int reg1 = item1.getRegisterNumber();
    int reg2 = item2.getRegisterNumber();
```

```
    if (reg1 == reg2 && reg1 != -1) {
      kind = SQUARE;
    }
  }
  if (seen == Const.DADD) {
    OpcodeStack.Item item1 = stack.getStackItem(0);
    OpcodeStack.Item item2 = stack.getStackItem(1);
    if (item1.getSpecialKind() == SQUARE &&
        item2.getSpecialKind() == SQUARE) {
      kind = SUM_SQUARES;
    }
  }
  super.afterOpcode(seen);
  if (kind != NOT_SPECIAL) {
    stack.getStackItem(0).setSpecialKind(kind);
  }
}
```

Check if we are about to sum two squares.

Now, we are finally ready to detect and report our expression. We can do this inside the `sawOpcode()` method. All we need is to match the `invokestatic` instruction, which calls `Math.sqrt()` on the sum of squares:

```
Public void sawOpcode(int seen) {
  if (seen == Const.INVOKESTATIC &&
      getClassConstantOperand().equals("java/lang/Math") &&
      getNameConstantOperand().equals("sqrt") &&
      getStack().getStackItem(0).getSpecialKind() == SUM_SQUARES) {
    BugInstance bug = new BugInstance(
                this, "MATH_USE_HYPOT", NORMAL_PRIORITY)
            .addClassAndMethod(this)
            .addSourceLine(this, getPC());
    bugReporter.reportBug(bug);
  }
}
```

Here, we're reporting a bug pattern named `"MATH_USE_HYPOT"` with normal priority, which is attached to the current class, method, and source line. Note that to match the class name of the `Math.sqrt()` method, you need to specify it in JVM format: `"java/lang/Math"` instead of `"java.lang.Math"`.

We also need to register the detector and the bug pattern inside findbugs.xml and add textual descriptions of the detector and the bug pattern into messages.xml. You will find these files in the src/main/resources folder of the project. Also, it would be prettier to rename the `MyDetector` class to something more appropriate, like `Manual-HypotDetector`.

To build the plugin, you can use the `mvn package` command, and you'll get the jar file inside the `target` directory. Now, all you need is to use the plugin. The procedure for including your plugin in the analysis depends on where you are using SpotBugs itself. For example, if you use it inside Eclipse IDE, you can navigate to Window > Preferences > Java > SpotBugs > Plugins and misc. Settings and add your plugin jar file there, as shown in figure B.2.

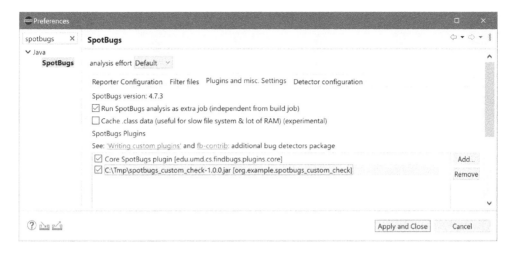

Figure B.2   Enabling a custom SpotBugs plugin in Eclipse IDE

Now, when you run the analysis, the bug will be displayed in the editor (figure B.3).

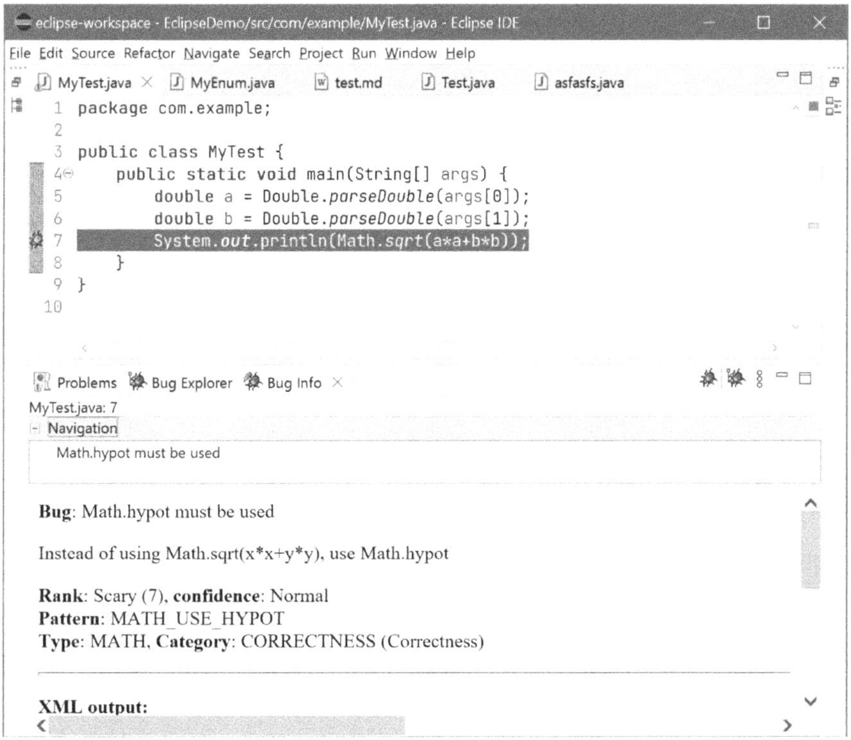

Figure B.3   SpotBugs plugin warning shown in Eclipse IDE

Similarly, you can configure it in other IDEs. If you are using SpotBugs as a part of your Maven or Gradle build process, you'll need to deploy your plugin to the Maven repository and specify the coordinates. You can find all the details in the SpotBugs documentation https://mng.bz/6ndG.

B.3   IntelliJ IDEA plugin

IntelliJ IDEA also allows you to create plugins for static analysis and various other purposes. Many plugins are publicly available at JetBrains Marketplace, adding support for specific Java libraries. They provide library-specific inspections that highlight the code if it uses a library incorrectly or inefficiently. There are also many in-house plugins distributed inside companies to help develop internal projects. Online documentation for the IntelliJ plugin SDK is available at https://plugins.jetbrains.com/docs/intellij/. The easiest way to create a plugin is to use the new project wizard in IntelliJ IDEA and select the IDE Plugin generator (figure B.4).

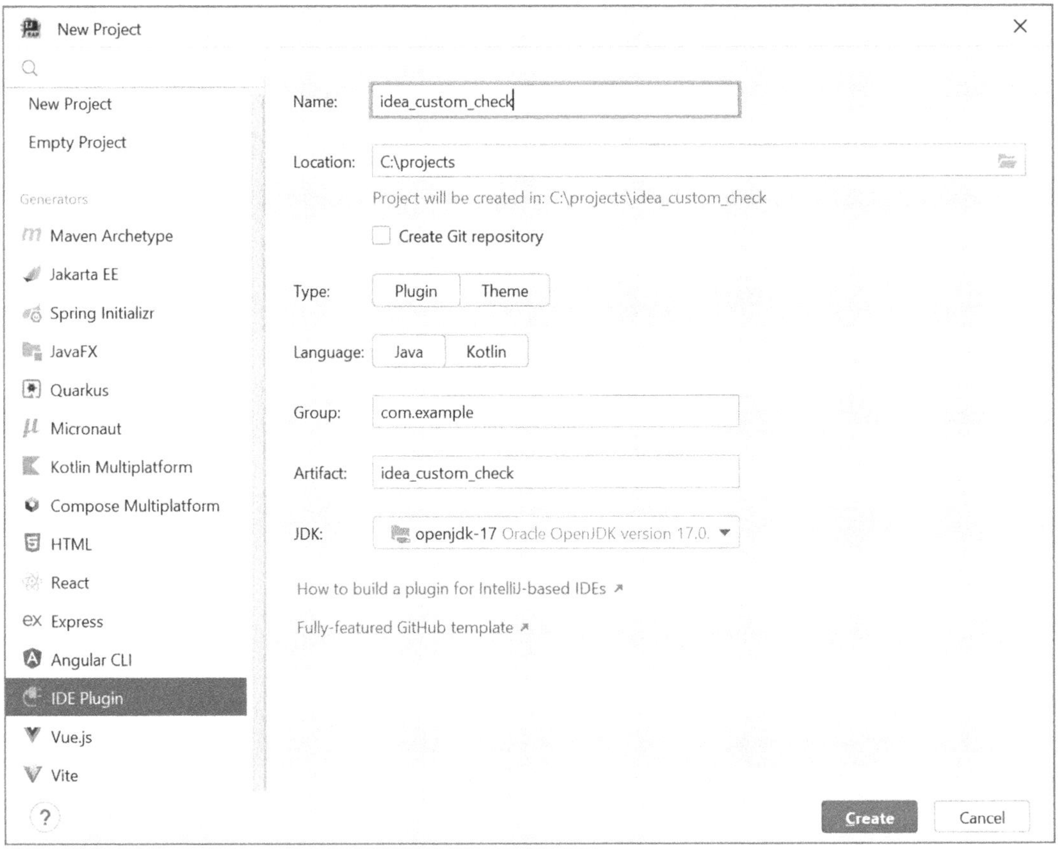

Figure B.4   Creating an IDE Plugin project inside IntelliJ IDEA

It will generate a sample project for you. You can find this sample in the idea_ custom_check directory. Now, we need to tune the configuration a little bit. First, a dependency to the "java" plugin should be added in the build.gradle.kts file, as we want to write a Java inspection. Find the `intellij {}` section and set the dependency there:

```
intellij {
    version.set(…)
    type.set("IC") // Target IDE Platform

    plugins.set(listOf("java"))
}
```

Here, `"IC"` refers to *IntelliJ IDEA Community Edition*, which means your plugin will be available in the free version of IntelliJ IDEA. Next, open the plugin.xml file, and add a dependency on the `com.intellij.java` module from the IntelliJ SDK somewhere under the `<idea-plugin>` tag:

```
<depends>com.intellij.java</depends>
```

You may also want to edit other parts of plugin.xml and build.gradle.kts, such as a plugin description, the vendor email, or the minimum IntelliJ version required. Now, let's create an inspection class. To do this, you need to extend the `LocalInspectionTool` abstract class and implement a `buildVisitor()` method:

```
public class HypotInspection extends LocalInspectionTool {
  @Override
  public PsiElementVisitor buildVisitor(ProblemsHolder holder,
                                        boolean isOnTheFly) {
    return new Visitor(holder);
  }
}
```

Now, let's implement a visitor itself. It accepts a `ProblemsHolder` object, which is used to finally report the warnings. For Java, you can extend `JavaElementVisitor` and visit a kind of element we want to report. Here, we need to examine method calls to find a potentially applicable `Math.sqrt()` call, so you should override the `visitMethodCallExpression()` method:

```
private static class Visitor extends JavaElementVisitor {
  private final ProblemsHolder holder;

  Visitor(ProblemsHolder holder) { this.holder = holder; }

  @Override
  public void visitMethodCallExpression(PsiMethodCallExpression call) {
    …
  }
}
```

The `visitMethodCallExpression()` method accepts a *Program Structure Interface* (PSI) element that represents the call. The PSI is the layer of IntelliJ API responsible for parsing files and creating syntactic and semantic models. For `PsiMethodCall-Expression`, you can find exactly which method is called here and which arguments are passed. The easiest way to match a Java method is to create a `CallMatcher` constant:

```
private static final CallMatcher SQRT_CALL =
    CallMatcher.staticCall("java.lang.Math", "sqrt").parameterCount(1);

@Override
public void visitMethodCallExpression(PsiMethodCallExpression call) {
  if (!SQRT_CALL.test(call)) return;
  …
}
```

The `SQRT_CALL` matcher will ensure the given call is a call of the `Math.sqrt()` method with a single parameter. Now, we can safely obtain that parameter (removing the parentheses if necessary) and check whether it's an addition operation represented as `PsiBinaryExpression` with the operation token +. Finally, we should check that both operands are squares. If both conditions are met, we can report the problem:

```
@Override
public void visitMethodCallExpression(PsiMethodCallExpression call) {
  if (!SQRT_CALL.test(call)) return;                          ◁──── Check that we are calling
  var arg = call.getArgumentList().getExpressions()[0];              Math.sqrt() with a single argument.
  arg = PsiUtil.skipParenthesizedExprDown(arg);              ◁──┘ Remove parentheses,
                                                                   if any.
  Get the                                                          
  argument.

  if (!(arg instanceof PsiBinaryExpression sum)) return;     ◁──── Check that it's a
  IElementType token = sum.getOperationTokenType();                 binary expression.
  if (!token.equals(JavaTokenType.PLUS)) return;
  Check
  that it's
  actually
  a sum.      if (isSquare(sum.getLOperand()) &&              Check that both operands
                  isSquare(sum.getROperand())) {             of sum are squares.
                holder.registerProblem(call, "Use Math.hypot()");
              }
}
```

The `isSquare()` implementation is relatively straightforward. You need to once again check that the expression is a binary expression, but now, you should check for a multiplication token (named `ASTERISK` in IntelliJ API). You can use the `Equivalence-Checker` utility to ensure both operands are equivalent to each other:

```
static boolean isSquare(PsiExpression expr) {                Remove parentheses,
  expr = PsiUtil.skipParenthesizedExprDown(expr);       ◁──┘ if any.
  if (!(expr instanceof PsiBinaryExpression mul)) {     ◁──── Check that it's a
    return false;                                              binary expression.
  }
  IElementType token = mul.getOperationTokenType();
  if (!token.equals(JavaTokenType.ASTERISK)) {          Check that it's actually
    return false;                                       multiplication.
  }
```

```
    PsiExpression left = mul.getLOperand();
    PsiExpression right = mul.getROperand();
    var eq = EquivalenceChecker.getCanonicalPsiEquivalence();
    return eq.expressionsAreEquivalent(left, right);
}
```

> **Ensure both operands of the multiplication are equivalent expressions.**

Now, you need to register the inspection as an extension inside plugin.xml. To do this, you need to create a `<localInspection>` entry inside the `<extensions>` tag:

```
<extensions defaultExtensionNs="com.intellij">
  <localInspection implementationClass=
            "com.example.idea_custom_check.HypotInspection"
    language="JAVA" displayName="Math.hypot() could be used"
    groupBundle="messages.InspectionsBundle"
    groupPath="Java" shortName="Hypot"
    groupKey="group.names.verbose.or.redundant.code.constructs"
    enabledByDefault="true" level="WARNING"/>
</extensions>
```

Here, the predefined inspection group Java > Verbose or Redundant Code Constructs is used and the inspection short name `Hypot` is specified, which will be used to identify the inspection inside the inspection profiles and suppress the inspection warning, if necessary.

That's basically it. Now, you can ensure the plugin works by using `gradle runIde`. To create an installable package, use `gradle build`. After that, you'll have a plugin jar under the build/libs directory. It can be installed using the Install Plugin from Disk option in the Settings > Plugins dialog. Alternatively, you can publish the plugin on JetBrains Marketplace at https://plugins.jetbrains.com/, making it publicly available for all IntelliJ IDEA users.

This appendix hasn't covered how to create an automatic quick fix or test the inspection. These tasks are not very hard either. Of course, a single plugin may implement as many inspections as you want.

B.4   *Using structural search and replacement in IntelliJ IDEA*

Creating an IntelliJ IDEA plugin is useful if you want to add complex static analysis inspections. However, for simple inspections, like the one described here, it looks like overkill. IntelliJ IDEA provides a much simpler mechanism to do this. It's called *Structural Search and Replacement* (SSR).

Essentially, it's a search mechanism, but instead of searching by substring or regular expression, you can search for a specific fragment of the Java program's abstract syntactic tree, ignoring unimportant details like comments or formatting. It also allows you to create a custom inspection, so every found occurrence will be automatically highlighted in the source code. Finally, it allows you to specify a quick fix, so you can apply the change automatically.

Let's create an SSR template to find `Math.sqrt(x * x + y * y)` calculations and suggest a replacement. You need to visit the Editor > Inspections settings page, and then press the + toolbar icon and select Add Replace Template. Now, you can just type a template referring to variable parts via `$identifier$`, like this:

```
Math.sqrt($x$ * $x$ + $y$ * $y$)
```

Next, you can specify the replacement template:

```
Math.hypot($x$, $y$)
```

The resulting window is shown in figure B.5.

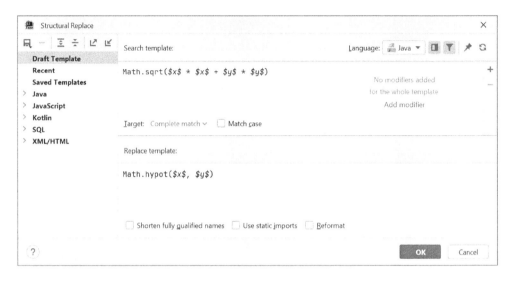

Figure B.5   Configuring a structural search and replacement template in IntelliJ IDEA

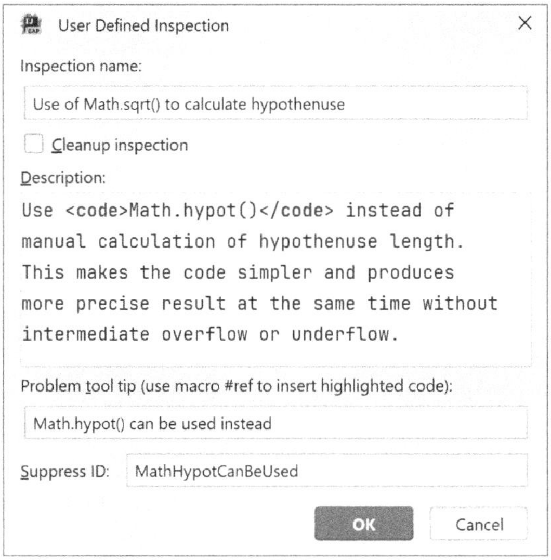

You can create additional filters for the whole expression or for individual placeholder variables. For example, you can set it to find a match only when variables have a specific type.

After pressing OK, you'll be asked to enter new inspection meta-information, such as name, description, and suppression string. You can write something like what is shown in figure B.6.

Figure B.6   Specifying SSR inspection metadata

Now, the new inspection is stored inside the project inspection profile, and it will highlight all the expressions that match the pattern (figure B.7). Note that x and y can match complex expressions, not only single variables.

```
System.out.println(Math.sqrt((x1 - x2) * (x1 - x2) + (y1 - y2) * (y1 - y2)));
```
| Math.hypot() can be used instead | ⋮ |
| Replace with 'Math.hypot((x1 - x2), (y1 - y2))' Alt+Shift+Enter   More actions... Alt+Enter |

Figure B.7 A structural search warning in IntelliJ IDEA editor

If you commit the inspection profile (usually, stored inside the .idea folder) together with your project, other developers will be able to use this new inspection as well. You can also reuse the same profile for static analysis on a CI/CD server, using JetBrains Qodana (https://www.jetbrains.com/qodana/). In general, SSR is a powerful mechanism to aid in preventing project-specific bug patterns or augment existing static analyzers. You can refer to the IntelliJ IDEA documentation for further information on SSR (https://www.jetbrains.com/help/idea/creating-custom-inspections.html).

index

RELATED MANNING TITLES

Troubleshooting Java
by Laurentiu Spilca

ISBN 9781617299773
328 pages, $59.99
February 2023

The Well Grounded Java Developer,
Second Edition
by Benjamin Evans, Jason Clark, and Martijn Verburg
Foreword by Heinz Kabutz

ISBN 9781617298875
704 pages, $69.99
October 2022

Modern Java in Action
by Raoul-Gabriel Urma, Mario Fusco,
and Alan Mycroft

ISBN 9781617293566
592 pages, $54.99
September 2018

Spring in Action, Sixth Edition
by Craig Walls

ISBN 9781617297571
520 pages, $59.99
January 2022

For ordering information, go to www.manning.com